Praise for *Japan and the United States*:

"I was fortunate to have met Yukio Okamoto early in my tenure as U.S. Ambassador to Japan. As a titan in U.S.–Japan relations and our alliance, Yukio quickly became a trusted advisor and friend with an invaluable perspective on issues of critical importance to our two countries. This book is a testament to his incredible legacy."

—John Roos, *former U.S. Ambassador to Japan*

"Yukio Okamoto's savvy record of his career underscores his extraordinary legacy. He supported Prime Ministers, Presidents, and other leaders in managing decades of political, security, and economic relationships between our two nations and others. As efforts to maintain or alter the status quo in Asia intensify, we'll wish that Yukio was here to tease out solutions."

—Paul Tagliabue, *former Commissioner of the NFL (1989–2006)*

"This book is a compelling account of how a son redeemed his father's and his country's bitter defeat with a life committed to Japan and its American ally. From this closely-observed account of U.S.–Japan relations emerges a portrait of a good man racing to put out the fires of conflict and war."

—Suzanne Berger, *Professor of Political Science, MIT*

JAPAN and the UNITED STATES

The Journey of a Defeated Nation

A Diplomat's Memoir by
Yukio Okamoto

With Reminiscences by
Richard L. Armitage *and* **Joseph S. Nye, Jr.**

Edited by
**Elisabeth Rubinfien, Richard J. Samuels,
and Daniel Sneider**

TUTTLE Publishing
Tokyo | Rutland, Vermont | Singapore

Table of Contents

Introduction

by Richard J. Samuels, Massachusetts Institute of Technology & Daniel Sneider, Stanford University

YUKIO OKAMOTO was an accomplished Japanese diplomat, an advisor to prime ministers, and a public intellectual who acted throughout his long career as a bonding agent in holding together the postwar alliance between Japan and the United States. At key moments during the sweep of postwar history, he was a significant actor in adapting that alliance to the challenges of his time—from the rethinking of Japan's role in global and regional security as it struggled with its postwar pacifism and its Cold War cheap riding on U.S. security guarantees, to the creation of a true security partnership in face of new threats from China and North Korea. Few public figures were more trusted in Tokyo and Washington and none was more respected as a maintenance engineer of this postwar alliance than Yukio Okamoto.

Okamoto, a boundlessly energetic, unconventional, pragmatic, charismatic, and accomplished public servant, was sadly an early victim of the Covid-19 pandemic. He was a young 74 when he passed away in April 2020. But he left behind this important memoir which offers uniquely thoughtful insights into modern Japanese foreign policy, and especially of Japan's relationship to the United States. As was true in his lifetime, Okamoto offers a refreshingly frank assessment of the alliance—a sometimes critical look at both countries—a personal trait that was prized by senior American officials for decades.

This book is the product of a benkyōkai (study group) that first convened in 2013 at the MIT Center for International Studies, where Okamoto was a Robert E. Wilhelm Fellow and at which he vetted his draft chapters for study group participants Suzanne Berger, Joseph

Nye, Ezra Vogel, Kenneth Oye and Richard Samuels, a co-editor of this volume. As the manuscript began to take shape, Okamoto brought in co-editors Elisabeth Rubinfien and Daniel Sneider. All the seminar participants and each of the three co-editors were decades-long friends of Okamoto's—and Professor Oye actually was his undergraduate classmate at Swarthmore College in the 1960s.

The book sets the postwar alliance within the framework of a complex and often difficult history between our two nations, beginning in the events that led to war. Those who knew him, as we did, were often treated to his passionate examination of the War, including Japan's own responsibility for war crimes. But it will be a revelation to others to listen to this former senior Japanese official weave the story of the postwar alliance within a complex tapestry of personal and international history. His memoir examines his parents' wartime experiences as well as the fateful decisions that led to war—and their subsequent lessons—and the way Japan and the U.S. were able to reconcile, forging a postwar partnership out of devastation and deep mutual enmity. Indeed, this volume contains a very personal reckoning with that wartime past, one that might be a revelation even to those who knew him well. Okamoto describes his coming to understand and confront his father's own participation in one of Japan's most notorious war crimes—the creation of Unit 731, a secret operation to develop chemical and biological weapons by using captured POWs, Chinese, Koreans and others as experimental subjects.

The title Yukio Okamoto chose for this memoir speaks to his worldview—"The Journey of a Defeated Nation." He offers Americans a complex and nuanced understanding of how the War shaped Japanese thinking, one that remains critical today and corrects the rather simplistic view of Japan that unfortunately prevails among some American policy makers and parts of the American public. Readers will find his "transwar" approach—i.e., explaining the present by illuminating the past—especially effective. As we discovered after his death in notes Okamoto scribbled as he was conceiving this volume: "Japan went to war with China and the U.S. because of militarism. It was a tragic affair and confronting it became my DNA."

Attempts to place Yukio Okamoto in a fixed location on the Japanese political spectrum always failed. He never saw himself as a partisan figure, as a conservative or a liberal, but rather as a patriot. Nowhere is this truer than when it came to the painful and still deeply contested issues of Japan's wartime history. He could be scathing in private when talking about Japan's responsibility to put things right with its neighbors, but also tough on those he thought were using the past for other political purposes, including Japan's neighbors in China and Korea. He never shirked from acknowledging Japan's wartime transgressions—or its occasional Cold War failures of courage and resolution—but neither did he soft-peddle his frustrations with America's often ham-fisted diplomacy, a too-casual posture he believed some in Washington considered its privilege as the alliance's senior partner. He would have no truck with their view of Japan as an obedient lapdog or mere "cash dispenser." Indeed, he told us that "my first motivation for writing [this book] was to let people know the unfair treatment by the Americans at the time of the Gulf War," and in notes found after his death his determination that this volume would "candidly criticize the United States without alienating his readers, whom he wished would "feel that Japan is still a true American ally."

Okamoto arrived at his views by following—indeed, at times inventing—a winding path, one he reveals to us on these pages. Born in the seaside province of Kanagawa, boating and diving would remain enduring diversions throughout his life. His father, Shuzo, brought him, his mother, Kazuko, and his two brothers, Katsuya and Yasuo, to Malaysia in 1958, barely a dozen years after all but a handful of Imperial soldiers left its jungles in defeat. As Okamoto tells it, he was in elementary school there when he first encountered anti-Japanese sentiment in the schoolyard. Being called "beast," "pig," and "executioner" stayed with him his whole life, powerfully informing his view of how history shapes the present. After high school back in Japan, he flirted with what he declares was a callow but fashionable "pseudo-leftism" at university during the Vietnam War. Upon graduation in 1968 from the Law Faculty of Hitotsubashi University, a prestigious feeder for careers of Japan's top diplomats, he joined the Japanese Foreign Ministry on an elite track. Actually, once Okamoto caught the eyes of his superiors, he was put into the fastest lane of that fast track—and, as he describes on these pages, he may at times seemed to some a reckless driver. His diplomatic career included stints in Paris, Cairo, and Washington—and back in Tokyo, eventually as Director of MOFA's Second North America Division, the most senior official responsible for the relationship with the United States. All this positioned him one day to become Administrative Vice Minister and Ambassador to Washington—the two highest posts in the ministry.

But, frustrated by Japan's sluggish response to President George H.W. Bush's call for it to join the "coalition of the willing" in response to Saddam Hussein's invasion of Kuwait in 1990, Okamoto chucked his formal career at the peak of his promise. Still, prime ministers and corporate chief executives would not let him get away. They valued his insights and courage, and recruited him to serve them—and Japan—offline, as their consultant and board member. Officially and unofficially, Okamoto advised, prodded, represented, and educated. He wrote books about international affairs, took an entrepreneurial turn in Tokyo and Silicon Valley, and was a regular personality on Japan's most influential weekly news shows.

Understood in this context, it is easy to see the development of Okamoto the iconoclast. This would be less remarkable in other nations' foreign services perhaps, but Okamoto was a Japanese diplomat in a particularly hidebound Japanese bureaucracy. He could no more countenance failures of imagination or careerism by tentative officials than he could violations of international law. By all accounts—his own on these pages and the reminiscences of others—Okamoto knew how (and was ever willing) to defy convention in the service of Japan's national interest. He might cut a corner or two or make a pest of himself in the land where nails that stand out are famously hammered down—actually there are dozens of rich examples in this memoir—but he always did so fully cognizant of the difference between insubordination and initiative.

Many senior government officials everywhere—particularly those who operate in the foreign policy arena—appear to be somehow everywhere all the time. They participate in, and attempt to solve, widely diverse and difficult global problems. None was more ubiquitous than Okamoto. For decades, long after he left the Ministry of Foreign Affairs, there was virtually no significant Japanese foreign policy lacking his fingerprints; no Japanese prime minister—whether those who were awkwardly incompetent or those who were visionary and determined—was denied access to his advice. And there was no foreign official whose trust he failed to earn and retain. Readers will be impressed by how his paths as a diplomat, business consultant, and venture capitalist took him to conference rooms and parlors with so many of the most powerful Cold War (and post-Cold War) actors on the world stage.

What comes alive on these pages is how he wrestled with many of Japan's most difficult policy problems, all while understanding his counterparts' concerns, yet without undermining Japan's interests. Okamoto's central mission after joining the Foreign Ministry was to guide Japan away from the constrictions of postwar pacifism, seemingly enshrined in the American-authored constitutional restrictions on Japan's war making ability. He played a central role in the evolution of Japan's security policy to allow for Japan to participate beyond the narrowest definitions of self-defense, beginning with the decision in the early 1990s to join United Nations peacekeeping forces and extending later to the revision of security laws to permit Japan to offer logistical support to U.S. military operations in Afghanistan and Iraq.

When the terrorist attacks of September 11, 2001 occurred, Okamoto was sitting in the Prime Minister's office, serving as an advisor to Prime Minister Koizumi Junichiro. He was determined that Japan not repeat the mistake of the first Gulf War when it offered only money—"checkbook diplomacy"—in support of its ally and its "coalition of the willing." This time Japanese naval vessels dramatically escorted U.S. naval vessels out of their Japanese home port, a protective measure. And he helped rush through legislation in the Japanese Diet that permitted Japanese naval vessels to offer refueling and other support in the Indian Ocean to the U.S. operation against Al Qaeda in Afghanistan.

While Okamoto supported the broad goals of the United States, he was not afraid to be sharply critical of its handling of the wars in Iraq and Afghanistan. He also was a player on relations with Iran, seeking to use Japanese influence and relations with Tehran to open doors to negotiation. In Iraq, he was closely involved in the decision to send, and place, Japanese peacekeeping forces there, though they had to operate under very restricted rules of engagement. As he reports in this memoir, in this operation he worked closely with a Japanese diplomat, Oku Katsuhiko, who was tragically killed carrying out his mission.

Okamoto was also deeply involved, as a Foreign Ministry official in charge of security relations and later as an advisor to several Japanese prime ministers, in managing the difficult problems of American bases on Okinawa. He traveled to Okinawa frequently, seeking to mediate between the island's political leadership and Tokyo and the American forces based there. His passion on this issue knew no bounds.

As this memoir details, Okamoto was deeply concerned about Japan's wartime past and the need to respond to the calls for still unresolved issues of historical justice. As an advisor to Mitsubishi, he played a key role in helping to settle a suit for compensation filed in Chinese courts by Chinese forced laborers who worked for the company's materials firm during the wartime period. At the same time, he was agonized by the issue of Japan's system of wartime brothels and the "comfort women" brought there from Korea and elsewhere. While acknowledging the injustice, he felt strongly that claims of forced sexual slavery were not fully supported by historical records and was involved in attempts to find a solution to this wrenching issue. We have described Okamoto as an engineer, rather than as an architect, because there are so few of the latter on the world stage. Yet his grand strategic vision should not be underappreciated. Indeed, this vision was on clearest display in the last decade of Okamoto's life—something this memoir communicates only in part. In his later years, he actively shaped Japanese public opinion on national security issues by teaching at Ritsumeikan University and, as noted above, by appearing regularly on Japan's most widely viewed public affairs television shows. His vision was further advanced abroad, where he committed his energies to secure Japanese government funds to endow university chairs in Japanese diplomacy and politics in order to nurture the next generation of U.S. and Canadian scholars committed to teaching and writing about Japanese politics and diplomacy.

Above all, perhaps, Okamoto was a student of leadership. He acknowledged Japan's leadership deficit and believed that its political class needed to be bolder and more creative, and—while he admired many—he was concerned that too many others—politicians and bureaucrats alike—could be callow, narrow-minded, and avaricious. He was bold—and, as we have suggested, he was much more. Okamoto knew that successful diplomacy and grand strategy require empathy as much (or more) than they require rational analysis of a partner or competitor. They require leaders to be unconventional and creative—traits he found in short supply in Japan as elsewhere, but which he possessed in abundance.

NOTE TO READERS:
In the period since Okamoto-san's death in 2020, there have been important changes that he would have addressed had he had the chance. The Russian invasion of Ukraine ended Tokyo's efforts to improve bilateral relations with Moscow, the election of a conservative South Korean president enabled Seoul and Tokyo to retry building a more cooperative posture, a stable Tokyo–Washington alliance relationship returned at the end of the Trump presidency, and former Prime Minister Abe's assassination—each had an impact on the dynamics addressed on these pages.

We have not inserted ourselves into his original text to reflect these developments or to impose our own interpretations of them. Instead, we advise the reader to appreciate that Okamoto-san's observations are those of an influential and thoughtful diplomat who was deeply engaged in world affairs at an important historical moment. With Elisabeth Rubinfien, we have edited his memoir with fidelity to his views of a world he knew intimately, which has shifted in important ways. We believe the reader will benefit from this rare insight into Japan's foreign and security policymaking, and that many of the lessons he imparts remain valuable as Japan and the United States approach together our new world order.

Photos courtesy of Okamoto Associates, Inc.

Reminiscence

by Richard L. Armitage

Former U.S. Deputy Secretary of State, USG (2001-05)

YUKIO OKAMOTO, along with his mentor Ryozo Kato, are the two finest diplomats whom I have had the honor to know. Notice, I said "diplomats"—not "Japanese diplomats." I am speaking of all international diplomats. Their combination of experience, historical knowledge and dedication made them so.

For me, Yukio was quite special. I was at the wedding reception when he and Kyoko were married in Washington. They were the first Japanese family to invite me into their home. It was at the old Gaimusho (Ministry of Foreign Affairs) housing complex, quite small, and I was honored beyond recall. The small size of the housing was much less important than the conversation with two wonderful people.

During the first Gulf War, Yukio was sorely embarrassed and angered by the Government of Japan's reluctance to participate in some manner, except as a source of funds, which became controversial because of the yen–dollar exchange rate. Okamoto-san did not view his country as a piggy bank. He wanted a Japan fully engaged in all notable endeavors.

Okamoto-san took it upon himself to come to Washington to learn what sort of assistance might be most useful for the U.S. and coalition troops. Then he begged, borrowed and cajoled donations to provide generators, water purification equipment, etc., to assist the coalition. This was on his own!

That is the action of a real Japanese patriot. He was keeping Japan in the game.

Okamoto-san was quite active in Taipei. He realized earlier than most that Taiwan's freedom and survival is essential to Japan. It is my belief that Japan's recent warming of relations with Taipei began with his efforts. He was not antagonistic towards China but did understand the gravity and consequences of China's rise. True to form, he would not abide "bullying" of other countries.

His serious demeanor, combined with his reasoned thinking, was responsible for some resolution between Japanese conglomerates and former slave laborers in Korea—government could not do this but a patriot like Okamoto-san could.

After leaving the Foreign Ministry, Okamoto-san started a very successful business. But he continued to be invited to present to various Diet study groups. The combination of his knowledge, experience and confident delivery made him a very busy man as far as the Diet was concerned. He added enormously to the maturation of thinking in Japan's Diet at a time when it was most needed.

Prime Ministers sought his counsel, valued his advice, and were often guided by his views and suggestions. This dual role of businessman and advisor did not sit well with some in the Gaimusho. Yukio bore the criticism well and kept on doing what was right and pressed on. Although this rankled some, his advice was always "spot on" and always furthered Japan's interests.

One of the driving factors of Okamoto-san's energy, I believe, was the fact of his father's participation in the infamous Unit 731 in World War II. He had confided this to me one evening and this drove him to want to defend those who couldn't defend themselves. To some extent he worried that the sins of the father could be passed to the sons. This kept him always attuned to follow the right path. It led him to want to correct what he considered unjust, hence his efforts in the Republic of Korea, his efforts to support Uighurs in China, his efforts in the first Gulf War, etc. He felt keenly the frustration of the people of Okinawa and visited there many times. Subsequent visits by Japanese Prime Ministers are a direct result of his urging.

American diplomats learned quickly not to ask a question if they could not stand the answer. Okamoto-san believed deeply in our alliance, defended it when needed and criticized if he felt things were tilting out of balance—both in Japan and the U.S.

It was always a pleasure to arrive at a conference and see that Okamoto-san was on the agenda. You knew then that this was going to be a serious and weighty discussion. His demeanor was quiet. When he had heard quite enough, he would speak up sensibly and directly.

Yukio almost always had a serious expression on his face. But when he smiled, it was magic. Both those faces are etched in my memory forever. And we must not forget Kyoko, who was always at his side, as charming as he was, and most supportive of her husband. I saw them as two for one.

Previously, I mentioned that Yukio was a passionate defender of the U.S.–Japan alliance. Various Indo-Pacific Commanders (as it is now known) relied on his wisdom. In no way did he take second place to anyone when it came to defending our alliance. He was not, however, reluctant to speak out when he felt either Japan or the United States was getting a "little wobbly," to use Margaret Thatcher's famous phrase. Okamoto-san felt that the best chance for peace and stability in Asia lay in the body of our alliance. This was true in 1960, when Prime Minister Kishi and President Eisenhower signed our treaty. This was never more true than now, as authoritarian and anti-democratic urges are showing around the world. Yukio's passion for the alliance was outshone only by his passion for democracy. On this he was fervent. He realized that Japan needed a vibrant opposition in the Diet so that policies could be discussed, and the people of Japan could have real choice. He was not partisan, only professional.

This is a man who could have been a meteor in the Japanese Foreign Ministry but gave up that career track because of frustration with Japan's lack of participation in many global activities. Now, as Prime Minister Kishida strides ever more confidently on the world stage, Yukio's wisdom and experience could surely find footing with him.

On a personal note, how I loved his Christmas cards featuring underwater life—a highlight of the season for me. After Kyoko, Japan, and the U.S.–Japan alliance, he seemed to love the ocean the most!

I miss him deeply, mourn his death, and treasure his memory. He certainly knew John Donne's epic poem, "For Whom the Bell Tolls." It ends "And therefore never send to know for whom the bell tolls; it tolls for thee."

Okamoto-san was involved in mankind. Therefore, when the bell tolled, he answered it. The world was a much better place with him among us and we are the less for his loss.

Reminiscence

by Joseph S. Nye, Jr.

Former Chair, U.S. National Intelligence Council, USG (1993–94)

YUKIO OKAMOTO was a national and international treasure. I first met him at a Pacific Forum Conference on Japan–U.S. relations in the 1990s. It is hard to remember, given the strength of the alliance today, that it was under challenge in that period. The Cold War had ended, and many in Tokyo and Washington regarded it as a historical relic to be discarded rather than a guiding policy. Some in Japan were urging the government to move to a security policy that would rest upon the United Nations rather than the United States. Some in Washington believed that the Japanese economic challenge to the U.S. economy was a greater threat than the rise of China or the uncertainty posed by North Korea's nuclear program.

Yukio was a kindred soul in believing that the alliance was not obsolete because of the end of the Cold War and instead could become the basis for stability that would foster economic growth. Security is like oxygen. We tend to take it for granted until we begin to miss it, and then nothing else matters. Yukio and I shared this view, and we worked together to make it a reality. He was then outside the government but in constant contact with officials on both sides of the Pacific and a constant source of good ideas and support.

I was then working in the Pentagon developing an East Asia Strategy Report and negotiating with Japanese counterparts to obtain as high-level declaration reaffirming the alliance. The Japanese government of the day included Socialist members with a long history of skepticism about the alliance with the U.S. There was reluctance to issue a declaration reaffirming the alliance. Nonetheless, in 1996 the two governments issued the Hashimoto-Clinton Declaration in

Tokyo affirming that the Japan–U.S. alliance was the basis for stability in the East Asian region.

Yukio and I continued our friendship after I left government and returned to Harvard. We would visit each other's houses when he was at MIT or I was visiting Tokyo. In addition, we shared countless podiums at conferences in both countries over the years. Like others, I always benefited from his wise perspective as well as specific advice. Thus, it was not surprising that I said yes when Yukio asked me if I would read the early drafts of the chapters that comprise this memoir. I found it a fascinating and important story and learned a great deal from it, as other readers will as well. I was struck by its profound honesty, particularly in coming to terms with his father's generation. Equally important was his wise perspective about the future. That was the mark of the man and why we miss him so much. We are fortunate that he has left us these words.

Prelude

Emperors and the Gengō System

THE NEW ERA OF REIWA started in Japan on May 1, 2019, after the era of Heisei, which lasted for 30 years from 1989. According to the government, *Reiwa* means that a culture is born as people bring their hearts together. Delegations from 183 countries attended the enthronement ceremony of Emperor Naruhito on October 22.

In the Constitution that held until Japan lost World War II, Article 1 stated that "The Empire of Japan shall be reigned over and governed by a line of Emperors unbroken for ages eternal." As the Sino-Japanese War started in 1931 amid the whirlwind of fascism, the deification of the "living god" emperor gained momentum.

But Japan lost the War, and on January 12, 1946, the year after the War came to an end, the Emperor himself denied divinity and issued a rescript commonly known as The Humanity Declaration:

I and the People have an eternal connection based on mutual trust and affection that does not depend upon legends and myths. The connection is not founded on the false pretense that the Emperor is divine, or that the Japanese people are superior to other races and fated to rule the world.

Under the recommendation of General Douglas MacArthur, who was in charge of the occupation of Japan, the United States decided to leave the imperial system in place as a "symbol of the unity of the people," but the way that Emperor Hirohito was to be accepted by the public after ruling Japan through the War was not fully defined.

It was Emperor Akihito of Heisei, the first emperor to ascend the throne as a human emperor, who established his presence marvelously. In search of what it meant to be the Emperor as a symbol of the State, Emperor Akihito visited battlefields of the Asia-Pacific War in memory of the fallen, sat with the people who were suffering from natural disasters as they happened, tried to contact as many common people as possible, and earned the affection and respect of the citizens. The present imperial system has been accepted and now has a stable position among the people of Japan.

In Japan, eras are named after the Emperor in reign. These years are called "*gengō*." After the Meiji Restoration put an end to the Edo Shogunate that had lasted for 265 years from 1603, the Meiji and Taisho Eras followed under their respective emperors. Emperor Hirohito's 63 years from 1926 to 1989 were called Showa. This was a turbulent period for Japan.

Emperor Hirohito died in 1989 and the new era under Emperor Akihito, Crown Prince during World War II, was called Heisei. Heisei ended after 30 years with the first abdication by an emperor in 202 years. The new Emperor of Reiwa, Naruhito, was born 15 years after the end of the War.

Gengō is not compatible with the western calendar. We cannot make comparisons with world events without having to pull out a conversion table every single time. Still, our government continues to use *gengō*. Under *gengō*, Japan marks its own time with its own clock, and the days go by. Japan's temporal axes and era classifications are not completely integrated with the international community.

On the other hand, *gengō* era names are convenient when simplifying periods to describe them. For example: Meiji, when the modern state was formed; Taisho, when democracy flourished for a short time; Early Showa, the 20 years dominated by darkness and madness; defeat and reconstruction in Mid-Showa; growth and prosperity in Late Showa; the collapse of the bubble and stagnation of Heisei, and so on. We are yet to know how the Reiwa Era will be remembered.

This book depicts events that took place mainly during the Showa and Heisei eras.

Part One is a story centered on the first half of Showa, the age of darkness, described by Japan's noted 20th century historical novelist Ryotaro Shiba as when "Japan wandered into a magical forest and got lost."[1]

PART ONE

MY PARENTS' WAR

MY FATHER SHUZO'S WAR

A Rebellious Agricultural Engineer

MY FATHER SHUZO was born in Meiji 42 (1909) in Osaka, the largest city in western Japan. Shuzo's father Tsunetaro was born in 1885 to a poor farmer in Harima (in present-day Hyogo Prefecture bordering Osaka to the west). After serving in the Russo-Japanese War, Tsunetaro moved to Osaka, where he built an ironworks, then expanded his business and later established a shipping com-

pany that operated between Osaka and Shikoku. He also ran a railway, albeit small, and bought ships from the United States that he used to make big profits on trading with Qingdao, China. However, he lived a turbulent life and lost everything when his business ultimately failed.

Japan transformed from a feudal to a modern state during the Meiji Era (1868–1912). It was a period of emergence when the country was overflowing with hope and shining most brilliantly. In the grand serial novel of six volumes *Saka no Ue no Kumo* (*Clouds Above*

Yukio Okamoto's mother and father, Kazuko and Shuzo, at their wedding on November 17, 1937, at Meguro Gajoen in Tokyo.

the Hill)[2], Ryotaro Shiba starts the epic by saying, "A very small nation is about to enter a great cultural flowering." Meiji, which started out with a modern nation winning the Sino-Japanese and Russo-Japanese Wars, was described vividly through the story of two brothers who were army and navy officers. "Looking at the white clouds shining in the blue heaven on the hill going up"—it was an optimistic period for the citizens to progress.

Shuzo was born near the end of this Meiji Era. While he was attending high school under the former education system, he met Nobuo Origuchi, a poet and one of Japan's leading scholars, and started visiting at his home. Origuchi was more than 20 years older than Shuzo and lived in Osaka, teaching at a junior high school. Shuzo was impressed by how passionately Origuchi explained the importance of agriculture, and started to consider agricultural administration as a career.

The person that Origuchi looked up to as his lifetime mentor was Kunio Yanagida, the father of Japanese native folklore studies. Even though people continue to read his writings on the ethnic uniqueness and homogeneity of the Japanese today, Yanagida was originally an official in the Ministry of Agriculture and Forestry (MAF). He believed that the quality of life of poor farmers should be improved by increasing the productivity of Japanese agriculture through scale expansion and technological innovation. However, opponents to Yanagida's policy were powerful, both landowners who wanted to increase yields by increasing the number of peasants, and industrialists who valued mass production in agriculture.

Landowners dominated the Imperial Assembly, Japan's first Western-style parliament. Voting rights were given only to those who could pay a tax of five yen or more annually. Policies that MAF designed to save poor farmers were continually crushed by the Imperial Assembly.

Through Origuchi, Shuzo became a great believer in Yanagida's ideas. Considering it his mission to improve the lives of poor farmers, he entered the Faculty of Agriculture at Kyoto Imperial University and in 1932, joined MAF.

The first job he was given was to study rice production growth at the experimental agriculture station in Nagano Prefecture, where many poor farmers lived. After that, he returned to the Ministry headquarters and worked for the Agricultural Products Division of the Ministry's Bureau of Agriculture. His job was to increase the productivity and output of Japanese agriculture. Yanagida had worked in a division of the same Bureau before Shuzo joined the Ministry.

At the time, a major conflict ensued over agricultural policies. On average, Japanese farmers were cultivating just 0.5 hectares (1.2 acres) of land, and most worked as peasants under their landowner. The peasant life was harsh and poor. Their main crop was rice, but they sold all the rice they raised and lived on millet, barnyard grass, and daikon radish, much as they had 100 years before. Even after Yanagida retired, MAF had carried on his approach, believing that expanding farmland and increasing productivity was the best way to increase farmers' income and enable Japanese agriculture to survive. But then, MAF teamed up with the military to expand Japanese interests in Manchuria and started sending Japanese farmers there, where there was vast farmland.

The Manchurian Migration Policy, which began in 1932, was a policy of MAF that attempted to protect peasant farmers who were being exploited by landowners. However, it also was a policy designed to support the Imperial Army's ambition to solidify its reign over Manchuria. Naturally, it led to clashes with the landowners who opposed having their peasants sent overseas.

MAF promised to give 10 hectares (24.7 acres) of land to Japanese farmers who migrated to Manchuria, while forcibly purchasing the farmland for practically nothing from Chinese and Koreans who were settled there. The goal was to move rice farmers from Tohoku and Nagano as well as silk farmers who had suffered devastation during the Great Depression.

In reality, however, few farmers left their homes for Manchuria. Seeing that its original plan had failed, the Ministry announced that it would provide subsidies for agricultural infrastructure to municipalities that cooperated with the program. This prompted a large number of mayors to persuade farmers in their districts to go to Manchuria.

Soon after, war went into full swing on the Chinese continent and many farmers in Japan were drafted, leaving a shortage of farmers in

Japan. Because of this, the initial plan of the Ministry—to move one million of the 5.5 million farming houses across Japan to Manchuria—was eventually downsized to 100,000. This process is detailed in Kazuhito Yamashita's "*Revival of Kunio Yanagida's Agricultural Policy Reform*."[3]

This Ministry of Agriculture and Forestry policy later led to tragedy. With the final defeat of Japan in the War, the Chinese who had formerly owned the farmlands attacked the Japanese farm households, where only women and children remained after the men had been drafted as soldiers. Facing carnage and rape, many of the women killed their children and committed suicide.

Yamashita believes that sending pioneers to Manchuria was a blemish on the pre-War history of the Ministry of Agriculture and Forestry.

That my father Shuzo consistently thought it was most important for Japan to increase agricultural productivity was obvious from his responses at Diet interpellations after the War.

His teaching had been correct, but Shuzo, who sat at the top of the class until he graduated university, was intellectually arrogant and stubborn. He did not listen to the opinions of others. A former colleague of his told me that Shuzo remained committed to Yanagida and opposed the MAF policy of sending poor farmers to Manchuria. It must had been noticed by the military.

Moreover, Shuzo was critical of the war itself. His wife Kazuko repeatedly heard him say, "I am against this war." She said that at the government office, they called him an "anti-military element."

In July 1940, the Ministry abruptly rescinded a promise it had made to send him to England to study. Instead, he was suddenly drafted and dispatched to the Soviet-Manchurian border. There was no strong need to draft a 31-year-old bureaucrat at that early stage of the war. And worse, although Shuzo had a title of *Koto-kan* (Senior Official) in the Central Government, the rank usually deemed the same as Colonel in the Army, Shuzo was drafted as a Private, the rank given to 18-year-old boys with no education. Kazuko believes that the MAF sold Shuzo to the Army as an anti-war element because he opposed sending farmers to Manchuria.

Draft notices were sent to men across Japan. In 1936, the year before the Sino-Japanese War went into full swing, there were 320,000 men in the Army. By the time Shuzo was drafted four years later, the Imperial Army had 61 Divisions with 2.4 million soldiers. Combined with the 430,000 in the Imperial Navy, Japan's military force was 2.83 million strong. This is 10 times the strength of Japan's Self Defense Forces today. Later, as the war situation deteriorated, more and more men were drafted and by the end of the war in August 1945, the Imperial Army had 5.5 million troops in 172 Divisions, while the Navy had 1.7 million. It was an enormous inflation of numbers with the total number of troops at 7.2 million, when Japan's population was a mere 72 million.

Between the two of them, my father and mother had eight brothers and sisters, five of whom were drafted. Shuzo was ordered to appear in the 37th Regiment of the 4th Division Infantry in his hometown Osaka. Osaka was originally a commercial city, and the people had a good reputation for business but were not deemed suitable for combat. The 4th Division was chastised as the weakest division in Japan, known for always being the last to arrive in the battlefield when ordered to make a sortie and terribly weak at battle.

In addition, his military classification was "transport soldier," a soldier who transports food, ammunition, and fuel. The Japanese Army, which put 'Infantry First' and disregarded logistics, considered this the lowest job in the military. Transport soldiers were ridiculed within the Army with a saying: "If a transport auxiliary is a solder, then butterflies and dragonflies are birds, broiled fish will start swimming, and flowers will bloom on telephone poles." Indeed, this extreme neglect of the transport division became a major cause of Japan's repeated defeats in the War.

The day before his departure, a crowd gathered at Kazuko's father's house to celebrate Shuzo's new beginning. Shuzo leaned alone against a window with his eyes closed, not saying a word to anyone. The next morning, he went on his way walking through the throng of neighbors who came out to see him off, waving their miniature Japanese flags. Kazuko says that he did not utter a word.

My Hero Who Lived Next Door

Shuzo was sent to Sun Wu, in Heihe City on the Amur River at the Soviet-Manchurian border. Across from Heihe lies Blagoveshchensk, capital of the state of Amur in the Soviet Union.

To explain Japan's actions at the time, it would be most appropriate to introduce the story of a Japanese soldier by the name of Makiyo Ishimitsu. Ishimitsu lived through the turbulent periods of Meiji, Taisho and Showa—from the birth of modern Japan to its destruction by war. I was captivated by Ishimitsu's memoir, a book that stood in my father's bookcase when I was a boy, and he became my hero. (In 1958, his bereaved family published the massive diary that Ishimitsu had attempted to incinerate just before he died in 1942, as a more than 1,100-page memoir. Its content and narrative make the diary one of the best autobiographies of modern times.)

Ishimitsu served in the Sino-Japanese War as an Army Lieutenant, fighting Chinese troops in Taiwan. After one battle, he heard a voice coming from a mountain of dead bodies of the enemy. It was the voice of a little girl, crying. She had been tied to the back of a female soldier. Ishimitsu took this girl with him to fight the next battles. His unit supported Ishimitsu, who never let go of the girl on the battlefield. Until he was able to entrust her to a village chief, he lay down by her side while thoughts of the cruelty of war kept him awake at night. This was the figure of a Japanese Meiji soldier.

After that, Ishimitsu had come to think that Russia was the true threat to Japan and he moved to Blagoveshchensk in 1899, where he studied Russian. Later, in mainland China, he scurried around the fields of Manchuria collecting information, disguised as a laundry shop owner, or a coolie, or even a mountain bandit.

When the Russo-Japanese War started in 1904, Ishimitsu returned to the Army as a Major and fought the Russian Army in Mukden. He felt troubled by the tragedies that the devastating war was causing people in China and Russia, however, and he started to put the people whose lives were trampled above his loyalty to the Army.

In October 1917, a socialist revolution took place in Russia. Citizens feared Bolsheviks, whose rampage rose in rebellion against the Cossack, in the state of Amur. They asked Ishimitsu, who had returned to Blagoveshchensk for the first time in 20 years, for help. After some serious contemplation, Ishimitsu stood up to support the people who opposed the revolution. He bonded with not only the civil vigilantes and Cossacks, but also with the Bolsheviks. His personal purpose was to do his utmost to lead the Japanese militia to avoid bloodshed.

Blagoveshchensk eventually fell into the hands of the revolutionary army and the Great Russian Empire collapsed. But Japan, along with seven countries including the United States, China, and Italy, sent troops to Siberia to crush the revolutionary army. While the other countries all sent fewer than 10,000 troops, Japan stood out with 73,000.

Ishimitsu was skeptical of the Japanese military's policy to gain independence for Amur and make it a buffer country between revolutionary Russia and Manchuria. Not only that, Japanese soldiers stationed in Siberia repeatedly invaded, assaulted and looted homes, so the residents who had initially welcomed the Japanese military started to turn against on them. Ishimitsu was infuriated by the behavior of the Japanese Army and went to Vladivostok to discuss this with Lieutenant General Shigeru Oi, the Commander-in-Chief of the Division there. Ishimitsu expressed his opinion to Oi, even telling him that if the situation were not to change, Japan should gracefully withdraw all troops.

Later, he wrote this in his diary:[4]

Commander Oi stood up with his face burning red: "That's it! I've heard enough!"

My heartbeat was hammering. It was all I could do to swallow my words.

"Who, pray tell, are you working for? The Russians?"

"I beg to be pardoned of my mission. I am unfit for this job."

"Fine. Quit, then."

I turned my back to the door and headed straight to Vladivostok Station, where I boarded a train. I was boiling with anger. The station was still swarming with Japanese soldiers.

Is it loyal to make sacrifices, knowing that the objectives of intervention in Siberia will not be met? If it fails, would it be correct to pass it off as a mistake made by the higher officials, saying that I was loyal to the responsibilities I was ordered to fulfill, therefore am not at fault?

Through the window, the fields, rivers, and hills were completely dressed in white, painting the same scene day and night, then again at dawn. Everything was frozen white.

I was approaching the end of my journey. What waited for me there was a thick wall that no amount of striking or throwing myself at could tear down. Even if I pulled myself back to reorient, on my next approach, the unbudging wall still stood in my way. I collapsed at the wall and laid my dishonorable self down.

Ishimitsu had seen through the nature of the Japanese Army. Finally, disillusioned with the Japanese military, he left Blagoveshchensk. Japan continued to station troops in Siberia even after each country had retreated. It even temporarily occupied Irkutsk in the western part of Lake Baikal.

In the end, however, things turned out just as Ishimitsu had feared they would. The Japanese Army fell under siege by the Red Army in Siberia, suffered great loss, and retreated in 1922. Prime Minister Yuzaburo Kato proclaimed the dispatch of troops to Siberia as a "history of misappropriation rarely seen in diplomacy, not resulting in the least bit of national interest."

After experiencing more adverse fortune, Ishimitsu returned to Japan and lived in the ancient capital of Kamakura for eight years, taking care of his sick wife. He recalled: "*The limitless sky and boundless ocean, ceaseless breezes and consistent waves of the Pacific became my only comforting friends.*"

This surprised me. Not many houses had been built along the beach in Kamakura at the time. One of them was where I spent my childhood. Ishimitsu had passed away in 1942, amidst disappointment and poverty, a few years before I was born, but the address his grandson gave me was in my immediate neighborhood. My hero had lived just next door.

31-year-old Transport Soldier

Transport soldier Shuzo was assigned to the 18th Field Army Arsenal in Sun Wu County, Heihe City, Heilongjiang Province. Heihe City was a place Ishimitsu had frequently visited from Blagoveshchensk across the river.

Although Japan had withdrawn from Siberia, it expanded control of China on partial leasehold rights of the Liaodong Peninsula acquired in the Russo-Japanese War. Then, on September 18, 1931, the Japan's Kwantung Army blew up Japan's own Manchurian Railway at Liutiaohu Lake near Shenyang. Japan blamed the incident on the Chinese Army and used it as an excuse to immediately take full control of Manchuria.

The war that started this way dragged in all of the citizens of Japan and China until 1945. In 1932, Japan established "Manchukuo," a government that would dominate the current Chinese provinces of Liaoning, Jilin, Heilongjiang, and the autonomous region of Inner Mongolia.

Now that Japan reigned over Manchukuo, its biggest enemy became the Soviet Union. Japanese forces had withdrawn from Siberia in 1922 but continued to clash with Stalin's Soviet Union. In May 1939, one year before Shuzo was assigned to Sun Wu, Japan launched a large-scale battle against the Soviet Union along the Soviet-Manchurian border. This was the famous Nomonhan Incident (aka the Battle of Khalkhin Gol). Some 58,000 soldiers were mobilized on the Japanese side, against 69,000 from the Soviet Union. The battle began with a unilateral attack by the Japanese Army, which later suffered great damage from a Soviet Army counter-attack in August. A ceasefire agreement was signed on September 15, 1939.

Originally, this was no more than a small conflict on the border in the wild, which the Kwantung Army did not have a strategy to bring to an end. The Army expanded the battle without even notifying the Imperial headquarters in Japan and ended up being defeated in the face of the Soviet Army's overwhelming ability to outfit and replenish.

It was between the Japanese Forces' spiritualism that says, "We won't know until we try. It will work out somehow," and the Soviet troops' rationalism and overwhelming material advantage.[5] (Ryoichi Tobe, et al.)

This battle that historians evaluate as the "first modern war and first major defeat for the Japanese Army" was an important milestone. Shuzo was stationed at the Soviet-Manchurian border for military service in July 1941, two years after the Nomonhan Incident.

The 18th Field Army Arsenal that Shuzo belonged to was secured and managed supplies necessary for field battle, based on lessons learned from the Nomonhan defeat. The specific mission he was given is unknown, but being a private, it likely had to do with simply pushing carriages and carts.

Or perhaps he was given a different mission, as I will explain later.

In any case, Shuzo very likely could not put up with the situation. Wanting to learn Russian like Makiyo Ishimitsu, he requested entrance into the Kwantung Military Russian Language School in Harbin. His commander probably also found it difficult to use an elder transport soldier who was isolated from the others. Fortunately, Shuzo was admitted to the school despite being a soldier of the lowest rank. After graduation, he became an interpreter based in Harbin. This was one year after his assignment to Sun Wu.

The Kwantung Army needed people who understood Russian for another reason, which Shuzo had no way of knowing at the time.

Shuzo completed the one-year Russian language course, graduated at the top of his class, and received a silver watch from Kwantung Army Commander-General Yoshijiro Umezu for his performance. After the War ended, many books written in Russian lined his bookshelf. The only war stories my father told his sons—as he showed them this watch—were about how hard he had studied Russian.

General Umezu was surprised at the grades achieved by a mere transport soldier. He investigated Shuzo's history and strongly urged him to apply for an officer's status with a simple exam, saying it was not too late. Like Shuzo, his older brother Shoichi and his younger brother Shigeki had both graduated from Kyoto Imperial University, took the test as soon as they were recruited to the Army, and enjoyed privileges as second lieutenant and lieutenant, respectively, even without any military training.

Shuzo fervently refused Umezu's recommendation. His anti-military spirit made him stubbornly reject promotion. For this reason, older veteran soldiers often beat him, saying, "We'll beat that pretentious attitude out of you!"

General Umezu apparently took time to talk with Shuzo, who later recalled, "Mr. Umezu was a decent person in the military. There were some human-like humans among professional soldiers."

Toward the end of the War, as Army Chief of Staff, Umezu said that Japan should fight a decisive battle with the United States on the mainland. However, it seemed that his real intention lay elsewhere. In June 1945, he explained to Emperor Hirohito that the Army had absolutely no capability to carry on. This reporting was believed to have moved the Emperor in the direction of peace. At the Supreme Council for the Direction of the War, over which the Emperor presided, Umezu was sympathetic with Navy Minister Yonai's reconciliation policy with the United States. After the War, Umezu remained silent throughout the Tokyo Trials and was sentenced to life imprisonment. He died while serving his sentence.

After completing Russian school, Shuzo did not return to his original unit but instead worked as "interpreter personnel" at the 4th Army Command. Later, he told his children that while he was in Manchuria, he had intercepted Russian broadcasts and translated them into Japanese. He was probably referring to this period.

The circumstances of how Shuzo was sent to Manchuria are as I explained above, but there remains a mystery. Would the Kwantung Army stationed there actually waste a technical bureaucrat over the age of 30 on pulling carts as a transport soldier? Expelling Shuzo from Tokyo in a humiliating position should have been punishment enough for his unacceptable attitude. There was no reason to send him to the Arsenal in Sun Wu as a transport soldier.

My conjecture is this: Unit 731's Branch 673 was in Sun Wu, in close proximity to the Arsenal. That branch was collecting large numbers of wild rodents by order of the Unit 731 headquarters in the Pingfang district of Harbin. The purpose was to collect rats and cultivate fleas to propagate the plague-causing bacteria *Yersinia pestis*.

It is possible that Shuzo was forced to engage in the capture of these rodents at Branch 673. The MAF knows best about rats, the enemy of agricultural products. It would be natural for the Kwantung Army to think that they could use Shuzo in that way. After the War, Shuzo often told Kazuko how much he hated rats. While ranking as a transport soldier, Shuzo Okamoto might very well have been working at the Unit 731 Sun Wu Detachment and not at the Arsenal.

From Sun Wu, Shuzo was transferred to Army Unit 731 in Pingfang, a suburb of Harbin. There is no doubt that he was at Unit 731 in January 1945, but the specific date of his relocation is unknown.

All Japanese Army units were serially numbered. The number 731 was assigned to the Epidemic Prevention and Water Purification Department Headquarters stationed in Pingfang. The Unit worked under the pretense of conducting research for the prevention of epidemics among soldiers and securing a water supply system accordingly. However, the reality was that human experimentation of biological weapons was being conducted on prisoners. The prisoners were called *maruta*, or "logs." The Unit cultivated pathogens of diseases such as plague, typhoid, and paratyphoid, bred infection vectors such as fleas and rats, then applied them to actual battle. The lives of about 3,000 prisoners, including Chinese, Russians, and Koreans, were sacrificed in this Unit, which later came to be known as the Devil's Unit. Its commander was Surgeon General Shiro Ishii, chief medical officer of the Imperial Army.

Bacterial Unit 731

Unit 731 was established due to Ishii's paranoia about bacterial warfare. He persuaded the Army's top-ranking officials that Germany, the U.K., and the U.S. were all researching bacterial weapons, and in 1932, had the unit established based on his ideas.

By early 1945 the unit had grown into a huge organization with a total of 3,552 members consisting of 1,344 military servicemen and 2,208 civilian army employees. The budget related to Unit 731 reached roughly 30 billion yen in current value.

The large-scale expansion of Unit 731 was the result of the weakening of the powerful Kwantung Army. As the Japanese Army became outnumbered in Southeast Asia and the Pacific, the Imperial Headquarters ordered the Kwantung Army to send troops to the southern battlefront as reinforcements. As a result, the Kwantung Army, which had been 700,000-strong, significantly weakened and lacked equipment. This is when military leaders came up with the idea that "the only powerful weapon is a bacterial weapon."

The Soviet Union had placed a force of 1.2 million men on the Soviet-Manchurian border. The Soviet Union had a Neutrality Pact with Japan in order to concentrate on the European front against Germany, but the Kwantung Army knew that this was only temporary, that it was only a matter of time before Soviet troops would start pouring into Manchuria. Unlike the Tokyo government, which unrealistically expected the Soviets, as a neutral country, to mediate peace with the United States, the Kwantung Army's outlook was not optimistic. The Army was all too aware of the overwhelming difference in strength, which they learned from the battle in Nomonhan. For this reason, they quickly leaned toward a forbidden bacterial war to fight the Soviet Union.

Surgeon General Ishii was correct in his argument that every country was studying bacterial weapons, but Unit 731 was conducting research that other countries were not.

First of all, the experiments on humans were an organized effort. Secondly, they set the principal object of these experiments to research and grow *Yersinia pestis*, an extremely lethal and contagious bacteria, which no other country did. Thirdly, they actually used these weapons on the battlefield, such as when it dropped bacterial bombs on Ningbo and Changde between 1940 and 1942.

What Unit 731 was doing was the work of the devil.

Ishii thought that only bacterial weapons could enable the Japanese forces to compete with the United States. Toward the end of 1944, the Navy joined Ishii in an attempt to attack the United States with bacterial warfare, called Operation PX. The plan was for a submarine to approach the U.S. mainland. The submarine would carry a special airplane, which would be used to sprinkle bacteria on the west coast.

It was Yoshijiro Umezu, who by then had become Army Chief of Staff after giving Shuzo the silver watch in Harbin, who adamantly opposed this strategy. He forced the plan to be canceled, saying, "A bacterial war against the United States means war against all humanity."

Today, he will not stand the test of anti-racism as he did not say the same thing against using bacterial weapons in China. Such was the limit of the Japanese notion of human rights at the time.

It was doctors and medical researchers who led the cruel human experimentation and the practical application in battle at Unit 731.

In August 2017, the Japanese public broadcaster NHK conducted a thorough investigation of Unit 731 and revealed the cooperative relationship that existed between the Army and universities at the time.[6] The military provided major research funding to at least ten universities and research institutes, with the medical departments of the top two universities—Tokyo Imperial University and Kyoto Imperial University—at the center. In exchange, the universities sent many medical professors and researchers to Unit 731.

The school that sent the most researchers was Shuzo's mother school, Kyoto Imperial University. By 1942, the number of researchers from there had reached 75.

There were various reactions to the NHK report, but many of them were positive, praising NHK for reporting the truth. Japanese were finally facing this issue from their past.

Shuzo went from Sun Wu to Harbin's Russian language school, but as irony would have it, it was likely because he graduated at the top of the class that he was assigned to Unit 731 Headquarters in Pingfang. Added to that, the Kyoto Imperial University group that was sending the largest team of doctors to Unit 731 may have lured him into the secret facility, relieved that he was an alumnus.

Kazuko thinks that in addition to interpreting, Shuzo was also made to research how to wither crops, such as with blight. She says that Shuzo had hinted at this. If so, the agricultural engineer who wanted to join the MAF to increase agricultural production found himself turned to the opposite, to destroying farming. A truly ironic fate.

How did the fact that Shuzo worked for Unit 731 become known to his wife Kazuko? The reason is quite simple. Being the passionate person that she was, Kazuko went to Harbin to see Shuzo in 1945.

After Shuzo's death, Kazuko revealed this to her children for the first time.

"Shuzo-san told me he was working to prevent infectious diseases. I had no reason to doubt this, but I thought there was something strange going on, too. I mean, why would Shuzo-san have the kind of freedom to leave his duty to come and see me? But I just figured that he was promoted to a higher position. Yes, I heard he was working in the Kwantung Army Quarantine Water Supply Department. When I learnt long after the War that this was another name for the infamous Unit 731, was I ever surprised!

"It was then that I knew the reason why Shuzo's personality became so distorted. But you've got to promise me: Don't ever talk about this to other people."

I wanted to research further, but I had to respect my mother's plea to keep Shuzo's history hidden from the outside world, so I gave up. However, in April 2018, the Japanese government, at long last, released the list of the 3,607 men who belonged to Unit 731 as of January 1945. I could "officially" find my father's name in the National Archives, and my mother could no longer object. Unfortunately, by then, too much time had gone by and no survivors remained who had known Shuzo at the Unit.

In the early 1940s, there were 80,000 Russians living in the City of Harbin. As Japan was not yet at war with the Soviet Union, there were no POWs, but Shiro Ishii and the Unit 731 military police were extremely afraid that rumors about human experimentation would leak out. Using citizen informants, they secretly sought any Russians who showed interest in the mission of Unit 731 and caught them and sent them to prison on the grounds of spying on the Unit. So, Shuzo might have been used to interpret for Russian prisoners who ultimately were to be used for human experimentation.

Interrogation of the Russians was harsh. A trial held in Khabarovsk after the defeat of Japan indicted Japan for many charges including conducting human experimentation on a Russian woman holding an infant. Did Shuzo have to be at the place of interrogation to interpret her words, too?

As Shuzo refused to talk about anything concerning Manchuria other than receiving his silver watch, we children had no idea what he had experienced.

What I do know for sure is that Shuzo suffered personally as a result. Any intellectual elite is vulnerable to collapse. His initial humiliation and his abominable experiences cramped and contorted his personality. The War changed the gentle literary youth, the one who loved to play the flute whenever he had time, into a man who was perpetually depressed, antisocial, and constantly dissatisfied with the contradictions of the world.

Today, the only people who can talk about Unit 731 are those who belonged to the Boys' Brigade of Unit 731. That is because they were assigned to the Unit from the age of 14, meaning that more of them are still alive today. These boys were those who had earned excellent grades in school, whom Shiro Ishii had selected from across the country in 1940, when Japan did not expect to lose the war, to train as future bacterial war leaders. They entered a special program where students took chemistry, physics, medicine, and pharmacology, among other subjects, while they were trained in Unit 731 and received a salary.

I visited one of them, 91-year-old Kikuta Sunaga. Today he lives quietly in Karuizawa, 170 kilometers from Tokyo, with his son's family.

Young Sunaga had no idea what Unit 731 was or what they did. All he wanted was to help the country, so he applied for the Boys' Brigade and passed. He went to Harbin with 106 others who had also passed the exam. As soon as he reached the Unit in Pingfang, however, he saw a sign at the gate and was struck with an ominous feeling: "Those who enter without permission will be shot dead." Luckily, he was sent into the manufacturing department that made containers for bacterial bombs, so he did not have to encounter the cruel scenes of human experimentation. Still, he was stunned when he witnessed prisoners with their legs chained.

Sunaga can still clearly hear Ishii's voice in his speech when they arrived at the Unit. "Japan's enemies are developing new weapons. The weapons that Japan can win with are bacterial weapons. I want you boys to study here so that you can eventually become the leaders of Japan's bacterial warfare."

Sunaga was in the Unit at the same time as my father Shuzo. He

escaped Harbin on the same day, but there was no contact between
the two.

The Devils' Escape

On July 31, 1945, when the defeat of Japan became inevitable, Unit
731 received a sudden mission order: "Blow up and destroy all buildings, equipment, and machinery on unit grounds, cremate every
prisoner in the prison, completely destroy all evidence, and return
all troops to the mainland."

From that moment, destruction work continued day and night.
Prisoners were gassed or shot to death. Tremendous quantities of
explosives, dynamite, and 200-kilogram bombs were brought in.
Masaru Shimoyama, who was assigned to Unit 731 at the age of 18,
wrote later that it was "work beyond imagination" and explosions
resembling battlefields resounded on the base day after day.[7]

On August 9, as large-scale demolition work continued at Unit
731, the Soviet Union abrogated the Soviet-Japanese Neutrality Pact
and charged into Manchuria with furious momentum. By August 13,
just before the Soviet Army reached Harbin, the facilities and POWs
had been completely erased and the Unit 731 generals and doctors
had escaped out of sight.

Commander General Shiro Ishii and his staff fled aboard seven
planes. Shuzo and the other soldiers withdrew from Harbin on August 13, two days before Japan surrendered. Many nurses and female
employees who had worked in the Unit escaped. The base had been
developed enough to even include an elementary school, so there
were many other women and children as well. Those people took
the first train out. Sunaga jumped on an open wagon transporting
coal and headed south toward the Korean Peninsula, determined. My
father Shuzo escaped the same way, probably on the same day, too.

As the train approached Pyongyang on August 15, Sunaga learned
the news that Japan had surrendered. Sunaga recalls that at that very
moment, the scenery changed. All the Japanese flags that had been
flying everywhere had been replaced with the Korean flag. When
they got off the train, the Japanese soldiers started to feel very vulnerable.

Meanwhile, many Japanese soldiers who did not know that Japan had surrendered were heading north toward the Kwantung Army Headquarters in the new capital Xinjing (now Changchun) to join the battlefront. Shuzo later muttered to his sons, "Why couldn't I just shout to those soldiers 'Japan has lost the War. Don't go!'"

Many of the soldiers who headed north were captured by the Russian Army and sent to Siberia and Central Asia. The exact number is unknown. Estimates range from 350,000 to 650,000. Of those, at least 60,000 died from forced labor and malnutrition.

Russia then captured vast numbers of Japanese soldiers across Manchuria, taking them prisoner. They encouraged the POWs to become informers and sought out those who had been with the top-secret Unit 731. This led to the trial in Khabarovsk of 12 members affiliated with Unit 731, including Kwantung Army General Otozo Yamada, who had succeeded Yoshijiro Umezu, and his men. The fact that we now know the reality of the human experimentation conducted by Unit 731 is largely through statements of the defendants during this trial.

The main reasons for Japan's continued animosity towards Russia are two; only six days before Japan surrendered, Russia entered the War; and even after Japan surrendered, Russia surged in and took four islands in the north, inherent territory unrelated to Japan's aggression.

And a third—the Siberian detention.

After changing trains a number of times, Shuzo and his colleagues arrived in the Korean Peninsula's southernmost city Pusan. There, they slept outside for a few nights waiting for a ferry to Japan. They sailed from Pusan on August 24 and arrived at Senzaki Port in Yamaguchi Prefecture. Senzaki later served as the entry point for more than 400,000 Japanese soldiers returning from the continent. My father's group, one of the first to return to Japan, ran back before anyone else because the Unit was notified of the coming debacle, days before others were. When they arrived, they burned every document, abandoned their weapons, and returned to their homes.

It was around midnight, just two weeks after Japan's official surrender that Shuzo quietly came home to his wife who had temporarily evacuated, with his head hung low. My mother Kazuko recalls screaming from fright believing she had seen a ghost, but it was actually Shuzo, totally exhausted, standing in the doorway.

As such, my father's homecoming was not a festive occasion. The Unit that may as well have been the devil was the first to pull out for classified reasons and as a result, all members were home safe and sound before anybody else. The guilty sinners left other soldiers and made a cowardly escape. Years later, Kazuko felt that this was what continued to torment Shuzo.

After the end of the War, Commander General Ishii negotiated with the United States Occupying Force GHQ to avoid arrest and prosecution by the Tokyo Tribunal by agreeing to hand over all of the data on biological experimentation. Ishii, who was very cautious and suspicious, still did not feel safe. He pretended to have died from illness and even faked his own funeral before going into hiding. He was a typical example of the Japanese military leader who refused to take responsibility.

In 1981, Kyo Shimamura called on Japan to take responsibility in his book, *Live Experiment on 3,000 Human Beings.*[8] Shimamura had been a reporter for the Japanese newspaper "Manchuria Daily Paper" before the War and had dug into the facts regarding Unit 731 while he was detained in Siberia after the War. He wrote:

> *Even many survivors of Auschwitz, Treblinka, and Majdanek were rescued after the War ended. None of those taken to Unit 731 ever returned home alive. Post-War Germany conducted and is still conducting a thorough pursuit in this area and exposing the facts. Why has Japan failed to do so?*

I visited the Unit 731 site in 2004, more than 60 years after Shuzo and the others withdrew.

The Chinese government had erected a large stone sign that read, "Site of Unit 731 of the Japanese Army that Invaded China," and the facilities were well kept. Under the hot summer sky on a clear July day, some white flowers were in bloom, but they did nothing to soften the scene.

The 731 soldiers had supposedly demolished the facilities, but many of the buildings remained. As I descended into the basement of the main building, I felt enveloped in a chill. The Chinese government had restored the facility as much as it could, and life-sized mannequins were placed in the room where human experimentation had been conducted to show visitors what had occurred. Torture instruments were on display.

The empty rooms without displays were actually more horrifying to me. Terror ran through me as my imagination created the vividly distorted faces of prisoners suffering in pain. In the dead silence, chills ran up my spine. My wife had accompanied me, but she could not stand the atmosphere any longer and escaped to the outside.

I, too, went outside. The summer sun and overgrown grass enveloped the area. There, the Japanese who had fled, including my father, and the captives who were unable to leave the facility alive—people on opposite ends of the spectrum—breathed the same air in the same place. Sunlight poured from between the leaves of the trees. How did the prisoners with their feet chained perceive this light?

The biggest shock to me came when I entered one narrow and shabby facility. It was as if it had been abandoned and left just as it was back at the time. The light from outside came through windows along the wall, evoking the scenes of this gloomy room. Inside was a concrete structure 20 meters long and 4 meters wide that resembled a water tank with no water. The tank was divided into about 100 compartments, each covered with a net lid. It was all covered in fallen leaves.

There was no explanation posted, but I intuitively felt that this tank had been used to breed rats. The rats that Shuzo adamantly hated would have been raised here as hosts for fleas, to spread the plague-causing bacteria *Yersinia pestis*. As Shuzo was sent to the Unit as an interpreter, he might have been lucky enough to avoid breeding rats as he had in Sun Wu (assuming my imagination is correct), but I could almost hear the cries of tens of thousands of rats coming from the tank. I felt my knees would crumble.

The War in the Pacific

Pearl Harbor Attack

WHILE SHUZO was at the Manchurian Front, in Tokyo, a decision was being made that would destroy the nation. It was the campaign to go to war with the United States. With the attack on Pearl Harbor on December 7, 1941, the Sino-Japanese War that had begun on September 18, 1931, at Liutiaohu in Liaoning, became the Asia-Pacific War.

The Japanese "Army" has long carried a cloud of suspicion and shame over its dubious strategy. Troops were sent to Siberia with the purpose of creating a buffer nation at the Soviet-Manchuria border. The Nomonhan battle started as a one-sided attack on the Soviet Union by Japan. The Manchurian invasion began when the Kwantung Army blasted the Manchurian Railway trains run by Japan, and made it look as if the Chinese Army had done it. And then the Pacific War began with no declaration of war, with the surprise attack on Pearl Harbor on a Sunday morning, when people were on their way to church.

The Japanese people found out after Japan's defeat in 1945 that the Army had been deceiving them all along. The anti-military sentiment deeply penetrated their awareness and remains unchanged today. Even a debate on national security, which would normally be an obvious thing to conduct, is considered taboo.

As a nation, if people could look back and proudly say that it had been a "war of justice that was fought fairly," this hatred of a military system would probably never have taken root.

In Japan, one key idea remains very much alive—that "the reason the U.S. condemns Japan for the 'sneak attack' on Pearl Harbor is that the Japanese Embassy in Washington did not deliver the declaration of war to the U.S. Government on time." This explanation is used to show the U.S. is unreasonable and Japan is misunderstood.

However, this trivial argument only captures the slight time lag in the final phase.

To begin with, the Memorandum against the United States that Japan delivered to the U.S. Department of State said, "The Japanese Government regrets to have to notify hereby the American Government, that in view of the attitude of the American Government, it cannot but consider that it is impossible to reach an agreement through further negotiations."

This was no more than an "intention to break off negotiations." It was only after the bombs were dropped on Pearl Harbor that the State Department understood it as an ultimatum stating a declaration of war. After all, even the Japanese Embassy that was decrypting the telegrams received did not think this statement was a declaration of war. It was surely disingenuous. The Japanese government tried to hide its intention to attack until the bitter end.

Secondly, the plan was that the Memorandum would be delivered to the U.S. Department of State at 1300 hours on December 7 (Eastern Standard Time). However, at 11:30 EST, 183 bombers had already taken off from a fleet of aircraft carriers off the coast of Hawaii. Bombing started at 13:20 EST. It doesn't make sense to claim Japan is being unfairly criticized when it had started scattering bombs just 20 minutes after delivering its "intention to break off negotiations."

In the first place, the Imperial Fleet, with a mainstay of five aircraft carriers, set sail from Hitokappu Bay on Etorofu Island (now a part of the Northern Territories held by Russia) to attack Pearl Harbor on November 26. On December 2, the fleet heading to Hawaii received a command from Imperial Headquarters to attack Pearl Harbor. Was this fair and legal under international law?

This is how the Pacific War with the United States began.

My mother Kazuko's two younger brothers were sent to Guadalcanal and Okinawa. My father Shuzo's elder brother was sent to the Ogasawara Islands, close to the tragic Iwo Island (Iwo Jima).

Defeat at Guadalcanal

Kazuko's younger brother Subaru was six years her junior. He graduated from the Toba College of Merchant Marines and took a job at Osaka Shosen (now Mitsui OSK) to become a navigator. However, the ship he boarded was requisitioned by the Navy and incorporated into a transport fleet headed for Guadalcanal Island and was sunk by a U.S. torpedo off the coast of the island. Subaru drifted at sea for two days, waiting to be rescued, and swallowed a large amount of heavy oil, which ruined his lungs. He survived but had become too weak to go to sea again and eventually he died of lung complications. As far as Kazuko was concerned, it was the war at Guadalcanal that killed him.

Guadalcanal was the first place where the Japanese Army confronted the U.S. Army head on. It was also the beginning of Japan's defeat and subsequent withdrawal from the Pacific Islands.

On August 7, 1942, the U.S. landed in Guadalcanal to take over the airfield that the Japanese Army had built. The Imperial headquarters dispatched troops—916-strong—led by Kiyonao Ichiki to make a surprise attack and recover the island. They thought it would be easy to destroy what they thought would be a small number of U.S. forces, and that the Imperial Army was undefeatable.

However, what was waiting for them was a huge unit of 19,000 men with powerful equipment, chiefly of the U.S. Marine Corps First Division. Japanese troops were dispatched intermittently after the Ichiki troops were annihilated, but Japan lacked information and military logistics, and ended up increasing the number of victims by repeating the tactic of surprise attacks and night attacks. Before withdrawal orders were issued in January 1943, the number of military men sent totaled 30,600 soldiers from the Japanese Army and 4,700 from the Navy. Of those, 25,000 died or went missing. It was a huge loss.

There are various explanations for the defeat of the Japanese Army at Guadalcanal, such as its incremental approach to increasing fighting strength. But the real reason was simple: the U.S. military overwhelmed the Japanese Army in all aspects, including the number of troops, firearms, ammunition, logistics, and aircraft support.

However, the arrogant Imperial Headquarters concluded that the reason for the loss was that "the dispatched troops were weak," as they repeated the exact same tactics over and over again.

Nonetheless, Japan's strategy to secure Guadalcanal Island, about 4,000 miles away, where the supply line was stretched to its max, did not make sense to the U.S. and Australia, considering the enormous expense involved. It was natural for the U.S. to strike there. Pursuing an impossible operation, many Japanese transport vessels were sunk by U.S. aviation forces.

Subaru's merchant ship had been one of them.

Annihilation at Iwo Jima

My father Shuzo's elder brother, Shoichi Okamoto, was a recruited civilian. Unlike Shuzo, he took an exam for promotion to officer and was sent to a small island just next to Iwo Jima in the Ogasawara Islands, as army lieutenant garrison captain. In February 1945, the U.S. forces were headed for the Ogasawara Islands, covering the surface of the sea with its enormous fleet. Shoichi and his men prepared for their honorable deaths, but the U.S. military turned all of its units toward Iwo Jima.

In 1933, the Japanese Navy built an airfield on Iwo Jima, a small island 4 km north to south by 8 km east to west, some 1,200 km south of Tokyo, as a base for seizing islands in the Pacific. U.S. forces advanced to capture Iwo Jima to turn it into a base from which bombing raids on the Japanese archipelago could be launched. Given its strategic location, Iwo Jima was destined to become a fierce battleground.

On February 16, 1945, the U.S. forces began a total attack of Iwo Jima. It is said that in the three days prior to landing, the amount of ammunition that rained on Iwo Jima was enough to cover the entire island with an iron sheet 30-centimeters thick.

The 20,000 soldiers under the command of Lt. General Tadamichi Kuribayashi defended the island. They spent half a year before the U.S. attack digging tunnels that twisted and turned for several kilometers throughout the island. Iwo Jima is a volcanic island, and the escaping steam made tunnel-digging extremely challenging. The soldiers had to take turns every five minutes. For one month, the garrison took cover in the underground tunnel network, which spread over a total length of 18 kilometers, dodging U.S. bombardment. The all-out assault by 75,000 U.S. Marines began on February 19 and they were met with heavy fire from the Japanese garrison. The battle was beyond gruesome.

At the southernmost end of the island is Suribachi-yama (lit. "bowl mountain"), a 169-meter-high mountain that looks like an upside-down bowl. The fighting began with the U.S. trying to capture the mountain. A famous bronze statue depicting four American soldiers raising the Stars and Stripes after the fierce seven-day battle stands today as a monument in front of the Pentagon.

Lt. General Kuribayashi, a renowned family man, had studied for a short while in the United States and knew the true strength of that country all too well. Baron Takeichi Nishi, who had won the show jumping gold medal at the 1932 Los Angeles Olympics was also on Iwo Jima. In June 1944, Nishi was ordered to command the 26th Tank Regiment there as Lieutenant Colonel. He was also an honorary citizen of Los Angeles and had many celebrity friends there.

A theory remains strong that the Imperial Headquarters disliked the pro-American Kuribayashi and Nishi and dispatched them to Iwo Jima knowing there was little hope of returning alive.

The American military men who knew Lt. Colonel Nishi well tried to save him from an honorable death, calling out to him over a loudspeaker, "Baron Nishi, you are too great for the world to lose." However, Nishi, who was well-known for looking out for his subordinates, naturally would not accept their mercy, and he was killed with his men in the bombardment from an American tank. It is said that in the end, he stood in front of the U.S. military tank, holding a hand grenade.

Kazuko's younger brother Akira, who had been dispatched to Okinawa, had won several equestrian trophies during his student days and naturally, Lt. Colonel Nishi was his hero. It is possible that Akira had the chance to encounter Nishi at some point.

When Nishi died, Akira was in Okinawa and felt great shock and grief. Akira himself was killed in action two months later, as if to follow Nishi.

My uncle Shoichi, who was in the Ogasawara islands, was preparing and awaiting orders from the Imperial Headquarters to join the Kuribayashi Division on Iwo Jima. However, before the battle order came, Iwo Jima was annihilated. Upset, Shoichi sent a telegram to the Imperial Headquarters asking, "What are we to do?" The reply he received missed the point. "Raise moral support. Pray for the soldiers of Iwo Jima."

At daybreak, Shoichi took his men to the top of a hill to look out toward Iwo Jima in the ocean and they worshipped for a very long time. That was all he could do.

Of the 22,000-man strong Iwo Jima garrison, 21,788 were killed. The U.S. Army also sustained significant casualties—6,821 died and some 16,000 were injured. It was the only battlefield in the Pacific War where the American side suffered more total casualties than the Japanese.

The soldiers from both sides were ordinary citizens—greengrocers, bakers, newspaper-delivery shop owners, etc. It is said that because the Imperial Headquarters were aware of the inevitable fate facing Iwo Jima, the number of professional soldiers was low.

I first visited Iwo Jima in 1986. The opportunity came while I was seconded to serve in the Secretariat of the Cabinet Security Council headed by the Prime Minister. Two hours on a C-130 from the Japan Air Self Defense Force (JASDAF) Iruma Air Base near Tokyo took me over a solitary island floating in the deep blue sea. The ocean seems to keep people at bay. Nobody is there except for a few SDF and Japan Coast Guard personnel. A large runway separates the east from the west. Precipitous cliffs surround the island. The landing point is a 3-kilometer coast on the east side. The sand on the beach is black because of the volcanic nature of the island. The U.S. Marine Corps landed here and were pinned down under the counterattack of the Kuribayashi Division. Their blood was sucked down into the black sand.

There are only rocks and grassland on the island. As the volcano is still active, steam rises here and there. I entered a tunnel that the Japanese soldiers had dug but I couldn't stay inside for more than 10 minutes. I broke out in sweat, as if in a sauna. My camera instantly clouded over. It was like being inside a kiln from hell. I couldn't stand it any longer, so I went outside to the grasslands where the wind was blowing and watched the white wave crests coming in layers to wash the steep cliffs. Desolate nature surrounded by indigo blue. Compared to the heat underground, this was heaven. They say that the garrison soldiers wished to just get out of that heat hell, even if it meant being shot dead.

From that time on, I developed a desire to show this place to young Japanese and Americans. In August 1995, with the cooperation of the Japan Air Self Defense Force, I took 32 Japanese and American youth to the island. They were students who belonged to the Japan–U.S. Student Conference, a student exchange program started in 1934. I visited former Prime Minister Kiichi Miyazawa, who had a strong interest in Japanese–U.S. student exchanges because he had participated in one in his youth, to ask him to accompany us. He said yes on the spot and joined us on this Iwo Jima trip, which was not easy for him. Gathering around Mr. Miyazawa, both the Japanese and American students pledged their friendship into the future.

I left the group to rest my eyes on the Pacific Ocean without joining the discussion.

There are three types of seas. The benevolent sea that helps and coexists with humans in harmony; the sea dominated by a turbulent god that bares its fangs toward humans; and, the sea like the one surrounding Iwo Jima, which witnesses all human behavior while denying any relation.

I gazed over the endless ocean enveloped in silence, thinking of the innocent Japanese and American soldiers who had lost their lives there.

Tragedy of Okinawa

After taking over Iwo Jima, the American forces headed for Okinawa.

To capture the islands of Okinawa located in the southernmost part of Japan, U.S. forces mobilized a mighty force of 548,000 troops and 1500 vessels. In the first stage, more than 180,000 men landed, commanded by Lt. General Simon Buckner. It was April 1, 1945.

Imperial Headquarters developed a strategy to make Okinawa a breakwater for mainland defense and ordered the defending Divisions to prolong the battle as long as possible to buy time to prepare for a final battle on the mainland. The defense force had 116,000 under the command of Lt. General Ushijima and 20,000 recruits from among the islanders. Kazuko's equestrian brother, three years her junior, was one of them.

There were 450,000 residents living on the main island of Okinawa. U.S. military shells and flame-throwers were sprayed over the residents without distinction, killing 120,000 islanders, or almost one-fourth of the entire population of Okinawa. The death toll of the Japanese Army was 94,000. It was a rare tragedy in world history, where the number of civilian deaths in a single battle exceeded that of the army.

Many of the islanders were killed alongside Japanese soldiers in the southern part of Okinawa. Opinion is divided over whether the Japanese garrison deliberately moved in among the residents to use them as shields in case of a U.S. attack, or the residents were simply too scared to leave the side of the soldiers and move to non-combat zones. Both were likely true. At any rate, Okinawa became the most tragic battlefield of the entire Pacific War.

It was not only U.S. forces that killed civilians. There were cases of Japanese troops killing local residents for reasons such as constraining military operations or possibly passing information to the U.S. military. In some instances, soldiers would force mothers to kill crying babies lest they give away their location.

Whether or not it was a direct military order is still debated in Japan, but many residents were driven to commit mass suicide under military intention. One after the other, families took their own lives, sitting together around grenades provided by the military. Even in this extreme situation, husbands protected their wives and wives protected their children as they calmly faced death.

In contrast, once the U.S. forces took over most of the island, they were relatively kind to the Okinawans who surrendered without fighting. Many mothers and their children were rescued by the U.S. military from fighting that continued in the south.

One cannot talk about present-day Okinawa policy without taking into account the Imperial Headquarters' policy to sacrifice Okinawa and the suffering of the Okinawans that followed. The antipathy of Okinawans toward the mainland is rooted in the tragedy of this time and has persisted. Years later, while U.S. soldiers stationed in Okinawa were allowed to run in the island marathon, Japan Self-Defense Forces members still were not permitted to participate, showing that the grievance of Okinawa remained stronger toward the mainland forces than toward American soldiers.

The cleavage still exists between Okinawa and the mainland. I have been to Okinawa more than 70 times, but I am still a *Yamaton-chu* (Okinawan dialect for "mainlander").

Lt. General Mitsuru Ushijima killed himself at Mabuni Point on the southern edge of the Island, and the Battle of Okinawa ended on June 23, 1945.

Kazuko's younger brother Akira was killed in action on Okinawa. Kazuko was grief-stricken at losing the family member who was most dear to her. Akira, who loved horses deeply, had volunteered to take care of his unit's horses. This is what killed him.

After the War ended, Akira's comrade came to tell his wife and two daughters about how he had died. When the U.S. military attacked, Akira ignored orders to retreat to the air raid shelter and went to evacuate the horses. He was caught in a hail of Grumman machine-gun fire and died with the horses. His comrades' story was that he did not hide behind the horses, but rather faced the attack to protect them—he loved the horses that much. He died in action in April 1945, four months before the Pacific War ended.

As an epitome of the Battle of Okinawa, let me tell you about Ie Jima, where I am designated as an honorary citizen.

Ie Jima is an island nine kilometers from the main island of Okinawa, about 20 minutes by ferry from Okinawa's northern port of Motobu. Heading out over the cobalt sea, a scenic ship-terminal appears on the western bank of Ie Jima. You can always count on the islanders welcoming or wishing farewell to their guests. Under the bright blue sky and the dancing rays of sunlight, the road opens out to Ie beef-cattle sheds and sugar cane fields. At night, the dark fields are dotted with bright electric lights used for chrysanthemum cultivation, inviting an early bloom.

With a population of roughly 4,400, Ie Jima is a peaceful island with a calm appearance that has left the scars of war behind. Of all the facilities the government constructed on Ie, the crematorium was most welcomed by the residents. Live out life earnestly and return to the ancestors—that is the ultimate wish of the people.

The island, however, has a cruel and devastating history. On March 26, 1945, the U.S. military began firing at this island from a fleet that covered the sea to capture the Japanese Navy airfield on the island. On April 16, two weeks after landing on the main island of Okinawa, an overwhelming 21,000 soldiers of the 77th Infantry Division landed on Ie Island. The Japanese garrison consisted of 2,700 men, with an additional 1,200 island residents recruited as combatants.

Ie Jima is flat except for a 172-meter rock hill called Gusuku-yama at its center, and there is no place to hide. Many islanders, desperate amid the fighting, died in vain. This island was one of the most tragic battlefields, and a microcosm of the Okinawan War. Rear Admiral Lawrence Reifsnider is quoted as saying that this war was neither the Pacific War nor the Okinawan War, but the Ie Jima War. That is how intense this battle was.

Men 65 and older, women 60 and older, along with children 17 and younger were evacuated to Nakijin across the sea, but 3,600 residents remained on the island. The Japanese military used these people to assault U.S. military men with explosives, grenades, and bamboo spears, regardless of their age or gender. This battle lasted six days until April 21, killing 4,000 people, including the Japanese garrison and 1,500 islanders. There were 1,120 U.S. casualties.

The islanders today will not voluntarily speak about the war. They do not want to ever be reminded of that hell. They have promised themselves that they will never speak of it. The people of Okinawa feel very strongly about this.

I visited Okinawa many times. After continued interaction with the people, the elderly began to open up to me.

The Japanese Army had forbidden the islanders from surrendering to the Americans. The Japanese Army that came from the mainland treated Okinawans as an inferior ethnic group and suspected that they would leak classified information, such as about the construction of bases. The Army told the Okinawans that American soldiers would kill them all by "cutting up the men into small pieces and running over the women with their tanks after they were finished doing what they want with them."

The situation of the inhabitants hiding in caves was particularly horrendous. Many people died pleading, "Water, water" until they breathed their last breath. If a baby were to cry, the mother would be forced to make a choice: Suffocate the child to death so that the Americans wouldn't find them, or leave the cave and fall to American gunfire, if fate were to choose so. One day, I was having a drink alone with Governor Masahide Ōta and we got into a discussion about the mothers who hid in caves with their babies. Governor Ota told me that on Okinawa, the mothers fed their babies their own urine because there was no water, and when the urine didn't come anymore, they died together.

Across Ie Island, too, desperate residents used explosives and hand grenades, given to them by the military, to commit mass suicide. Meanwhile, the U.S. pacification unit also rescued many. Some 2,100 residents hiding in caves were protected and transported off the island. The people living on Ie Jima now are those who had left the island before the U.S. military attacked and returned after the War.

Shimabukuro Seitoku, who spent 16 years as Mayor on the island of Ie from 1989 is one of them. He left just before the Americans attacked, when he was seven years old, and escaped to the main island. Carrying his heavy luggage tied to his back with straps, he walked for three days without rest into the Nakijin forest. He said that he always remembers the long distance he covered, walking without rest, carrying luggage along the main highway for three days and nights.

The fires burning after such exhaustion, were far, far away. The mountains ran past and even became boring. Ie Jima, wrapped in a red pillar of fire, was far away.

Two years later, the residents were allowed to return to the island. Their buildings were abandoned or had turned to ash, and bodily remains were scattered throughout. Islanders used pickaxes to restore the farmland that the U.S. military had reinforced with coral rock to create military installations.

But in 1953, the U.S. government forcibly expropriated 68% of the island and cleared the farmland once again. The islanders started a major opposition movement and Ie Island came to be known as "home to the anti-U.S. military base struggle."

Shimabukuro, who had served a total of 20 years as deputy mayor and then mayor, was faced with a dilemma. He had the choice of confronting the peaceful anti-military policy of the Japan–U.S. Security Treaty that was run by the central government or cooperating with the local government's military base affairs leaders to regenerate the island with subsidies. Shimabukuro chose the latter path.

The people of Ie were living on their beautiful island, tending to their pastures and horticulture, while Okinawa's other cities, towns, and villages were turning a cold shoulder to Shimabukuro.

As elsewhere in Okinawa, the people on Ie have little negative feeling towards Americans. Although one-third of the island is still used as an auxiliary airfield for the U.S. military, under Shimabukuro's leadership, the island has always taken the stance of cooperation with the Japan–U.S. security system. The islanders have always had an agreement amongst themselves that they will cooperate with the U.S.–Japan security alliance.

White lilies and colorful hibiscus are planted everywhere on the island, filling the air with their fragrance. Among them lies the spacious Ernie Pyle Memorial.

A war correspondent for the *Washington Daily News*, Ernie Pyle won the Pulitzer Prize in 1944 for his dispatches from the Pacific. He died during the Ie Jima landing operation, on April 18, 1945. The people of the island still hold a memorial service every year in front of his well-maintained monument.

My Mother Kazuko's War

The Free Woman—A Creation of the Times

LIKE SHUZO, my mother Kazuko was born in Osaka in 1914. She came from a family of longevity, in which women had power. Her grandmother, my great-grandmother Tane, was born in 1862, the second year of Bunkyu during the years of Edo Shogunate, and lived to be 92. Her mother Tei was born in 1893 and died at the age of 95. As of 2019, Kazuko is 105 years old.

Kazuko grew up in the Taisho era, which only lasted from 1912 to 1926 because Taisho Emperor Yoshihito, who was always in poor health, died at 47. In that short span, democracy and culture flourished in an atmosphere of freedom known as Taisho Democracy.

When Kazuko was 96, she wrote a collection of essays titled "*Namba no Yuyake* (Sunset in Namba)" in which she spells out in detail the special features of the times. A long dirt road when there were no automobiles, where old men come and go, pulling their carts of luggage. Grandmother Tane gives her one *sen* (about 6 yen or 5 cents U.S. in today's currency) for allowance every day, which she spends on peanut rice crackers or sweet starch dumplings. The sunflowers beside the railroad crossing guard's hut shine brightly. She takes a rat that she caught at home to the neighborhood police station and receives 2 *sen* as an extermination reward.

Taisho Democracy was brought about by dramatic economic growth. Japan's exports quadrupled during World War I, and it monopolized the Asian market after the war. After the war, heavy industries including steelmaking, machinery production, and electricity grew substantially. The *zaibatsu* (business conglomerates) and financial capital expanded. This economic growth led to a larger urban middle class that found itself with greater political power. Proletarian parties emerged in the Diet. The Japan Communist Party was established in 1922, followed by the Labor Farmer Party in 1926.

The wave of democracy led by the urban middle class became a widespread civil movement aimed at liberation from repression. This included general elections, liberal education, freedom of speech, assembly and association, suspension of colonial rule, the right to strike, liberation of discriminated communities, and university autonomy. The general election was introduced in 1925, open to all male citizens over the age of 25. There was a feeling of reform and liberation throughout society. Literature and drama flourished in such a free atmosphere.

In the rest of the world, too, revolutions were happening—the Xinhai Revolution in 1911, the Russian Revolution in 1917, and the German Revolution in 1918. This global momentum boosted Japanese democracy and liberalism. This window, which was open until the military seized political power, became a precious moment in time for the advancement of Japanese democracy.

Kazuko grew up during this period. "It was an era when women had the freedom to do just about anything, you know. Women felt more freedom than now," she recalls.

After she was separated from her busy mother, Kazuko learned many things from her grandmother Tane, who looked after her.

"Money only buys grudges. Use your mind and body, not money."

The atmosphere of the times along with her grandmother's guidance and discipline, nourished an air of positivity and activism in her character.

The Russo-Japanese War ended in 1905, and Japan entered an era of imperialism. However, Japanese national sentiment toward the U.S. was quite favorable.

I asked my mother what the citizens at that time thought about America. Having recently been baptized as a Christian at 99, she replied with a mischievous look, "'Will you come into my parlor?' said the spider to the fly. "You boys don't know this, do you? It's a poem by William Wordsworth that I learned in grade school." She was so proud of herself that she could recite something she had learnt almost a century earlier. "We all liked America. And Roosevelt mediated peace with Russia."

What she recited was not William Wordsworth, but a passage from a children's nursery rhyme. Besides, Wordsworth was British—but that was not important to her.

Kazuko's goal was to enter Osaka City Ogimachi Girls' High School, a progressive five-year school where many of the teachers had studied in the United States. She worked hard, studying late into the night. Her primary school held classes until 8 o'clock in the evening, so she would carry two meal boxes to school. There were no electric lights in the classroom, so when it grew dark, the children studied by candlelight. By the time she arrived home and finished her homework, it was midnight. That was when she was 12 years old.

It was a time of upward mobility with many opportunities, when ambitious young people were motivated by the phrase, "You'll be a PhD or a Cabinet Minister." The nation itself was rising while Meiji's momentum continued.

Kazuko successfully won admission into Ogimachi Girls' High School. It was a very liberal school where Principal Jinnosuke Sudo would say to the girls, "Do anything you want, as long it's not stealing. Challenge life with all your might." He told them that he would be there to help them whenever they were in trouble.

Once, when the students heard that Principal Sudo was being forced to leave, they stood up in protest. Believing that he was being removed because of his liberal ideology, they staged a lockout of the principal's office and took the case directly to the Mayor of Osaka. Mayor Hajime Seki took it upon himself to serve tea to these rampaging schoolgirls who sought to occupy the principal's office, listening intensely and warmly to their story. "So what is it that you girls want done?" Kazuko and her friends felt abashed. Evidently, their principal's transfer was not a demotion due to his liberal ideas. He was actually being promoted.

Another group of her friends even went to Tokyo to meet Tokugoro Nakahashi, the Minister of Education. It was an amazing era when a Cabinet minister would meet with the type of high school girls who organized demonstrations, not to mention actually listen to them. Still, the girls went on strike for six months and held their own classes at the YWCA while the school was closed.

Soon the Communist Party intervened, which surprised them enough to cool them down, and the turmoil subsided. When the girls finally returned to school, there was no punishment or blame of any kind. That was the kind of era Taisho was.

After graduating from high school, Kazuko, whose family business was in pharmaceuticals, entered Osaka Women's College of Pharmacy (presently Osaka University of Pharmaceutical Sciences) at the instruction of her mother. However, she was more interested in the world outside of Japan, and studied Esperanto.

But soon after she began corresponding with European pen pals, the police paid a visit to her parents.

"Your princess is heading to get herself mixed up in trouble," they warned.

It was 1934 and the times were changing. Kazuko's hopes for an overseas exchange were halted by her shocked parents. "My youthful dream disappeared along with the green flag that symbolized the Esperanto movement," she said.

The military installed the Manchukuo puppet regime in Manchuria, enthroning Aixinjueluo Puyi. Condemned for its invasion of Manchuria, Japan withdrew from the League of Nations, heading toward a collision with the rest of the world. Japan had already entered its era of fascism.

Kazuko was not loved by her mother, Tei Yoshiki, who came from an established family that went back for generations. The family business was a pharmacy, and Tei's father was the editor of the Asahi Newspaper. In Tei's neighborhood, there was a lumber shop where an apprentice named Saburo worked. He was from Totsugawa, a poor village in Nara. Tei fell in love with Saburo, but as wealthy merchants, her parents would not allow their daughter to marry a poor apprentice, of course. So, they eloped.

Eventually, Tei became pregnant with Kazuko. At this point, Tei's parents had no choice but to accept the marriage, but by then Tei was regretting having married a man who had only a fourth-grade education. She behaved coldly toward Kazuko, telling her, "If only I hadn't gotten pregnant with you, I could have married a better man."

Unlike Tei, Saburo loved his daughter Kazuko deeply, but having married into the Yoshiki family, his power was obviously much less than Tei's. When he gave Kazuko some pocket money, he had to do it behind Tei's back.

Although he did not have much schooling, Saburo was a bright man. He eventually succeeded as a large pharmaceutical wholesaler in Osaka and became a prominent figure after publishing a medical journal. His prosperity grew to the point where he was able to own racehorses. After the War, his horse *New Ford* won the Grand Prix at the Kikuka Sho in 1948. Another one of his horses won graded race championships at Kyoto Race Course three years in a row from 1956.

They were a horse family. The children became infatuated with horseback riding at an early age. Kazuko became captain of the equestrian club at her college and her younger brother Akira became captain of the equestrian club at Ritsumeikan University, winning the Kansai regional championship.

In 1932, when Baron Takeichi Nishi and his beloved horse Uranus won the equestrian gold medal in the Los Angeles Olympics, the excitement was tremendous. All of Japan cheered at Nishi's accomplishment. Kazuko was in her first year of college and Akira was still in high school, but the story of Baron Nishi brought them even closer to their horses. In their privileged family environment, they took every opportunity to ride horses in a spare moment. Eventually, this love for horses took Akira's life on the battlefield.

Marrying Shuzo

Having been treated coldly by her mother Tei, Kazuko couldn't wait to leave home. While attending college, she went to study at an extra-curricular school, where she met Shuzo, a Kyoto Imperial University student who had come to teach part time. He taught her English and mathematics, and she started to develop feelings for him.

Shuzo had a strong interest in literature and was studying under the famous writer Nobuo Origuchi, a leading poet of the time. Shuzo told Kazuko that his favorite *waka* poem by Origuchi was "*Kono michi wo ikishi hito ari. Hagi no hana fumikudakareshi ato ari.* (There were those who followed this path. There are traces of the trampled bush clover)." It is a famous poem that is still taught in high school Japanese classes, but the rationalist Kazuko found this hilarious and burst into laughter. "So *waka* poetry is putting on airs about what everyone already knows in a complicated manner, is it?" she laughed. Shuzo laughed and found her to be an interesting and liberated woman. For Kazuko's part, watching him seriously advocating the art of the poem made her want to marry him.

In 1937, the wedding that Kazuko's mother did not bless was small and frugal. Shuzo was 27, Kazuko, 22.

However, their happiness did not last for long. After four years of marriage, the army drafted Shuzo and took him away from Kazuko. A military man came, and Shuzo was taken from Kazuko's parents' home to somewhere unknown. Kazuko wrote about this in her book, *Namba no Yuyake*:

> *Two days after Shuzo left home to be dispatched to Manchuria, I received a frantic call from my father Saburo. "I found out where Shuzo is now! It's Sakuramiya Elementary School! Go there immediately."*
>
> *With my child on my back, I took two trains and walked along the long road from the station to the school under the hot sun. Asking passersby to give me directions, I finally arrived at the elementary school gate to find soldiers standing guard on both sides, holding rifles with bayonets. Just then, I saw some flickering in the windows on the second floor. This child's father, my husband, is up there! This might be the last time in this life that I will ever see him!*
>
> *A pitiful hedge that even I could climb stood as an overbearing invisible iron wall called the empire.*
>
> *Near the gate, many tired people had laid out straw mats and fabric cloths, just waiting in hopes that they might catch a glimpse of their loved one's face when the soldiers were transported. I decided to go home for the night. When I returned in the morning, the school was empty, and the windows were all open. A lady at the stationery store by the gate told me that the soldiers had been transferred in the middle of the night and loaded onto a ship at the nearby Chikko Harbor. Nobody knew where they were headed.*

This was happening all over Japan. Kazuko later found out that Shuzo's ship headed for Busan, on the Korean Peninsula. From there, the railway led to Manchuria.

Three months had passed when Kazuko received her first military postcard from Shuzo in Manchuria. Written on it was a single sentence: "After snapping off the frozen buds in the mountains and bringing them back to my room, the red azaleas started to bloom." That was it.

Kazuko was disappointed, but as the years went by, she could not bear missing him any longer, so she decided to go and see him. It was January 1945.

To reach Manchuria, she had to go to Shimonoseki by rail from Osaka, board a Kampu Ferry and cross over to Busan. From there, she would travel through the Korean peninsula to Harbin.

To make a difficult trip even harder, the war situation had worsened. The same ferry she was intending to take, the 8,000-ton Kampu Ferry *Konron Maru*, had been sunk in 1943 by a torpedo from the U.S. submarine Wahoo, killing most of the 655 passengers and crew on board. It was the first civilian passenger liner sunk by the U.S. military, and many more were to follow.

In the early autumn of 1944, on August 22, just when Kazuko declared that she would travel to Manchuria, the Tsushima Maru, a 6,700-tonne ship evacuating Okinawan children to the mainland was destroyed by the American submarine Bowfin, on its way to Nagasaki. Some 1,476 civilians were killed, mostly children. This escalated her family's opposition to her planned journey, but her determination to make the same voyage as the sunken ferry remained firm. Despite great opposition from those around her and amidst the chaos of the war, Kazuko headed off with her six-year-old first son Katsuya, my elder brother. The Japanese troops were being cornered and it was no place for a young woman to be traveling with a child, but her determination brought them to Shuzo.

On the train from Busan to Harbin, Kazuko and her son were the only non-military passengers. After two days on the train, they arrived in Harbin, where they stayed for one month. All that Katsuya remembers is the beauty of the Russian Orthodox Church in Harbin and the sour bread he ate every day.

During that time, I was conceived.

Life had become even more difficult by the time Kazuko returned home. After the U.S. soundly defeated Japan in the Battle of the Philippine Sea in June 1944, seizing all sea and air control, ships were sunk one after another. From the beginning of the Pacific War in December 1941 to its end in August 1945, total Japanese losses amounted to 2,394 ships, or 8.02 million tons. Transport of resources and food from the south, from China, and from Indonesia had all ceased.

Everyday life was sacrificed. To manufacture ships and aircraft, household pots and pans, cooking utensils, manhole lids, temple bells, and all other products made from iron or steel were collected and thrown into blast furnaces. The streetcar rails also disappeared. In industries, too, distribution was extremely biased toward munitions. According to the economist and historian Takafusa Nakamura, nearly 70% of Japan's approximately one million tons of textile facilities had been melted for steel production by March 1944.

As a result of the national mobilization of even high school students, the volume of shipbuilding in Japan that had been 600,000 tons per year at the start of the war increased to 1.74 million tons by 1944. But no matter how many ships they built; the number of vessels plummeted under American attack.

As for fighter aircraft, including planes with buckling in the riveting, 26,500 were still produced each year. But whatever Japan did, there was no way they could compete with the U.S., which had eight times the aircraft manufacturing capacity of Japan.

Kazuko's life was difficult, too. Having been brought up as a prosperous merchant's *itohan* (little princess), she was never taught to cook and had brought along her maid when she married Shuzo. After the maid left because of the War, Kazuko had no idea how to keep her life together. No matter where she went, there was no food. Each day was a battle for survival. With a young son in the house and then me on the way, daily life was no easy task. However, she had no choice but to persevere, both for her beloved husband and for her children.

The damage to lifestyle was the same throughout Japan, but the hardship on housewives was exacerbated in urban areas where food was hard to come by. Like many others, Kazuko often took a kimono into a farming village to exchange for food.

Kazuko still feels bitter towards the "countryside." She cannot let go of the humiliation she felt when women on the farms all but snatched away her precious kimono for a mere handful of rice.

Kazuko's Battlefield

Kazuko lived under constant air raids by U.S. military aircraft. They were intense and inhumane.

General Curtis LeMay, who commanded the Great Tokyo Air Raid of March 10, 1945, ordered the pilots to "reduce the most congested residential complexes and railway transport facilities to rubble and ashes." Although the war was continuing without any regard to how the Japanese citizens felt about it, the United States thought that undermining citizen morale would lead to ending the war. LeMay told his subordinates that he wanted Tokyo to be "burned down—wiped right off the map."

The Great Tokyo Air Raid was carried out by 334 B-29 bombers dropping 1,665 tons of incendiary bombs on five million citizens. It targeted residential areas where there were no military-related facilities, killing more than 100,000. One U.S. Air Force officer boasted, "The air raid on this day alone killed more people than any military strategy in world history." Kazuko had moved to Tokyo from Osaka, and their home on the hill was also burnt to ashes that day.

Kazuko said, "Our house was burnt down while Shuzo-san was in Manchuria fighting. There was absolutely nothing I could do about it, and I felt so bad for him."

Wearing an air raid hood, pregnant Kazuko took her son Katsuya in her arms and ran to wherever she could go.

The U.S. air raids were thorough. Over the next several months, some 130 air raids followed, burning down more than half of the vast city of Tokyo. Air raids targeted not only Tokyo but also nearly 200 cities across Japan and continued for more than six months. Some 43% of urban areas were lost. Most Japanese homes were wooden structures and their density contributed to the scale of sacrifice—many millions of dead and injured victims and 2.36 million homes lost.

The bombing of Dresden on February 13, 1945, was carried out by 769 British Lancaster bombers and 527 American B-17 bombers over three days leaving an estimated death toll of 25,000. Altogether, 350,000 people were killed by air raids across Germany. In 1943, Japan too, had indiscriminately bombed Chongquing, capital of the Kuomintang government. The bombing of London by the Nazis was the same. In other words, the U.S. was not the only country carrying out indiscriminate bombing.

Nonetheless, in the case of the United States, the firebombing of Japanese citizens differed from other bombings in terms of magnitude and cruelty. More than 800,000 Japanese civilians were killed during the War and most of these deaths resulted from air raids.

Japanese citizens were informed through news reports only about the invasions in China and the attack on Pearl Harbor. Battles in the Pacific were reported only as victory battles. The war that Kazuko and other ordinary citizens experienced was U.S. military aircraft raids.

The men were away as soldiers at war, so the victims were women, the elderly, and children. Firebombing is cruel. Its purpose is to kill the residents of a particular district by first dropping incendiary bombs to surround the target area and create a wall of fire that makes it impossible for people to escape, then attacking them with small bombs and machine guns. Fires created by incendiary bombs are not like forest fires. They produce hot air that reaches 1,500 degrees Celsius. The strong wind that accompanies such heat scoops people up into the air and draws them into the flames. The terror that citizens across Japan experienced was frightening enough to convince them that the War was bringing their world to an end. The scenes of Hiroshima and Nagasaki go without saying.

For the air-raiders, dropping a bomb from the sky over a city makes it unnecessary to look at the victim's face, distorted by pain. Thus, there is little to make them feel the pain as a human being. For Air Force soldiers, the sensation was probably much like the battles being fought these days in computer games.

This is the image of war that Japanese people hold to this day. It is the immutable foundation of their continued aversion toward militarism.

In addition to the incendiary bombs, many Japanese people were subjected to the horror of machine-gun strafing. In the spring of 1945, as Kazuko was making her way to Tokyo, her train was attacked by a Grumman just as it was about to cross the Yodogawa railway bridge in Osaka. The passengers all got off the train and ran through the railroad bridge. The Grumman circled and returned, showering them again with gunfire. Some of the passengers were hit by the bullets and fell, but my mother was lucky. She lay face down on the iron bridge, and as she watched the Yodo River flowing way below, she was sure that she would die. To this day, she remembers the way the murky river looked as she saw it through the crossties.

This was the second time she was caught in machine-gun strafing. The first time was when she was riding horseback with her father along a lane in the suburbs of Kyoto and a Grumman plane appeared, shooting. The family immediately dismounted and hid in the grass. My mother attests that she clearly saw the Grumman pilot's face. I was skeptical that a pilot's expression could be seen from below, but she says she vividly remembers.

The Air Raid Bombers

The strafing went on in cities across Japan.

My older brother Katsuya, who was seven years old by then, was not exposed to the machine-gun strafing, but after moving to the city of Kamakura when the War ended, many of his friends told him stories of the attacks they experienced in the city. Evidently, on their way back from attacking Tokyo and Yokohama, the Grumman planes would swing by Kamakura on their return to Iwo Jima or to aircraft carriers, perhaps to lighten their load or to use their leftover ammunition for target practice. They were regularly seen strafing before flying off over the sea. The Grummans also showered children playing on the beaches with machine gun bullets.

The United States had complete control of the airspace over Japan and anti-aircraft firing no longer existed in Japan, so the Grumman planes would fly at very low altitudes over the suburbs of major cities, aiming their fire at the people. Residents of Kamakura say that the faces of laughing pilots sitting in the passenger seats were clearly visible because they flew so low.

Many of my older friends had similar experiences. Prominent

writer and politician Shintaro Ishihara (known later for writing the book *Japan That Can Say No*) talks about being attacked by a Grumman fighter. He was a number of years ahead of me at the same high school. A Grumman plane came strafing towards him on his way to school one day and he dove into a rice field. Ishihara also declares that he clearly saw the pilot's face. This formed the psychology at the root of his harsh views of the United States. For some American military pilots, Japanese civilians must have been seen as prey for hunting.

These attacks were not limited to Tokyo. My wife's family lived in Nagoya, where the firebombing was fierce. They ran a pharmacy that was completely burned down by B-29 bombing. They lost their entire estate. U.S. military aircraft raided Nagoya 63 times, killing 7,800 people and destroying 135,000 houses by fire.

Some of the American B-29s that bombed Nagoya were shot down and 28 crew-members were captured and executed. After the war, Tōkai District Commander Lt. General Tasuku Okada was held responsible and sentenced to death by hanging by the Yokohama Allied Forces Court.

Upon admitting to having approved the execution of the American flyers and thereby taking full responsibility for the decision, Okada appealed to the court against the cruelty of indiscriminate bombing.

"The scenes of indiscriminate bombing are likely unimaginable to many of you. Small bombs are mixed with incendiary bombs to hinder firefighting by the residents. Women and children's limbs hang from electric wires. Corpses are blown up onto rooftops of broken homes. In the end, the slate is wiped clean by the whirlpool of fire that closes in. It is a picture of hell. I approved the execution because these crew members were criminals who had violated this caliber of international law, 7-to-20 times."

When he was given his death sentence, however, Okada asked to speak and said something quite surprising.

"I would like to thank this court for giving the Defendant the opportunity to speak in-depth regarding the United States Air Force inland bombing issue. I believe that this gratitude will play a very important part in the unity (of the two nations)." His hatred toward the enemy in the war he had fought had disappeared.

In Japan, many find the death penalty unjust for Okada.

Professor Sabata Toyoyuki, a well-known Japanese historian and an honorary professor at Kyoto Prefectural University of Medicine writes about the Nagoya incident as follows: "After murdering a large number of innocent citizens with repeated indiscriminate bombings, the American crew members wished to save their own lives by escaping with parachutes and demanding protection as Prisoners of War. This type of nerve is very different from the Japanese."[10]

He goes on to argue that the cultures of the two nations are built on completely different historical foundations: The Japanese people value Buddhist aesthetics, while Americans place greater value in the fight itself. However, while the Japanese view of forgiveness is based on Buddhist thought, there is also a forgiveness that comes from intellectual laziness, when nobody can be held responsible because there has never been a reckoning with the War in the first place. Surprisingly, in 1964 under the Sato cabinet, the Japanese government awarded Japan's highest-ranking medal, the First Class Order of the Rising Sun, to General Curtis LeMay, who commanded the indiscriminate bombing of Japanese cities, for "cooperating with the development of the Japan Air Self Defense Force."

The first American I ever met was Staff Sergeant Jacob DeShazer, a bomber pilot who had carried out air raids on Nagoya. He was a member of the famous Doolittle Raiders conducting the kind of Nagoya bombing that the condemned Lt. General Okada had so reviled.

DeShazer was born in Salem, Oregon. He was devastated by the Japanese attack on Pearl Harbor and vowed to take revenge for his colleague soldiers who were killed, so he volunteered and received air-raid training. In April 1942, he took off from the aircraft carrier Hornet in a B-25 bomber and bombed the city streets of Nagoya. On his way back to the U.S. military base in China, however, the flight he was on ran out of fuel. He parachuted into an area controlled by the Japanese military and was taken prisoner. What followed was the harsh fate of 40 months as a POW in Japan. Nevertheless, after reading a Bible lent to him by one of the guards, he came to forgive the Japanese who had been so harsh to him.

Three years after the War ended, DeShazer returned to Japan as a missionary at a church in Osaka. The person requested by the church to host DeShazer and take him into their home was none other than Saburo Yoshiki, Kazuko's father.

DeShazer lived on the second floor of Saburo's big house for several years. There, Kazuko listened to his stories about God and was deeply moved. I met Reverend DeShazer in the summer when I was 11 years old. I don't remember what he said to me then. Jacob had a son, Paul, who was about the same age as me. Strangely, the beauty of his blond hair is the only thing I remember.

DeShazer later moved to Nagoya, the city he had bombed, where he built a church and worked in the Christian mission for 30 years. Many documents and writings that describe his character are available in the United States.

Japan's Surrender

Road to Early Realization of Peace

WHEN I JOINED THE MINISTRY OF FOREIGN AFFAIRS (MOFA) in 1968, my colleagues who started the same year included Kazuhiko Togo, grandson of Shigenori Togo who was the Minister of Foreign Affairs at both the start and the end of the Pacific War. One year ahead of me was Koreshige Anami, son of Korechika Anami who was the most powerful general in the Imperial Japanese Army and War Minister at the end of the War.

Because Togo and I joined in the same year, we became good friends right from the start. He told me that he joined the Ministry in order to resolve the northern territorial issue, but he became embroiled in a confrontation between MOFA and a certain politician, and never became Ambassador to the USSR as everyone had expected. In 2001, he was appointed Ambassador to the Netherlands but was discharged after only one year.

As the star of the Ministry's China School, Anami became Ambassador to China. He was a man of grand presence. His wife was Ginny Stibbs, originally from New Orleans, LA. She was an active person and popular as the first lady of Japan in China. The Chinese people who met her would at first be surprised that this blonde Ginny represented Japan, but after that, everyone liked her.

Togo's grandfather and Anami's father had been on opposite sides over surrendering or continuing to fight after the Okinawa defense forces were totally defeated in June 1945. From the beginning of 1945, at every meeting of the Supreme Council for the Direction of the War, Shigenori Togo and Korechika Anami engaged in intense arguments.

Foreign Minister Togo thought that defeat was inevitable and tried to finish the war with a conditional surrender by moving in the direction of peace at an early stage. Anami argued that Japan was not losing the War because it had not lost its territories overseas and that they should fight to the end.

Some recent studies show that Anami personally wished for an early peace but superficially developed the war theory in order to successfully guide the bellicose young army officers to surrender. What is the true story, I wonder.

By the beginning of 1945, most of the leaders could recognize Japan's defeat. There was a way for Japan to reach peace earlier.

Shigenori Togo and Navy Minister Mitsumasa Yonai thought that they should be working on peace initiatives as soon as possible. However, Togo, despite being a Foreign Minister, misunderstood the international situation and devised an unrealistic strategy to end the War by asking the Soviet Union to mediate. Meanwhile, Yonai, the other advocate for peace, did not have a strong voice in the Supreme Council for the Direction of the War because the Navy had already lost most of its ships.

The most promising road to the early realization of peace was being negotiated by Naval Attaché Yoshiaki Fujimura, who was stationed in Switzerland, and Allen Dulles, the elder brother of John Foster Dulles, who became U.S. Secretary of State in the 1950s. In its May 1951 issue, the monthly magazine *Bungei Shunjū* revealed the complete content of these negotiations through interviews with the people involved, who were alive at the time.

In April 1945, Lt. Colonel Fujimura reached Allen Dulles through a German contact, Dr. Friedrich Wilhelm Hack. On May 3, Dulles received a reply from the State Department stating that "direct peace talks with Japan may proceed."

Fujimura immediately sent a telegram to Navy Minister Yonai and military commander-general, Admiral Soemu Toyoda, using a Navy-exclusive encryption machine brought in by an Imperial Navy submarine. He wanted permission to negotiate with Dulles. Fujimura sent 12 telegrams in all, continuing to stress that Japan had no prospect of winning the war.

There was no reply from Tokyo. Meanwhile, a suggestion came from Dulles: "If you can bring a representative with the status of

Minister or Admiral from Tokyo, the United States is prepared to cover transportation from Japan to Switzerland." Still, there was absolutely no response to this.

Within the Navy, Navy Minister Yonai and Zenjiro Hoshina, Director-General of the Navy's Military Affairs Bureau were in favor of the talks, but General Toyoda and Deputy General Takijiro Onishi of the Military Command were against the idea, saying that it was an American plan to divide the Japanese Army from the Navy. Moreover, "The suggestion is coming from a mere Lt. Colonel!"

The possibility of early peace talks finally evaporated. Three months later, it was August 13, two days before Japan was forced to make an unconditional surrender. Fujimura was surprised to receive a call from the Tokyo Navy Command. "Is that story of the negotiation with the United States still alive?"

Fujimura shouted in anger, "You are two months late!"

In February 1945, Japanese army officers stationed in neutral countries such as Spain and Portugal had captured details of the secret treaty made in Yalta between Roosevelt and Stalin regarding Soviet participation in the war with Japan. However, this information was not released outside the army. This was to advance the strategy called "*ichigeki kowa* (lit. one final strike and make peace)," which they claimed would go as follows: After September, they would let the U.S. forces land in mainland Japan and they would beat them soundly once, and then prioritize peace negotiations.

At around the same time, in the spring of 1945, peace efforts had been underway in Stockholm between former Swedish Ambassador to Japan, Widar Bagge, and Japan's Ambassador to Sweden, Suemasa Okamoto. However, Foreign Minister Togo dismissed these efforts. Togo ultimately chose not to negotiate directly with the United States but instead to request mediation from the Soviet Union, with which Japan had a neutrality treaty since April 1941.

Why did he choose the Soviet Union? Togo and other pro-Soviet members thought about it in this way:

Directly offering the U.S. peace will likely force an unconditional surrender on Japan. (This thinking was wrong. In fact, the U.S. was flexible, as we saw in Burns' response on August 12 regarding acceptance of the Potsdam Declaration.)

The Soviet Union on the other hand had its hands full on the European front and was surely most afraid of Japan striking from behind on the east. Japan had its hands full with China and French Indochina and it would be a big problem if the Soviet Union started making threats. The two nations had similar strategic interests.

What Togo did not realize, however, was that the Soviet situation had already changed after the German army surrendered in Stalingrad in February 1943, two years before.

The Fujimura–Dulles connection occurred through the Navy channel, and the Foreign Ministry had not been notified. The Foreign Ministry had the Okamoto-Bagge channel, but Togo ignored it.

Meanwhile in the Soviet Union, during his Revolution Day speech of November 1944, Stalin strongly criticized "the invading countries Japan and Germany for what they did to peace-loving nations such as Britain, the United States, and the Soviet Union." Even after this, in 1945, the Japanese Ministry of Foreign Affairs was still relying on that Stalin.

Even if Japan had not uncovered the secret agreement that the Soviet Union planned to participate in the war against Japan, Soviet Foreign Minister Vyacheslav Molotov told Ambassador Naotake Sato on April 5, 1945, that because Japan assisted Germany in carrying out war against the USSR and was presently at war with Soviet allies the U.S. and Great Britain, the Soviet–Japan Neutrality Pact could not possibly survive. Having said that, he gave notification that the neutrality treaty would not be extended beyond its end date of the following March.

Sato sent several telegrams saying that it would be impossible to ask the Soviet Union to help with the peace effort. Togo did not listen. At the meeting of the Supreme Council for the Direction of the War on June 22, a policy to negotiate a request for mediation by the Soviet Union was approved.

The Soviet army was already on its way from Europe to the Far East to prepare its attack on Japan, but on July 8, Togo asked the former prime minister, Prince Fumimaro Konoe, to travel to the USSR to request mediation. Abandoning the peace channel that the U.S. offered, the government placed its hopes on Soviet mediation. While countless numbers of soldiers and citizens were dying on the

Pacific islands and mainland Japan, this was the sort of pitiful drama that was playing out in Tokyo.

The Soviet Union ignored all of Japan's requests and entered the War on August 9.

The Army was against a peaceful resolution. The peace advocates in the Navy and the Ministry of Foreign Affairs had been proceeding individually with peace efforts. Everything was disjointed.

Emperor's Intervention and Unconditional Surrender

There is no doubt that the Emperor personally wanted an early peace, but he never commanded the military, which insisted on continuing the War even after huge loss of lives.

There is no denying that the Emperor did not have objective information to enable him to order peace negotiations. The first time the Emperor came into contact with the facts was on June 9, when Army Chief of Staff Yoshijiro Umezu, the man who had presented a silver watch to my father in Manchuria, returned from a visit to the Chinese front. He reported, "Our vigorous Army in China, which Army Headquarters is planning to use in the decisive mainland battle, has almost exhausted its supply of equipment and ammunition. The ammunition will only last for one big battle."

Similarly, Navy Admiral Kiyoshi Hasegawa reported to the Emperor on June 12 that the Navy had lost its combat ability, stating, "The Navy no longer has any soldiers or ships."

After these reports from Umezu and Hasegawa, the Emperor was decisively leaning toward peace efforts. But how would he convince the military, particularly the Army, to give way to peace? War Minister Anami, who considered surrender and retreat as humiliation, continued to insist on fighting.

All in all, the Emperor did not show strong leadership. To the end, he did not show the strong determination he had espoused while wearing a commander-chief's uniform during the suppression of rebels at the 2.26 incident in 1936.

The Emperor's intention to pursue peace was only indirectly communicated through Kantaro Suzuki, who was a weak prime minister, and Togo, a foreign minister whom the military did not listen to.

On July 27, 1945, Japan received the Potsdam Declaration through the Japanese Embassy in Switzerland. To buy time to confirm and understand the content of the declaration, Prime Minister Kantaro Suzuki declared that Japan would continue fighting. If the Potsdam Declaration had been accepted at the time, the atomic bombings of Hiroshima and Nagasaki likely would not have taken place. Responsibility lies heavily on Prime Minister Kantaro Suzuki for declaring silent contempt (*mokusatsu*) of the Potsdam Declaration and pushing forward (*maishin*) war efforts even as he was already willing to surrender. The responsibility of the Army and some members of the Navy who insisted on continuing the War is even heavier.

Some of the junior officers were determined to continue the War. But by then, it is likely true that Navy Minister Yonai and War Minister Anami had been trying to suppress these hard-liners.

On August 14, 1945, when the Supreme Council finally decided on unconditional surrender, Anami went to see Togo and apologized for his behavior up until then. In the early morning on August 15, the day of the Emperor's radio broadcast accepting the Potsdam Declaration and unconditional surrender, Anami committed suicide by *harakiri* (disembowelment). In this way, the entire Army was informed of Japan's defeat in an intense manner, and the theory that the War could be continued came to a halt. In this most Japanese form of self-determination, Anami enforced the Emperor's instructions throughout the Army and communicated the prohibition of armed resistance.

It should be noted however, that immediately before his suicide, Anami's final words to Lt. Colonel Takeshita, who witnessed the *harakiri*, were "slash Yonai," directing him to kill the peace-advocating Navy Minister. Did he also say this to dramatically convey defeat to the public?

However, none of these episodes justifies the U.S. dropping an atomic bomb on Hiroshima on August 6 and another on Nagasaki on August 9. Roosevelt and Churchill had already agreed at Hyde Park in September 1944 to consider Japan as a location to drop the atomic bomb when it was completed. Not only that, they made the final decision to drop the bomb the day before the recommendation for Japan to surrender under the Potsdam Declaration was delivered. We cannot completely dismiss the suspicion that the U.S. hurried the decision to attack because if Japan had surrendered, the opportunity to test the effects of the two atomic bombs, Little Boy and Fat Man, would have been lost.

In particular, if the Americans had thought that dropping the bomb on Hiroshima would decisively push the Japanese government toward unconditional surrender, dropping a second bomb on Nagasaki three days later without even trying to gauge the impact of Hiroshima was totally inexplicable. Albeit with a few diehard opponents to peace in Tokyo, it was apparent that Japan was going to surrender in a matter of a few days, not weeks, without using the bombs that killed more than two hundred thousand people in the two cities.

On August 14, the Emperor recorded the Imperial Rescript of the Termination of the War, informing the public about Japan's unconditional surrender. This was broadcast over the radio the next day, August 15, and is remembered as the *Gyokuon Hoso* (Royal Voice Broadcast). For the first time ever, the citizens heard the actual high-pitched voice of the Emperor, who was telling them that Japan had lost. The War that destroyed every corner of the nation ended in the sizzling heat of August, leaving only burnt fields and blue skies.

Could There Have Been "Another History"?

The discussion of what would have happened if Japan had ended the War earlier can only be theoretical. A country that is dominant in a battle can achieve favorable conditions if they can bring about a ceasefire while winning. On the other hand, while a country is winning, the greedy advocates of continuing the war have the stronger voice. Meanwhile, the inferior party in the war is wary of being forced into adverse peace conditions, making it difficult for that side to call for a ceasefire.

Even after losing every battle in the Pacific, its garrison annihilated on Iwo Jima, Okinawa devastated, and major cities on the mainland reduced to ashes, the Emperor and the Army did not make the decision to surrender until the bitter end.

However, we still have to think about it. What would have happened if the War had ended earlier through peace negotiations or surrender?

In retrospect, the most convenient timing for Japan to propose peace would likely have been when Singapore fell in February 1942 and a British intelligence agency sent a peace feeler through the Turkish Embassy. At the time, however, the Japanese government was too victorious and arrogant to pay attention.

If Japan had not chased the mirage of Soviet mediation and instead engaged in the peace negotiations that Fujimura and Allen were trying to realize, there would have been much less physical damage to Japan. Civilian casualties drastically increased after March 1945. Even if it had been too late for Iwo Jima, the apocalyptic battle of Okinawa might have ended in a ceasefire part way through. And, of course, the history of Hiroshima, Nagasaki, and Soviet involvement would have looked quite different.

The Army planned to win favorable peace conditions after striking the United States in a total counterattack in Japan after September. The condition that they were hoping to achieve was the protection of national polity centered on the Emperor.

The Japanese leadership only worked according to the logic of their own organizations. Neither the military nor the bureaucracy shared any information that was inconvenient to itself, and they did not provide the Emperor, who was in the position to make final decisions, the entire picture of the war situation.

The Emperor lacked the power to bring the nation together, the Army could not restrain the young officers who insisted on a final battle on the mainland, the Navy was not able to move toward peace after most of its ships had been sunk, the Ministry of Foreign Affairs entrusted its hopes to Russian mediation, and the Emperor's vassals were determined to uphold the national essence. Given this, the Japanese government was unable to make the decision to surrender, clinging to hopes of a conditional surrender that would protect national polity and its own interests. It very much resembled the legendary serpent-monster *Yamato no Orochi*, which had eight heads.

In the course of procrastination, millions of soldiers and citizens were killed.

On the other hand, consider what would have happened if Japan had surrendered earlier. An early surrender would probably have been a conditional surrender. Part of the Japanese imperial structure, such as invaded territories and military organizations, might have remained. The severity of punishment for war responsibility would likely have been lighter.

In the first place, if Japan had accepted the 1941 Hull Note, an ultimatum by Secretary of State Cordell Hull, Japan and the United States would not have gone to war. Not only that, the Korean Peninsula, Taiwan, Southern Sakhalin, and all the Kuril Islands would have remained Japanese territories or colonies.

Would this have been in the national interest for Japan? Of course, international politics thereafter should have given Korea and Taiwan independence, but until then, would the continuation of colonization or annexation over the years have been in the interest of the Japanese nation, not to mention the Korean and Taiwanese people? Would Japan have been able to become the modern state that it is now? If pre-War rule and the Meiji Constitution remained as a condition of surrender, would freedom and democracy have taken root in Japan today? After all, wasn't it the drastic reform that General Douglas McArthur inflicted on Japan that served as the basis of modern Japan?

But here, we come to a big dilemma: In the face of a huge number of victims, it is not permissible for a nation to say, "It was a good thing that we lost the war." In addition to stabilization in East Asia, the peace, prosperity, and democracy that we enjoy in Japan today rest on the precious sacrifices of ordinary soldiers and citizens who died in the War. The military leadership that was preying on Japan and destroying the country would never have been banished without these sacrifices. The blunt truth is that the ordinary soldiers who died in this wretched war took the nation back from its inner enemy's hands. The level of sacrifice it took to accomplish that was too heavy.

PART TWO

THE JAPANESE AND THE AMERICANS

WHAT WAS LEFT FOR JAPAN AFTER THE WAR?

Who and What Started the War?

ON AUGUST 14, 1945, Japan surrendered after accepting the Potsdam Declaration, and the war that destroyed the nation ended. (Despite Japan's surrender, the Soviet Union advanced and occupied the four northern islands that had always been part of Japan. This state of affairs continues today, and although 75 years have passed since the War, Japan and Russia have not concluded a Peace Treaty.)

I was born three months after the War ended. So, in effect, the history of post-War Japan is the story of my life.

Japan recovered from the physical loss and the psychological damage of the War with incredible speed. However, there were two things that Japan neglected to do in the process. In my view, these still haunt the nation.

First, Japan should have convicted itself for its war actions. Instead, Japan left it to the International Military Tribunal for the Far East, the war crimes trial of Japan's leadership, held in Tokyo by a tribunal of the victorious allied countries. In the court, the allies assumed the role of prosecutor, and Japan the role of defense counsel, whose mission was to defend and justify the acts of war criminals. Thus, from the very start of the post-war period, Japan was required to justify the course of the war actions.

Yes, there were people like U.S. Major Ben Blakeney who, as a defense attorney for the Japanese war defendants, defended Japanese officials at the Tokyo war crimes trials. I am not raising the issue of nationality. I am simply pointing out that one of the major reasons Japan still has not faced directly the war of more than 70 years ago is that Japan itself has never conducted its own trials of its war criminals.

Secondly, military actions throughout the War needed to be thoroughly examined and verified. This examination has not been done either.

Military leaders knew from the start that Japan would lose a war against the United States. Nonetheless, nobody tried to stop the situation from evolving into the tragedy. Nobody objected to individual battles either, like Iwo Jima, where all 20,000 soldiers had no choice but to face death.

Toward the end of the War, everyone in the command knew that defeat was inevitable. Instead of surrendering, however, they sat back and procrastinated, letting millions of soldiers and citizens die, especially in the U.S. scorched-earth campaigns after March 1945, in Iwo Jima, Okinawa, Hiroshima, Nagasaki, and countless cities on the mainland that were reduced to ashes.

No one had the courage to change the flow.

It was exactly as Makiyo Ishimitsu had written in his diary.

Did post-war Japan break away from this idiosyncrasy—its incrementalism and difficulty making tough decisions? The answer, unfortunately, cannot be a proud "Yes." In terms of the percentage of GDP, fiscal deficits now are worse than at the end of the Pacific War. The Supreme Court continues to demand re-distribution of parliamentary seats by region to equalize the distribution of votes, but the Diet continues to neglect the demands. Japan's social security and medical systems are on the verge of bankruptcy and diminishing, as people do not want to pay taxes for their future under the current uncertain system. Other than minor reforms, the basic structure and pension and medical payment levels remain intact. Japan's structure of extreme incrementalism has not changed to this date.

What started the War? Aside from the obvious reason that Japan needed to secure natural resources in Asia, there was also, in the deep layers of Japan's psyche, a sense of repulsion against the negative American sentiment toward Japanese.

At the post-World War I Paris Peace Conference, Japan worked hard to promote the Racial Equality Proposal in the League of

Nations. The major goal of the Japanese Government was to end the exclusion of Japanese immigrants from the United States. The Japanese delegation appealed for the Racial Equality Clause to be incorporated in the League of Nation's Covenant.

Nobuaki Makino, Japan's delegate, was the father-in-law of Shigeru Yoshida, who would later become Prime Minister during the period of Japan's reconstruction after WWII. Makino appealed directly to his personal friend President Woodrow Wilson, who promised to cooperate, but the prime ministers of the United Kingdom, Australia, and Canada strongly opposed the proposal. The U.S. Congress also opposed it, saying that Japan's proposal suggested amendments to U.S. domestic laws, thus interfering with internal politics. The League of Nations supported Japan with a vote of 11-5, but the chairman, President Wilson, overturned it on the ground that a unanimous vote was needed.

This inflamed political groups and public opinion in Japan. Anti-American sentiment spread further to the citizens' level when the Immigration Act was enacted in the United States in 1924, prohibiting all immigrants from Japan. The warm sense of familiarity that people had for the United States when my mother Kazuko was growing up, rapidly cooled, accelerated by the military leadership.

However, anti-racism could not be the major reason to start a war.

The War with the United States was reckless no matter who looked at it. The U.S. was a super-giant with an economy many times the size of Japan's, including in crucial industrial output such as electrical power, coal production, steel, shipbuilding, aircraft and motor vehicles, and also in the number of factory workers. Never in modern history has a small country launched a war against another with a gap of this scale.

Who started the War? To me, this question is important. Was it the Army's rampage, as many in Japan now believe—that the unrefined Army began the reckless war, which the Navy, a bunch of sophisticated internationalists, was unable to stop? If this is the case, historians will have an easier task, simply to analyze the special culture of the Imperial Army and the rebellious young officers in that hierarchy. As the German case has been completely attributed to the acts of Nazis, the Japanese case could be attributed to the Imperial

Army, a unique institution with rare intellectual arrogance.

On the other hand, if the Navy started the War, there will be different and more complex implications that necessitate a wider analysis of Japan's idiosyncrasies because in that case, the War was no longer the act of an isolated group of elites within the Japanese ruling system.

The public wants to believe the picture of bad guys (the Army) versus good guys (the Navy) and take a consolation in the story that the good guys representing the average common-sense Japanese were simply outnumbered by the others and lost the tug-of-war. In other words, the body had a cancer, but other than that, its other parts were OK. But was it really so?

The school of people who call the Army the culprit asserts that Army General Hideki Tojo was the one who directed the war as Prime Minister, and the powerful Army General Korechika Anami opposed peace talks right to the bitter end. Even in the International Tribunal for the Far East, while there were 15 Class-A war criminals from the Army, there were only three from the Navy.

Kiyoshi Ikeda, Professor Emeritus of Tohoku University, fortifies this argument by saying that the War was initiated by the Army and the Navy was dragged into it. In *Kaigun to Nihon (The Navy and Japan)*[11], he writes about his own experience as a naval officer:

An Army soldier's goboken sword had a bright glow while the Navy officer's dagger was no more than a trinket. This contrast vividly symbolizes the difference between the Army, which prided itself on deep roots in rural Japan and considered itself the leader of the Japanese Empire, and the Navy, which was detached from the people and was devoted to Westernization.

I found my father's *goboken* (lit. 'burdock sword') when I was a child and brought on the thunder-like anger of my father. About 50 cm in length, it was used as a bayonet and was the symbol of the assault army. On the other hand, the Navy daggers were ornaments worn by officers who were never engaged in hand-to-hand combat.

Top-ranking naval officials were originally pro-U.S. and U.K. However, the dissatisfaction among subordinate officers regarding the unfavorable restraints placed on Japan's naval shipbuilding compared with those placed on the U.S. at the Washington Conference in 1922 and the London Conference in 1930, gave more power to the pro-German members of the Navy. Ikeda states as follows.

> *The Army, which had lost confidence in the war with the Soviet Union in Nomonhan, was intrigued by Germany's dominance in Europe and rushed into a German-Japanese alliance. The Navy was dragged into it and ended up as an accomplice. In other words, suppression by the United States and the United Kingdom on Japan became a backdrop for planting a spiritualism that did not agree with the nature of the Navy's rationalist and mathematic thinking marine engineers, who operate complex machines.*

This idea sounds persuasive, but my father Shuzo often said, "It was the Navy that started that war with America. They are the ones that brought the country to destruction."

It must have been his post-war analysis because as a mere soldier, there was no way he would know the actions of the upper military ranks.

Historian Masayasu Hosaka also asserts, "The true criminals who started the war against the U.S. were the Navy Ministry Military Bureau and the officials in the Navy's General Staff," and mentions a few by name.[12]

Hosaka says that the Navy strongly resented the ratio of warships allowed to Japan, the U.S., and the U.K., adding that when pressured by the American oil embargo, the Navy attempted to use resources from French Indochina by conducting the so-called Southern Operations. Furthermore, he highlights that compared with the Army drawing popular praise with its flashy activities in Mainland China, the Navy was feeling left behind in the dark.

Many researchers point out that the Navy had a serious shortage of fuel and that the rapidly growing argument within the Navy was that action must be taken before oil reserves were depleted in two years.

To me, Hosaka's theory seems closer to reality.

Ever since the Imperial Defense Policy of 1907, the Army and Navy had different perspectives: the Army considered the Soviet

Union virtually an enemy nation, while the Navy considered the U.S. and the U.K. to be that. In the first place, the Japanese Army had no interest in the Pacific islands and besides, they would have to rely on naval transport for battles on the islands. It does not make sense to me that the Army would have been enthusiastic about risking operations on the Chinese continent in order to stage a war in the Pacific Ocean.

On September 4, 1945, Chief of Army General Staff Yoshijiro Umezu accompanied Minister of Foreign Affairs Mamoru Shigemitsu as the Army representative for the signing of the Japanese surrender on board the *USS Missouri*. The Navy, however, which regarded the United States as its main enemy until the end, only sent a subordinate admiral to the signing ceremony because the top admiral, Soemu Toyoda, refused to attend. It was a display of the Navy's hostility that still was there.

Looking ahead to the start of the Pacific War, perhaps what the Navy was seeing was not the 1:5 ratio of economic scale between Japan and the U.S., but rather the ratio of number of naval vessels, the closest difference in terms of capability between the two. Japan, dissatisfied with the warships allocation ratio of U.S. 5 to Japan 3 at the Washington Conference, had unilaterally abandoned the agreement in 1934 to promote its own shipbuilding. So, the actual difference in naval power between the two was even narrower, more like 1.5:1.

On top of that, the Navy must have thought that the U.S. would have to divide its fleet between the Pacific and Atlantic, which, in the Japanese view, would even the two navies' warship resources. With the added spiritual element, the Japanese military, united under the Emperor and fighting under the protection of the gods, could not be defeated. This is probably how the Japanese Navy thought.

But the Navy had not understood the level of American solidarity and ability. Admiral Kichisaburo Nomura, who was Japan's Ambassador to the United States at the start of the War, wrote in his memoirs:[13]

American people work a couple of times harder than Japanese. That means Japan, with a population of 80 million, is actually a state of only 20 million.

The attack on Pearl Harbor was devised by the famous Isoroku Yamamoto, the Imperial Fleet Commander, revered as a hero in Japan. Quite a lot of research literature has been written about him. When the decision was made to initiate the War, Yamamoto told the Imperial Headquarters-Cabinet Joint Conference on November 27, 1941, and the Imperial Council on December 1, that he and his men could "run wild" for six months.

Yamamoto was originally strongly opposed to war with the United States. For this reason, many contemporary researchers interpret his words to mean that Japan would only last six months and therefore should not start the war. It is explained that his reason for proposing the Pearl Harbor attack was his belief that Japan would surely lose against the U.S., but since it had been decided to go to war, it was the duty of military personnel to create a strategy that would deliver a maximum blow.

I have little doubt, however, that even Yamamoto, a wise admiral, failed to understand American prowess, despite living in the U.S. for four years as a Naval Attaché. It is undeniable that he made two big mistakes.

First, he had not understood the American national character—that if anyone directly attacked their territory, the entire nation would come together like a fireball. Yamamoto had insisted early on, "At the onset, Japan must launch a fierce attack on the enemy's main fleet, depriving the U.S. Navy and the Americans of their morale to the extent they can never recover." He was utterly wrong.

The second was the delay in, or rather absence of, a declaration of war. Yamamoto had reiterated a number of times that the attack on Pearl Harbor must not be a "sneak attack." Indeed, the delay in delivering the "notification of war" was due to the slow work of the Japanese Embassy in Washington, as I recounted earlier. Even if it had been handled with alacrity, however, the intended plan was to deliver to the U.S. State Department an oblique diplomatic note to cut off negotiations 30 minutes before the bombardment. If Yamamoto thought that was a "legitimate and respectful attack," he was insensitive.

The attack on Pearl Harbor enraged America, and these two faults eliminated the possibility of an early peace and led to the ruin of Japan.

In the "*March of Folly: From Troy to Vietnam,*"[14] American historian Barbara Tuchman writes:

> *Here was a strange miscalculation. At a time when at least half the United States was strongly isolationist, the Japanese did the one thing that could have united the American people and motivated the whole nation for war. So deep was the division in America in the months before Pearl Harbor that renewal of the one-year draft law was enacted in Congress by a majority of only one vote—a single vote. The fact is that Japan could have seized the Indies without any risk of American belligerency; no attack on Dutch, British or French colonial territory would have brought the United States into the war. Attack on American territory was just the thing—and the only thing—that could. Japan seems never to have considered that the effect of an attack on Pearl Harbor might be not to crush morale but to unite the nation for combat. This curious vacuum of understanding came from what might be called cultural ignorance, a frequent component of folly.*

The above actions by the Navy reveal a part of Japanese idiosyncrasy that can still be seen today: The obsession with form, how Japan is seen from the outside, and the euphoria that comes from a belief in their own superiority. The Navy's world-class shipbuilding technology and lineup of military vessels resulted in over-confidence and arrogance toward the U.S., leading to the decision to fight a war. Japan completely ignored what lay beneath the enemy's surface appearance—comprehensive power, wisdom, and the rich life of the people who supported their nation.

This mentality was not corrected even after the reconstruction of Japan. During the revival period, Japan pursued only 'the numbers' to exceed Europe and the United States, under the slogan, "catch up and overtake."

In the 1980s, the country gained the status of the world's leading producer of goods, falling into the cult of production technology, downplaying the importance of software and services that cannot be expressed in numbers. This religion of production turned Japan's economic competitiveness toward recession after the mid-90s.

The Total Lack of Strategy of the Army and the Navy

For anyone who tries to analyze the basic nature of war, the Japanese military leadership, both Army and Navy, decidedly lacked the ability to carry out modern warfare. Military history is not the main purpose of this book, but have these flaws that led Japan to a succession of defeats totally disappeared from the country today? Or, are they still in the present-day Japanese structure? In order to know, one needs to touch on a number of battle examples. I will mention only two.

(1) Army—Imphal

My father Shuzo never spoke of Manchuria, but when he drank, he would express his fury over the Battle of Imphal, which killed one of his best friends. He likely spoke of that to his sons because he was not involved.

The operation was designed in early 1942 when the Japanese Army still had momentum. It was based on an unfounded hopeful prediction that Japan could launch a "sudden attack on India from Burma, team with Indian pro-independence forces to take the Assam region, and demolish British morale, thus dropping them out of the Allied front."

The operation was implemented in March 1944, two years behind the original plan, by which time the situation had completely changed. By then, with the invasion of Normandy only two months off, Britain had no reason to withdraw from the Allied front. Japanese leaders were under the misunderstanding that spiritual strength only belonged to Japan; they had no idea that the opponent's willingness to fight was equally strong.

On March 8, 1944, 100,000 Japanese soldiers left Burma for Imphal, India. It was a cruel 470-kilometer march over the 2,000 m-class Arakan Mountains, through jungles, and across the great Chindwin River. The Japanese Army underestimated the strength of the British Army. Knowing that the British had 10 divisions, they still thought they could win with a force of three divisions. The amount of heavy firearms and ammunition the soldiers carried was reduced to a minimum in order to make the march. Only three weeks' worth of rations were prepared for the soldiers, who were sent to the land of tropical diseases, where the Allied Forces had air control. General Renya Mutaguchi, 15th Army Commander, would not allow his completely exhausted soldiers to withdraw.

The battle resulted in 30,000 Japanese soldiers dead and 40,000 injured or struck by disease. Some 60% of the deaths came after withdrawal orders. They did not die fighting, they died from fatigue, hunger, and sickness.

About his friend, Shuzo spat out, "It was the Japanese Army that killed him, not the British."

(2) Navy—Battleship *Yamato* sortie

When it came to forced operations with no strategic purpose, it was the same with the *Yamato* sortie. With a displacement of 64,000 tons, the *Yamato* was the largest battleship in world history. Armed with nine 46-cm main cannons, the ship brought together the Japanese Navy's finest technology.

But when fighting in Okinawa became intense, the *Yamato* was ordered to beach itself and support the Japanese army as a field artillery fortress. A field artillery fortress? This was not a sane strategy.

To begin with, anyone could see that it was impossible to reach Okinawa through waters that were completely controlled by the U.S. military. Still, Navy Chief of Staff Lt. General Ryunosuke Kusaka went against Fleet Commander Vice-Admiral Seiichi Ito's protest and ordered the sortie for reasons of absolutely no military rationality, saying that it would be "the first of 100 million special attacks."

The *Yamato* left the Port of Kure in the Seto Inland Sea on April 6, 1945, and headed for Okinawa. The next day, the battleship was bombed by 400 U.S. planes in the East China Sea, and it sunk there with its accompanying ships, taking Ito and his 3,700 men down.

Renya Mutaguchi, who forced the Battle of Imphal, returned home without taking any responsibility. After the War, he lived out his life giving lectures justifying his strategy.

Ryunosuke Kusaka, who ordered the *Yamato* sortie, lived a peaceful life as an advisor to a chemical fertilizer company until his death in 1971.

Shiro Ishii, who commanded the Devil's Unit 731, continued to interact with his former subordinates without ever being judged, until he died in 1967.

My father Shuzo, with his eyes shut, calmly told his sons, "Only the soldiers who are drafted die. Professional soldiers are always safe. It's always the cowards who bring a country to destruction."

The Army leaders of the Imphal Operation symbolized the excessive self-confidence that came from the theory of fighting spirit. The Navy leaders of *Yamato*'s sortie symbolized the over-confidence in an object called the world's mightiest battleship.

The Japanese military was convinced that it could win a war against a stronger military power, as long as Japan was mentally superior. The leadership's war guidance, which ignored reality and stressed such notions as "kamikaze in the sky, flesh on the ground," "blessings of the gods and Buddha," and "divine grace," went unchallenged. It did not look like a modern war at all.

Japan never had the resources or ability to start a war with the United States. The only thing the Japanese military had was arrogance that made them believe that the Japanese military always wins.

A few months after attacking Pearl Harbor, the Japanese military in the Asia-Pacific was defeated in every battle against the United States, one after another. Any victory against the United States, the Soviet Union, or the United Kingdom—countries equipped with military resources—came through surprise attacks. The wins in Pearl Harbor, Indochina, the Philippines, Indonesia, and the six-month period after Japan started the War were all the result of insufficient preparation by the enemy. By the stage of head-on combat against a battle-prepared opponent, Japan's defeat was already visible.

Imphal and the *Yamato* sortie clearly indicate that the Japanese military did not have a "strategy." Neither the Army that initiated the Sino-Japanese War nor the Navy that started the Pacific War had a clear strategy. Japanese war meant individual battles started by *ad hoc* decisions and then expanded. There was no plan for how to execute and how far the operation should go.

The Imperial Council made the decision on November 15, 1941, to initiate war with the United States: "Quickly destroy the foundation of the U.S., Britain, and the Netherlands in the Far East, then encourage the Chiang government to surrender, collaborate with Germany and Italy to make Britain surrender and finally force the

U.S. to lose its will to continue war." It was a plan to make all nations surrender so that the U.S. would give up, which was not a military strategy for embarking on a war. There was absolutely no thought put into how to end the war.

The same was true for individual battles. Because there was no war strategy, everything was thrown together in an ambiguous way. The strategy for the Midway battle was to "capture Midway Island and seal the enemy's maneuver from Hawaii, destroy the enemy fleet." That is tantamount to saying, "Win all battles!" Without a strategy, one cannot make a specific operation plan.

The U.S. military was different. Its basic strategy was thorough in terms of ending the war with direct hits on mainland Japan. The Japanese military had five divisions in Taiwan but this meant nothing to the Americans, who skipped Taiwan and came directly to Okinawa. In individual battles, there was always a specific plan. In the Midway Battle, for example, Nimitz focused all of his power only on sinking Japanese aircraft carriers.

Present-day Japan also does not often evaluate itself objectively amid long-term trends. The national character we saw during the War, which assessed its own power only in terms of superficial numbers, has not changed very much.

"Anti-militarism" in Japan that the War Left Behind

On the other hand, the War has changed the Japanese perception of the security that Japan needs to possess as a nation.

The firebombing that targeted citizens, the use of flamethrowers to burn soldiers and citizens alive, the atomic bombs, and the total devastation caused by the delay of surrender—the picture of hell and hardship forced upon Japanese citizens was terrifying, even compared with the people of the similarly defeated nations of Germany and Italy. The image Japanese people carry in their hearts to this day is:

"War is an abomination—something we don't want to remember. We never want to see another military uniform or weapon, ever again. No matter what battles are taking place outside of Japan, we cannot allow a single compatriot to be sacrificed. We want to keep the military and war as far away from our daily lives as possible. We don't even want to talk about it...."

This is the reason why the Japanese people have not compre-
hensively examined that War. We haven't even given it a name. The
government and the media sheepishly refer to it as *Saki-no Taisen*
which means "the previous big war." That War has no proper noun!
Textbooks mention it as "World War II," but this doesn't reflect the
nature of this War. Why can't we simply call it the "Asia-Pacific War"?
Because of the reason mentioned above: Japanese simply don't want
to talk about it. They don't want to get involved in the polemics of
ascertaining anew the political nature of that War.

The Japanese government disposed of wartime materials and
documents without even verifying what went wrong. There has been
no debate about who should be responsible for the War. In the Diet
from 1952 to 1953, the House of Representatives and the House of
Councilors passed a total of five resolutions requesting the release
of war criminals sentenced overseas and at Sugamo Prison, saying
that further detention only makes it hard for the public to endure.

The most sensitive part about the War responsibility debate has
concerned the Emperor. The focus has been on how much Emperor
Hirohito knew about the status of the War. There are two volumi-
nous books by American scholars on postwar Japanese political
history that thoroughly examine the Emperor's War responsibility:
Embracing Defeat by Professor John Dower,[15] and *Hirohito*[16] by Professor Herbert Bix.

Many scholars have established that the Emperor himself was
willing to abdicate to take responsibility for the War. However, General MacArthur needed the Emperor in order to implement a stable
occupation policy, and he opposed the Emperor's abdication. There
is no doubt that in the undercurrents of some military leaders' not
taking responsibility, there was a feeling regarding the Emperor, who
remained on the surface unchanged, questioning why a person of
lower rank should be made to take responsibility when the highest
ranking does not.

In the United States, there were many calls to punish Emperor
Hirohito as the head of state, but in January 1946, MacArthur wrote
to General Eisenhower, the Chief of Staff of the Army[17]:

If (the Emperor) is to be tried, great changes must be made in occupational plans. ... His indictment will unquestionably cause a tremendous convulsion among the Japanese people, the repercussions of which cannot be overestimated. He is a symbol, which unites all Japanese. Destroy him and the nation will disintegrate. ... It would be absolutely essential to greatly increase the occupational forces. It is quite possible that a minimum of one million troops would be required.

Washington accepted MacArthur's opinion and put an end to the idea of holding the Emperor responsible for the War. However, other Allies that fought against Japan continued to be dissatisfied with the American policy.

After Emperor Hirohito's death in 1989 brought an end to the Showa Period, his son Akihito was enthroned, and a new era of Heisei began on January 8 of that year. At a time when all of Japanese society was beginning to forget about the War, Emperor Akihito visited many former battlefields, mourning the victims. It was as though he was on a mission fueled by his own guilt. Under the constitution that says the Emperor is a symbol of national integration, Emperor Akihito was not allowed to express a political view. In my eyes, in this way, he seemed to reveal his liberal values to the extent he could within the constitutional limitations.

The Emperor and Crown Prince have a series of study events known as *go-shinkō*, where leading experts and scholars mostly from the academic community deliver lectures to them. I also was given the opportunity a number of times. While I am not allowed to discuss the contents of our discussions, I will only mention that I came to develop a deep respect for Emperor Akihito and Empress Michiko as exceptionally conscientious human beings.

The International Military Tribunal for the Far East was convened between May 1946 and November 1948 and held trials to judge the War responsibility of the leaders. Seven who were charged as Class A war criminals at the tribunal for the crime of prosecuting the war, and 934 who were charged in other trials as Class B and C war criminals on counts of savage acts such as mistreatment of prisoners of war, were sentenced to death. The execution of 941 people was a heavy price for responsibility compared with the far smaller number of war criminals executed in Germany.

The Tokyo Trial, after all, was a case of the winner unilaterally convicting the loser. The Japanese people were not willing to accept it as a fair trial. Large-scale killings and atrocities performed by the Allied forces were never mentioned. General Curtis LeMay, who had indiscriminately bombed each major city in Japan, told his subordinates the truth. "If we'd lost the war, we'd all have been prosecuted as war criminals," he mused after the War.

The government and military, which did not delve into their War responsibilities, passed on the responsibility to all Japanese citizens, under the doctrine of "Confession of war guilt by 100 million Japanese." The people, who were continuously deceived by false pronouncements by the military, who had their families drafted and killed, were all forced to take responsibility for the War. Unlike the Germans, who clearly defined that the Nazis were at fault and the German citizens were victims, the Japanese have had to face the world with their heads down because they were taught to accept their guilt. This despondency of Japanese that remained across generations has hindered the establishment of the external relations of a healthy nation. Japan, thus, has been shrouded in excessive pacifism.

The national sentiment of a country that has lost a war is difficult. Why did my beloved son, husband, and father have to die on the battlefield? They did not succeed in protecting the country, but the cynical truth is that the war-torn homeland actually became free, democratic and prosperous after the war. Did it become a peaceful modern nation through defeat? If so, what was the purpose of our beloved ones dying in the war?

For individual Japanese soldiers who continued to fight desperately in the Pacific islands and in Asia, the battle was one of self-defense, to protect their families from the overwhelming enemy advancing to their homeland. These soldiers were simple good citizens. In war movies, soldiers die shouting, "Long live the Emperor!" In reality, however, the strong feelings of those soldiers lay with their families. The wills and testaments that they left behind were mostly written to their families and stated that they were happily on their way out to die for their wives, mothers, and sisters.

In 1941, Hideki Tojo, who led the war, issued the *Senjinkun* military code (Instructions for the Battlefield) for the entire military to follow. "Do not live to be humiliated as a prisoner of war."

It was a cruel instruction. If the soldiers ran out of food, their only choice was to die of hunger or to commit a suicidal battle known as the "banzai attack." Of the approximately 2.5 million combatants killed in the war, 60% died of illness or starvation, according to the late historian Akira Fujiwara, Professor Emeritus at Hitotsubashi University.[18]

"No food for two nights and three days and the steel helmets in the pouring rain"—my mother Kazuko says that she cannot stop her tears from flowing whenever she remembers the soldiers singing this song.

The military leaders and staff who ordered suicide attacks were always doing so from a safe place. But the bereaved cannot accept the notion that their loved ones were simply killed due to wrong decisions made by cowardly officers.

Even though each battle includes many heroic actions, the war dead in defeated countries are never "heroes who fought and won the peace and prosperity of today" as they are in victorious countries. The bereaved have no salvation. They must accept the death of their family members always with the qualifier: "It was a wrong war."

The majority of Japanese, who cannot accept the glorification of the causes of the Asia-Pacific War and convince themselves that the War emancipated Asian people from Western colonialism, have no choice but to curse and deny the very existence of war itself.

This was, indeed, the biggest legacy left by the War in Japan. Anti-military sentiment in a defeated nation is much stronger than in a victorious country.

This feeling is especially true among Japanese women. The outrage of being robbed of family in a logic-defying war in the absence of suffrage is rooted in Japanese women as a powerful antiwar feeling.

This is the basic premise of contemporary Japan, which will be discussed throughout the rest of this book.

A New Start for Japan

Hope amid Poverty

THE HOUSE IN TOKYO my father and mother had lived in was burned down in the infamous firebombing of March 10, 1945. The family moved after the War, to the ancient capital, Kamakura, where the Shogunate of Japan had been located for over a hundred years from the end of the 12th century. It lay an hour west by train from Tokyo.

People were poor and the town was enveloped in a sad melancholic atmosphere that even a small child could feel. Shops were lit by bare light bulbs and strips of flypaper hanging from the ceilings were black with captured flies. A strong smell of ammonia wafted from public toilets situated around town.

Still, although Kamakura had been subjected to machine gun sweeps, there had been no firebombing, so its appearance was unchanged. Residents kept the streets clean. Wounded soldiers in white gowns stood on street corners playing the accordion, soliciting charity. The country was flooded with such wounded soldiers, men who had lost their limbs.

Still, people's faces were bright, as they were free from the fear of death. There were no more air raids to destroy their lives. Compared to death, enduring poverty was easy.

In the country as a whole, especially in urban areas, food shortages were serious. Prior to the War, Japan had imported large amounts of key resources and rice, the staple food, from Korea, Taiwan, and Southeast Asia. In addition to not being able to pay for imports after losing the War, 1945 was a bad year for crops, which further exacerbated the food shortages. Rations were limited to about 300 grams per person per day. Malnutrition, fleas and parasites spread, and many died from starvation.

Life in my home was frugal. There were always tiny pebbles mixed in with the rationed rice and it was my younger brother and I who had the job of removing them one by one before our mother started cooking. The meat on the table was often whale meat because it was the cheapest, but there wasn't much of it, either. A small piece of margarine would be sitting on top of the rice and that, mixed with a bit of soy sauce would often be our only dinner. For children who don't know any other life however, there was nothing better than the taste of fragrant steamed white rice topped with savory margarine.

Japanese citizens lived in poverty. In addition to lack of supplies, inflation raged. Prices increased 100 times in the three years after the War.

In Kamakura, our house faced Yuigahama beach at the end of the street that stretches straight from the famous Great Sitting Buddha. The Great Buddha sat next to Kōtoku-in Temple, which owned the statue. Yukio Sato (former U.N. Ambassador), who later befriended me like an elder brother at the Ministry of Foreign Affairs, was the second son of the family that had run the temple for generations.

Our house was built on top of a stone wall. Today, a major road runs between the house and the beach, full of cars, but there was no road at the time and the stone wall extended straight down to the sandy beach and out to the sea. The beach was where my hero, Makiyo Ishimitsu, took his walks.

Despite the poverty right after the War, the sun and the sea in Kamakura were extra special. The sun spread layers of bright light that danced on the sandy beach and the blue sea stretching to infinity. The sea was so transparent that I could see schools of large fish from a nearby quay.

It was a sad, colorless era, but there were good quality picture books and stories by authors like Mimei Ogawa and Joji Tsubota, who gave lasting dreams to children. The songs people often sang were about war orphans living a happy life, and about positive feelings toward America.

Akai kutsu haiteta on'na no ko   (The little girl wearing red shoes)
Ijin-san ni tsurerarete icchatta   (Gone away with Mr. Foreigner)

Yokohama no hatobakara fune ni notte	(On a boat from the wharf in Yokohama)
Ijin-san no okuni ni icchatta	(Gone away to Mr. Foreigner's land)...
Imagoro wa aoi meni natchatte	(By now her eyes are surely blue)
Ijin-san no okuni ni irundaro	(Living in Mr. Foreigner's land)

Although it's difficult to convey the nuance to Americans, this popular song reflected the Japanese sentiment, with a sense of sadness and longing for America flowing through. The usage of the word "Ijin-san (Mr. Foreigner)," as Americans were called, conveyed a warm feeling toward the people against whom the country had fought and lost.

Japan was poor, but there was hope and cheer in the hearts of the children. Large numbers of GIs of the Occupation Forces came to visit the ancient capital of Kamakura with its Great Sitting Buddha and hundreds of temples. They came in station wagons decorated with wood panels on the sides. They symbolized civilization and abundance. At the time, chocolate was something Japanese people could never eat, but GIs gave Kamakura children Hershey's chocolates. One of them gave me a Disney comic book, too. How gorgeous Mickey Mouse and Donald Duck looked in all natural colors. I started dreaming of the day that I, too, would cross to the other side of the ocean in front of my house. Thinking of the world outside excited me.

I was lucky to meet such GIs, but not everyone was so fortunate.

My senior in high school and university, author and politician Shintaro Ishihara who experienced Grumman strafing during the War, recalls walking along a street in a neighboring city of Kamakura as a young teenager when suddenly a GI slapped him in the face with a popsicle. He loathed Americans ever since.

My friend who served as the Vice-Minister of Economy and Industry (MITI) remembers a GI firing at him from a jeep at close range when he was a child. Another friend who was the Vice-Minister at a major Ministry confided that his mother was nearly raped by a GI. Every country has its bad soldiers.

The good thing about the United States is that the "good soldiers" outnumbered the "bad" by far, and many of them had a high sense of morality and mission, like Jacob DeShazer.

Japan was destroyed by the United States, but most Japanese people did not harbor anti-American feelings. The public thought the War was caused by the Japanese military. Incredibly, the Japanese did not fire a single bullet at the occupying U.S. Forces throughout the country. It was an amazing development that nobody could have anticipated.

After Japan surrendered, Douglas MacArthur landed at Atsugi Base on August 30, holding a corn pipe in his mouth. Only two months later, American soldiers were walking around Ginza busy streets completely unarmed. Japanese society had completely changed from battle mode to peace psychology in an instant.

The acceptance by the Japanese of American rule without resistance cannot only be attributed to the reasons above and the gentle and good nature of the people.

The Emperor himself declared the surrender and the end of hostilities to the entire nation. The lack of a strong religious spirit among the Japanese gave power to the Emperor's words. Buddhism and Shinto are polytheistic and do not have a centripetal force. The only powerful god that could control the lives and deaths of the citizens was the "living god" Emperor. This person made a "human declaration" of defeat and preached to the public about compliance with the Occupation.

The popular feeling against their own military leadership made the U.S. military forces look like liberators. Japanese civil society, which had never won freedom or revolution on its own, did not feel a great resistance to following the orders of the victors who reigned.

There is a Japanese saying, "If it's long, let it wrap around you," which means, "If you can't beat them, join them." It is wisdom that advises not to rebel against strong authority. It can also easily lead to changing loyalties. Japanese POWs surprised the U.S. military when they became cooperative and easily shared secret information soon after they were captured.

When I turned six, we moved from Kamakura to the neighboring city of Fujisawa where I started elementary school. Times were still harsh, but I was not aware of that. The radio brightened up people.

When I got sick, I was allowed to eat a banana. It tasted like heaven. Water flavored with a few drops of a liquid called "Essence" was the best drink ever.

Elementary school lunches were served with skim milk. It tasted awful but the nutritional value was high. The skim milk powder that Japanese children grew up on in good health was aid sent by the United States. Postwar Japanese hygiene and food conditions were terrible, and many children suffered from malnutrition and illness.

The U.S. and United Nations' assistance prevented that situation from developing into a disaster.

From Recovery to Stability

Approximately 2.5 million Japanese soldiers and 800,000 civilians were killed in the War. More than 200 cities were firebombed, and of these, more than 60 were reduced to burnt fields. Nine million people had their homes burnt down. Thirty-five percent of the national wealth was lost.

The industrial blow was devastating. Heavy industry, chemicals, mines, and cotton-spinning facilities were halved by U.S. bombing.

However, the Japanese have a unique adaptability to cope with disasters. During the 2011 Great East Japan Earthquake and Tsunami, too, the victims got right back up with impressive courage and order.

Japan's reconstruction became possible because many of the Allied countries, headed by the United States, abandoned demands for war reparations. The U.S. further donated roughly 1.8 billion dollars over six years beginning in 1946, through the Government Appropriation for Relief in Occupied Area Fund (GARIOA) and the Economic Rehabilitation in Occupied Areas (EROA) program. Without this assistance, Japan would not have recovered for a long time.

The United States was a special country, for rewarding with favor and philanthropy, not punishment, an enemy country that had attacked its homeland. This is something that many Japanese people felt. In virtually all postwar public opinion polls, the countries with an overwhelmingly large proportion of people who like the United States are Japan and Israel. In regular polls, strong majorities expressed a liking for the United States. The foundation of the pro-American sentiment among Japanese that continues to this day was built during the five years of MacArthur's reign.

Japan relinquished 44% of its pre-War territory due to its defeat, and as a result, 3.3 million military personnel and 3.3 million civilians pulled out of China, Korean Peninsula, Taiwan, and Southeast Asia. Many repatriates returned home with nothing but what they were wearing, pulling on the hands of their small children. The return of repatriates from overseas and POWs who survived capture in the Soviet Union continued until 1957.

During the War, Japan had a total population of approximately 72 million, of which 9% lived in Japanese occupied territories overseas. These people returned to mainland Japan all at once, seeking new workplaces and residences. The defense-related industries had been dismantled, so there were no jobs available. Cities overflowed with the unemployed.

Black markets bustled. Supplies stocked up by the military in preparation for a decisive mainland battle, along with food and materials that remained in the villages and factories, were released and found their way into the black market. As long as you had money, you could fill most of your needs in the black market, but the prices were prohibitive. Rice cost 130 times the official price, potatoes 60 times, and sugar 270 times the rate fixed by the government.

After the War ended, my father Shuzo returned to the Ministry of Agriculture and Forestry.

The fate of those people who expelled him to Manchuria was uncertain, but Shuzo was satisfied with his new position.

His first job was to distribute *tatami* mats fairly among consumers. *Tatami* is a type of flooring unique to Japan, made from multilayered rice straw, tightly fastened and compressed, covered with woven igusa, a type of reed. Japanese culture is often referred to as "*tatami* culture."

Some 2.36 million homes were lost in the war, but without *tatami* mats, houses could not be built. *Tatami* farmers did not put the material on the market at the official price, but instead sold it on the black market and made huge profits.

Shuzo's mission was to make the farmers ship *tatami* to the public market. The record of testimony that Shuzo gave at the House of

Representative in the first National Diet held in 1947 remains. The minutes of the long interpellations with an opposition party suggest that he had a hard time with the farmers. These farmers ignored the demands of the MAF and continued to sell *tatami* mats on the black route at high prices.

The same was true for other materials essential to living. Before the War, MAF had helped the peasants fight against landowners. Expecting the farmers to cooperate with the Ministry in return turned out to be naïve.

The world had changed. The Imperial Diet, which had been dominated by the landowner class, was abolished, and the peasants gained power through the release of farmland, creating politically influential agricultural cooperatives. Farmers no longer needed the backing of MAF. From this time on, MAF would constantly be subjected to tension with politically powerful farmers' organizations.

The release of *tatami* to public markets finally began, but at a lagging pace.

Shuzo had always felt superior to those who were less capable than he, and his experiences in Manchuria made him stubbornly righteous to the point that he lost his ability to cooperate. There was no way that he would be able to get along with farmers who were only interested in making profit. Kazuko said that Shuzo never had a nice thing to say about the peasants, whose interest he was supposed to look after.

The MacArthur GHQ issued reform directives one after another, which the Japanese government faithfully followed. Inflation eased and the foundation for economic reconstruction was laid. On the other hand, many small and medium enterprises went bankrupt and the number of unemployed increased due to the rationalization directives.

What saved the day was the Korean War. Japan suddenly became the logistics base for the war on the Korean Peninsula that broke out in 1950. Booming with munitions orders, industrial production recovered to the pre-War average level.

In April 1951 President Truman dismissed Douglas MacArthur, who had revived Japan, when he advocated using an atomic bomb on China in the Korean War.

People across the nation regretted MacArthur's departure. Some 200,000 citizens filled the streets leading to Haneda Airport, seeing him off with waving flags of Japan and the United States. His departure was broadcast live on the national radio network, with the announcer calling him "the Marshal who saved Japan from chaos and hunger!" After five years and seven months in Japan, MacArthur was sent off, showered with the respect of the Japanese public.

After the Korean War, the Japanese economy took off into miraculous growth.

Cheerful songs became popular in towns, and barrack homes were built one after another. Vigor returned to Tokyo, which had been flattened by firebombing. Popular culture developed from what little entertainment had remained.

Ten years had passed since the Asia-Pacific War. The lives of the Japanese people had become visibly enriched. Electric vacuum cleaners replaced straw brooms, electric fans replaced handheld fans, washing machines took the place of washboards, and iceboxes became electric refrigerators. Every time a new appliance arrived, cheers ran through the neighborhood. Refrigerators, washing machines, and TVs came to be known as "the Three Sacred Treasures." The economic white paper of 1956 stated that the country was "no longer in the post-War period."

Black-and-white TVs came to fortunate homes, where townsfolk gathered. I went to an affluent friend's home, and it was exciting to watch Rikidozan, the national hero of professional wrestling, beat American wrestlers. The Japanese people became unified, and exuberant about various things. Almost nobody missed the TV broadcast of the wedding of Crown Prince Akihito (who later became the Emperor of *Heisei*) in 1959.

In 1957, I entered a municipal junior high school. School lunches were served in elementary schools but from junior high, we had to bring our own from

Yukio Okamoto in the garden of the Osaka-Namba home of his mother's parents, his entry into junior high school.

home. Nobody's lunchbox was elaborate. Mine consisted of white rice, a piece of fish and maybe a few rape leaves. There was no juice or tea. Students were given hot water to pour into the lunchbox lid. Nobody complained, though, because they had no way to compare it to a richer life.

At that time in Japan, there was an accumulation of good quality and abundant labor due to increasing higher education and a rapid increase of urban residents. In addition to that, society was filled with aspiration and enthusiasm for growth. The longing for richness that resulted from the prolonged shortages of supplies and food became the driving force for economic growth. Post-War Japan had strength because it had nothing to lose. It was an era when everyone could rise if they worked hard, just like in the era of *Meiji*.

Japanese people are strong when given a direction. They have tenacity of purpose and are diligent and elaborate, and they brought about high growth in both production and consumption. The 1964 Tokyo Olympic Games and the construction of infrastructure that preceded it completed Japan's economic recovery.

In the 1970s, more than 90% of the population considered themselves middle-class, giving rise to a rare phenomenon—a homogeneous mass society called the "entire 100-million population becoming middle-class." In 1947, the average life expectancy in Japan was merely 50 years for men and 54 for women. At the end of 1974, it had increased to 71 years for men and 73 for women. Today it is the highest in the world, at 82 for men and 88 for women, in 2020.

There were of course several reasons for the Japanese economic miracle, but I will leave that to other resource materials.

Post-war Days of My Parents

When my father returned from Manchuria and returned to the Ministry of Agriculture and Forestry, he had already become a different man. At home, he did not speak much and was often lost in thought or criticizing others. His personal relationships did not go well. He was short-tempered and easily got into fights with those around him.

Japanese customarily send gifts in the summer and at year's end, usually processed or fresh food. Civil servants, especially those who have supervisory functions, including the distribution of *tatami* mats, would receive many such gifts. Shuzo, however, made his wife Kazuko return all the gifts to their senders. Naturally, the senders would feel insulted. When Kazuko said, "We don't have much to eat, I wish we could keep it," he scolded her like there was nothing worse. To care for the children, Kazuko had no choice but to cleverly increase the household funds by selling the kimonos she had from before she married.

Shuzo was tormented by war ghosts. As a child, I once found a *Goboken* sword, the kind issued to solders, in the closet.

"Have you ever killed a man, Papa?" I asked.

I will never forget his face. "Don't you ever ask such a stupid question again or I will throw you out of the house!" He chased me out of the house as I screamed and cried.

He was never promoted in the Ministry of Agriculture and Forestry (MAF). I, myself, became "Division Chief," the basic first rank for bureaucratic ascension, at the Ministry of Foreign Affairs at the age of 40, but he never earned even that title at MAF. Thinking that was unusual, I once jokingly commented to Mr. Watanabe, one of my father's few friends and colleagues, "I wonder why my dad never gets promoted."

Mr. Watanabe responded in all seriousness.

"Yukio-san, do you know what your father's experience was during the War?"

"Yes, I heard he was an interpreter in Manchuria."

"Hmm, you don't know anything? Never mind, then. But let me tell you, I really sympathize with the situation your father was in."

I had no idea what he was talking about.

A long time passed before I learned about my father having served in Unit 731, and that people who had been in that Unit were forbidden to hold public offices after the war. MAF naturally knew Shuzo's military history. He was fortunate to be able to return to the Ministry, but the organization could not possibly have promoted him to a higher rank. Or perhaps he deserved the non-promotion, having changed into a bigoted and opinionated man.

The biggest thing the War took from my mother Kazuko was the love between her and her husband. The War turned Shuzo into a man who could not relate to others. Advancement in his career at MAF was cut off, and he lost his desire to work. He drank alcohol and came home late every night, never spoke a kind word to Kazuko, and when he arrived home, he shut himself up like a clam.

Shuzo retired from the Ministry of Agriculture in 1962. Eleven years later, he died at the age of 64 of lung cancer caused by years of heavy smoking.

From the day he returned from the War until the day he died in 1973, the relationship between the couple remained estranged.

When Kazuko turned 100, she said for the first time, "Shuzo-san was a good person only until the War started. After that, it seemed that he was always fighting with something that I could not see. Then, no matter how hard I worked to raise you three children, no matter how hard I tried, he showed no appreciation. If I were to make a mistake, he would blow up. He totally became a selfish person with no thought of anyone but himself. He's dead and gone now, but I dislike that man."

Shuzo was naturally strict with his children. My brothers and I were not allowed any mischief whatsoever. He couldn't even over-look the bad manners of others in town, and he yelled at strangers. It almost seemed that his mission became to correct the injustices of the entire Japan. I hated going out with my father. The only time I would sit face-to-face with him was when my school marks fell. To me, he was frightening, and I never felt loved.

However, I started thinking later that this was all because he had become a person who could not express himself. How did a man with such a strong sense of justice endure the pain that he had to witness every day in Unit 731, the brutality and the cruelty? No, because he could not endure it, his character was distorted.

I now believe he actually loved his sons. I once came down with the flu and had a high fever. My father came to my bedside and held my hand tight for a long time. I was already an adult, so holding my hand was not something he could have ever done in normal circum-stances. He probably thought I was unconscious.

Through my fever I slightly opened my eyes and saw his tears streaming down his cheeks.

My parents never told us three brothers to get along and be nice to each other. They raised us to compete, as individuals with different personalities. My mother Kazuko often said, "You don't have to be loved by others. But be respected." I did not like her teachings, but that's the way it was, so my older brother Katsuya, younger brother Yasuo and I never experienced a happy family gathering.

The three of us went to the same high school in our neighborhood. After that, my elder brother studied shipbuilding at Tokyo University and took a job at Mitsui & Co. My younger brother also went to Tokyo University, where he studied law and then went to the United States to become a Wall Street lawyer.

I don't have any children, but both of my brothers have been blessed with wonderful children. Perhaps as a reaction to their childhoods, they have raised very warm families.

After we had all reached our sixties, we agreed that our mother had long played a "divide and rule" strategy, and we confessed our biased views to each other. Now we are very close brothers, as if to regain the past decades of aloofness.

Kazuko gained freedom after Shuzo's death. She had graduated from university, but to continue her schooling in a new field, she joined a correspondence course at the same high school her sons had attended. She attended the school every weekend for several years. She was 73 years old when she graduated and served as valedictorian at the ceremony representing her teenaged classmates, which was featured in a newspaper.

She then entered Tamagawa University, at the age of 77 to pursue a degree in Education. In P.E. class, she took swimming lessons with classmates who were younger than her grandchildren. It took her four years to complete most of her curriculum, but she stumbled at the end. To obtain a teaching license, she needed to go through hands-on training at a school somewhere, but no schools would entrust their pupils, even for a short period, to a trainee-teacher over 80 years of age.

We sons had not been aware that she was seriously trying to become a schoolteacher and were quite surprised at her deep disappointment. She did not give up, though, and tried to find a way to become a teacher in Indonesia. When she could not find what she desired, we felt relieved.

Instead, she started traveling around the world alone. Because of her age, her applications to join tours conducted by travel agencies would be turned down, so she took off on her own with a backpack.

Indonesia was her favorite destination. In Japan, elderly travelers on their own are not looked upon kindly. In Indonesia, however, hotels said the older you are, the more welcome you are. This was the opposite of Japan in showing respect to elders.

In Bali, Indonesia, she set off into town straddling the back of a motorbike driven by a young girl who had no driver's license. The two were caught and taken in by the police, and my mother's face beamed when she told us about the very warm welcome the police gave her at the police station. At the street stalls, there was no stopping her from eating all the raw food she wanted, without a care about hygiene.

Every time she went to Indonesia, she returned full of energy, but once she was back in Japan for a while, she would wither, her energy gradually sapped. This was because Japanese society has determined that elderly people have elderly ways to behave. When she was 90 years old, people around her laughed at her because she applied for a 10-year passport. She cursed their laughter.

Japanese society likes to cram people into pre-defined boxes. Japan's education system creates collaborative people convenient for corporations, its society makes obedient wives to serve men, its families send children to extracurricular schools that only serve the purpose of passing university entrance exams. It is not a society where old people or women can step outside of the societal norm and live as they like.

When I complimented my mother for living a way of life that wasn't bound by stereotypes, her reaction was terse and critical:

"I'm just acting normally. If you think that's unusual for elders, you're the one trapped in the incurable social framework!"

At the age of 105, she is reading books every day in her retirement home. Her rebellious spirit remains the same. [Ed. note: Mrs. Okamoto passed away in 2022 at 107.]

My Student Years as a Pseudo-leftist

In September 1953, the San Francisco Peace Treaty was concluded between Japan and 48 countries of the allied camps. Japan regained its independence and sovereignty. Later, conflict deepened between the U.S. and the Soviet Union, and the U.S. shifted to a policy of making Japan an economically independent communist-breakwater rather than a demilitarized and harmless country. Many U.S. troops stationed in Japan were dispatched to the Korean Peninsula during the Korean War, creating a vacuum in Japan's national security. The GHQ, which had until then pursued a complete demilitarization policy, instructed the Japanese Government to create a police reserve. This was the birth of the Japanese Self-Defense Forces.

In 1960, Prime Minister Nobusuke Kishi signed a new Treaty of Mutual Cooperation and Security between the United States and Japan (aka Anpo). However, there was strong domestic opposition, and Tokyo was wrapped in the largest postwar demonstrations led by students chanting, "Anpo will drag Japan into American wars."

In the final phase of adopting the treaty, 300,000 students surrounded the Diet. My older brother Katsuya, who was a third-year university student, went to the demonstrations every day and came home after colliding with the police. I was in ninth grade with no idea what Anpo was, but when my elder brother talked about the demonstrations, he seemed like a hero. My mother asked him not to go to stay safe, but he wouldn't listen. My father just sat with his arms crossed and said nothing.

Amid the anger and confusion, Nobusuke Kishi drove the U.S.–Japan Security Treaty through the Diet on June 20, 1960, in exchange for his own political career.

Under the treaty, Japan formed an equal alliance with the United States.

The fierce demonstrations made it look like the U.S.–Japan relationship was in danger, but once the treaty was finalized, movement leaders who had lost their fighting goals left without planting any revolutionary momentum in society. Interest in economic gain got the better of the students and my brother too, joined a large company. The subsequent administration turned the people's attention exclusively to economic growth. Before we knew it, Japan's "national security" became as natural as air, something we would die without, and yet invisible.

However, the students' anti-power energy was not completely burned out. The activists developed a strategy to revitalize the opposition, targeting the timing of the automatic extension of the Japan–U.S. Security Treaty in 1970. Inspired by the atmosphere of the times, I, too, became a student who was classified as "Left-hearted." You could not have conversations with friends unless you had read *The German Ideology* by Karl Marx and Friedrich Engels. I started joining the demonstrations at the height of the Vietnam War. I thought it was a student's duty to oppose war.

That was as far as activities went for pseudo-leftists like me, students who were referred to as "non-political" with an air of contempt. It was an age of continuing rapid growth for Japan and people believed in the all-middle-class concept. There was no sense of reality in the class theory that said workers were being exploited by the capitalist class. The Marxist idea that if capitalism develops, it inevitably becomes socialism, was far removed from the reality of the times.

The peak of the student movement came in 1968 when I joined the Ministry of Foreign Affairs (MOFA). Some students became even more radical in their search for a "revolution" under agitators who advocated anti-American anti-Stalinism. Terrorist attacks on companies, clashes with police and occupation of universities continued.

Haruhiko Shibano had been my best friend in elementary school and junior high school. He was smart and lively. After school, we would spend time at my house or his, doing homework together. His mother had died early and my mother, who was sympathetic, was especially kind to him. He lived with his father, who was a writer, and his sister, who was skinny and wore glasses. It was a simple house, but it felt warm.

After we started high school, we grew somewhat remote. Then after I graduated from university, I met him by coincidence at Yokohama Station. He was wearing a denim jacket and looked defiant. We went into a coffee shop and talked. He still had his friendly smile, but I felt a distance. As we were parting, he said: "Oka-chan (that was my nickname), I guess we're going separate ways now. Thanks for being a good friend when we were kids."

I later found out that he had become a leader of the Keihin Anti-Anpo Joint Force (*Keihin Anpo Kyoto*) at Yokohama National University, which was aiming for armed revolution. In December 1969, he led two members into a plan to ambush a police escort car that was to carry his comrade to prison. Shibano needed a gun to do that, so armed with an iron pipe and knives, they attacked a koban police box in lower downtown Tokyo, and Shibano was shot to death. He was 24 years old. The extremists looked up to him as the first revolutionary to be shot and killed by the police. He became their hero.

Shibano's friends were insidious. They sent a bomb to the home of a National Police Agency official who argued that the shooting by the policeman was a legitimate act of self-defense. His wife died when she opened the package and it exploded.

I read on the internet that half a century later, people still gather to hold memorials for Shibano. I am angry at them, those who took Shibano, who was once my best friend, into terrorism.

The activities of the revolutionary left were intensified by Shibano's death. The Keihin Anti-Anpo Joint Force joined the Japanese

Yukio Okamoto (center) with university friends.

Red Army to become the United Red Army that had a shootout with police in February 1972 after taking a hostage in a mountain lodge. This was called the Asama-Sanso Incident, the largest incident in the postwar history of domestic security until the 1995 Aum Shinrikyo Sarin Attack. The battle at the lodge was broadcast live on television for 10 hours and from the statements of the arrested members, it was disclosed that 12 of their members had been killed by peers because their thoughts were not communized enough.

This sent a message across the nation that student movements were terrifying, and as a result, the heated left-wing movement rapidly cooled off. With this incident, organized student movements, in effect, came to an end. In a sense, Shibano's terrorism escalated the insanity of the extremist students' "make-believe revolution" and ended it with self-destruction.

Okamoto (second from left) was a member of the yacht club at university and he enjoyed going to the beach whenever he could.

WORKING BETWEEN JAPAN AND AMERICA

Starting Life as a Diplomat

I JOINED THE Ministry of Foreign Affairs (MOFA) in 1968. It was an elite community where everyone who entered through the same category of exam was eventually appointed as an ambassador to some country. All the members of my class, too, were eventually appointed as ambassadors, except for me and one other who quit midway.

After working for one year in Tokyo, I was sent to the United States as a "trainee diplomat" together with five colleagues from the same class.

My first sight of America was the Golden Gate Bridge in San Francisco from the sky. To think that the bridge had existed before the Pacific War shocked me: How could anyone even have thought about starting a war with this country? That was my very first impression. This impression grew stronger in Washington, where we reported ourselves to the Embassy. The sight of suburban homes and wealthy lifestyles, I was told, was the same since before the War. Did Japan challenge the United States, knowing what these houses looked like?

The intense impression I got in the U.S. was how diligent the people were. That impression was reinforced 15 years later when I was posted to the Embassy in Washington and saw the work of American government staff. High ranking officials started work as early as 6:30 in the morning and even worked on Saturdays. It reminded me of the statement of Kichisaburo Nomura, the Ambassador to the U.S. during the War: "Americans work twice as hard as Japanese."

I entered Swarthmore College on the outskirts of Philadelphia as a trainee in 1969. When I was signing up, I had to declare my income. My salary at the MOFA was 24,000 yen, which with the exchange rate of that time, was 80 dollars a month, in addition to a rent and tuition stipend. I was told, "No, not your weekly income, write your monthly income." Today's monthly income for a MOFA trainee is 230,000 yen, or roughly 2,500 dollars in 2020. That's not bad for a student. In other words, the salary level of trainees in terms of dollars increased 25 times compared to my time.

I obtained a loan of 1,000 dollars from the Bank of Tokyo in New York, paying back 50 dollars a month for two years. With that money, I bought a used Mustang for 700 dollars and drove all over the United States.

It was the generation of hippies and Flower Power and just after the Watts riot. Racial animosity on campus was intense. Black students called white students "sons and daughters of slave-masters."

A strong wave of anti-Vietnam protests swept across America. Anti-war became part of the campus decor. The Kent State shootings happened in Ohio the following year. For the students, "We Shall Overcome" just wasn't powerful enough, so they started raising their fists. Then Watergate followed. The nation split in two, and cracks between the citizens regarding Vietnam spread wide. The United States was hurting.

A lot of students used marijuana. A 17-year-old girl who was in my class advised me, "Yukio, alcohol is bad for your health, you should stick to marijuana." Meanwhile, young people were free and had a sense of mission. The youth were sincere in their search for ideals and peace. They could hear the wind blowing high in the clear blue sky.

My best friends at school were Art Brock and Steve Arbuthnot.

Art was admitted to Harvard Law School but he chose to become a teacher in Harlem in New York. He created a unique curriculum for kids who were not interested in studying. "A man who ate seagull soup threw himself from the quay. Why do you think he did that?" The children would spend a week with eyes aglow, discussing this with each other and coming up with their stories. Art's own story was that "He was a deckhand and the ship he was on wrecked. His shipmates gave him the soup saying it was seagull soup, but in fact, it was made from the flesh of the others who died. He couldn't handle the memory, so he threw himself from the pier."

That answer is correct. There are other correct answers, too. The story can be anything. He taught the children creativity. "Even juvenile delinquents dream and imagine. You know, we have to make those dreams come true," Brock told me one time in his converted loft in Manhattan.

Steve did not go to graduate school, even though he had excellent grades. He became a police officer in Washington because he could not stand the mounting crime rate, saying, "I will choose a career that is more direct than Art's." He was trained to always aim at the opponent's chest when firing a handgun, and he patrolled the city every day, and luckily for him, he never had to kill anyone or suffer injury himself. He took early retirement and went to live peacefully with his family in Washington D.C.

Many young men went to Vietnam. The biggest concern among my classmates was how to avoid the draft. At that time, my friend Jim Webb, who became a senator after serving as Secretary of the Navy, was serving in Vietnam as a second lieutenant in the Marine Corps. There he lost four communication men in a row. The communication soldiers were always the first to be targeted in battle. The fifth man who put aside his fear and volunteered for the communications position was a fellow named McGarvey, who lost his arm. He did not regret offering his services, though, and had the remaining part of his arm tattooed with a black dotted line (the cutting line). He never completed high school and later became an automobile mechanic. He and Webb remain best friends.

Webb told me a story: One day at Webb's house, McGarvey became so angry that his nose started to bleed. It happened when he read the memoirs of a journalist who wrote about his opposition to the Vietnam War and how he dodged the draft while he was a student at Harvard. The journalist's name was Jim Fallows. He had become the editor-in-chief of the Atlantic Monthly and a speechwriter for President Carter. Webb set up a meeting between McGarvey and Fallows. The two sat silently glaring at each other for 10 minutes. Then they started talking. It took time, but they became friends at the end.

I don't need to remind you that the biggest problem America continues to face is racism. When I first went to the U.S. in the late 1960s, I experienced a certain amount of unpleasant treatment.

Today, 50 years later, I don't see the same behavior. Civil rights movements and globalization have created a new society. Above all, this is the result of education provided through the conscious efforts of the United States as a nation. There are those in Japan who say, "It's just a superficial change. Many people hold racism in their hearts," but nobody can refute the fact that more than half of the people at polling stations, where no one could peek, wrote the name Barack Hussein Obama on their ballots. No country can criticize the United States for being racist.

It is sad to witness a divided America under President Trump. Whatever political changes may occur, I just pray that America's direction as an institution that proceeds towards freedom and democracy never changes.

After completing my training in the United States, I was transferred in 1971 to Paris to work for the Permanent Delegation of Japan to the OECD. The European view of America was quite different from what I had experienced until then. I was taken as an Americanized foreigner and sometimes faced sneers, but it helped me, from time to time, to see the United States from another perspective.

Yukio Okamoto visits Sharm El Sheikh, Egypt, a resort on the Red Sea that he especially enjoyed and looked forward to visiting on his rare vacations, whenever he could.

I returned to the Ministry in Tokyo after two years. Eight years later, in 1981, I was sent to Cairo.

It was the most fulfilling time of my life. I saturated myself in the Middle Eastern climate and Islamic culture, which were completely new to me.

The most profound thing I learned there—belatedly—was about religion. I had lived my life

During his tenure in Cairo, Yukio Okamoto attends a meeting between Japanese Ambassador Toshio Yamazaki and Egyptian President Hosni Mubarak.

knowing Buddhism, which guides the ordinary person to gain merit until he becomes a "buddha," and Shinto, which teaches that souls dwell in everything on earth. The impact of facing the monotheistic religion of the Middle East was remarkable. The austere environment, with the inherent dichotomy of life in an oasis and death in a desert under scorching sunlight, left no room for ambiguous and gentle polytheism as in Japan.

The feelings for God that exist there permit no compromise. In the Japanese climate, even experts maintain the simplistic idea that "since we are a Buddhist country, we are best at mediating between Israel and Palestine." Working in the Middle East taught me the importance of Japan responding resolutely but respectfully to the Middle East.

In 1983, I returned to the United States as Counselor in the Japanese Embassy in Washington. This time I was not a trainee, but a diplomat.

The political tide had changed since the Flower Power era that I had seen before. McGovern and Mondale had both been defeated, and it was the age of Ronald Reagan's conservative-centralism. Economically, the "trilemma" of inflation in the late 1970s, the balance of payments deficit, and high unemployment had stripped Americans of their vitality. There was the closure of Youngstown, the Penn Central and the crisis of Chrysler. Overseas, national prestige was being trampled on in Iran and Sudan.

After the storm of economic struggles passed, a completely new group of young people emerged. The conservative yuppies. These young people did not bring back the traditional values of family, work, and patriotism that Reagan advocated. They escaped the great recession of 1979, seeking a new life and wealth. Many venture businesses were created. The people who made up this so-called "Atari Generation" were copies of each other, invariably dressed in navy blue jackets, white shirts, and striped ties. Reagan emphasized "rugged individualism," but this young generation was not that kind of tribe.

Perhaps this was peculiar to Washington, but human relationships were also stylized effectively. An American friend told me that when they received business cards at a reception, they instantly evaluated the person and separated the cards into their left or right pockets, depending on whether the person seemed useful to them or not.

Dating also did not start with love at first glance. When men and women met, they would first ask each other their addresses. If they lived too far from each other, they would label the other as GU, Geographically Undesirable. For young people, the priority was work and career advancement. Traveling a distance to take a date home would affect work the next day. Instead, they chose partners who lived at a comfortable distance. GUs were excluded, no matter how attractive they might be. Meanwhile, they also knew that love doesn't grow from one-night stands, either because of herpes or AIDS.

So, the hippies were gone and the young people were better behaved. There weren't many young people dedicating their lives to society like Art Brock or Steve Arbuthnot. The number of law school and business school applicants had increased, with the aim of becoming rich.

In Japan too, it was an era of young people seeking materialistic, decadent pleasures. Discos were filled with young women in one-piece body-skimming dresses, and men did everything they could to improve their techniques for attracting the women for the night.

Support for the Self-Defense Forces among young people with this reasoning: "We are safe and rich in Japan. All the violence happens in foreign countries. We're scared. We need the SDF to protect us from the dangers overseas." The Japanese were in a frenzied bubble era and hardly paid much attention even to the collapse of the Cold War.

Western countries started saying that Japan was selfishly seeking only its own economic benefits. "Japan is a heretical nation so there is no choice but to contain them," French Prime Minister Edith Cresson, a tactless European politician, said without hesitation. She referred to the Japanese as "ants," going so far as to say, "Japanese are short yellow people who stay up all night thinking of ways to screw the Americans and the Europeans."

Later, after I returned to Tokyo from Washington and started to work for Japan–U.S. relations at the Ministry of Foreign Affairs, I went to visit Jim Fallows, a leading American advocate of "Japanese heterogeneity." Fallows was the man who had that glaring match with McGarvey, the Vietnam vet who had a dotted line tattooed on the stub of his arm. Fallows and I got into a deep conversation at a park near his house in the suburbs of D.C. I found out finally that he actually was fond of Japan. He wanted to do something about Japan and wanted Japan to do something, and he was frustrated with the unchanging Japanese nature and so he was criticizing the country. Many of his criticisms were not unfounded.

Who are the Americans and the Japanese

When I was in the United States at the end of the '60s, I traveled all over the country, trying to get to know as many Americans as possible. I even tried hitchhiking as a way to meet people. At the time, it was a common means of transportation among students. I wondered if people would willingly give a ride to an Asian they had never met before.

I stood by the road holding my thumb up and many cars did stop. Such goodwill! The openness was incredible. In Florida, I was standing by the road with a sign that said "Key West" and a Cadillac stopped for me. The driver was an executive at a television station in Miami. As we talked, we found ourselves getting along, so he took me straight to his home. His wife, who was in the middle of changing, shrieked, but the whole family welcomed me. I spent the night in their big house, and the next day went diving with the family at John Pennekamp Coral Reef State Park.

What kind of a country is this? The United States must be the only country in the world where people would treat hitchhikers who are complete strangers this way. It was fifty years ago.

I realized that this attitude probably had a lot to do with the origin of the country. My strong impression was that, in the United States, where pioneers struggled with nature to cultivate the wild west, strangers were basically partners. The area you can reach by throwing stones becomes your territory. You move forward from there. In an agricultural society with a small land area like Japan, it is most important for everyone to live without confrontation. From childhood, we are taught that "stepping back" takes priority over "moving forward." Communities are organized in compact areas, and there is less room to accept strangers from outside.

I heard a Japanese friend lamenting. He and his wife moved to the United States with their children, who had no knowledge of the English language. They were worried that the kids would be bullied because they couldn't speak. Forgive me, children, for subjecting you to such a situation because of my work …

But their worries were completely unnecessary. The classes at school warmly accepted them and the children had a very happy life in America. The problems started after they returned to Tokyo. The children were told by their cautious parents that they should not be conspicuous and should not talk about their experience in the United States. But when they unconsciously uttered a word with an American accent, their classmates bullied them for showing off. The father gave a big sigh, "We are welcomed in a foreign country and then rejected in our motherland. Is this the country called Japan?"

I heard similar stories from other friends. It is the exclusivity seen everywhere in Japanese society. The problem is somewhat abated but still exists today. The future of Japanese society will be decided by whether or not Japan can accept heretics and geniuses.

The thinking behind the Japanese education system is to formulate uniform classes that do not create either dropouts or heroes. Some elementary schools intentionally do not produce winners in the 50-meter race. They make the children all hold hands and cross the finish line together, side-by-side.

The child of an acquaintance of mine was disliked by his teacher because not only did the child ask questions outside the box, he also sometimes disagreed with what the teacher said. His mother, a university professor, was startled when she was called to the school and found her son studying in the special education class because he did not understand the meaning of what was being taught. The child was given the lowest grade in every subject he was good at, including math. His mother had to quit her job in Japan to take him to Australia to be educated. There, he was finally able to enjoy learning at school. He went on to graduate from an Australian university with good scores, without returning to Japan.

The Japanese are patient and persistent. They are serious and honest. And their submissive nature makes them harmonious and cooperative. This is the reason Japanese excel when it comes to manufacturing and crafting things (*monozukuri*), where uniform, consistent production is important.

The Japanese are also kind and generous. The problem is that these virtues are basically contained within and not usually directed in an outward fashion. The kindness stays within the community, among friends and the workplace. Not much is expressed beyond these boundaries, to people outside. Furthermore, Japanese shyness restricts them from explicitly expressing compassion to strangers.

When I'm speaking to an audience of citizens in Japan, I ask them this question: "In the past month, have you received from or given kindness to a stranger?" Only a few hands go up.

From my experience of teaching at Japanese university, young Japanese are less inhibited and more open. They can turn their kindness outward universally. Still, it will be a long road.

Japanese people show their virtue in a completely different way than Americans do.

One extreme example occurred when I was invited to dinner by Takeshi Hemmi, who was the president of a major oil company in Japan. It was only my third encounter with him, and I was 45. There was a heavy rain that day and I arrived at the restaurant soaking wet. Mr. Hemmi, who was already there, looked at me in surprise and told me to take off my jacket and even shirt. I obeyed.

Then he told me to take off my trousers. When he saw my hesitation, to my shock, he took off his trousers, which weren't wet. "Okamoto-san, let's make this an underwear banquet."

I had to go along, eating dinner wrapped in bath towels that a waiter brought to us. By the time the dinner ended, my clothes were clean, dry and pressed.

Taking off his trousers for a much younger lad? This was Hemmi's individual manners, not Japanese. But still, such behavior could happen only in Japan.

This takes me back to the economic environment of a society. Virtue in America cannot come without the affordability brought about by rich nature and material fulfillment. Obviously, kindness to others and magnanimity are only possible with financial and mental surplus.

In Japan, when playing golf, it is an intrusion to hit your ball into the neighboring course. If you do, you usually go to the course you invaded, take off your hat, and apologize to the people playing there. I am not good at golfing, so I always have to go to the next course and apologize. Once I did the same thing in the U.S. and apologized to the men who were walking towards me on the course. They couldn't understand what I was doing and said, "Apologies? We are just walking in the sun." This is my favorite story to tell Japanese audiences.

These generosities are not common among all Americans. Many workers worry about their job security and try to protect their position rather than being kind and flexible with others. Once the manual is decided, it is forced upon the other party, regardless of the collateral damage. The incredible rigidity of workers, especially those who hold the right to command, often surprises Japanese.

Just one example: Recently, there was a line drawn on the floor of a passageway at New York LaGuardia Airport. By the time I noticed a sign next to it that read "Do Not Pass," I had inadvertently crossed the line by one foot. I said to the officer who was watching me, "Oops, one step too late. I am sorry," and immediately retreated. But the situation was serious. She said in a definite tone, "No sir, you already stepped over the line. You must go outside." She wouldn't let me simply step back. I pleaded with her that I had left my passport and boarding pass with my wife at the boarding gate and explained that if I were to go outside, I wouldn't be able to get back in.

"If I go out now, I will miss my plane."

"That's your problem."

I had to start an argument of physics. "But officer, it was only one-half of a step when I realized my mistake. At that moment, half of my body was still within the line. The rest was because of inertia."

She did not find my argument amusing, and declared, "If you refuse to comply, I'll call the police."

She actually picked up the phone and started talking to the police.

I surrendered and left the security area. I will skip the rest of the story about how much difficulty I had to go through to get back to the gate without my papers.

This sort of thing would not happen in Japan. Workers on-site are flexible. Perhaps it is because they are not in a competitive environment and don't have to worry about job security. The flexibility and kindness of the people is probably among the best in the world. Then why such inflexibility at the policy level, a vestigial trait from wartime? I will discuss this in Chapter Seven.

But anyway, the superior part of Japanese society is not so much at the leadership level as at the level of the people on the ground.

I observe the competitive society of the United States. It is a nation that covers a vast expanse in terms of people and geography. Moreover, the society is not a collaborative agricultural society like Japan, but a hunting society where individual abilities are the priority. If you don't excel, you cannot rise in society.

There are intensive competitions at the top of the tier, as well, which often appear as a contest of loyalty to the Stars and Stripes. It is completely the opposite in Japan, where even the word "patriotism" has become sensitive. The simplicity and speed with which an American citizen unites when confronted with an opponent nation or organization is amazing. Japan has had to encounter the American fireball-like unity: at Pearl Harbor, in sanctioning Iran in 1979, and during the Gulf War.

The biggest difference in the social structure between Japan and the United States is that of an egalitarian society versus an unequal society. In a 2018 Cabinet Office survey in Japan, 93% of the citizens said they belonged to the middle class.[19] The U.S. figure in the same year was 68% (Northwestern Mutual).[20]

For example, what is the difference in salary between the president of a company and its employees? According to a survey by the AFL-CIO, CEO compensation in a major U.S. company (S & P 500 Index firm) was on average 361 times that of the average employee's wage in 2017.[21] In Japan, the annual remuneration of the president is no more than 12 times the model for a 25-year-old employee, according to The Institute of Labor Administration.[22]

Sony's Chairman Akio Morita once happily told me, "We held a contest for a proposition to improve in-house productivity and do you know who won the first prize? A gate guard! Having such people on the ground is our great strength."

I always talk with taxi drivers in Tokyo. Many drivers listen to the Diet debates on the radio in their car. Their interest in current events is surprisingly high, including topics of international geopolitics. It is not often that I can have these conversations with drivers in other countries.

As I said earlier, this is where the foundation of Japan's power lies. What is missing is strategic decisions at the top.

Intense Economic Friction

When I arrived at my post in Washington in 1983, my cheerful and hardworking friends had their desks lined up side-by-side at the Embassy: Ken-ichiro Sasae, who later became Ambassador to the United States, Ken Shimanouchi to Brazil and Spain, Yasuo Saito to France, Russia and Saudi Arabia, and Mitoji Yabunaka, who became the Vice Foreign Minister. We were particularly close to each other. Almost every night, we gathered at someone's house for drinks.

In Washington, Japan–U.S. economic friction had begun. It was even regarded as the eve of war. I started visiting Congress members and explained Japan's position. I was only a Counselor at the Embassy, but I figured that junior legislators who were not very concerned with the hierarchy in the Embassy would meet with me.

So, I went to see all the freshmen and women who were elected to the House of Representatives in the 1984 election. After that, I began visiting second- and third-year congress members as well.

Altogether I met with more than 150 members, many of whom I visited several times. Most of them left a very deep impression on me, including John McCain, who was a sophomore in the House at the time.

The 99th Congress in 1985 had issued sanctions resolutions on Japan that condemned Japan for raising the level of its voluntary restrictions on automobile exports, and I went around appealing for the Japanese position. It was like an avalanche, with the House passing the Rostenkowski resolution by 394–19 and the Senate the Danforth resolution by 92-0.

I was discouraged, but there was something that secretly impressed me. Most of the 19 congressmen and women, an absolute minority, who voted against the resolution in the House were those I had visited and to whom I had explained Japan's view. I never told anybody about that, nor did I report it to Tokyo.

Still, these 19 legislators left their stakes and expressed their independent opinions before an overwhelming majority. I developed a deep respect for the heritage of American society that supports individual decision-making.

If I now know Americans better than the average Japanese does and if my respect for Americans is deeper, it comes from this experience of meeting these congress members individually. Each one of them was a special person, someone who could get more than 100,000 voters to write their names. I was overwhelmed by their open attitude, how they would listen to a foreigner and try to understand the opponent's position, their ability to compose their own opinions concisely, and above all, their pursuit of fairness.

The Japanese economy was enjoying the height of the bubble at that time. The Nikkei Index on the Tokyo Stock Exchange had climbed to 20,000 yen in 1987 from 10,000 yen in 1980, then jumped past 30,000 yen in 1988 and hit an all-time high of 38,957 on December 29, 1989. Indeed, the Japanese people worked very hard. They worked from morning to midnight with an implicit disregard for their family at home. Japanese came to be known as the

"economic animal" and workers were called "corporate warriors."
The Japanese became intoxicated with success, and the nation became overconfident.

For instance, there were ridiculous discussions citing the expen-
sive land prices in Japan, saying "One Japan would buy four United
States" and "Canada could be bought at the price of the Tokyo Imperial Palace grounds." That year, a Japanese real estate company
bought Rockefeller Center in Manhattan and the image that Japanese
people were rich and conceited took hold. America's rebellion against
Japan reached all levels.

I attended a seminar held at the Wye Plantation in Maryland in
April 1990. One night, an American participant came to visit me in
my room. He was a businessman from Chicago. Assuming he wanted
to continue the afternoon discussion, I welcomed him in and offered
him a chair and a drink. Without a smile, he stood there and spoke
in a low threatening tone.

"I came here to tell you something. Let's talk *kendo*. America
taught the Japanese martial art *kendo* to the Japanese people—very
gently, using bamboo swords, *shinai*. The Japanese learned quickly
and began to beat America, their master, with wooden swords, *bo-
kuto*. Bleeding, America begged Japan to stop striking, but you Japanese wouldn't have any of it. Now America is going to fight with
real steel swords, *shinken*. We're not going to go easy on you until
you bleed. Please don't forget that."

Then he quietly closed the door and left, leaving me dumbfounded, standing there with the bottle of whiskey I had intended
to share with him.

Meanwhile, the Japanese did not feel rich. Japanese corporations
made a lot of profit and corporate savings soared. But the blue-collar
workers' share was low. Per capita GDP calculates total national income divided by the number in the population; on a personal level,
people did not have much wealth and could not see the strong accusations by the U.S. of an economic invasion as a problem of their
own. The big companies' profit was circulated overseas once again.
In short, Japan is a country where there are few visibly super-rich
people, even before one examines the Gini coefficient, a measure of
income inequality.

Speaking of the super-rich, on June 10, 1990, as MOFA's division chief dealing with the U.S., I was invited to a party aboard a private luxury cruiser that was anchored in Tokyo Bay. I was flabbergasted at the wealth that U.S. citizens could enjoy at an individual level. In Japan? No way. Why should Japan have to be apologetic?

The owner was a tall, handsome man in his forties. He greeted his Japanese guests with a handshake and a nice smile. His name was Donald Trump.

PEOPLE PUSHING AHEAD

The Most Powerful Diplomat

MY MENTOR was a man named Nobuhiko Ushiba. He served as vice-minister for Foreign Affairs, Ambassador to the United States, and Minister of External Economic Affairs in the Japanese Cabinet. The late Prime Minister Yasuhiro Nakasone called Ushiba "the greatest postwar diplomat." In *Transformation and Patriotism—The Life of Diplomat Nobuhiko Ushiba*,[23] the author Tamotsu Asami says, "His overwhelming presence still remains in the memories of many. … Ushiba made full use of all energy, always running at full speed, making sure that his banners are very clear."

Ushiba was appointed to Washington as Ambassador in September 1970, but was dismissed in May 1973 by Foreign Minister Masayoshi Ohira, who later became a prime minister, allegedly for criticizing Prime Minister Kakuei Tanaka's pro-China policy. He returned to Japan after an unusually short term of two years and nine months.

During my nearly 30 years of public service both at MOFA and the Prime Minister's Office, I had the luck of meeting or knowing every prime minister since 1970, if only for a moment. It was a bonus that came with being an official in the Japanese bureaucracy. But I did not hold much respect for Ohira or Tanaka, simply because they fired Ushiba.

Prime ministers are naturally all different from each other. Some were impressive and others less so. My conclusion, looking up at the prime ministers from my bureaucratic position, was that the most important requirement for a leader in the end is the passion and philosophy of how they want to run the country.

Kakuei Tanaka, who served as Prime Minister from 1972 to 1974, was one of the special prime ministers for Japan.

After his resignation as prime minister, he was charged in a criminal trial for accepting a bribe from Lockheed Aircraft Corp. In April 1979, I accompanied Henry Kissinger, who wanted to see Tanaka even after his indictment. The Tanaka mansion in Mejiro, five miles northeast of central Tokyo, was dubbed "Mejiro Palace" by the press. There was a big pond in the garden, filled with carp. Tanaka was the owner of a local bus company and a typical example of the nouveau riche. People called him "Imataikō (Contemporary Regent)." He was known to have bought up dry riverbeds at low prices from the government and resold them at a high price, making big profits. He was an overwhelming character and when it came to the stage of implementation, I would say he had more presence than any other prime minister. People called him a "computerized bulldozer."

Kissinger wrote in his memoir about Tanaka:[24]

Like Nixon he had exceptional abilities; like Nixon he was very insecure and, what is even more remarkable for a Japanese, he showed it. He was Prime Minister for only eighteen months. I found him extremely intelligent, unusually direct. He came closest of any Japanese leader to speaking in the idiom of personal power that is conventional among heads of government of other countries.

When the meeting in Mejiro had ended and I was preparing to leave, Tanaka called me back. "Can you talk for a moment?" Then for an hour-and-a-half, he continued to talk to me with passion.

"Japan is no good the way it is. We first have to make the local regions strong."

I was taken aback at how much energy he was willing to pour into one young person like me, but I still had to ask a question that had been on my mind.

"Mr. Prime Minister, why did you fire Ambassador Ushiba? That was very unfortunate."

Mr. Tanaka grinned, without getting angry. "Hey, I don't know anything about that."

Ushiba and Tanaka were similar when it came to passion and action.

Among past ambassadors to the United States, Ushiba's tenure in Washington remains legendary. His ability goes without saying, and the Americans found his personality attractive. Although his style was different, he had the character of Tanaka that Kissinger described.

Ushiba was well aware of the true power of America. In 1971, he sent a telegram to Tokyo that said, "Do not mistake American capability." Several years later, he showed me that telegram. It went something like this:

"Recently, our country has become overconfident toward the United States. There are shallow debates in Japan that U.S.-made vehicles are not dependable, or that American vacuum cleaners and washing machines break down easily. That is not where true American power is. American power lies in leading-edge technologies that are protected by defense classification and cannot be seen by other countries: aviation, space development, weapons manufacturing, and information processing—this is where American wisdom is concentrated. If Japan doesn't understand this, Japan will have great regrets in the future."

Ushiba knew America's comprehensive power, which had put a man on the moon in the 1960s. In the 1990s, his predictions turned out to be true.

Despite his warning, Japan after the 1970s became euphoric. At the same time, it depended on the United States for its national security, and its international competitiveness was helped by a low fixed exchange rate.

Japan overcame the Nixon shock of 1971 and the oil crisis of 1973. In the mid-Showa Era, 30 years after the War, Japan had come to recognize itself as a world-class nation. But Ushiba had a different perspective. He felt that Japan's confidence was much greater than life-size.

When Prime Minister Takeo Fukuda, who highly appreciated Ushiba's ability, formed his Cabinet in November 1977, Fukuda telephoned and requested of Ushiba to become the Foreign Minister. Ushiba strongly declined. I was with him at the time of the phone conversation and asked him why.

His answer: "I've never dealt with issues of national security."

I thought he was just being humble. However, come to think of it, there was no way that Ushiba, who had served as the ambassador to the United States at the forefront of the Japan–U.S. Security alliance, would not have any knowledge about security. I figured the real reason he turned down the request of the Prime Minister was his sense of guilt for having tried to pull the country toward the Germany–Japan Axis before the War.

Ushiba had become a diplomat in 1932. In 1941, he was stationed in Berlin where he leaned heavily pro-Axis under Hiroshi Oshima, Ambassador to Germany. As a young secretary, Ushiba criticized the pro-British and pro-American diplomats in Tokyo. He claimed that in order to help Germany, Japan should attack the Soviet Union from the east so that the Soviets could not concentrate their efforts on the German front.

After the War, there was strong criticism of his wartime ideas. How could such a person sit at the center of Japan's postwar diplomacy? Ushiba did not say much to me about what happened before the War, but he must have thought he was not fit to do the job. He was not ready to forgive his own policy failure from when he was young.

Full-force Negotiations, Ushiba Style

Prime Minister Takeo Fukuda did not give up on making Ushiba a cabinet minister. He created a new ministerial post for Ushiba, called it Minister of External Economic Affairs, and asked him to take it. At that point, Ushiba could not refuse, and that is how he became invested in the fierce trade negotiations with the U.S.

The biggest issues in Japan–U.S. trade relations at that time were beef, citrus, and procurements by Nippon Telegraph and Telephone Corp. (NTT), the Japanese telecommunications company that was state-owned at the time. To what extent could Japan expand its beef and citrus import quota? Ushiba negotiated with Minister of Agriculture and Forestry Ichiro Nakagawa, whose nickname was "Northern Bear." Ushiba used his typical manners to reach right into the heart of the other guy. Nakagawa liked Ushiba's personality and he gave Ushiba the maximum ammunition to use in negotiations with his American counterpart, U.S. Trade Representative Bob Strauss. Ushiba's negotiation style reflected his character. He did not salami-slice his concession proposals but instead, disclosed all his cards to Strauss at the beginning and never took a step backwards.

In May 1978, Ushiba and Strauss decided to meet away from Washington and chose to negotiate privately at the Beverly Wilshire Hotel in Los Angeles. The exchange between the two, who sat on sofas facing each other across the coffee table in Strauss' room, was very intense. Both were so excited—I had never seen a negotiation that involved pounding on the table at each other. But there was a human relationship there, too, one of trust. Strauss obviously felt this and clasped Ushiba' s hand at the end, presumably thinking, "If Ushiba says this is the best Japan can deliver, I guess we'll have to accept it."

Once Strauss agreed, he would turn himself to spending all of his energy on persuading the U.S. Congress. I was given the rare opportunity to witness the essence of a fierce but trusted diplomatic negotiation.

Another thorn in U.S.–Japan trade was procurements by NTT. To symbolize the opening of the Japanese communications market, the U.S. was pushing hard for NTT to treat American suppliers the same way as Japanese suppliers when it came to procurement. When it was reported that a company executive had remarked that all they could purchase from the U.S. was a bucket and a mop, the comment took on a life of its own.

At the end of June 1978, Strauss said he wanted to resolve this problem with Ushiba when they were to meet in Geneva five days later. On the evening of July 5, representatives of several ministries gathered at Ushiba's office on the fourth floor of the MOFA to deliberate. The Ministry of Posts and Telecommunications, which had jurisdiction over NTT, was not forthcoming, and the meeting ended without a conclusion.

As I was about to leave the room with other attendees, Ushiba called me back.

"We're getting nowhere with the MPT. Can you go and deal directly with NTT?"

This was a crisis. Strauss had given Japan a deadline. What would happen if Ushiba went empty-handed? Strauss was not known for his patience. The final agreement negotiated through all that dialogue between Japan and the United States would evaporate, just like that.

Strauss carried a lot of weight in Congress. Depending on his response, the U.S. might take a very strong line on Japan that could end in a trade war. However, there was absolutely zero response from the Ministry of Posts and Telecommunications, which was supposed to represent the position of NTT. But I had never met NTT people before. Could I convince them that very night to change their adamant position?

"Excuse me? You're asking me to go directly to NTT and persuade them?"

"That's damn right. Go and clash with them."

I prepared myself, as there was no other choice.

"Understood, sir. I will go then."

"Thank you. I'll trust you with the results, but don't confront them. Make friends with them."

Facing a crisis, a good commander's order is always simple. I had to face a much more acute crisis more than 10 years later, when trying to transport 800 four-wheel-drive vehicles as the first Japanese contribution to the Gulf War and was blocked amid the swirl of international attention. The instruction I received then from Deputy Foreign Minister Koji Watanabe, a man I respected, was exactly the same as Ushiba's: "Go. Make friends with your opponents." Would they become friends with me at this late hour?

The boss was demanding the impossible, but negotiating Ushiba-style might be my only option, I thought.

Ushiba taught me to face my counterpart with all my might. There is no need for bluffing or tricks. If your head-on approach doesn't communicate to the other side, it's simply a "no deal."

I telephoned the MPT and asked if I could talk with NTT directly. It is the rule to get the approval of the Ministry in charge if you want a direct contact.

"Fine," they said, "but don't hold out much hope. NTT will be tough."

At eight o'clock that night, I crossed Hibiya Park from the Ministry to NTT on the other side of Hibiya Avenue. The park was enveloped in the dark of night.

I was received by Deputy Director Moriji Kuwabara of the Technology Bureau, which determines the standards for procurement of materials.

After I shared stories about the difficulties of U.S.–Japan negotiations, I went straight to the point.

"I'm not asking for all of it. Can you make at least part of your procurement non-discriminatory both within and outside the country, and as a result purchase about 20 billion yen worth of foreign products?"

I knew nothing about telecommunications technology, but I persisted.

"Please increase it a little bit more?"

I was repeating myself.

Later, Koji Maeda, Director of Technology, joined us. The two Technology Bureau executives responded to me upfront. Finally, they said:

"We might be able to cooperate if you think that is the minimum figure you will need to conclude the negotiations, but we cannot accept it at our level. It might be possible at a political level."

My Ushiba-style negotiations had opened their door. Our talk began at 8:00 p.m., and by the time it finished, it was 2:00 a.m.

After that, the three of us drank whiskey and we emptied a bottle. When I left NTT, it was 4:00 a.m.

I went straight to Ushiba's home in Oyamadai, Setagaya, at the outskirts of Tokyo, and waited for the gate to open. The Ushiba family's day begins early. At around 6:00 a.m., Mrs. Ushiba came to open the gate and was surprised to see me sleeping by the gatepost. She invited me inside and served breakfast. I reported to Ushiba that NTT had brought out the maximum munitions.

He was very happy and immediately called Prime Minister Fukuda on the phone. "Mr. Prime Minister, would you kindly speak with NTT's president Akikusa and say that NTT needs to procure 20-billion-yen worth of foreign made products?"

Prime Minister Fukuda called Akikusa on the telephone, and President Akikusa accepted.

That afternoon, NTT's powerful Vice-President Yasusada Kitahara, went to see Minister Ushiba. Kitahara looked at me with a grin. "Sounds like you all had a bit to drink last night."

After Kitahara left, Ushiba asked me what the drinking was all about.

I just replied, "It's nothing special, sir."

Ushiba entrusted me, a simple desk officer, with negotiations to seek the limit that NTT could accept. Then he took those figures directly to the top to settle. Always in search of the fine line of compromise, he laid out his entire position on the table for his opponent to see and reached an agreement. This method was only possible if the other party placed full confidence in Ushiba. That is how he pushed forward. I copied his style thereafter.

In December that year, Ushiba visited Washington, armed with the Fukuda Cabinet's comprehensive economic measures. After negotiations with the U.S. government, Strauss took Ushiba to visit the Senate with Fumihiko Togo, Ambassador to the United States, who was the son-in-law of Foreign Minister Togo at the time of Japan's surrender in 1945. There, more than 20 senators were waiting with Senator Russell Long, chairman of the Senate Finance Committee. The atmosphere was tense.

"My electorate says we should break all ties with Japan."

"Japan won't listen, no matter what we say. We have no choice but to restrict imports."

The harsh words continued. When the senators had finished, Togo rose and said, "Our two nations are facing some difficult problems right now, but with our mutual efforts, we will surely be able to solve them."

It was a polite remark, but the kind of cliche that did not settle the air. Nobody said anything.

Then suddenly Ushiba stood up. I thought he was going to thank the Senators for the meeting, but he didn't. There was a hint of anger in his voice.

"I have never heard of such foolishness. Surely, Japan is also at fault, but we are trying to fix that. What you people are talking about is trade protectionism. That is communism. Japan and the United States are fighting against communism, are we not? I came here to protect free trade."

For a moment, the room fell into dead silence. Then it filled with thunderous applause. Afterwards, everyone wanted to shake hands with Ushiba. The host Strauss was smiling happily.

Lonely Leaders of the World

The first summit of the Group of Six (G6) was held in France at the Château d'Rambouillet near Paris in November 1975, as proposed by President Giscard d'Estaing. The United States, United Kingdom, France, Germany, Italy and Japan participated. The summit later added Canada and became the G7, which has continued for more than 40 years, to this date. For Japan, who is not a permanent member of the U.N. Security Council, this is the most glamorous place for international discussions.

In order to make this summit meeting successful, a group of so-called "wise men" from each country was formed to hold what we know today as the "Sherpa Meeting."

Ushiba was Japan's representative. The U.S. was represented by former Secretary of Finance George Schulz (later Secretary of State) and his assistant Helmut Sonnenfeldt. From France was former EC Vice-Chairman Raymond Barre (later Prime Minister), and from the United Kingdom was Ushiba's good friend, Sir John Hunt (later Cabinet Secretary). Germany was represented by Deputy Finance Minister Karl Otto Pole and Italy, by Bank of Italy Deputy Director General Rinaldo Ossola. I accompanied Mr. Ushiba alone as his aide. The preparatory meetings were held at the Carlton House in New York.

At the meetings on October 5 and 6, the dates and location for the Summit were scheduled and the agenda was set to include economic recovery and sustainable growth without inflation, currency stability, and assistance to developing countries. The representatives agreed that the basic idea of the summit would not be to draw concrete conclusions, but to provide a place for national leaders to freely philosophize.

A major issue that arose at Carlton House was Canada's participation. Ushiba, who had served as Ambassador to Canada, argued that Canada should naturally be included, but Tokyo had instructed him to tune into the positions of the other countries, which decided to proceed without Canada for the time being. Ushiba was enraged and banned me from transmitting telegrams that I had drafted to inform Tokyo of the discussions. MOFA in Tokyo continued to pressure me to send a telegram, but Ushiba would not sign my draft, no matter how many times I asked him to.

Around 9:00 p.m., in Ushiba's suite, I was unable to stand it any longer and said, "Minister, I have left two telegraph officers stationed at the U.N. Mission just for this telegram. Please sign it so that they can go home."

He was miffed.

"Telegraph officers? Send them home!"

After about an hour, he asked, "Did you send the telegraph officers home?" He wanted to be sure.

"Yes, I did, sir." I lied.

At around 11:00 p.m. he stood up and announced that he would be heading to bed. I stood and blocked the door to his bedroom, saying strongly, "Please sign this. I won't move until you do." He signed it without even reading it and disappeared into the bedroom. Then I ran to the U.N. Mission and handed the draft telegraph to the officers who had been waiting there for long hours.

The next morning, Ushiba was still in a bad mood, but gave me 200 dollars.

"You must have kept those telegraphers waiting, didn't you? Give this to them with thanks."

That is the kind of person he was.

The Rambouillet Summit was held from November 15 to 17, 1975 without Canada. The members present were President Valéry Giscard d'Estaing, President Gerald Ford, Prime Minister Harold Wilson, Chancellor Helmut Schmidt, Prime Minister Aldo Moro and Prime Minister Takeo Miki.

The talks began with only the leaders, but they decided that records were needed, so they summoned one notetaker from each country into the meeting room. Hideo Kitahara, Ambassador to France, went into the room first as Japan's notetaker, but came right back out saying it was too onerous, passing the job on to a MOFA Director General.

Soon, he too, came out of the room, saying it was too much work. So, luckily for me, I was sent into the room to take notes. This is how my job as a summit note-taker began. After France, while taking turns with other colleagues, I filled this role for five more summits—

in London, Puerto Rico, Bonn, Tokyo and Venice.

Taking minutes for such an important meeting was not an easy task. I started out scribbling as fast as I could, intending to make a verbatim record of what was being said, without missing a word.

The result was miserable. I was unable to decode my enormous volume of notes, much less report a succinct summary to the officials eagerly waiting outside.

Thereafter, I worked hard taking two sets of minutes simultaneously—one for the official record and the other for the briefing to the waiting senior officials. My eyes were bloodshot.

At the Puerto Rico Summit, the American note-taker sitting beside me was Alan Greenspan. A man of his position probably didn't need to take detailed notes. I was envious of him, occasionally jotting a note while apparently enjoying the leaders' discussions. (Or, was the U.S. secretly recording the discussions electronically, against the original agreement?)

Either way, for me, the whole job was exciting. Only two meters away from where I sat taking notes, seven national leaders were having frank and personal discussions. It was the ideal place to think deeply about what type of people became leaders and which qualities they needed.

Without staff to assist them, the leaders discussed matters among themselves, drawing only on their own intellectual abilities. It was a battle of knowledge and philosophy. The size of the country or even the status was irrelevant. It was a place that tested the individual's ability to develop deep dialogue.

At a summit meeting, after reading from the prepared memos in Round One, participants have to build their own mental framework and speak in their own words as the arguments roll on. If they are not successful in jumping in at the beginning of the first round of discussion, they will inevitably find themselves further behind by mid-meeting.

The G7 summits, although no two were the same, left me strongly feeling that one cannot resort to a hasty cramming of the knowledge, much less philosophy, needed for a national leader. It won't work.

The bottom line is obvious: A country's system must constitute a mechanism by which leaders are chosen from among candidates who already possess the basic qualities, *ante factum*, not *post*. Otherwise, a leader who is only talented at empty rhetoric will end up leading the country to no direction.

Overall, the discussions were not only extremely interesting, but intriguing, even if somewhat pedantic in their use of words like "ignis fatuus," which embarrassed an ignorant note-taker like me.

At the same time, I realized that being a leader is a lonely job. In each country, the leader has no peers at the top, and they must make decisions independently. The summit was a place where lonely leaders could pour their hearts out and share their feelings with each other.

One European leader said:

"I envy the U.S. and Japan. You can freely use money for the advancement of science and technology. In Europe, young people are easily influenced by the socialism that their countries border, so we need to spend our money on welfare. Accordingly, our industrial competitiveness is weakened. I hope the U.S. and Japan will fully consider the troubles of Europe."

Naturally, because it was a discussion among people like Giscard d'Estaing, Schmidt, and Wilson, the contents would evolve through the course of the meeting to another dimension. If discussions converged on expanding the effective demand of a country in the morning meeting, in the afternoon it would develop into: "Given too much emphasis on social security and unemployment insurance as today, people will tend to focus on welfare rather than labor value. Perhaps Keynes' demand theory is no longer valid." Remarks prepared by the bureaucrats of each country are useless when it comes to such discussions that move to new plateaus.

Both Schulz and Ushiba were very high-level aides for the U.S. and Japan, but American and Japanese leaders are not always good at answering questions that were not prepared in the briefing book. The leaders, who were isolated to begin with, became further secluded in the heated discussions.

Ushiba was not entirely confident that Japanese representatives would be accepted by their Western peers, who already enjoyed a strong sense of friendship. He knew well the limits to Japan's level of ability for international engagement.

In the aforementioned book by Tamotsu Asami, the author wrote that Japan has not reached the level of aiming to take charge of international order, and that only Ushiba truly understood that there was no prospect of reaching that level in the near future.

Asami's description of how Ushiba must have felt was correct.

To Ushiba, I honestly reported how other leaders at the summit received the Japanese prime minister, including one episode in which, when the Japanese prime minister was speaking, French President Giscard d'Estaing took out his newspaper and started reading it.

Ushiba smiled and said, "Young man, that is still where Japan is."

Ushiba passed away on December 31, 1984, at the age of 75. Many Western newspapers carried obituaries about him.

PART THREE

ALLIANCE OF THE DEFEATED AND THE VICTORIOUS

Japan–U.S. Alliance: Contingency Favors Japan, Peacetime Favors America

Director of Security Affairs, North American Affairs Bureau, Ministry of Foreign Affairs

IN 1985, seventeen years after I joined the Ministry of Foreign Affairs (MOFA), I became the Director of the Security Affairs Division in the North American Affairs Bureau. This division had jurisdiction over the U.S.–Japan Security System. In Japanese bureaucracy, the role of a Division Chief is very important.

For me, it was the busiest and most fulfilling season of my career. Overtime hours exceeded 200 hours per month. This was 200 hours on top of the normal 180 work hours per month, so on an average weekday, I was working until 2:00 a.m. and until 10:00 p.m. on Saturdays. I sometimes went to work on Sundays, too, so my line of duty was quite inhumane.

There are a number of reasons that we had so much work. The first reason was that it was during the final confrontation of the Cold War. The United States was in fierce competition with the Soviet Union and the standoff was at its peak. Throughout the 1970s, the Soviet Union continued its arms buildup. Its Pacific Fleet alone had 840 ships totaling 1.85 million tons. Among them were 70 nuclear submarines. In contrast, Japan's Maritime Self-Defense Force had 250,000 tons and the U.S. Navy's 7th Fleet deployed in the Pacific had 700,000 tons. Even together they fell far short of the Soviet force.

We often received intelligence briefings at the Department of

Yukio Okamoto, 39, consults with colleagues as Director of the National Security Affairs Division, North American Bureau, Ministry of Foreign Affairs. He recalled it as the busiest and most fulfilling posting of his career.

Defense and were amazed by the satellite photos we were shown. The images projected on the screen were of Soviet missiles, military aircraft, surface ships, and submarines. Great expectations were placed on Japan's role as an ally. President Ronald Reagan, who called the Soviet Union the "Evil Empire," valued Japan, but his demands increased accordingly.

The second reason was that Japan had begun to respond to American demands that Japan back up its commitment to the alliance with action, or at least greater defense spending. In Japan, Prime Minister Yasuhiro Nakasone strongly advocated for the U.S.–Japan Alliance. The United States too, had a mind to ask its wealthy Japanese ally to do a lot more. After the American Embassy hostage incident in Iran and the Soviet invasion of Afghanistan, it was finally time for Japan to advance its security policy. The personal "Ron and Yasu" relationship boosted this.

In my days there, I saw weapons technology transfer to the United States, Japan's participation in the Strategic Defense Initiative (SDI), the elimination of Japan's limit on defense spending to 1% of its annual GNP, the abortive dispatch of patrol boats to the Persian Gulf, the modernization of the 7th Fleet, the conclusion of a special agreement on labor costs, and much more. In each case, Mr. Naka-sone's judgment was clear.

The third reason was the trade and investment friction that raged between the United States and Japan in the late 1980s. As Japan's sur-plus with the U.S. continued to increase, Japan came under intense criticism. This criticism extended to the realm of security, and Japan was in a position to at least fulfill its security obligations as an ally.

After Prime Minister Nobusuke Kishi, the Japanese leader who signed the Security Treaty with the United States in 1960, the politi-cian who best understood the importance of international action to protect democracy was likely Prime Minister Masayoshi Ohira, who made the decision to boycott the 1980 Olympic Games in opposition to the Soviet invasion of Afghanistan. This prompted an uproar in Japanese public opinion for abandoning a people's event, but Prime Minister Ohira declared in his policy speech to Diet in January 1980 that "there are times Japan has to make sacrifices for world peace." This was when Japan decided to pursue a policy in which freedom is more important than money or national entertainment. It was a watershed moment.

Japan's security system had clung to the coattails of Prime Min-ister Kishi's legacy. It was repeatedly held back by the opposition when the LDP Cabinet was weak, and thus became distorted. Few prime ministers tried to return it to what it should be. In my personal judgement, their names are Yasuhiro Nakasone, Ryutaro Hashimoto, Junichiro Koizumi and Shinzo Abe.

The 1980s was the honeymoon of U.S.–Japan defense cooper-ation. Soldiers call the enemy a "bogeyman," and in this case the common Japanese and U.S. bogeyman was the Soviet Union; this made operation of U.S.–Japan security relations psychologically comfortable. Japan's defensive power against the Soviet bogeyman was directly linked to America's security. Japan deployed 100 P3C anti-submarine and maritime surveillance aircraft on its limited na-tional terrain which, in terms of density, is the world's highest. Their potential role was to block the three channels, Soya (La Perouse), Tsugaru, and Tsushima, in anticipation of Soviet nuclear submarine activity in the waters surrounding Japan.

Due to the blockade of the three straits, the Soviet nuclear submarine fleet would be bottled up in the Sea of Japan and would not be able to sail to Los Angeles or San Francisco. In other words, during this period, the improvement of Japanese anti-submarine warfare (ASW) capability was directly linked to the security of the United States as well as to the safety of Japan.

Under these circumstances, security talks between Japan and the United States were always held in a friendly atmosphere. That is, until the Gulf War tore the two nations apart. As Director of Security Affairs my first job was to draw up the implementation provisions for transferring weapons technology from Japan to the U.S., as agreed between Nakasone and Reagan. At first glance, this agreement looked fairly low key, but it had great significance in correcting Japan's prior security policy. After clearing this up, the main topic became the SDI research program, or the so-called Star Wars program. The idea was that if the Soviet Union were to launch any of its 20,000 nuclear warheads at the United States, the United States would launch an SDI system from 4,000 kilometers away to destroy the electronic circuits on the Soviet missiles. It would fly at a speed of 8 km/second and deploy lasers or kinetic means. It was explained to me that this was a precision technology that could hit the eyeball of a mosquito 10 kilometers away.

Japan's participation in SDI had a symbolic meaning for the alliance. An American newspaper at the time wrote, "European allies participate in SDI because they want American technology but only Japan has participated as a true ally." Unlike theater missile defense systems that could be used to defend specific targets, such as missile silos or bases, SDI was not something that would directly defend Japan, but it became the key to the United States winning the Cold War.

With the participation of the Defense Agency, the Ministry of International Trade and Industry, and the Science and Technology Agency, MOFA took the lead in dispatching a total of 55 large missions to the United States at the end of March 1986 to learn about SDI. When we visited several research laboratories and defense companies, what surprised us more than the SDI concept itself was to see how American researchers and engineers were infatuated with their research. They truly believed that this grand SDI concept could be realized technically, and they pursued their research with full confidence.

Japanese experts were unanimous in saying that they were thankful knowing the level of technology the Americans think is possible: "If we know the American target value, we can develop the technology with peace of mind." I was slightly disappointed at the lack of independent goal-setting, but the overwhelming technical power of the United States made a strong impression on the Japanese team.

In September 1986, the government made the decision for Japan to participate in the SDI program. We prepared a large volume of material to answer Diet questions from the opposition who would undoubtedly speak out. However, perhaps due to the government's resolute attitude, there was little dispute.

Three years later, SDI contributed to the decision by the Soviet Union to give up its search for nuclear supremacy and to accept coexistence with the liberal camp. Ultimately, the Berlin Wall came down, ending the Cold War structure. Having achieved its original purpose, SDI quietly faded away without advancing to the development and deployment stages. However, the impact that this research had on the development of general-purpose technology was immeasurable.

Structure of Japan's National Security

Japan is engaged in the Security Treaty with the United States. This Treaty is based on a concept whereby attacks on Japan are considered attacks on the United States. In other words, a country that is thinking about invading Japan must prepare for war with the United States. For this reason, Japan has been able to live surrounded by peace in a region where hostile military forces are heavily concentrated.

On the other hand, in accordance with the Japanese Constitution, Japan prohibits itself from using the right to collective self-defense beyond its borders because that would be fighting for another country, so if the United States were to be attacked, Japan cannot fight for the United States. Some people say this is a one-sided alliance.

A typical example is President Trump. On June 26, 2019, in an interview with FOX Business Network ahead of the G20 Osaka Summit, he said: "If Japan is attacked, we will fight World War Three ... with our lives and with our treasure. If we're attacked, Japan doesn't have to help us at all. Japan can watch it on the Sony television…"

In 1983, the Ministry of Foreign Affairs and the Cabinet Legislative Bureau (CLB), the agency that interprets Japan's constitution, were in conflict over the right to collective self-defense. The question being discussed was this: When Japan is attacked and turned into a battlefield, can Japan's SDF protect the American warships that have come to defend Japan?

"Of course, yes" was MOFA's answer and "Of course, no" was the Cabinet Legislative Bureau's, which said it would violate the Constitutional limit on the right to collective self-defense. This alliance wouldn't work if you listened to the CLB.

The controversy was finally brought up to Prime Minister Yasuhiro Nakasone, who gave strong instructions to the Legislative Bureau. The Executive Secretary to the Prime Minister told me that Prime Minister Nakasone told the CLB Chief to amend its opinion. When he replied that he would take the issue back to the Bureau to re-examine the position, Nakasone tersely said, "No. Correct it now." I was impressed. When I think about the confrontation between MOFA and other ministries, the existence of a strong prime minister is a sine-qua-non for Japan–U.S. relations.

Mr. Nakasone's instruction was regarding an "emergency," that is, whether the SDF could protect a U.S. ship when Japan was under attack. In this case, the interpretation was treated as "the right to self-defense" in that protecting a U.S. ship that came to rescue Japan under attack would be nothing other than protecting Japan itself. However, when Japan is not being attacked—that is, if a U.S. ship were attacked during "peacetime"—the interpretation did not allow the Self-Defense Forces to protect it. That had to wait for the Prime Minister Shinzo Abe's reform of Japan's security laws in 2015.

We used to say in MOFA that the impediment that stood in the way of a righteous defense policy in Japan was the steel pants called the "View of the Cabinet Legislative Bureau." In fact, the source of the problem was the lack of a political decision to remove the CLB from the discussion. The Cabinet Legislative Bureau is not an independent organization. It is a part of the Cabinet under the direction of the Prime Minister. It all depends on how the Prime Minister instructs them.

Under the Treaty, Article 5 stipulates American defense of Japan, and Article 6 requires Japan to provide the U.S. with military bases for peace and security in the Far East. As a result, U.S. forward deployment strategy is established, which can expand into the Indo-Pacific.

Thus, even if it is incomplete, it is a bilateral alliance. In addition, Prime Minister Abe finally enabled a mechanism to allow the partial use of collective self-defense. Now, in some vital situations, Japan can use force to defend the U.S. military.

Japan's Scale of Defense

What scale of defense force does Japan need? The concept of "Required Defense Force" means that the power of defense is determined based on the level of surrounding threats. In the 1970s, however, it was impossible for Japan to increase its defense capacity in response to increasing Soviet military power. As a result, in 1976 Japan changed to the concept of "Standard Defense Force," which holds that Japan will maintain the minimum defensive force necessary to prevent a power vacuum that invites aggression.

What this means in terms of fiscal logic is that no matter what occurs around Japan, no more than a fixed amount can be spent on defense. Today's concept of a Mobile Defense Force has a number of modifiers, but after all, it just describes how to effectively use the standard defense. This defense system is like putting the cart before the horse, in which surrounding threats are determined to be at a level that can be handled by a defense force that is possible within a fixed budget.

1% of GNP

In 1976, the Cabinet of then-Prime Minister Takeo Miki limited Japan's defense spending to 1% of annual GNP. The fiscal authority's position that it was necessary to stop the increase in defense spending. This limit was finally removed a decade later by Prime Minister Nakasone. This happened because no matter how hard the government tried, defense spending that year would exceed 1% of

GNP by a little, going over 13.4 billion yen.

First of all, the 1% of GNP was an illogical limit. Japan's nominal economic growth rate in 1976, when this limit was set, was 12.4%. If the Japanese economy had continued to grow without the second oil shock, the GNP would have been two-thirds higher in a decade or less, and this would have raised the defense budget by the same percentage, regardless of actual necessity.

In other words, even if the economic growth rate were low, a small defense budget would exceed a 1% GNP limit, and arithmetic alone would define Japan as a "military state," potentially raising security concerns in neighboring countries. If the economic growth rate were high, however, even if the defense budget were to increase drastically, Japan would still qualify as a "peaceful nation." It is silly for the upper limit of the defense budget to be determined by the economy. The removal of the 1% definition was the earnest desire of both the Defense Agency and MOFA.

The man with the most discerning opinion regarding Japan's defense policy was a member of the House of Councilors, Motoo Shiina. He was the Japanese politician most respected by American security officials. Shiina devised a formula for setting the total amount of defense spending in advance, to replace the 1% of GNP.

In this method, a five-year defense plan would first be established, and the budget necessary to realize it would be determined annually without reference to GNP. This method was approved by Prime Minister Nakasone and Chief Cabinet Secretary Masaharu Gotoda. With this, the linkage of defense spending to GNP was finally removed. I went to Shiina's home nearly every day to receive instructions from him and ran around coordinating with the relevant ministries. As expected, the Soviet Union criticized Japan for "taking a big step toward becoming a military power."

Techno-nationalism: Selection of Japan's Next Generation Fighter Plane

The U.S. attitude toward Japan in terms of the military was superb. I've always felt a secure commitment to the defense of Japan by the American men and women in uniform. When Washington lets

American defense industrial interests get tangled up in the alliance, it's a different story. A typical example was the FSX, Japan's next generation fighter plane.

Aside from the Gulf War (next chapter), the FSX was the most acute conflict between the two nations over the administration of the security alliance. The Air Self-Defense Force and Mitsubishi Heavy Industries engineers naturally wanted to make their own fighters. Moreover, this was the last opportunity to pass on the legacy of the engineers who had inherited the technology of the Zero Fighter planes.

Itsuro Masuda, chief engineer at Mitsubishi Heavy Industries Nagoya Works, came to MOFA carrying a model of the FSX carefully wrapped in a *furoshiki* cloth. He appealed for domestic production. I was moved by his arguments. "Even Brazil and Israel are making their own fighters," he pleaded. "Why can't we do the same? We have the necessary technological capabilities." I had to convince him that the U.S.–Japan Security System required that interoperability be secured. Yet, while I could sympathize with the chief engineer's arguments, Washington was very aggressive about selling F-16s and F-18s off the shelf.

In the end, Washington and Tokyo agreed upon a "joint development" formula. The work would be divided, with the U.S. covering 60% and Japan, 40%. Japan would pay the entire development cost estimated at 165 billion yen and would give up areas that it could have developed independently, and Japan even moved closer to the American side by agreeing that the F-16 would be its base model.

The U.S. Congress, however, ignored this process and denounced Japan for trying to steal American fighter technology: "After our automobiles, now they want to steal our prized aviation industry!" A great chorus of "Don't give our technology to Japan," led by Senators Byrd, Danforth, Helms, and others, triggered another discussion of how ugly and unfair Japan is.

Japan and the United States finally settled an agreement on the FSX in April 1989 after making the conditions of development and production even more advantageous to the United States. The issue left many bitter memories for Japan.

Allegations of Bringing Nuclear Weapons into Japan

Nuclear weapons are something that Japanese people absolutely reject. This is a natural national sentiment after the bombing of Hiroshima and Nagasaki. But Japan needs the protection of the American nuclear umbrella. The constant conflict between these two facts complicates Japan's defense policy.

Japan has a resolution called the "Three Non-Nuclear Principles" that states, "Japan shall neither possess nor manufacture nuclear weapons, nor shall it permit their introduction into Japanese territory." Not possessing or manufacturing poses no problem, but Japanese opposition parties have constantly attacked the United States for ignoring the three principles when American warships come to Japanese ports of call loaded with nuclear weapons.

The Japanese government has avoided dealing with this problem head on by replying that since the United States knows the Three Non-Nuclear Principles, it surely would not violate them. The U.S. avoids it by explaining its NCND (neither confirm nor deny) policy regarding the existence of nuclear weapons on ships. I too, had to use this explanation to respond to Diet questions. It was the New Zealand Lange administration that addressed the NCND policy and strongly urged the United States to clarify the existence of nuclear loads on individual ships. Eventually, the ANZUS security treaty among Australia, New Zealand and the U.S. fell apart because the Lange administration would not yield on this point.

There were strong counterarguments made by people like former U.S. Ambassador to Japan Edwin Reischauer and U.S. Navy Rear Admiral Gene LaRocque from the early 1960s that the "transition"—not the "introduction"—of nuclear arms through Japan had been allowed, and that calling the United States a liar would only hurt the alliance. Later, a document supporting Reischauer's arguments was released. This controversy continued until President George W. H. Bush stopped the loading of nuclear weapons onto surface vessels in 1991.

Being summoned to the Diet many times on this issue was my biggest headache, and after I left the Ministry, I was relieved to hear the news that these documents were released. It was a seemingly sterile dispute, but the Japan–U.S. Security Treaty system was maintained, despite differences of opinion between the ruling party and the opposition. Otherwise, Japan would probably have ended up like New Zealand, whose alliance broke up after it refused to recognize the U.S.'s NCND policy.

All in all, anti-military and anti-nuclear sentiments have their roots in the Pacific War. The country that wins a war will soon forget it, but the country that loses will let the memory of that war define the way its people live for the next 50 to 100 years. There are voices overseas that express concern about the nuclear armament of Japan. In fact, according to some polls, 17.7% of Japanese citizens think that Japan should have nuclear weapons. (Sankei FNN survey, September 2017) The phrase "at a technical level, we have the ability to own nuclear weapons at any time" tickles Japanese self-esteem and "we can do it but we won't" can be a diplomatic trump card. However, for Japan to become nuclear-armed is 100% impossible.

First, there are Hiroshima and Nagasaki, and the Japanese have a greater aversion to nuclear weapons than anyone in the world. Second, even if there were no such feelings, it is not realistically possible. Japan would first have to withdraw from the NPT, become the second North Korea, and receive sanctions from around the world. Few other people are as vulnerable to such pressure as the Japanese. Japan cannot withstand isolation from the world.

Thirdly, if Japan were to start developing nuclear weapons, the United States would stop supplying uranium fuel to Japan, in accordance with the Japan–U.S. nuclear agreement. Japan's nuclear power generation, even if dramatically reduced after the Fukushima disaster in 2011, would completely fall.

Fourth, where would nuclear missiles be deployed? There is no place in Japan to build a base or underground silo to store nuclear missiles. Building an infrastructure for safely holding nuclear weapons in Japan is unrealistic. I strongly felt this when I visited an air force base in Wyoming.

Frances E. Warren Air Force Base, Wyoming

In the summer of 1987, I invited Yasuhiko Okada, the examiner in charge of the defense budget at the Ministry of Finance, to join me on a visit to U.S. nuclear facilities. I wanted him to see for himself the weight of America's responsibility to maintain nuclear deterrence and to see what the U.S.–Japan Security Treaty established under extended deterrence really looks like.

After a meeting at the Department of Defense in Washington, we went to Minot Air base in North Dakota, where we were shown how the B52 strategic bombers carrying nuclear Tomahawk missiles flew. After actually flying in them, we went to the Frances E. Warren Air Force Base in Wyoming, where 50 ICBM Minuteman Peacekeeper missiles were kept. (The Peacekeeper missiles at Warren Air Force Base were retired in 2005 and now the base has 150 Minuteman III missiles.) From there, we visited Bremerton Naval Station in Washington State (now named Naval Base Kitsop), where we were shown the inside of a strategic submarine loaded with nuclear-armed Poseidon missiles.

This experience made me think hard about the meaning of deterrence. At a dinner hosted by the Warren Air Force Base commander, Col. Gary Curtin, I explained Japan's three non-nuclear principles. He smiled as he listened. After having seen the base, I felt that I understood the meaning of his smile. "See for yourself, just how hard it is to have nuclear weapons," he was telling me.

The following morning, we were guided to a conference room where the people who controlled the missile launchers were gathered. They worked in 24-hour shifts, and every morning, they had a briefing on the latest Soviet situation. These were young people in light blue uniforms with orange scarves around their necks. I was overwhelmed by their seriousness. A tense atmosphere dominated the room, far removed from the peaceful and laid-back pastoral Wyoming landscape. I was told that these young people were not soldiers selected to take charge of missile launchers, they were brought here on rotation. At the exit of the briefing room, I saw a poster they had made. In great big letters, it said: "OUR BOTTOM LINE, NOT TODAY, IVAN."

In other words, the world will be peaceful as long as they stand at the front lines of deterrence to prevent nuclear war that day. The next day, another team will secure peace for another day. Then, peace will continue day after day. So, they make it their duty to protect peace that day. This is what goes through their minds as they descend to the fire command room in the basement of each silo. The silos that house the missiles are distributed across a vast area so they cannot be destroyed at once by an enemy attack. They sit nestled in forests, farmlands and mountains. The land they are spread across would cover the entire area of Shikoku, one of the four major islands that make up Japan. This lone incident reminded me once again that for Japan to arm itself with nuclear weapons was an unrealistic idea.

When we were guided to the missile launch command room deep underground, I was especially impressed with the safety mechanisms that were set in layers to prevent missiles from being fired without a Presidential order. Missiles cannot be fired unless dozens of procedures have been processed. There is no possibility of an accidental nuclear war as in a movie. I sighed, imagining the enormous amount of money, personnel and education needed to create and maintain this safety system.

In short, safely owning nuclear weapons requires much more infrastructure and human resources than you would think. A country without such a system should not ever own nuclear weapons.

I sometimes meet brave commentators who argue that Japan should possess nuclear arms. Before I say, "As a country of peace, Japan should not have nuclear weapons," I first make a point of saying, "Don't do it, because the amount of money, manpower and space would be impossible." Deterrence costs money. I wonder how much is spent at Warren Air Force Base alone. Then-Secretary of Defense Casper Weinberger always talked about the "paradox of peace." War can only be deterred with unremitting effort and a quick response system. Only then can peace be maintained. However, if peace is maintained, it will be said that "deterrence" is unnecessary. This paradox is the fate of all democracies.

U.S.-Japan Alliance Milestone: INF Medium-range Nuclear Negotiations

The Decoupling Crisis

WHAT IS AN IDEAL ALLIANCE? I could probably explain the whole thing with one single episode: the milestone incident between Japan and the United States that took place in February 1986.

Negotiations between the U.S. and the Soviet Union regarding intermediate-range nuclear forces (INF) began in 1981. The intermediate-range nuclear weapons referred to were the missiles with a range of 500 to 5,500 kilometers, distances shorter than the intercontinental missiles (ICBMs) that could be used by the U.S. and Soviet Union in a direct war and the short-range nuclear weapons called "tactical" nuclear weapons. The main ostensible use for the INF weapons would be in a war between Russia and Europe.

European nations took it very seriously when Russia began deploying 130 SS20 intermediate-range nuclear missiles to the west of the Ural Mountains in 1976. It was a move designed to divide NATO. The Soviet Union's existing ICBMs would have been sufficient for it to attack Europe. The deployment of INF missiles that could reach Europe but not the United States was an intentional act designed to decouple America and the European members of NATO.

Each time the United States negotiated with the Soviet Union, President Reagan sent Ambassador Edward Rowny to Tokyo to explain the progress of the negotiations to the Japanese government. This showed just how highly President Reagan and Secretary of

Defense Weinberger valued the alliance with Japan. In the years that followed, there were several times when the atmosphere of U.S.–Japan security relations became intimate, but the days when the U.S. would go so far to detail to Japan the contents of its nuclear negotiations with the Soviet Union were exceptional.

On the evening of February 6, 1986, a personal letter addressed to Prime Minister Nakasone arrived from President Reagan, stating his intention to propose a plan to the Soviet Union to abolish all SS20 missiles deployed in European Russia west of the Urals and reduce 50% of the SS20 missiles in the Asian theater in exchange for U.S. withdrawal of Ground Launched Cruise Missiles and Pershing II nuclear missiles deployed in West Germany. It was possible that the proposal would be relayed to General Secretary Mikhail Gorbachev the following week.

This unleashed a crisis in Tokyo. Many feared the population would feel abandoned by the United States, and trust in the alliance would crumble. Even if NATO unity was maintained, there would be a "decoupling" between Japan and the U.S. Added to that crisis of perceptions, the Japanese side argued, an extremely difficult problem would arise. In the future, if negotiations for the reduction or elimination of Soviet SS20s in Asia were to happen, the Soviet Union would ask for the removal of U.S. nuclear forces deployed in Asia in return. This would destabilize U.S. nuclear strategy in East Asia.

The trouble was that as the basis of these negotiations, Washington would have to reveal its Asian nuclear forces to the Soviet Union and the NCND "neither confirm nor deny" policy would have to be altered. The Government of Japan, unlike New Zealand's, had been cooperating with the U.S. to sustain its NCND policy. Such a Japanese position would become untenable.

This presented a grave problem for Japanese security. For the United States, there was a fear that if the Asian SS20 issue were added to the American proposal, the Soviets would back off their earlier concessions and return to square one.

Meanwhile, frustration with Japan was growing in Europe. The West Germans particularly felt that Japan, which didn't want to take any political risk, shouldn't be interfering. It was an understandable feeling—the government there was in danger of collapse and concessions from the Soviets had only just been won by the placement of American nuclear weapons on German soil.

In such cases, countermeasures are discussed first at the level of the division chief. General Affairs Director Yukio Sato (later Ambassador to the U.N.) summoned Treaties Division Director Ryozo Kato (later Ambassador to the U.S.), Disarmament Divisions Director Yuji Miyamoto (later Ambassador to China), and me, Director of Security Affairs, to his room. Sato said: "This is a crisis. Let's handle other work flexibly and deal with this immediately." His orientation never wavered.

On September 6, 1976, when Sato was Director of the Security Affairs Division, a MiG-25 piloted by Lieutenant Viktor Belenko defected to Hakodate Airport and caused a huge commotion. The Soviet Union demanded with ferocious pressure that the aircraft be returned untouched. The U.S. military, of course, urgently wished to see the airplane. To avoid provoking the Soviet Union, the consensus in MOFA was to return the aircraft to the Soviet Union while Belenko could seek asylum in the United States.

As security chief, Director Sato instead insisted on a thorough inspection of the aircraft, saying that a country that could not even inspect a defected plane had no right to pretend to be a close ally of the United States. The Soviet Union was furious, but Sato remained adamant. With the support of U.S. Air Force engineers sent to Japan, the MiG was taken apart and examined with a fine-tooth comb before being handed over to the Soviet Union in its dismantled state.

Sato, who was affectionately known by the nickname "Great Buddha" was idolized by many MOFA staff members. In any organization, the true nature of a man can only be grasped by speaking with the people below. Sato earned enthusiastic reviews from his subordinates. His popularity earned him the nickname "Mr. MOFA." Everyone was sure that his career would thrive. He was on track to become the Vice Minister and after that, Ambassador to the United States. However, while he was kind to those under him, he spoke with bluntness to his seniors even on unpleasant topics. Some of his superiors objected to this trait, so his career ended in New York.

Treaties Director Kato was a pleasant guy with a sense of humor. I knew he worked hard and kept excellent records because I was his successor in various positions at the home office and overseas. Disarmament Director Miyamoto served in Beijing for four years from 2006. He was the man who directed a "strategic reciprocal relationship" between Japan and brought about stability in Japan–China relations at the time.

Sato led the discussion. After we discussed the situation from all angles, we came up with our conclusions:

1) Japan should respond to the U.S. immediately.
2) We must point out to the U.S. that there would be controversy in Asia regarding the nuclear balance and this would backfire on Washington's security strategy in the Pacific.
3) Japan must not interfere with the establishment of the U.S.–Soviet agreement, so we will prepare a realistic alternative rather than simply expressing opposition.

Finally, Sato said: "Let's think of a formula where we don't have to mention the words Europe or Asia."

I went back to my room and thought about whether there could be a miracle formula to erase the name of Europe and Asia. I spread out a map of the Soviet Union and discussed it with my staff members. I asked if there is a base located in central Russia where we could hope to gather all the SS-20s that are likely to be deployed east of the Ural Mountains. A junior officer who had been seconded from the Ground Self-Defense Force, grinned and said, "Okamoto-san, how about Barnaul?" "Bingo! That's the answer," I said. "Barnaul in central Russia can be named without mentioning Europe or Asia. Or the missiles could be deployed nearby at the Kansk and Novosibirsk bases. Don't mind about the military implications, this game is all about 'political perception.'"

I asked for an immediate meeting at Director Sato's office. When I mentioned the name Barnaul, Sato's face lit up. We agreed on the proposal to be conveyed to the U.S. Government: Please do your best to make the Soviet Union agree to a formula under which SS20s will be deployed in Barnaul, which will not be called either Europe or Asia. Japan will not stand in the way of U.S. negotiations and will do its best to support the U.S. in whatever way possible.

We each explained this proposal to our respective superiors over the weekend. On Monday we got the approval of Vice Foreign Minister Kensuke Yanagiya, and then Prime Minister Nakasone, to draft a personal letter to President Reagan from Prime Minister Nakasone. Time was of the essence. The following day, we received information that Reagan was likely to present the American proposal to Gorbachev at any time.

We worked over the weekend. Miyamoto drafted the letter to Reagan from Nakasone. I drafted a long directive with instructions for Ambassador Nobuo Matsunaga on how to convince the U.S. side of the Japanese position. We thought we had done our job and it would be up to the Embassy to make a demarche to the U.S. side, but that wasn't the end of it. Sato summoned Miyamoto and me. "Okamoto-kun, I'm sorry, but would you please fly to Washington immediately to explain the Japanese proposal?" "Miyamoto-kun, I'm sorry, but please go to Europe to explain Japan's position."

Sato seemed to think that as long as he preceded an order with the phrase "I'm sorry, but ..." he could get away with anything. I ended up having my wife bring my travel-kit to the office, and one hour after Sato gave the order, I left the MOFA building and headed to the airport.

Reagan Accepted Nakasone's Appeal

This operation had to be kept an absolute secret. All of us knew very well that if the process of diplomatic negotiations were to become known, even if the outcome was not bad, somebody later on would make a big deal about who lost or won.

It was not easy keeping it confidential. At the time, MOFA was relaxed and allowed reporters to enter rooms with a simple knock on the door. If a reporter became suspicious and started asking my staff questions about my sudden absence, along with Miyamoto's, it would be very risky. If the media came out with a headline like, "Japan, dissatisfied with the INF negotiations, asks to renegotiate," the U.S. Congress and Europe would react strongly, making it difficult for the American government to shift ground.

My assistant Hiroshi Inomata (later Ambassador to the Netherlands), who always comes up with inventive and witty solutions for everything, set up a camouflage for me by hanging his or someone's jacket on my chair and telling inquiring reporters that I was in a meeting elsewhere in the building.

In Washington, Ambassador Matsunaga took me first to see Michael Armacost, Undersecretary of State for political affairs. A few years later, Armacost moved to Tokyo as the Ambassador to Japan, where he became known as "Mr. External Pressure," because of his straightforward approach to Japan's trade surplus. But this is natural as an ambassador. I liked his humanity. When he moved to Tokyo and I visited him in his office at the Embassy, I addressed him as "Mr. Ambassador" because it was the protocol. He replied, "What's that? I have a name!" He was that kind of a man. Armacost said, "I can understand Japan's position well. The State Department supports Japan."

After that I visited a number of disarmament officials and explained Japan's proposal. I went to The State Department, the Defense Department, the Arms Control and Disarmament Agency, and the White House. Most importantly, I spoke with Air Force Colonel Bob Linhard, Special Assistant to President Reagan for nuclear issues and arms control. He was a gentle, big man in his early 40s, and a confidant to the President in the INF negotiations.

Linhard said, "If Japan had come just to say 'no' we probably would have sent them right back, but this specific alternative plan of a 'concentration in Barnaul' is extremely refreshing." Other American officials were surprisingly positive too, saying that Japan had brought a concrete proposal for the first time, instead of its usual abstract remarks.

A high-ranking Pentagon official even said that he would take Japan's proposal up to the White House as a Department of Defense proposal. Japan's quick reaction surprised the U.S., as Rowny had traveled to Japan only the Friday before. On the following Tuesday, an official from Tokyo was accompanying Ambassador Matsunaga with Prime Minister Nakasone's reply. I was asked how the Japanese government was able to respond so quickly. "Tell us your secret," they said. This was probably the first time the American government made such a comment about the fast action of the Japanese government. This was because of Yukio Sato. Linhard, the shadow behind the American side, was later promoted to Major General at the young age of 47, but sadly passed away a few years later.

Shortly after I returned to Tokyo, a reply came from the United States saying that Washington would respect Japan's position. Then finally, in 1987, at the U.S.–Soviet summit in Reykjavik, Reagan persuaded Gorbachev to concede and reached the landmark agreement on the Zero-Zero option. This meant the total removal of the Soviet Union's SS20s, both from West and East of the Ural Mountains. This was more than what Japan had hoped for. Later, in his autobiography *Fighting for Peace*, Casper Weinberger wrote that the speed and clarity of (Japan's) response strengthened President Reagan's decision that verification (of an agreement with the Soviet Union) would have been difficult any other way than with 'Global Zero.'

Objectively speaking, the SS20 was not the only nuclear threat to Japan. The ICBMs and nuclear missiles on Soviet strategic submarines were bigger threats. Only American strategic nuclear missiles on its mainland and carried on its strategic submarines (SLBMs) could serve as deterrents.

The U.S. could have resorted to all kinds of political gestures and rhetoric when Japan asked for the elimination of SS20s from Asia. However, the United States, which would normally never negotiate over strategic nuclear arms with another country, not only discussed matters with Japan constantly but also deeply sympathized with our position.

An alliance is truly about human relations. There was a trusting relationship at the top level, symbolized by the Ron-Yasu connection. Based on that came Secretary Weinberger's unprecedented commitment to Japan. We were able to do our job at our working level because of the basic stance of the U.S. officials who were willing to listen to Japan.

In contrast was the U.S.–China agreement reached in 1998 during President Clinton's historic nine-day visit to China. The agreement was to de-target Chinese nuclear missiles pointed at the United States, and a grand announcement was made celebrating a new era of U.S.–China relations. However, nuclear missiles aimed at Japan weren't even mentioned, let alone discussed. Japan was not notified regarding the U.S.–China missile agreement in advance or after the fact, and the missiles aimed at Japan remained. Perhaps due to lingering effects from what transpired in the Gulf, this was a period of penetrating cold for Japan–U.S. relations.

AMERICAN SOLDIERS STATIONED IN JAPAN

Forty-thousand Soldiers

IT IS THE U.S. NAVY, Marine Corps and Army stationed in Japan that make the language in the Security Treaty effective. In sharp contrast with South Korea, U.S. Army units in Japan are small, with only 2,000 men and women in management units. The Army's main mission is to keep an eye on the Korean Peninsula. The U.S. Air Force defends the air space in the Far East. Of particular importance is the Navy.

The 7th Fleet with Yokosuka as its home port, and auxiliary facilities in Sasebo, covers the entire West Pacific and the Indian Ocean, along with the Marine Corps under its command. Without Yokosuka and Sasebo, the U.S. Navy would have to be based in Hawaii. The closest cooperation with Japan's Self-Defense Forces is by sea, followed by air space.

This is natural, seeing that the Army would enter battle formation only when Japan is directly invaded and the enemy has landed in Japan, which would happen, generally speaking, as the result of a war fought elsewhere in Asia. In Korea, on the contrary, the Army is naturally the most important part of the U.S. forces. It was my mission to help the U.S. military in Japan work in a stable environment. This is what I spent the most time on.

Put simply, the purpose of the U.S.–Japan Security Treaty is to "continue to show deterrence to neighboring countries." Deterrence can only exist through constant effort. The U.S. military is a strong deterrent for Japan, all the more so because its forces are stationed in

Japan. For example, the 7th Fleet's nuclear-powered carrier Ronald Reagan in Yokosuka probably costs about two trillion yen, including its aircraft. Add escort ships and a nuclear sub and the monetary value will climb over three trillion yen, perhaps. Neighboring countries see this level of U.S. military assets placed right next to the Japanese capital as a strong commitment by the U.S. to protect Japan. The same applies to the 5th Air Force and the 3rd Marine Expeditionary Force.

It is not about what function each unit has, but about how the U.S. commitment to Japan is sustained that informs neighboring countries that the U.S.–Japan Security Treaty is not just a piece of paper but an effectively functioning partnership. In Japan, there is a contingency theory that the U.S. military should stay in Guam or Hawaii during peaceful times and come to help Japan only in an emergency. This was debated frequently after opposition party leader, Yukio Hatoyama, became Prime Minister in 2009.

The concept to station military troops in Japan only during emergencies is like trying to snatch bits of the Security Treaty. In my lectures in Japan, this is what I say:

> It's the same as a husband telling his wife, "I don't want to see your face anymore, so get out. But when I get sick, be sure to come back and take care of me." Will this kind of relationship hold the alliance together?

My audience shake their heads and laugh because they know this selfishness won't work.

Cooperation and Non-Cooperation of Localities

Ensuring full military capability in Japan is not easy. During the Great East Japan Earthquake on March 11, 2011, 100,000 Self-Defense Force personnel were mobilized to save lives, search for corpses, and deliver food and water. The dedication of the troops during this time sharply increased public acceptance of the SDF to 90%.

That is not all. The U.S. military sent 24,000 Marines who devoted their support. Likewise, this greatly raised the popularity of the Japan–U.S. security alliance among the Japanese people to 82%, according to a Cabinet Office survey in 2015.

For many years after the War, the military was viewed as an organization that has a zero-sum relationship with the civilian population. In Japan, the military has never fought on the side of citizens as it has in the West. The Japanese people have a strong anti-military feeling because they think the military destroyed their country.

For this reason, "peace" has been equated with "non-military." Keep anything that smells like gun smoke as far away as possible. For a long time, people avoided anyone in a military uniform. Military bases were the same. Even if they knew that the presence of U.S. Forces in Japan was ensuring Japan's safety, they have been reluctant to host military facilities in their neighborhoods, a form of NIMBY-ism.

Under such circumstances, to ensure that U.S. forces can smoothly carry out activities as guaranteed by the Status of Forces Agreement, it has been necessary to win the cooperation of the municipalities where the U.S. military is stationed. Sometimes it has worked, sometimes it hasn't. Let me give you some examples.

Example 1: Yokosuka City

The most successful instance that I dealt with was the improvement of the 7th Fleet's capability in Yokosuka. In the summer of 1986, a request came from Admiral Jim Cossey, the U.S. Navy Commander in Japan. He said that all the ships in the 7th Fleet would be replaced and many of them would become capable of carrying nuclear weapons, so please cooperate. He only said that the ships "were capable" of carrying nuclear

Okamoto meets with Admiral Jim Cossey, the U.S. Navy Commander in Japan, at the U.S. naval base in Yokosuka.

weapons, which didn't mean that they would actually be carrying them. However, depending on how the media reports the news, it could spark a major opposition movement in Yokosuka. Close co-operation with city officials was essential.

Of decisive importance was the mayor. My commute to Yokosuka began. Week after week, my wife drove me to Yokosuka from Tokyo, which took about an hour-and-a-half each way. I visited City Hall and spoke with Mayor Kazuo Yokoyama. While I reported on the progress of the U.S. military plan step by step, he consulted me on his explanations to the City Council. We made meticulous adjustments so that a standard fleet replacement wouldn't turn into a political problem due to opposition from anti-military activists. Thus, the 7th Fleet quietly replaced its ships one at a time, according to routine.

With quiet dialogue and paperwork, the ships were exchanged without becoming a media issue. It was an operation that did not become known to the world, but it was the greatest example during my tenure of emphasizing the need to establish the trust with host cities if you want issues to remain non-political and purely administrative.

Example 2: Fukuoka Prefecture

Cities like Yokosuka are exceptions. Most local governments do not want to become involved in security issues. In 1986, the Ministry of Foreign Affairs, together with the U.S. military in Japan conducted what was called the Article 6 Status Research to explore whether the U.S. Forces in Japan (USFJ) could effectively operate the way it should under Article 6 of the Status of Forces Agreement (SOFA). Scenarios were examined on how to evacuate U.S. military families from South Korea in the event a battle broke out on the Korean Peninsula. Fukuoka Airport was the natural place for families to evacuate to because it is the closest to Korea by distance. For that, we needed to understand how many evacuating families the city would be able to accommodate. We needed a lot of information—how many blankets and how much food were in the current stock, what was the shelter situation and the means of transportation, and so on.

My staff called the Fukuoka Prefectural Office. The response was cold.

"We don't want any involvement in such military operations. We will be criticized by our citizens. We cannot provide you with that information." I was very disappointed, but then I came up with an idea. I ordered one of my staff who was fresh from university and just in his first year at MOFA to pretend to be a student and ask the local officials what measures Fukuoka Prefecture has in place for a disaster emergency. He called the prefectural office and told them he needed the information for his university studies. Lo and behold, a great deal of material was sent to him along with a detailed letter. All of the information we wanted was there.

The small trick left a bad aftertaste. I should have been criticized for forcing my staffer to make a false call. It is against the law for a private person to pretend to be a government official. There is no mention in the law about the opposite situation—an official pretending to be a private citizen—but in ethical terms, it should be the same. I unfairly took advantage of the good will of the Fukuoka Prefectural officials. That said, the attitudes of public institutions that are more than willing to send materials to students while refusing to cooperate with national security policies, are imposing unnecessary strain on national security. The same was true with Yokohama a few years earlier.

Example 3: Yokohama City

There was a man who, as the chairman of the student committee of Tokyo University, led the anti-military movement and later became the head of the Security Affairs Division at MOFA four generations before me. His name was Yoshifumi Matsuda, a tall man who looked, and carried himself, like the actor Liam Neeson. He was a wonderful man, rich in humanity. He ended up becoming Japan's Ambassador to the Philippines but had started his career in the Ministry of Home Affairs after graduating from university. He was later transferred to MOFA where he was persuaded to stay rather than returning to his home ministry, as he had a rare quality. His work style taught me a hands-on approach and determination.

One of the major issues that arose when Matsuda held my position happened in August 1972, when the U.S. tried to transport M-48 tanks from the U.S. Army's Sagami General Depot in Kanazawa Prefecture to the Vietnam battle front through Yokohama's North

Pier. Yokohama Mayor Ichiro Asukata, who would later become Chairman of the Japan Socialist Party, would not allow the use of Yokohama city roads and stood on the side of the protesters against the tanks headed for Vietnam. The demonstration developed into a massive resistance movement, which delayed the transport of the M-48s for three months.

At one point during the turbulence, Mayor Asukata secretly gave Matsuda directions along national roads that could be used to transport the tanks. Matsuda was grateful, thinking that perhaps the socialist mayor, who on the surface strongly opposed transporting the tanks, offered a realistic compromise behind the scenes.

However, there was reason for doubt—perhaps the mayor intended to deceive him. So, Matsuda loaded a pole that was the same length as the tanks onto a truck and took the route suggested by the mayor. It wasn't feasible. At one corner, a tank simply would not be able to make the full turn, nor pull back once it had entered. It became evident that the mayor's alternative route meant the procession of military trucks carrying tanks would be brought to a standstill. Matsuda avoided the inevitable havoc as he well knew the leftists' tactics, having formerly served in the Ministry of Home Affairs.

Finally, at the end of October, the M-48 tanks, heavily guarded by Japanese police, were taken along the Murasame Bridge, which was reinforced especially for this mission, and departed from the North Pier, which was a USFJ facility.

"Always be friendly, but examine. Don't give them your heart." This was how Matsuda taught me to deal with adversaries. I would hear a similar phrase from an American Lieutenant Colonel in Baghdad twenty years later.

Yokosuka City cooperated with national security, Fukuoka Prefecture evaded, and Yokohama City tried to interfere. There were all sorts of municipalities.

Japan Coast Guard

The Japan–U.S. Alliance could not operate without the cooperation of the Japan Coast Guard (JCG) in charge of maritime security. The JCG has the same role as the U.S. Coast Guard and is administered by the Ministry of Land, Infrastructure, Transport and Tourism, not the Ministry of Defense.

The JCG is a paramilitary organization that legally serves as part of the Japan Self-Defense Forces during an emergency. Since the end of WWII, it has not been the Self-Defense Forces, but the JCG that has used force against opponents. Suspicious ships frequently come to Japan from North Korea, apparently for monitoring and sending operatives. In December 2001, a JCG patrol boat discovered one of these ships near Amami Oshima, north of Okinawa, and sank it after exchanging fire. When the suspicious ship was lifted from the seabed, large quantities of new weapons such as recoilless guns and high-performance machine guns were found in its hold.

However, the security system that the JCG works under is far from perfect. In 1987, a North Korean doctor and his family came to Japan on the fishing boat Zu-Dan, seeking asylum. Because Japan does not have a system for providing political asylum, the JCG decided to transport this group of 11 individuals to Taiwan on a YS11 cargo plane. North Korea strongly opposed this, and fearing air interference, the Japan Coast Guard asked for SDF escorts. The Self-Defense Force refused. My friend, who oversaw security, lamented: "What could the JCG do?" Its commanders lined up patrol boats along the flight route so that rescue operations could commence immediately in the event the aircraft was shot down by a North Korean fighter plane.

Despite its political disadvantages, the Japan Coast Guard is at the forefront of maritime security in normal times. They have a particularly strong sense of mission compared with other Japanese government agencies. Every time there was suspicion of nuclear arms being brought in on U.S. military vessels, I needed to request security for their entry and exit. Never once did the Coast Guard even hesitate to respond to U.S. military-related security requests.

In July 1986, as usual, Admiral Jim Cossey of the U.S. Navy came to my office. Cossey, a handsome man who looked like Gregory Peck, was professional and moved at a brisk pace. Carrier-born aircraft participating in night landing practice (NLP) at Atsugi Base were a constant source of friction with local residents because of the noise. It was Cossey's duty to hear my request when I said: "At least, please suspend flights during the New Year's holidays."

He wanted the safe entry of the battleship New Jersey, designed to carry nuclear missiles, into Sasebo port. He also wanted entry for the destroyers Long Beach and Merrill into Yokosuka and Kure port, respectively. He said that the simultaneous arrival of these three ships at bases in Japan would enhance U.S. Navy maneuverability in the event of an emergency with the Soviet Union in the Sea of Japan. So, this was an important military exercise.

I could foresee trouble, but I didn't ask a single question. "Yes, I will start the groundwork," I said. He seemed surprised that I agreed so easily and said he was truly grateful. As far as I was concerned, a case such as this was the Number One priority on the block in terms of the Alliance. To immediately reply "yes" was the natural thing for me to do. According to the Treaty, the U.S. Navy has the right to order port calls of U.S. battleships in Japan. The Alliance would not function if the Japanese government became reluctant to cooperate just because of an unproven assumption that the ships might be carrying nuclear cargo.

When this schedule was announced, the left wing raised tremendous opposition, citing concern that the USS *New Jersey* would be carrying Tomahawk missiles. They warned that on the day of the arrival, activists would not only protest from land, but also charter many fishing boats to gather in Sasebo for an offshore demonstration with the aim of blocking the entry of the *New Jersey*.

I went to the JCG offices, which are in the Ministry of Transport building just across the street from MOFA. Each of the central government offices in Kasumigaseki (the government buildings area) had its own restaurant. Everyone shared information about which one had the best, cheapest lunch and went there. The restaurant in the basement of the Ministry of Agriculture was popular for its rice and meat because of its jurisdiction, while the rumor was that the Ministry of Health and Welfare's restaurant served the most nutritious meals. I often went the cafeteria in the Ministry of Transport building because they had good noodles.

Director of Second Security Division Tomonori Nishiyama met with me. He was obviously a true man of the sea, with a well-tanned face of determined expression. When I asked for the protection of the

New Jersey, he said without pause, "This is our job. We'll take it." The two of us then went to see Vice Commandant Masakazu Henmi, who was the head of security. Henmi had a prominent nose, sharp eyes, and a dignified body that stood proud. I used to call him Neptune. "Okamoto-san, Japan is guarded by the Alliance. It is only natural for their ships to enter Japanese ports. We will ensure their safety."

I have had relationships with all sorts of government offices, but none of them responded to requests from MOFA with such determination as the Coast Guard, perhaps with the exception of MITI (Ministry of International Trade and Industry) during the first Gulf War. To prepare for possible sabotage on open water, Henmi and Nishiyama gathered patrol vessels from all over the country to Sasebo. Then, Henmi, who had overall responsibility for maritime security, went to Sasebo himself a few days in advance, and delivered a speech to the Coast Guard officers:

"The Japan–U.S. Security Treaty may appear to be structured as the U.S. unilaterally protecting Japan. However, by guaranteeing port entry of U.S. military ships in this way, we are turning the Alliance into a truly bilateral one."

On the day of the arrival, more than a dozen activist boats, mostly fishing vessels driven by or rented from fishermen, awaited the battleship *New Jersey* as it turned the bend at Kogozaki Point to enter Sasebo. Nishiyama, who was the general commander at the scene, ordered his warrant officer to use about 30 Coast Guard patrol boats to surround the *New Jersey* in a double ring. The patrol boats began simultaneously to run around the *New Jersey* in circles at high speed as the battleship continued to advance, creating a large swell. A double water barrier formed to protect the advancing battleship. It was masterful maneuvering. The protest boats were blocked by high waves and unable to even pull close to the battleship. The *New Jersey* crew members lined its decks watching this unbelievable sight. They were taken aback by this stunning act by the Coast Guard. I gave a photo taken by the Japan Coast Guard that day to the U.S. Department of Defense. I was told that the photo decorated Defense Secretary Weinberger's room for a long time.

The operation was fully carried out as planned, and Admiral Cossey was deeply grateful. The Japan Coast Guard was satisfied by the boost in morale and confidence it gained from completing this difficult operation. However, inside of me, I still sensed a shadow. The government, including Prime Minister Nakasone, accepted the *New Jersey* port entry knowing it could cause a major problem. However, the Prime Minister's Office was not aware that three ships, including the Long Beach and the Merrill, both of which were also capable of carrying nuclear weapons, were simultaneously entering the other ports of Yokosuka and Kure. Chief Cabinet Secretary Gotoda, who learned of this from the sensational headlines in the newspapers, hit the roof. Secretary Toshinori Shigeie (who succeeded me as the security chief and later became Ambassador to Korea) took the violent scolding in place of me. If he hadn't covered for me, I would surely have lost my job as Director of Security Affairs. The Long Beach and the Merrill also entered safely into Yokosuka and Kure, on the same day.

Without a doubt, if Mr. Gotoda had been aware of it, he would have opposed the three simultaneous port entries. As I knew Gotoda's reluctance, to say the least, I made individual reports separately on the arrival of the three vessels, each time with my opinion that the port call was intended to show the Soviets how "thick" the U.S.–Japan security system was. I did not mention that the three ships were coming on the same day. My approach went beyond the ethical rules of being a bureaucrat. Of the countless incidents I handled during my work at MOFA, this was a most blemishing act because the way I accomplished the result was dishonest.

In later years, after Mr. Gotoda had retired from politics, I became close with him. He always treated me kindly, but one day he pointed at me and Atsuyuki Sasa (a former Cabinet Security Affairs Office Director) and said, "You two are just too dangerous." Sasa seemed to enjoy that, but I could only look down in silence.

Importance of Not Making it Political— Cost Burden of 20,000 Employees

My teammates and I thought that it was our job to do as much as possible for the U.S. forces in Japan, who substantiate the words in the U.S.–Japan Security Treaty. We felt that Japan should foot the expenses of U.S. military bases, as much as possible. Japan's defense costs are low because the U.S. military has adequate resources stationed here so this is a matter of course.

The major costs were for labor, to pay the salaries of 26,000 Japanese employees working on U.S. military bases. Due to the rapid appreciation of the yen after the 1985 Plaza Accord, the U.S. military faced an additional expense of more than 30 billion yen ($225 million today) for labor costs alone. Under pressure, the U.S. government gave up and added to the on-going economic friction as voices from the U.S. Congress demanded that the Japanese Government pay the entire amount that U.S. military had been paying under the U.S.–Japan Status of Forces Agreement.

So, what kind of an elaborate demand would the United States ask of Japan? Would it come as a presidential request? The request came in a very simple form. One day in October 1986, First Secretary of the U.S. Embassy in Tokyo, Chris LaFleur, from the came to see me. He was smiling. LaFleur was thin and tall. He always had a gentle demeanor, that never put his opponents on guard. The MOFA Security Division didn't even have a meeting room. Twenty-three of us sat at desks lined up in rows and it was all you could do to pass between them. I offered a chair from one of the members who was away and asked, "What brings you here today?" "Yeah, well I was wondering if the Japanese side could consider sharing labor costs," "Labor costs? Is this an official U.S. government request? It's going to cost tens of billions. Shouldn't this discussion start at a higher level?" "I want to do this at the administrative level as quietly as possible, so I came to you," he explained. I was surprised by his casual approach, but I also understood the American government's desire to avoid making this a political issue. "Understood. I'll talk to my seniors," I replied.

I reported this to my boss, Hiroaki Fujii, Director General of the North American Affairs Bureau (comparable to an Assistant Secretary in the United States). I also discussed it with my colleagues in my division. What should we do? This is going to require a huge budget. How cooperative can the Ministry of Finance be?

There was a legal issue, too. Japan had already paid for all categories identified under the Status of Forces Agreement. Paying for the "labor costs" was an obligation of the United States. While I had my head wrapped around that, my deputy Kazuyoshi Umemoto (later Ambassador to Italy) provided a simple answer: All we had to do was enact a new agreement to supersede the existing agreement. I was surprised and impressed by this bold idea. If you can't find a way, make a way. That was our power.

No matter how much the U.S. did not want this to become a political issue, in order to take such major steps in Japan, it is absolutely necessary to have instructions from the political level. I went around asking various people to help. The most helpful politician was former Minister of Foreign Affairs and LDP Foreign Affairs Chairman Zentaro Kosaka. I liked him. While he was wealthy and noble, he was a thrifty man. At home, he had a collection of gifts of food that visitors had given to him, which he would eat a little bit at a time. Even if a treat became old and hard, he would force himself to eat it, saying it would be a waste to discard. There were many such people among the great at that time. Toshiba Chairman Toshio Dokō and NTT Chairman Hisashi Shinto—they all lived amazingly simple lives. I can't help thinking that this thrift was an enabling factor in Japan's miraculous growth after the War.

With Umemoto's proposal and Chairman Kosaka's support, not to mention the strong leadership of Prime Minister Nakasone, it was agreed within the Japanese government that Japan would provide a total of 100 billion yen for labor costs under a new five-year agreement. Creating this agreement became my job. Since then, the agreement has been revised and it remains valid today. The amount that Japan has contributed toward the labor costs of base employees totaled about 30 billion dollars as of 2020.

To accomplish my task, I telephoned the Department of Defense in Washington every day. The person on the other end of the line was Japan Desk officer Jim Auer in the Office of the Secretary of Defense. We put the agreement together without bringing it to a political level or even holding a single exaggerated negotiation. The new agreement was passed in May 1987 at the plenary session of the House of Representatives. So, former Secretary of Defense Weinberger got it wrong in his memoir, *Fighting for Peace*. He wrote, "… increasing Japanese support for American labor costs by $100 million—a commitment that Minister Kurihara and Prime Minister Nakasone forced on an extremely reluctant Japanese bureaucracy."[25] Leaving aside the incorrect amount of money, he got the entire picture backward. Regarding the labor cost burden, it was the administrative level that took the initiative and sought approval at the political level. Not a single official opposed. The story of Nakasone and Kurihara holding down a stubborn bureaucracy and making it a political reality was a stereotype that even the intelligent Weinberger, who understood Japan as well as anyone, fell into.

The Islands of Tragedy—Okinawa

Okinawa Summit

OKINAWA IS A GROUP OF ISLANDS, 1,500 kilometers to the south-west of Tokyo in the southernmost part of Japan. The population of Okinawa is 1.46 million, with the second highest population growth rate after Tokyo. It has a lot of growth potential.

Okinawa became a gruesome battlefield during the War and is still shackled by a heavy concentration of military facilities because of its geo-strategic location. It is a pivotal point for the U.S. security strategy in the West Pacific and Indian Ocean. The effectiveness of the Japan–U.S. Security Treaty depends on whether the U.S. military in Okinawa can perform its duty smoothly.

The 18th Air Force Wing is stationed at Kadena Air Base and the 3rd Marine Expeditionary Force is at Camps Hansen, Schwab and elsewhere on Okinawa. The total number of personnel changes constantly, but it generally is around 25,000. The Okinawan archipelago, which extends 400 kilometers from the main island of Okinawa in the north to the southernmost Hateruma Island, stands in the way of Chinese passage into the Pacific Ocean, and close to the Senkaku Islands, a theater of intense territorial dispute between Japan and China. Okinawa plays a crucial role not only for Japan but also for the security of the United States.

I have been concerned about these islands ever since I became involved with the Japan–U.S. security relationship at the Foreign Ministry. After leaving the Ministry in 1991, I thought about how, as a civilian, I might find a way to redress the situation. Five years later, having been working as a consultant to successive prime ministers and private firms, I was pondering the Okinawa issue when it occurred to me that the G-7 summit was scheduled to be held in Japan in 2000. How about holding the G-7 summit of the world's advanced economies in Okinawa? Previously, this was something that only Tokyo had hosted. For the U.S. President to visit Okinawa for the first time would have great political significance. If the President were to give a speech on reconciliation with the people of Okinawa Prefecture, I thought, it would finally bring an end to the Battle of Okinawa.

With that in mind, I published my opinion on the front page of Sankei Shimbun on July 11, 1996. The opinion was widely reported, and it drew an array of harsh responses. Even Prime Minister Nakasone, whom I greatly respected, opposed, saying that the U.S. would surely not want the concentration of U.S. military bases to be seen by the leaders of other countries.

I thought otherwise. To the contrary, it would show the Europeans the extent of the U.S. commitment to the security of East Asia. I later heard that Sandy Berger, National Security Advisor to President Clinton, a Democrat, had sought the opinion of Republican Richard Armitage. Armitage strongly recommended the Okinawa Summit, and the White House was in favor. On July 21, 2000, President Clinton stood on Mabuni Hill, the site of the final and bloodiest battles on Okinawa, and delivered a speech that became a part of Okinawan history.

The Chief Cabinet Secretary

For me, the fateful day that laid the ground for all this was May 17, 1996. On that day, I visited Seiroku Kajiyama at the Prime Minister's office. He was serving as Chief Cabinet Secretary in the Cabinet of Prime Minister Ryutaro Hashimoto, and he was also the Minister in Charge of Okinawa.

The work of a Chief Cabinet Secretary extends across all state affairs, but Kajiyama had never been involved in diplomacy. I had taken it on myself to periodically brief him on international affairs and security. Our talks extended to Okinawa that day.

Kajiyama, who had been carefully listening to what I had to say, suddenly set both of his hands on the table and bowed his head deeply. "Okamoto-san, help Okinawa. Please!" He wouldn't raise his head. I panicked. "Sir, please raise your head. I will help you." It was the only thing I could say.

As a graduate of the Imperial Naval Academy, Kajiyama was a military man at heart. Former Minister of Foreign Affairs Makiko Tanaka, who acted intuitively and caused controversies everywhere, once coined a phrase that became famous: "Kajiyama is the *gunjin* (military man), Koizumi (later Prime Minister) is the *henjin* (oddball), and Obuchi (former Prime Minister) is the *bonjin* (mediocre man)."

Kajiyama was a man of precise strategy and courage. He was defeated by Keizo Obuchi in the 1998 LDP presidential election before he passed away in 2000. In my view, he would have changed Japan completely if he had been Prime Minister. To this day, he is probably the Japanese politician I have most respected. He was passionate and wholehearted in his spirit of service to the country.

What surprised me was his strategy. For example, there was once a debate about whether Taiwan is included in the U.S.–Japan Security Treaty. In July 1997, Koichi Kato, then LDP Secretary-General, said on TV, "Taiwan is not included in the scope of joint defense under the Japan–U.S. Security Treaty." China welcomed the words of Kato, who had served as Japan's Defense Minister previously. Then Kajiyama was asked to appear on a similar TV show. I told him that the correct answer to the question is neither yes nor no. Inclusion or exclusion of Taiwan in the scope of the Security Treaty is left in a state of "strategic ambiguity." It would not be wise to encourage either a Chinese invasion or a Taiwanese declaration of independence. As Kajiyama appeared on the TV program, however, he made it clear that Taiwan is included in the defense perimeter of the Treaty, and that Taiwan's defense is a joint obligation between Japan and the United States. Naturally, China hated what Kajiyama said.

After the broadcast, I went to Kajiyama and asked why he made that sort of inaccurate statement. His response revealed his cleverness: "Just think about it. The Prime Minister is going to Beijing in one month. Suppose Jiāng Zémín asks him, 'Who is correct, Kato or Kajiyama?'" Then all Mr. Hashimoto has to say is, "Both Kato and Kajiyama are wrong. There is no clear understanding between Japan and the United States. This makes it very important for Japan and China to work closely together to prevent miscalculations on both ends."

If he were to have given the correct answer, the Prime Minister would be forced to tell China that it was not Kato, the good guy who delighted them, but Kajiyama, the bad guy, who was correct. But Kajiyama purposely gave the wrong answer on TV to secure diplomatic space for the Prime Minister so that the Japan-China summit would not fail. He was such a man.

My Visit to Okinawa

In response to Kajiyama's request, I wasted no time flying to Okinawa. It had been eight years since I had last been there. Two-and-a-half hours from Tokyo by plane, the islands stood out in the deep blue sea and summer heat. Over the next two years, I was to travel to Okinawa more than 60 times.

Whenever I visited Okinawa, which I had done a number of times as a MOFA official, it was my duty to experience the American point of view, to observe the neighboring towns and residents from inside the U.S. bases. I would be invited by the U.S. military as a guest, visit their bases, tour their equipment, be entertained in their cafeterias, and be escorted in their helicopters.

This time however, I made it a point to keep myself at the Okinawan eye-level, peering into the bases from outside the fences. I visited Kadena Town, which hosts the largest U.S. Air Base in the Eastern Hemisphere. There are 7,000 Air Force officers stationed at Kadena. If you include civilian personnel, Japanese employees, and families, it is a community of more than 24,000. Kadena base houses aircraft and other equipment such as ammunition worth $4 billion. The mainstay assets are two F-15C/D air-to-air fighters and 15 KC-135 refueling tankers. The 18th Wing is one of the most, if not the most, important bases in all of the U.S. Air Force. The U.S. military has explained that this is its largest operational group. To keep an asset that large in full readiness is not easy.

It is not easy for Kadena residents either. Each time an F-15 takes off, two 25,000-pound thrust Pratt & Whitney engines set off a deafening roar. Kadena Air Base and the additional munitions storage areas occupy 82% of the town's area. The people live densely crammed into a narrow strip of land along the Hija River. Small old houses crowd the Kadena Rotary Plaza in the town center. The mayor, Tokujitsu Miyagi, told me just how hard things have been for Kadena people.

I had a very long telephone conversation with Miyagi, and asked: "Would things improve if you had more money?"

"Why yes," he said. "We could resuscitate the whole town. I have big plans, but it will likely cost around ten billion yen. It's a far-fetched pipe dream."

I also visited Kin, a neighboring town where a 12-year-old girl had been raped in 1985 by three U.S. servicemen. The mayor took me to the scene of the crime. It bothered me that the streets of this town were dimly lit, even though it suffers a higher rate of incidents and accidents than other Okinawan towns. The mayor murmured, "If we had 200 million yen, we could light the entire town, but we don't have the budget."

When I returned to Tokyo, I first went to seek the support of the Ministry of Foreign Affairs. I visited my former colleague who held a high-ranking position and was virtually controlling negotiations with the United States. I asked him to talk with the U.S. military headquarters in Tokyo to help the towns and cities of Okinawa. I appealed to him—towns in Okinawa needed money.

His reply startled me: "We make the decisions here regarding base administration. Then we notify Okinawa. The national government decides, and local governments carry out the instructions. These things can only be determined by us bureaucrats who are concerned with the national interest 24 hours a day. Mr. Okamoto, you are a civilian now. Don't bother yourself about what you don't need to."

After I left the Ministry, I stood at the Kasumigaseki intersection for a while, watching passersby. It took time to recover from the humiliating blow inflicted by a man with whom I had worked closely. Still, my desire to help Okinawa remained strong. At the other side of the intersection stood the Ministry of Finance. Well then, I thought,

I'll make my appeal directly to the Ministry of Finance.

I went straight to the Budget Bureau at the Ministry of Finance to call on Deputy Director Masakazu Hayashi (later Vice-Minister). The Budget Bureau is the most powerful bureaucratic institution in Japan. Every initiative in the country costs money. The Budget Bureau makes an assessment and with the approval of the Minister of Finance, budget is appropriated, and thus an initiative becomes a part of the national policy.

I felt comfortable talking to Hayashi. We were the same age and we had worked together in the Embassy in Washington. He looked like a serious man at first glance but was actually a man of bold actions with many stories to tell. He was at his desk. I told him that Town of Kadena was in a deadlock. The streets of Kin Town where the rape was committed were too dark. The City of Nago needs money for its future. And so on. I asked him to help Okinawa.

Hayashi sat quietly listening to what I had to say, but gave no response. I figured he was no different from my former colleague at the Ministry of Foreign Affairs. He was probably bewildered by a civilian who had no responsibility to raise this subject. I stood up to thank him for his time. Hayashi stood up and walked me out of his office. He then looked me straight in the eye, shook my hand and said in a firm voice, "Okamoto, I'll help you."

With that in mind, I visited Kajiyama. I explained that we would set up a special committee to determine projects based on local needs. We must value the proposals of young people living in Okinawa's towns, we must take full advantage of the islands' resources, tourism, natural environment, and the prefectural character defined by a communal spirit and start a welfare operation that includes medical and nursing care.

Kajiyama took me to see Prime Minister Ryutaro Hashimoto. Mr. Hashimoto and I had had a close encounter during the Iran–Iraq War in 1986 regarding the dispatch of patrol vessels from the Japan Coast Guard. The Prime Minister's Office was in a historic building, but it was tiny. The executive office could accommodate only seven people at once. When Kajiyama took me into this small room, the Prime Minister pointed toward me, smiled, and said, "Kaji-san, hanging around with a dangerous guy like Okamoto will get you into trouble." Words of welcome, Hashimoto style.

In June, Prime Minister Hashimoto amended the law to allow two special advisors to the prime minister. One would oversee administrative reform and the other would be in charge of Okinawa. Two months after our meeting, he asked me to fill the latter position. Impressed with Prime Minister Hashimoto's bold yet practical positioning of Okinawa as the Cabinet's "top priority issue," I accepted his request.

So, on November 12, amid a battery of cameras, I went to the Prime Minister for the appointment ceremony. Hashimoto did not leave a good impression with people he met for the first time. He was basically shy, so he did not show a lot of affection. On top of that, he sometimes tried to make an opponent succumb intellectually right from the beginning, like a child. People ended up either

On November 12, 1996, Yukio Okamoto, 49, was appointed Special Advisor to the Prime Minister for Okinawa Issues. Looking nervous, he poses for a commemorative photo with Prime Minister Ryutaro Hashimoto.

fearing him or loathing him. The real Hashimoto was genuine and warm. This is what he said to me: "Hey, for better or worse, when you like each other, you're stuck with each other. And actually, we don't hate our jobs all that much either, right?"

Islands of Tragedy

Okinawa is an island of tragedy, whose hardships came in three stages. The first stage was, of course, the total destruction of Okinawa during the Pacific War, which I will not repeat. The second was when Japan recovered its independence in 1951 through the San Francisco Peace Treaty but Okinawa remained under the U.S. occupation. While Japan made a miraculous recovery in the late

1950's and '60s, Okinawa was left out of that economic growth as it had no freedom under the U.S. Occupation.

In the defeated land, especially where war comrades have shed blood in battle, the U.S. military sometimes tends to be harsh toward residents. In Vietnam, in Afghanistan, and in Iraq, the lack of consideration of the human rights of conquered residents was apparent. During the Korean and Vietnam Wars, the U.S. military massively enlarged its bases in Okinawa. Occupying U.S. Forces built new bases by simply bulldozing people's homes. There were even stories of sick people thrown into the streets wrapped in their *futon* (mattresses). Demonstrators holding sit-ins were rounded up, loaded in trucks and driven far away, then left there. In Nishihara, in Isahama, and in Maja (Iejima), Okinawans called the resistance movements "The struggle against bayonets and bulldozers."

The character of U.S. bases on Japan's mainland and on Okinawa are completely different. Without exception, U.S. bases on the mainland had existed since before the War, then were taken over from the Japanese Imperial Army after Japan's surrender. Residents came to settle around the bases afterwards, and only subsequently started raising complaints about noise.

In contrast, most of the bases on Okinawa were built after the War without the least consideration for residential circumstances, and administrative divisions and zones of public life were chopped up, imposing substantial damage on residents. Children were forced to take detours around the bases to get to school, walking distances several times longer than before. Farmlands, fishing areas, and businesses were left in a ruined state, and still are today.

When Okinawa was returned to Japan in 1972 and gained the freedom to grow, Japan's era of rapid growth as a country had just ended. As such, Okinawa never enjoyed the economic boom of mainland Japan. The wealth gap between Okinawa and the mainland has never narrowed.

The third stage of tragedy is the unfair treatment Okinawa had to endure after being reunited with Japan. Okinawa was returned to Japan in 1972 and came home full of American bases and soldiers. It provided, as it were, a bonus to the security structure of Japan. Naturally, one would assume that the Japanese government would reduce the number of bases on Okinawa, but that did not happen. On the contrary, the central government in Tokyo disregarded the oppressive situation in a distant region that had little political influence. Instead, it reduced the bases on the mainland, especially in the Tokyo metropolitan area. Indeed, 60% of U.S. military bases on the mainland were reduced in terms of area, whereas on Okinawa the reduction was a mere 15% as of 2020. As a result, 70% of the area of U.S. military bases in Japan came to be concentrated in Okinawa, whose land area is only 0.6% of all of Japan. Even today, there remains an unbridgeable gap between Okinawa and mainland Japan in their perceptions of what it means to share the security burden.

The first time I strongly felt this gap was when I was the director in charge of the Status of Forces Agreement and had to deal with the plan to build the Yokosuka U.S. Navy family housing compound at the Ikego munitions site. Standing at the forefront of the opposition campaign were local housewives. One of my classmates from high school was a leader in the blockade of the construction. The opposition's initial claim that "U.S. military presence will increase crime" was replaced by the "quality of life" issue. The dense Ikego forest had been preserved because it was used as a munitions depot for the U.S. military. Environmental protection became the cry of the opposition movement.

"Do not cut the beautiful forest!" "A calyptrogen clam fossil was found!" "This is the northernmost habitat of one species of praying mantis!" For residents who own homes built on land after developers have cut down entire swaths of trees, the green land preserved by the government had become a sanctuary that must not be touched. It took 10 years before the Ikego housing project construction finally started, with the number of trees to be cut down limited to 15%.

Ikego is located in a rich metropolitan suburb on the mainland. On the other hand, living conditions in Okinawa were far more dire. While I was struggling with Ikego residents, delegates from Okinawa's Kin Town Council came to see me. As I mentioned earlier, Kin houses Camp Hansen, the largest U.S. Marine Corps base outside the United States. The town has had its share of incidents and accidents in the past. One of the town representatives, an elderly woman, petitioned to me: "Mr. Director, please invite family homes of U.S.

military members to our town. The soldiers of the Marine Corps right now are all single. It would help to soften the atmosphere if family members were in town. We would feel more at ease."

The residents of Ikego were against U.S. military families moving in to protect the praying mantis habitat, while the people of Kin were inviting homes of military families to be built in their town, as a step better than single soldiers. This was the difference between the mainland and Okinawa.

As Prime Minister Hashimoto's Special Adviser on Okinawa, I had a secretariat of 16 members, and with the dedication of these people a "Committee for Okinawan Issues" was launched. My main role was to select the Committee members and when this was done, I was already convinced we would succeed. Our committee included an even number of members from Okinawa and the mainland; the presidents of the two major Okinawa newspapers that were critical of whatever the central government did; and unexpectedly, Keiichi Inamine, who became Governor of Okinawa two years later in 1998, to oversee the implementation of our projects.

If you looked at individual municipalities, the plight was even more pronounced. U.S. military bases and training grounds occupied 28 municipalities in Okinawa. They covered 82% of Kadena Township, 56% of Kin Township, 57% of Chatan Township, 53% of Ginoza Village, 57% of Yomitan Village, 42% of Higashi Village, 37% of Okinawa City, 35% of Ie Village, and 33% of Ginowan City that has Futenma Airfield.

Based on the recommendations of this Committee, 100 billion yen was delivered to the municipalities for various urban projects to compensate for the restricted economic growth caused by having so much land locked up for military use. Masakazu Hayashi of the Ministry of Finance kept true to his word and fully supported me throughout the process.

Some 23 billion yen was handed to the town of Kadena, which holds Kadena AFB, the largest U.S. Airbase in the Western Hemisphere, the town where Mayor Miyagi had told me with a sigh that 10 billion yen was a pipe dream. The funding enabled Kadena's rebirth into a modern town, attracting the immigration of IT venture companies from across Japan. Mayor Miyagi had been invited to run for Governor of Okinawa, but he declined. "How could I run away from this interesting project and go for the Governor?" he told me.

The township of Kin, which houses Camp Hansen, the largest Marines Camp outside the United States, and where the young girl had been raped by U.S. soldiers, undertook several projects to improve the town infrastructure. I had homework to do after I promised Mayor Katsuhiro Yoshida that I'd get help to light up the streets. I asked the prominent light artist Tomoko Ishii to install beautiful streetlights. With the approval of the Committee, now the streets of Kin are brightly illuminated with creative lights.

However, independent town development like this was not enough to stabilize Okinawa. I visited Washington D.C. in the spring of 1998 to convey the Okinawa situation frankly, and to ask for cooperation in improving conditions. With the full cooperation of our Embassy in Washington, I was able to meet the necessary people, but unfortunately, I did not get the reaction I had expected from officials in Washington. At the State Department, I asked an Assistant Secretary, "The U.S. military is carefully protecting the environment around training grounds in Hawaii by not firing cannons. Please give the same consideration to Okinawa."

Onna-dake, the highest mountain in Okinawa at 363 meters, stands in Camp Hansen. At that time, the mountain was almost bald due to the Marines' using it for target practice with 155 mm howitzers. Onna-dake had become a symbol of the destruction of nature by the U.S. military. I thought that if consideration for environmental conservation were shown by the U.S., the emotions of Okinawa residents would improve significantly. But there was not one bit of sensitivity in the blunt response of the Assistant Secretary: "We cannot stop the firing because there is no other place in Japan for artillery training. The U.S. has Alaska and deserts to shoot in. So don't compare Japan with Hawaii. Okinawa is a problem that you need to resolve."

I had begun to think that it would be impossible to make these guys understand Okinawa, but a ray of hope came my way when I met with people at the Department of Defense and the Armed Forces. The DOD was anxious to relocate the Marine Corps Air Station in Futenma because it thought that "if the problem is not concluded under the Hashimoto administration with its great interest in Okinawa, it will take a very long time to resolve, placing the U.S. military in an unstable situation." These worries unfortunately turned out to be true.

My meetings with people in uniform were much more fruitful. I met with Charles Krulak, the Commandant of the Marine Corps, (Vice) Admiral James Ellis, Jr., Deputy Chief of Naval Operations, and Air Force General Ralph Eberhart. Perhaps they had a sense of crisis that one mistake would cause them to be kicked out of Okinawa. They wanted to think through the problem together with the Japanese side, to see what they could do as human beings.

General Krulak, who stood at the top of the Marine Corps, was particularly sympathetic. Even as he was occupied with maneuvers in the Middle East, my friend Richard Armitage called him directly and arranged a meeting for me. Krulak was known as a strict commander, and I was warned that if I started off on the wrong foot, I would lose him.

The General took a great amount of time to listen to me. I wanted him to understand the needs of the residents as much as possible. I asked him to make every effort to eliminate incidents and accidents. The relationship between the Marine Corps and the residents of Kin township is of key importance, I said. I spoke about the work and projects the Japanese side had begun in the township and pleaded for help in changing the atmosphere in Kin. I needed his cooperation.

General Krulak spoke clearly: "You don't need to say anything more. That work is something we should have started first." He explained that he had lived in Kin for four years and said that if there was going to be a lighting project for the streets of Kin, he would fully cooperate by sending engineering corps and building materials from the Marine Corps. He spoke passionately of his desire to cooperate separately from the Special Action Committee on Okinawa (SACO), saying, "This is our own crisis." I heard later that he told his staff after our meeting, "I wish I could have met with that man earlier." That statement became my medal of honor.

Futenma

The September 1995, the rape of a 12-year-old girl by U.S. marines turned Okinawa into an island of protest. Incidents caused by U.S. soldiers were not rare, but this case was special. For Okinawans who had survived poverty and tragedy, the passion and love for children are especially strong. The victim was a girl walking home from a stationery store after buying a notebook for school. It sparked the people's long-felt frustration that no matter what, the military activities of U.S. Forces should not cross the boundaries of an ordinary citizen's life. Moreover, there was the fact that the culprits weren't handed over to the Japanese authorities. A wave of rage engulfed Okinawa.

Rallies drew 80,000 protesters. Resentment over the inequality between Okinawa and mainland Japan also boiled over. When he became prime minister in January 1996, Ryutaro Hashimoto had designated Okinawa as the top priority issue that the nation needed to resolve. It was a bold definition. One month later, during the Santa Monica Summit with President Bill Clinton Hashimoto requested the return of Futenma Marine Corps. Air Station, which had become a symbol of the Okinawa base problem. Although few thought it possible, Secretary of Defense William Perry decided it would be relocated. The historic "Return of Futenma" was announced at a press conference on April 12 by Prime Minister Hashimoto and U.S. Ambassador to Japan, Walter Mondale. But the return did not proceed smoothly and still today, more than twenty years later, the project is far from the completion.

Originally, my job was concerned only with the regional development of Okinawa. And I had been perfectly happy with the way my work was progressing, improving the situation of towns that had to live with American bases. One day, however, Chief Cabinet Secretary Kajiyama summoned me. "Please, Okamoto, help with Futenma too," he said.

To be honest, I did not feel good about this. Once I start working on something, it is my nature to go all the way until I see results. I knew that tackling this problem would worsen my relationship with the Ministry of Foreign Affairs, which is slow to move. I had never felt comfortable with the Foreign Ministry's approach to the return of Futenma. Why should I have to deal with this problem, which had become so tangled as a result of MOFA's preference for secrecy? I knew that if I were to move aggressively, I could collide with the Foreign Ministry. I told Kajiyama honestly, "I don't want to get caught in that office's jealousy anymore. Please just let the guys at the Ministry of Foreign Affairs handle it." But he wouldn't listen. "You can't get any work done if you worry about others badmouthing you!" he said.

The chief cabinet secretary did not trust the Ministry of Foreign Affairs. He often performed a routine he called "The MOFA Waltz." "MOFA only cares about cocktail parties, not the happiness of Okinawa," he said, pretending to dance with a partner while kicking away with his heels. "This is how MOFA kicks Okinawa away while dancing with the United States." Whenever he started this "MOFA dance," there was nothing the staff in the room could do but grin.

The job of Special Adviser on Okinawa wasn't easy to manage. In all administrative fields, one ministry is already designated to be in charge. Anything an aide tries to do will come up against one ministry or another. I had full political protection under the Hashimoto Cabinet, which had created the Special Advisor's position by enacting a new law. The powerful Chief Cabinet Secretary Kajiyama had told every ministry, "Please understand that Okamoto's words come from the Prime Minister and me." Given this protection, I had been able to perform my job as expected, with minimal friction with the existing bureaucracy. But this time was much more difficult.

Government offices other than the Ministry of Foreign Affairs provided maximum cooperation. It seemed that the entire government wanted to make amends for the miserable conditions Okinawa had been subjected to in the past. But the most difficult relationship came with my old nest, the Ministry of Foreign Affairs. MOFA had never hidden its displeasure with outsiders meddling in its affairs. Politicians were an exception. MOFA officials reckoned that angering a politician would only hurt them. Besides, they knew more about the content of an international issue than any politician so they could stay in control. When it comes to civilians, however, their attitude was, "Why are people from a lower rank sticking their noses into our business?"

The Ministry of Foreign Affairs did not like me negotiating directly with American officials. In fact, I had been told by my American friends that they were asked by the Foreign Ministry not to visit me at the Prime Minister's office. These friends confided to me that they were told at the Foreign Ministry that "Okamoto was taking money from Okinawa townships." My wrath toward them was not due to their invective or their whining about me, but to their not doing anything themselves to deal with Okinawa.

The Special Action Committee on Okinawa (SACO) agreement signed by the United States and Japan on December 2, 1966, included a clause to transfer the functions of Futenma Air Station. It stated, "The SBF—Sea Based Facility—will be located off the east coast of the main island of Okinawa and is expected to be connected to land by a pier or causeway," but a specific location was not mentioned. Of course, any municipality would object to becoming that location. Which ministry would take it on? Neither the Ministry of Foreign Affairs nor the Ministry of Defense dared pick up that hot potato. The relocation of Futenma, which was supposed to be Prime Minister Hashimoto's greatest political achievement, wasn't going anywhere.

Every time a relocation site was proposed, it was smashed down. Months of quiet ground-laying is essential before a location is mentioned in a newspaper article. The Ministry of Foreign Affairs' attitude—"the government should make the decisions about security policy and then tell the local people what's best for them"—will not work. Only on-the-ground effort sustained through blood, sweat and tears could resolve the base problem. At long last, in 2006, it was announced that Futenma Air Station, located in a densely populated patch of land near the capital of Naha, would move to an alternate location located on reclaimed seabed in Henoko-Oura Bay, in the northern region of Yanbaru.

The Old Mayor of Nago City

Instructed by Chief Cabinet Secretary Kajiyama to help with the Futenma move, I went directly to meet Tetsuya Higa, the mayor of Nago City, where the Henoko site was located. Three years before the Pacific War began, Mayor Higa had been sent to Vietnam as a Navy correspondent. He returned to Japan after the defeat. As Okinawa had been decimated, he worked in the Sakido Coal Mine in Nagasaki. The work was harsh enough to have killed him, so he fled to Kagoshima. He returned to his hometown Nago and lived a tumultuous life, hopping from one job to another, including rice milling, postal work, raising cattle in Hawaii, pig farming, tempura cooking, and working in a boarding house, before becoming a city council member and eventually, mayor.

Higa was raised in Yanbaru, the poverty-stricken northern part of Okinawa. As a youngster, Higa himself would tie a rope around his belly to help himself endure hunger. It was a time when the only food available was *sago*, a type of starch extracted from the Cycas palm. Poverty forged a strong bond within the community.

The people there are especially fond of children. Time and again, Higa said that he wanted to give the children a brighter future. I deeply sympathized, and at that point Mayor Higa, Deputy Mayor Takeo Kishimoto and I became allies on the Yanbaru development. I was certain that Mayor Higa would be willing to be consulted about the relocation of Futenma to Henoko, the only candidate site.

When Higa welcomed me at Nago City Hall, his face resembled one of the stern goblins on a traditional roof ridge tile. I asked, "Will you take in Futenma at Henoko?" His answer was, "Let's think of it as a problem for all of Yanbaru."

Right from the beginning, moving Futenma to Henoko was the most realistic plan. Futenma's 480-hectare vast airfield would be cut to less than half and moving the facility offshore would prevent accidents from happening in residential areas. The remaining issue was the political question of why another airfield needed to be located in Okinawa at all.

For four months after that, I traversed the northern region in an effort to build consensus. I knew that just trying to convince people in Nago would not be enough, so I used my holidays to visit surrounding municipalities and even remote northern islands such as Iheya, Izena and Iejima.

In the meantime, I began to see the complexity of the issue. It wasn't as simple as just telling people to rejoice because Futenma Airfield would shrink to one-third and the danger would move out to sea. It started to become clear that there would be no moving forward without understanding the Okinawan perspective on all the suffering they had endured in the three stages mentioned earlier.

I visited the legendary leader of the anti-base campaign, Shoko Ahagon at his home in Iejima. Mr. Ahagon, whose family was killed during the War and whose land was confiscated by the U.S. Occupation, led a non-violent anti-base campaign, and had great influence in Okinawa. From his sickbed, he asked me to take care of Okinawa. He died a few years later, at 101.

Gradually, the number of supporters and sympathizers increased, and in April 1997 Mayor Higa agreed to an environmental assessment that would become a prerequisite for accepting the construction of a runway. I went to report this to Prime Minister Hashimoto. He looked at me in disbelief. "Is this true?"

The problems started after that. Activists came to Nago in droves from the mainland to campaign against the project. This led to a referendum on December 21, 1997. There are 35,000 registered voters in Nago. Parents, children, brothers and sisters held deeply divided views. Collecting votes meant that the town would be split in two. Voter turnout was more than 82%. The winner was those who opposed relocation, 16,639 to 14,267—a difference of 2,372 votes. This made the relocation of Futenma to Henoko impossible. I felt that all prospects were lost.

I immediately flew to Okinawa to see Higa. That night, just the two of us sat together in a hotel on the coast of Nago, drinking *awamori*, the Okinawan sugarcane liquor, for a long time. "You've done all you can," I said, "so going forward, please just think of your own needs as you must continue to live in this community." Mr. Higa tightened his lips into a straight line and said, "I won't go home tonight, I'll spend the night here thinking about it.

The next day was Christmas Eve. Although Japan is not a Christian country, the entire nation is wrapped in hustle and bustle on this day. In the morning, Mr. Higa called me at my home in Tokyo. He said that even though the relocation plan had lost the popular referendum, he would accept the maritime base at Henoko so as to promote development of the northern region. "I will take responsibility for the confusion I have caused and resign," he said. "But I won't let the people who helped me and bet their jobs on national policy die like dogs. I've told Deputy Mayor Kishimoto and Director Bunshin Suematsu (later Deputy Mayor and Okinawa Prefectural assembly member) to believe in Mr. Okamoto and follow him as far as he takes you. I am on my way to Tokyo. Please let me meet Prime Minister Hashimoto."

Mr. Higa arrived at Haneda Airport in the evening. It happened to be that on that same day, Prime Minister Hashimoto had invited Governor of Okinawa, Masahide Ota, to the Prime Minister's Office to discuss the 2015 Base Return Action Program. I felt an urgent need to talk to Mr. Ota before he entered the Prime Minister's Office, so I asked him to meet me at the Capitol Hotel Tokyu next door. I appealed to him desperately. "Governor, the Mayor of Nago will announce his acceptance of the relocation plan tonight. For some time now, you have said that you would entrust Nago City to decide whether to accept the relocation. Won't you at least give a neutral statement now saying that you will 'now watch the discussion between the national government and Nago City' or something to that effect?"

As this was the first Mr. Ota had heard of Mayor Higa's decision, his expression changed. He flatly refused. "This will cause a big protest in Okinawa and it will run out of control. This is unacceptable," he said. From there, Mr. Ota went into Prime Minister Hashimoto's office at 5:30. I joined them with Deputy Commissioner Teijiro Furukawa and observed the discussion, which lasted until past 7:00. The prime minister said that he had done everything he could for Okinawa. "At this point, I must ask you, Mr. Governor, for a realistic response."

Mr. Ota was stubborn. "I must pull together the opinions within the prefecture," he said. "I can't say 'yes' right here and now. I will not have the understanding of the people." Mayor Higa had arrived at the official residence earlier but we had him wait in the office of the executive secretary to the Prime Minister so as to avoid a direct confrontation with Mr. Ota. After Mr. Ota left the office through one door, frowning, Mr. Higa entered through another door.

The prime minister approached Mr. Higa and clasped the elderly mayor's hands with both of his own. Mr. Higa, in his usual heavy tone tinged with convincing age, explained his decision. "The most desirable relocation would be outside the prefecture. However, if that is not possible, in order to save people suffering from the base, I will accept it. I ask that you assure us that you will promote development of this northern region that our ancestors protected. This is my will."

Mr. Hashimoto, an emotional man, was nearly driven to tears. The elderly mayor had written a *ryuka*, a traditional Okinawan poem, on a sheet of paper. He said it was his farewell poem: "*girin somukaran, arinshite raran, shian teru bashino watari gurisha*" (I cannot turn my back on my duty, I must cross the remaining bridge). Mayor Higa recited in a heavy, dramatic tone. "I must decide whether to move forward or to retire," he said. "Whichever I choose, I need to be prepared to live or die. I am ready to die politically and choose to accept that for the promotion of the region. This is what this *ryuka* means."

The next day, at the extraordinary cabinet meeting, Mr. Hashimoto handed out a paper summarizing Mayor Higa's words and reportedly read the *ryuka* aloud. The *Nihon Keizai Shimbun* reported, "After the Prime Minister read the remarks of Mayor Higa in a tearful voice, the Cabinet room fell so silent you could hear a pin drop."

Back in Nago, Mayor Higa read out the statement he had prepared. "While some 2,300 more people voted NO than those who voted YES, the number did not total 50% of the town's voters. After serious and careful consideration of the weight of each vote, I have accepted construction. The small burden that Nago accepts will eliminate the dangers of Futenma and lead to the downsizing of bases." Then the mayor submitted his resignation to the Nago City Council chairman and left the City Hall, saying, "Please let me disappear quietly among the masses."

Nago's mayoral election was held on February 8, 1998, with the entire nation looking on. It was a difficult election, but Deputy Mayor Kishimoto ran for Mr. Higa's seat and beat his opponent by 1,150 votes. With this, the move to Henoko was certain, I thought. It even looked as though a majority of the prefectural citizens would accept it. In the Okinawan Governor's election later that year, Keiichi Inamine, a member of our Okinawa round-table conference was elected to replace Governor Ota.

The Illusionary Ideal Proposal

Mr. Kishimoto thought that if certain conditions were met, Nago City should agree to the construction of a heliport for the sake of its economic growth. He was prepared to appeal to the hearts of the people personally if the prefecture was unable to use logic to persuade its citizens to support the relocation. However, amidst months of constant tension and hard work on the matter, my close friend, the new Mayor Kishimoto, died due to poor health. He was 62. A full year and a half had passed since the relocation announcement. Nobody ever imagined that more than 20 years later, it still would not be possible to decide when Futenma Air Station would be returned.

I left my post as special advisor to the prime minister in 1998, after two years, but the issue of relocating Futenma never left my mind. I was concerned that the SBF (Sea-Based Facility) plan that the government had decided on in April 2006 after difficult negotiations would cause too much friction with the citizens of the prefecture because, among other reasons, the project was too large and walls would have to be built, reclaiming an area underwater along Oura Bay where coral grows.

The Prime Minister's Office, the Ministry of Defense, Okinawa Prefecture, Nago City, the U.S. military, and a great number of politicians had become involved, rocking negotiations more than ever. They argued over the style of a Sea-Based Facility to be built. Fierce conflicts over the Nago Lite plan and Camp Schwab (interior and coastal) plan, in addition to L-shaped, X-shaped, and other runway plans continued, mostly between the Ministry of Defense and Nago City. Finally in 2006, an agreement was reached to pursue a V-shaped plan, in which two runways would be combined to form a V, but the Okinawan side continued to attempt further modifications. At the center of negotiations right from the start was Vice Defense Minister Takemasa Moriya. He was a friend of mine, but in 2007, he was arrested on suspicion of accepting golf invitations from businesses in exchange for favors and convicted of bribery and perjury. Japan lost a precious patriot.

The Democratic Party of Japan defeated the Liberal Democratic Party in the August 2009 elections, giving rise to a non-LDP government for the first time since the Morihiro Hosokawa administration in August 1993. The Cabinet was formed under Prime Minister Yukio Hatoyama. During his election campaign, Mr. Hatoyama's breakthrough was repeatedly making promises that the relocation of Futenma would "at very best" be outside of Okinawa prefecture. He stalled when the practicality of this became impossible. To add insult to injury, the new mayor elected in Nago City in January 2010 opposed the Henoko plan, once again triggering anti-base sentiment among the locals.

One day, Prime Minister Hatoyama called me out of the blue. He desperately wanted me to help him with the Futenma problem. I opposed most DPJ security policies because they had no understanding of the importance of deterrence. However, if the Prime Minister needed my help in resolving the Futenma relocation issue, which wasn't going anywhere, it was up to me to step away from my position and lend him a hand.

I had retained a number of drawings prepared by engineer bureaucrats that had been helping me when I was a special adviser to Prime Minister Hashimoto. One day during the summer of 1997, I took these drawings and submitted them to Chief Cabinet Secretary Kajiyama. "Special Advisor, you have made a good plan here," he said. "But right now, all sorts of people are coming up with all sorts of their own plans. Soon, the time will come when all of those proposals are rejected. Let's wait until then and settle the matter with this plan." After he spoke, he put my drawings in his safe in the Chief Cabinet Office. Mr. Kajiyama died three years later without ever using them.

Three months after the Hatoyama administration was established, I was summoned to Mr. Hatoyama's office to present an explanation of the Okinawa Issue. I complied on December 26, 2009, and at a subsequent meeting, Mr. Hatoyama asked me if there could be an alternative solution to the existing plan. I took out the old drawing I had proposed to Chief Cabinet Secretary and worked with my colleagues from back then to make further improvements. Prime Minister Hatoyama showed great interest in the drawing. At first glance, this plan seemed similar to the Nago Lite plan proposed by the U.S. military in August 2005, but the concept was completely different.

First of all, the construction would be on the reef farthest away from the shore and in direct contact with the open sea, as I had once agreed on with Nago Mayor Kishimoto. A single runway would be built there, connecting Camp Schwab on the other side with a pier, as per the existing SACO agreement. The entire Henoko reef is in shallow water, only about two meters deep, and the sun shining right through it was said to have made the seawater temperature too high for coral to grow. An avid underwater diver, I had thrown an oxygen tank on my back and dove in to see for myself. Other than a very small amount of seaweed, it was a barren shoal with nothing but sand and stone.

My engineers had come up with a stunning design, with a tunnel built under the runway. Seawater would flow through that with considerable driving force. The area surrounding the runway would be dug deeper, so the seawater escaping the tunnel would flow around the runway, creating a circulation throughout the shallows. As a result, the stagnant high-temperature seawater would be replaced by cold seawater from the open sea, dropping the water temperature of the entire reef. The coral breeding technology that the locals had already developed could be used to give birth to many new coral settlements on the Henoko reef. The idea was to transform the sandy bed into a rich coral reef. This plan would create a new environment, rather than destroying one.

The plan included another revolutionary construction method. Where would the sand to build the runway come from? We focused on the Haneji Inland Sea, also in Nago City, buried in sludge. It had reached the point where ships could no longer pass through due to the amount of sediment being washed down from the rivers. We decided to dredge this sludge and solidify it with a coagulant, then use that to build the runway. In the meantime, this would also revive the sea of Haneji. In consideration of the Okinawan people's sentiment, one more important feature was to make the runway removable. We designed the plan so that after decades, if the land were to be returned, the man-made island could be stripped of concrete and planted with trees, turning it into a natural island.

At the time, the government's plan was estimated to cost more than 600 billion yen, an estimate that soon ballooned to 940 billion yen, whereas the estimated total construction cost for our plan was 150 billion yen. The more I talked with people in Okinawa, the more

I became convinced that this was the only plan that would survive in Okinawa.

Our plan to stay true to the SACO agreement and reduce the burden on Okinawa was far superior to the government's plan. Mr. Hatoyama was pleased to see my drawings. Mr. Hatoyama asked me to explain my plan to the Foreign Minister, Minister of Defense, and Chief Cabinet Secretary, who were also happy with it. Quite a few government office executives also agreed.

Then why was it crushed? There was furious resistance from people I had never imagined. They were the Ministry of Defense engineers who had been working on the "V-shaped design." Our team answered all the technical questions they asked, but the Ministry of Defense never responded. In the end, these people reported to the Prime Minister's Office that this idea was not feasible, without even mentioning our rationale, and the plan was dropped before I knew it.

The Democratic Party, taking power for the first time, lacked knowledge and experience in many policy matters, inviting increasing criticism from the public. Inevitably, its political leadership was weak, and although the government had changed, it was not possible to overcome the resistance of the bureaucrats, who were unwilling to alter the existing plan. Prime Minister Hatoyama was unwilling to bear the burden of a negative legacy of the LDP era, which the Henoko relocation represented. But time ran out on him. In only nine months he had to resign as prime minister due to poor management—something he probably never imagined. After that, Naoto Kan became the new prime minister. Prime Minister Kan too, called me over and I went into the Prime Minister's Office through the back door late at night. The two of us talked alone for many hours. By then, however, we had already missed the opportunity.

On December 14, 2018, amid fierce protest by the Okinawan people, large amounts of earth and sand started being poured into Henoko and construction began. There was no place for me anymore. Why, then, am I again bringing up this story of defeat? Our plan was made by engineers who were former bureaucrats. This is to keep a clear record of the people who continued to work under criticism from their own ministries by making a plan that contradicted what the government wanted to do.

Outlook for the Okinawa Problem

Today, the so-called Okinawa problem is synonymous with the Futenma relocation issue. Most Okinawa-related problems are concentrated here. From the beginning, the Futenma problem was destined
to follow a long and complicated path. In 1996, what the U.S. and
Japan's governments agreed on in the first place was not the "return"
of Futenma, but the "relocation" of Futenma, which meant moving
Futenma Air Station away from a densely populated residential area.

Within the central government, the only people who knew about
that day's U.S.–Japan agreement were the Prime Minister's Office and
a very few in the Ministry of Foreign Affairs. The Defense Agency
and the Defense Facilities Administration Agency, who would have
to find a relocation site, were only notified one week prior to the
public announcement. The Defense Agency was shocked. Where
on earth did the Ministry of Foreign Affairs intend to relocate the
Futenma Marine Corps. Air Station?

Okinawa's Governor Masahide Ota, too, had only been informed
that Futenma would be "returned." Whether he took that to mean
"relocated" or "returned" was crucial. I confirmed this with Governor Ota when we were alone. His explanation was consistent and
clearly showed that he initially perceived this as an unconditional
return. Things had started off on the wrong foot right from the very
beginning. In other words, from the moment of the announcement,
Futenma became a "damage control" project, to minimize the damage caused by "the decision that was made without a relocation
site." From that moment, the Ministry of Defense developed a deep-
seated mistrust toward the Ministry of Foreign Affairs for the way
they grabbed the best part of the story, about the gorgeous "return,"
without telling the Defense Ministry about the difficult task of "relocation" that would be thrust upon them.

If Japan's central government had consulted with the Okinawa
Governor at the time of its agreement with the United States regarding the relocation of Futenma base, things would likely have turned
out differently. They should have told the governor that the U.S.
had agreed to relocate Futenma, and asked for the help of Okinawa
Prefecture in finding the best destination.

If the Governor had said "yes" at that stage, the people would have welcomed relocation of the Marine Corps. Air Station away from densely populated Futenma and the construction of alternative facilities would have proceeded smoothly.

If the answer had been "no," the government ought to have taken measures to reduce noise and accident risks, giving up on having the Futenma land returned for the time being. I can't help but think that if this had happened before Futenma had become a political issue, Governor Ota, who always said that it should never be all or nothing, would have chosen relocation as the next best option, and would have responded with a "yes."

Residents of Okinawa have a special character. The people there are patient. Once they are driven beyond their limit, however, resistance movements break out like wildfire. Okinawa was returned to Japan in 1972 by the decision of President Nixon, but in the background anti-base conflict had intensified. In 1968, a B-52 aircraft crashed at Kadena Air Base, igniting a fight against U.S. bases by the locals. While all of Okinawa was abuzz, the U.S. government concluded that "Okinawa should be returned to Japan and its security should be responsibility of the Japanese government. It would be to our benefit to use the bases in a stable fashion within that environment." This became Nixon's deciding factor in 1971 to return Okinawa to Japan.

After the Futenma base was designated for relocation, it became "rootless" and unstable. Without any specific prospect of having the land returned to Okinawa, an accident such as a Futenma helicopter crashing into the surrounding city would trigger uncontrollable mass protests. And if the Futenma relocation were to not go well, the US 7th Fleet, the 5th Air Force and the 3rd Marine Expeditionary Force that make up the U.S. forces in Japan would be left with no choice but to leave Okinawa. The Japan–U.S. Security Alliance would weaken at once. The basic message from the U.S. would be, "Okay, Japan, do it yourself now." This would be a welcome situation for China. That is why the Okinawan problem had to be settled in a stable manner no matter what happened.

With construction already underway, what is the next step? Okinawan sentiment towards the United States is generally positive. As remarks from Town Council members of Kin suggest, American military families are quite welcome in Okinawa. However, the current plan is to move Marine Corps administrative units and their families to Guam, leaving only combat units in Okinawa. If this decision were to be reversed, the attitude of the prefectural citizens would dramatically improve. I've heard that there's debate even within the Marine Corps about whether to leave "brain" or "muscle" in Okinawa. With political judgement at the highest level both in Japan and the U.S., deploying the troops so that the brains remain in Okinawa and the muscles move to Guam would not be impossible.

Another important thing is to arrange all bases in Okinawa for joint use by the U.S. military and the Japan Self-Defense Forces. This has been strongly advocated by Richard Armitage and Joseph Nye, former senior officials in the Clinton and Bush administrations and the authors of a series of influential reports on the U.S.–Japan alliance. I will not go into detail here, but there are many more steps that can be taken to improve the situation. More important than anything else is for the Japanese government to show its basic policy of collaboration with Okinawa—not through words, but through action. Leaders in Tokyo even told me that they were willing to put their lives on the line for Okinawa. There was an emotional sense of unity with Okinawa. This was also the case with Former Prime Minister Keizo Obuchi and Sadanori Yamanaka, former Director-General of the Administrative Management Agency.

The Hashimoto Cabinet positioned the Okinawan problem as the nation's top priority project along with the overall administrative reform of the country. Both Prime Minister Hashimoto and Chief Cabinet Secretary Kajiyama had strong feelings about Okinawa. Mr. Hashimoto often said to me, "Please work for Okinawa. I entrust my neck and Kaji-san's neck to you."

Kajiyama often cited words sent by World War II Navy Admiral Minoru Ota in his last telegram[26] before his suicide in 1945, which described the suffering and dedication of the Okinawan people: "The people of Okinawa Prefecture fought like this. Please give special consideration to the citizens of the prefecture in the future."

The Okinawan problem cannot be dealt with only by military rationality and technical theory. Unless a politician shows up who is willing to put his life on the line to save the plight of Okinawa, there is no moving forward. Now that Mr. Hashimoto and Mr. Kajiyama's generation is gone, there are no more politicians who will work with Okinawa with their kind of passion. With the future of Okinawa uncertain, the gap between the islands and the mainland is growing. According to a survey conducted by Asahi Shimbun in 2017, some 51% of Okinawans supported having a special governing body, surpassing the 35% who said they were satisfied with the way things were. Moreover, 4% said that Okinawa should become independent of Japan. This is something that must not be neglected.

PART FOUR

OPERATION DESERT SHIELD—JAPAN'S FAILURE AND U.S. ARROGANCE

PRELUDE TO DISASTER

The Plan to Dispatch Patrol Ships to the Persian Gulf

OPERATION DESERT SHIELD (the Gulf Crisis) began on August 2, 1990, after Saddam Hussein's invasion of Kuwait. Then, Desert Storm (the Gulf War) started on January 17, 1991, and ended in an overwhelming victory for the United States on February 28. Japan's poor response to this war is still remembered as the greatest failure in Japan's foreign policy since the end of World War II. Coupled with the unfair handling of Japan by the United States, it cast a shadow on the Japan–U.S. alliance for a long time.

Japan had seen the foreshadowing of failure three years before that. At a time when the Iran-Iraq War threatened the navigation of commercial ships in the Persian Gulf, Japan was unable to take part in the international effort to secure the freedom of navigation by sending military or non-military government ships. It is undeniable that this created *a priori* thinking within the Japanese Government that Japan's direct involvement in the Persian Gulf would not be possible. This is where the story needs to begin.

In July 1987, in an attempt to block maritime traffic to the Gulf Arab States and especially to Kuwait, Iran threatened tankers from all countries heading to Kuwait, using speed boats and Silkworm missiles as well as floating sea mines.

The Kuwaiti government asked the United States to guard commercial ships. The U.S. took charge of escorting commercial vessels in the Gulf, calculating that if they did not, Kuwait would go to the Soviet Union for protection and the Persian Gulf would become Soviet waters. In order to organize a multinational fleet to escort the merchant ships, the United States called on NATO, and the United

Kingdom, Netherlands, Italy and Belgium joined. There was a desire that Japan join as well. After all, Japan had the largest number of tankers sailing through the Gulf. Nonetheless, because the Japanese Constitution explicitly prohibits participation in multinational fleets under the right to collective self-defense, joining the fleet was not an option. The United States understood this.

Given this, the U.S. inquired: Could Japan dispatch minesweepers to remove the mines? American minesweeping relied on helicopters while Japan had powerful ship-based minesweeping capabilities, and sweeping the sea for mines is purely an act of defense, so Japan should be able to cooperate, thus the request.

At the time, Japanese tankers sailing through the Gulf displayed large Japanese flags painted on deck as if to say, "Don't shoot, we are non-belligerent Japan!" When I saw a big photo of this in a newspaper, I was dumbstruck but also felt that a civilian ship without the protection of its own navy really had no other choice.

I thought there was no way that Japan, the largest beneficiary of ensuring security in the Persian Gulf, could get away with not making any contributions at all. Officials gathered a number of times to discuss measures, meeting in the office of Takakazu Kuriyama, then-Deputy Minister for Foreign Affairs (U.S. equivalent of Deputy Under Secretary). At that time, I was the Director of the National Security Affairs Division, North American Bureau. After a meeting one day in September, Kuriyama kept me behind after everyone else had left. Once we were alone, he said to me, "Japan can't sit back and do nothing. That won't work internationally, either. Still, sending minesweepers to the battle zone to remove Iranian mines would be an act of collective self-defense, wouldn't it? Can you think of a good way to do this?"

Submerged in thought, Kuriyama gazed into the distance and the silence continued. I decided to suggest something that I had been thinking about for a long time: "If the Maritime Self-Defense Force can't do it, how about having Coast Guard patrol boats go near the Persian Gulf? The U.S. wants the Japanese government to respond with something other than just dishing out cash. They're not saying that we have to send our Self-Defense Forces. If we can send government vessels, it will have the same effect as dispatching the SDF."

The Japan Coast Guard (JCG) has a history of removing mines from the Japan Sea immediately after WWII. When the Self-Defense Forces were established, this mission was transferred to the Maritime Self-Defense Force, but maintaining contact with civilian ships is a specialty of the Coast Guard. When mines are found by the international navy in the Persian Gulf, the Coast Guard could act as an information center and send out notices to commercial ships of all the countries in the area, telling them to detour around dangerous areas. The patrol ships could remain on the outskirts of the Hormuz Strait. Couldn't they be used to send navigation information to civilian fleets in the Gulf? It doesn't matter how it would be done. What is important is for Japanese government vessels to participate in international activities for the safety of the Persian Gulf.

Kuriyama's facial expression changed. Smiling, he said: "You're right. There are no legal issues there. Good idea. Let's do it." I immediately went to the JCG to see Masakazu Henmi, Director General for Security and Rescue Operations, and Tomonori Nishiyama, Director for the Second Security Division. JCG is a part of the Ministry of Land, Infrastructure, and Transport (MLIT) across the street from the Ministry of Foreign Affairs. The two men were waiting for me in Henmi's office. We enjoyed a trusting relationship since the USS New Jersey had made its port call at Sasebo despite fierce opposition due to suspected links to nuclear weapons. One look at both Henmi and Nishiyama waiting for me in the room with smiles on their faces convinced me that they would cooperate in this operation as well.

Although I had made those suggestions to Kuriyama, I really wasn't sure if the Coast Guard had long-leg patrol ships with sufficient cruising distance to reach Hormuz. Until then, interpellations in the Diet had always implicitly assumed that the area of the Coast Guard's activity only extended as far as the Straits of Malacca. No matter how willing the Coast Guard was, without the cruising distance there could be no plan.

But the bald-headed Henmi, who stood out like Neptune, grinned and said, "Don't worry. For times like this, we have equipped large patrol ships over 6000 tons with one more tank. We have explained to the Ministry of Finance that it is a reserve tank, but by connecting the two tanks with a pipe, the ship can run forever. Just give us the order and we can make it to the Persian Gulf."

I was awed by their wisdom. It just might work. However, negotiating with the MLIT, which had jurisdiction over JCG, was not so easy. Discussions were tough. One lunch break in September there was an incoming call to the Ministry of Foreign Affairs from Transport Minister Ryutaro Hashimoto. Both Kuriyama and Hiroaki Fujii, Director-General of the North American Bureau, my immediate superior, were out of the office, so the phone call came to me. From the other end of the line came a threatening voice. "So this is the Director of Security Affairs, is it? I know your name. I hear you're trying to waste a bunch of my men."

It was a gangster-like threat. This was my unfortunate first encounter with Hashimoto, the man whom I would report to as special aide when he took the office of the Prime Minister of Japan nine years later. Anyone with a faint heart would be intimidated by his offensive opening remarks. This was his style. I figured he was calling from his office surrounded by MLIT subordinates, showing them how he could talk to MOFA, which he disliked. In that case, even though I was a mere director, I had to counter him on the spot.

"I know that this is a difficult decision for you, Mr. Minister. But unless you approve, Japan will have to face the same question in the future, and its commercial ships will have to stay outside, beyond the boundaries of the international community. It's for the safety of Japanese tankers. We cannot just sit and watch other nations protecting them for us. Minister, please!"

The good thing about Hashimoto was that if you stood up to him, he would listen carefully. In the end he said, "I'll keep your words in mind." Later, I received notice from the JCG saying that Minister Hashimoto now supports the dispatching JCG vessels, under the condition that he travels with the first ship. It was just like him—ever the kabuki actor.

Failure of the Plan and Secretary Weinberger's Support

We had the approval of Transport Minister Hashimoto, the minister in charge, and the stage was set to seek the approval of the Prime Minister. The gatekeeper was the Chief Cabinet Secretary, whose consent was required before bringing any policy decision to the Prime Minister. Masaharu Gotoda was the man in that position. If Gotoda, a pacifist, were to say yes, Prime Minister Yasuhiro Nakasone would most likely agree, since he had been quite positive about Japan cooperating in the field of international security. Well, I naively thought, Gotoda shouldn't have a problem with this as long as we send a patrol ship, not an SDF naval vessel, and remain outside the Strait of Hormuz.

I followed Kuriyama to the Chief Cabinet Secretary's office located next to the Prime Minister's office. Gotoda, originally a Commissioner General of the National Police Agency, was often called a "razor" for his sharp thinking and quick reactions, and had been feared by bureaucrats. It was unimaginable that I would become close to him in later years. His door was not open to accompanying officials, so I had to wait outside. After a long time, Kuriyama finally came out with a grimace on his face.

"He didn't go for it. He dared me to try and get anywhere with this, and if we did, he would stamp it out." Gotoda was not just saying no. He was vehemently against it. Gotoda told Kuriyama that sending Coast Guard patrol vessels just because we couldn't send the SDF would be circumventing the law—a cheap trick. Say we did send a patrol vessel. Any attack against a tanker would force the patrol ship to enter the Gulf to attempt to rescue. If that were to happen, Japan would find itself involved in combat. Gotoda stubbornly refused.

I had been speaking to Deputy Assistant Secretary of Defense Karl Jackson in Washington nearly every day. Jackson was a small man, with a good sense of humor. He did not intimidate others. When I first met him, he reminded me of Detective Columbo, the main character played by Peter Falk in the famous TV drama. He always wore a ragged raincoat, asking sharp questions as he scratched his head. Jackson smiled more than Columbo, but his stature and vibe were similar.

The theory that Japan was free-riding on U.S. security guarantees had begun escalating in the U.S. Congress. Jackson had kept Defense Secretary Caspar Weinberger updated in detail on Japanese deliberations. The entire Department of Defense watched with interest to see if Japan would reach the epoch-making decision to send patrol ships to the Gulf area. But the result was a firm NO.

A few years later, Gotoda told me the backstory: He had reminded Prime Minister Nakasone that such a grave decision must be approved at the Cabinet Meeting. Nakasone replied, "Of course." Then Gotoda threatened that he wouldn't sign at the meeting. By law, the Cabinet decision must be unanimous, which meant that any Cabinet member opposed to a measure must be relieved from duties. So, when Gotoda refused to sign, Nakasone would have to dismiss him, which in effect would destroy the proposal.

For a Chief Cabinet Secretary who opposes the Prime Minister's policy to resign, much less be dismissed, is unheard of. To begin with, Chief Cabinet Secretary Gotoda was a powerful man who was sent in by the Tanaka faction, the largest in Japan, at the request of Prime Minister Nakasone. Nakasone was the leader of the LDP's smallest faction and would not have become prime minister without the support of the Tanaka faction. By having control over the post of Chief Cabinet Secretary, the cornerstone of the cabinet, the Tanaka faction had been able to keep an eye on the Nakasone cabinet and exert influence. There was likely more to it as well.

I cannot go into detail, but in every cabinet, it is the Chief Cabinet Secretary, not the Prime Minister, who manages the treasury, also known as the secret funds of the Prime Minister's Office. For the Tanaka faction to take the post of Chief Cabinet Secretary in exchange for supporting the Nakasone cabinet meant that the Tanaka faction was in control of the secret funds.

If Gotoda were to resign, Nakasone could lose the support of the Tanaka faction, in which case his cabinet could not survive. In other words, Gotoda had veto power in the Cabinet. As a result, this story was finished. Of course, Deputy Assistant Secretary Jackson and the Department of Defense were greatly disappointed. Still, they did commend the efforts of the Japanese government; they knew that our efforts were not only words and that we did everything we could to dispatch our ships. Several days later, I received a call at home from Jackson suggesting that Japan could probably provide a "Decca System." "Decca?" I exclaimed, "You know we can't do weapons." He laughed.

"This one will be easy," he said. "Take it from me." I learned that

Decca was a radio lighthouse for navigation support. The device can pinpoint the location of a ship by transmitting radio waves from multiple locations. This would make accurate minesweeping possible. This, we could do. A ministry meeting was immediately held at Deputy Foreign Minister Kuriyama's office. Acceptance was immediate.

Director-General Hiroaki Fujii (later Ambassador to U.K.) took me to Prime Minister Nakasone at his residence right away. It was a Sunday. I knew that the best way to brief a person of esteem was to use a big map. I had my staff plot 10 locations of where Decca lighthouses would be located on a huge map of the Persian Gulf and laid it out on the Prime Minister's table. Nakasone was pleased. "This is good! No one should have a problem with it. Good plan."

Based on this sequence of events, Defense Secretary Weinberger made a formal request to Defense Minister Kurihara, who visited Washington on October 2, to install the Decca radio lighthouses. The system would cost only 1.5 billion yen (15 million USD) to install. It was a deliberately easy pitch.

The cost of the Decca lighthouses was trivial. The U.S. didn't need to ask Japan for the money. Secretary Weinberger gave Japan this easy role because Japan had done its best to dispatch patrol ships and should not be alienated. He strongly spoke for Japan to the American people and testified to the U.S. Congress that Japan too, was making an invaluable contribution. In his book *Fighting for Peace*, Secretary Weinberger wrote:

> *By this time we were getting very substantial help for our activities in the Gulf. All our allies benefited. We received several ships from the British, the Dutch, the Belgians, the Italians, and offers from the Germans. Also, Japan, although prevented from sending any combat vessels—its constitution provides for defensive activities only—agreed to provide a valuable and much needed navigational system to help our minesweepers as they methodically went about clearing the Gulf waters of Iranian mines. The system is now installed in Kuwait.[27]*

Weinberger was a Defense Secretary who understood the nature of our alliance and approached Japan by soliciting its spontaneous effort rather than a coercion. This approach worked well and brought great benefits, not only to Japan but also to the United States, as Japan would not ultimately get away with spending just 1.5 billion yen. His strategy toward Japan was formulated in large part on the advice of Richard Armitage, Assistant Secretary of Defense for International Security Affairs. The Government of Japan knew that this episode would not end with the petty amount of 1.5 billion yen ($15 million). Although no promises were made between Japan and the United States, Japan decided to increase its financial burden regarding the U.S. military stationed in Japan and boldly passed an agreement in the Diet the following year to cover all expenses for Japanese employees working on U.S. military bases in the country. These labor-related costs accumulated to equal $30 billion as of 2020. As I mentioned earlier, this was not treated as a political matter, but quietly settled at the administrative level.

Gotoda never did come around to our point of view. In his book *Sei to Kan* (Politics and Government),[28] he severely criticized the Self-Defense Force dispatch to the Persian Gulf area and even wrote that it was unconstitutional. Our concept was that of a patrol boat, but he wouldn't listen to us. I couldn't accept that. Which part of a patrol boat issuing navigation safety information from outside Hormuz is in violation of the Constitution? It never occurred to Gotoda to question the view that Japanese vessels, the largest fleet in the Gulf, should be protected by other countries at their own risk while Japan idly watches without raising a finger.

At the time, I hated Chief Cabinet Secretary Gotoda for crushing the only contributions Japan could make. Much later however, after I left the Ministry, the former head of the Cabinet Security Affairs Office Atsuyuki Sasa and the former Deputy Cabinet Secretary Junzo Matoba invited me to join their group, which periodically had dinner with Gotoda, and we became quite close as individuals. "Are you telling me that those things back then were all your doing?" he scolded. "You and (Atsuyuki) Sasa are dangerous as heck." Gotoda's face was smiling but his eyes were not. I suggested dispatching patrol boats on several occasions, but Gotoda, who is usually flexible, would not budge regarding this point.

In the United States, uniformed personnel are more cautious than civilians about using military power. This is because soldiers know the destructive power all too well. Gotoda, who had experienced war, was far more wary about dispatching the Self Defense Force than members of our generation were.

WHY WAS JAPAN DEFEATED?

President George H. W. Bush

THE EMPEROR SHOWA'S mourning ceremony was held on February 24, 1989, at a simple funeral hall set in a clearing in a wooded part of Shinjuku Gyoen. It was a freezing day, with cold rain and intermittent sleet. The attendees were seated under a tent, but a sharp wind blew through. During a break partway through the ceremony, the Japanese guests moved to an adjacent facility that was heated. One of the officials came to report to me because I was supervising the plan for how the Japanese side would treat U.S. President George Bush.

"I offered to usher President Bush inside the warm room, but he smiled and said, 'Oh, no. It's our duty to remain here,' and would not move from his seat in the freezing environment," the official told me. Apparently, President Bush, along with King Hussein of Jordan and a number of other heads of state continued to sit in the cold wind, with their coat collars turned up.

The way President Bush handled the U.S. Japan relationship was always from the strategic point of view. On February 1, 1989, just two weeks after taking office as president, Bush held a U.S.–Japan summit meeting in the East Wing of the White House with Noboru Takeshita, then Prime Minister of Japan. After discussions about international affairs in the morning, we moved on to a working lunch. The planned agenda was international security. Economic issues were not going to be addressed.

At lunchtime, however, the U.S. brought an army of economic ministers, including Commerce Secretary Robert Mosbacher, U.S. Trade Representative Carla Hills, and the Treasury Secretary. The Japan side felt defensive. Was the U.S. planning to negotiate rice and

Yukio Okamoto (at left, in the back), 43, attends a summit meeting between Prime Minister Noboru Takeshita and U.S. President George H. W. Bush in Washington D.C. in early February, 1989. Okamoto was then Director of the First North American Division of MOFA's North American Affairs Bureau.

semiconductors? Were they planning to take us by surprise? Then, as lunch began, President Bush said, "During lunch today, I would like to discuss the most important topic between Japan and the United States." Then he had Secretary of State James Baker explain U.S. policy toward the Soviet Union. In response, Prime Minister Takeshita had Foreign Minister Sosuke Uno explain Japan's Soviet Union policy.

For the next hour and a half, the discussion remained focused on strategies for how Japan and the U.S. should cooperate in relation to the Soviet Union and China. Not a word was mentioned about rice or semiconductors or anything else to do with economic issues. Later, I asked Karl Jackson, the detective Colombo, who by then had become an advisor to the President: "Why were so many economic ministers there, when the topic was international security?"

Jackson replied: "That was a direct order from the President. He wanted to show the economic secretaries two things: one, how broad and deep the U.S.–Japan relationship is, and two, how close the two countries are working at the top level. His message to them was: 'Conduct your individual economic negotiations based on this foundation.'" I was moved. The posture of the President will inevi-

Yukio Okamoto attends a summit meeting between Prime Minister Toshiki Kaifu and President George H. W. Bush in Palms Springs, California in March 1990, a time before the Gulf Crisis and the Gulf War, when Japan–U.S. relations were strong.

tably influence the basic stance of his secretaries and officials, and the American policy as a whole will place proper emphasis on Japan.

In March 1990, President Bush invited Prime Minister Toshiki Kaifu, who had succeeded Noboru Takeshita in August the previous year, to Palm Springs, California. The invitation had arrived only two weeks before the meeting. Setting up a U.S.–Japan Summit on short notice was not an easy task. How were we supposed to handle the logistics, especially back then, when Japan did not have a prime minister's special plane? What means of transport could we use? What must we prepare for the talks? How do we coordinate arrangements with the U.S. side? How do we get the press there? There was a lot of work to be done.

Not going was not an option. This would be the first time that the leaders of the United States and Japan would leave the big cities and meet in a relaxed atmosphere since the 1972 Nixon–Tanaka meeting in Hawaii. It had been 18 years.

"Is it possible to prepare for a summit in two weeks?" Director-General of the North American Bureau Hiroaki Fujii asked me. I was not confident, but I immediately responded, "We'll make it in time." Then after continued sleepless nights, my staff completed the administrative preparations. The Palm Springs Summit went well. It was a moment when the already close U.S.–Japan relationship from the Reagan days, when George Bush was Vice-President, became even deeper.

However, five months later, a tsunami washed over the U.S.–Japan relationship: Saddam Hussein's invasion of Kuwait and the subsequent Gulf Crisis and Japan's failed response. The disappointment toward Japan that spread throughout the United States shackled U.S.–Japan relations for a long time after that. Nonetheless, President Bush valued the relationship with Japan right up until the end of his term. Despite the headwinds of the U.S.–Japan relationship, President Bush invited Prime Minister Kaifu twice the following year, to his very special places, Newport Beach and Kennebunkport, continuing to send the message that Japan is an important country. The reason the U.S.–Japan relationship was not decisively severed over the Gulf War was because of a statesman named George H. W. Bush.

Outbreak of the Gulf Crisis

Operation Desert Shield started on August 2, 1990, when Saddam Hussein suddenly invaded Kuwait with 100,000 forces. I was then the MOFA director in charge of U.S.–Japan relations. President Bush decided to go to war with Iraq and naturally expected Japan to offer support. However, the Japanese government could not send the minesweepers, transport ships, aircraft and personnel that were expected by the U.S. The relationship between Japan and the United States fell to its worst level since World War II.

Takakazu Kuriyama, who fought to send Coast Guard Ships to the Gulf three years earlier, was my boss in several positions. This time he was the Vice Foreign Minister. He has written that every day of the Gulf Crisis had been a trial worse than any he had never experienced in his life as a diplomat. He said that Japan's postwar diplomacy had been questioned from the bottom up, and the very existence of the Japan–U.S. alliance was in jeopardy.

Initially, nobody thought that Iraq's invasion of Kuwait might have a major impact on U.S.–Japan relations. I, too, did not have a sense of impending crisis and had headed off on an official trip to China, entrusting my work in Tokyo to my talented deputy, Kenichiro Sasae (who later became Ambassador to the U.S.). However, the situation greatly changed when, on August 8, President Bush made the decision to dispatch 50,000 soldiers, including the 82nd Airborne Division, to Saudi Arabia and on August 14, called Prime Minister Kaifu on the telephone to request support from Japan's Self-Defense Forces.

I returned from Shanghai immediately, and Sasae filled me in on the details. He told me that there was no consensus at the meeting held under Deputy Minister Kuriyama because of the argument over the constitutional ban on the right of collective self-defense. The Director-General of the North American Bureau Shinichiro Matsuura had insisted that as an ally, Japan should make the move and dispatch the SDF without the use of force—such as minesweepers and SDF personnel—but could not get the consent of other attendees. The only remaining options were financial support for the coalition forces, dispatch of medical teams, and providing private ships and aircraft commissioned by the government for transporting materials and personnel.

I was feeling the after-effects of failing to send patrol ships to the Persian Gulf area three years earlier. First of all, not being able to dispatch patrol ships at that time had instilled the perception that dispatching SDF vessels to the Persian Gulf was impossible from the start. Secondly, three years earlier, we had successfully created a nice clean package that included Decca navigation system, plus cost-bearing of U.S. military base workers by Japan. Some politicians thought that since the U.S. gave us credit for installing Decca lighthouses without having to dispatch patrol ships, a financial way out would work this time, too.

However, that successful package was made possible by people in Washington, Secretary Casper Weinberger, Richard Armitage and Karl Jackson, who knew the delicacies and weaknesses of Japan. At the time of the Gulf War, there were no longer such people in powerful positions.

The GOJ's front towards the Gulf War had three dimensions. One was the enactment of the Law on Cooperation for United Nations

Peacekeeping Operations, which would allow Japan to dispatch Government officials people to the Gulf. Although politically it was the most important operation because it would expand Japan's future options for international contribution, the government could not reach consensus regarding how to involve the SDF, and the bureaucracy could not speak with one voice to the opposition parties. Although an enormous amount of time and energy were spent trying to make this work, the draft law was eventually scrapped on November 8.

In my view, MOFA should have spent more time on the 'groundwork' of explaining and soliciting opposition members, one by one, for the approval. Meanwhile, Washington didn't appreciate that the Japanese style of making arrangements was the Japanese government's top priority. In *The Gulf War and Japan*,[29] a book published by Asahi Shimbun in an attempt to keep a record immediately after the war, a U.S. government official is quoted as saying, "We don't know much about it. We are not particularly interested."

A second dimension was to make Saddam Hussein release the 213 Japanese he had taken as hostages on August 17. Former Prime Minister Nakasone visited Baghdad to negotiate directly with Saddam Hussein and as a result, the hostages were gradually released, and by December, the hostages from all countries had been released. As MOFA's overwhelmed Middle East Bureau was focusing on these hostage negotiations, I thought this gave our North America Bureau a chance to hijack the third dimension—Japan's contribution to the multinational forces in the Gulf. I seized the opportunity to focus on that. What follows is only the story of what I was in a position to know. It is the story of a mid-level officer, so to speak.

Prime Minister Toshiki Kaifu had canceled his planned trip to the Middle East on August 12 in order to take the lead in organizing Japan's response. This led to a rise in international expectations that Japan would make significant contributions. It was not so easy. After obtaining the approval of Director Matsuura, I went to see Vice Foreign Minister Koji Watanabe (later Ambassador to Russia), who was responsible for the entire Japanese contribution to the Gulf. Watanabe's room was on the 4th floor of the Ministry. It was a simple, spacious office with a big work desk, a sofa, and a conference table that could seat about 10 people. He was looking over some documents. I walked up to him and offered, "Please let my Bureau take over the 'contributions' job from the Middle East Bureau guys." He was delighted. "Will you really do that? Thank you!" Watanabe stood up and shook my hand firmly. Never did I imagine that four months of sleepless nights would follow.

The U.S. sent one request after another. They wanted minesweepers. They wanted transport ships and planes. They wanted Japanese personnel. They wanted Japan to show the flag. What was important was physical presence. Other countries were cooperating. They were trying to protect international legal order and the security of the Persian Gulf. Wouldn't Japan benefit the most? Look at the satellite photos. Most of the countries had pretty much decided to send soldiers, technicians, and medical teams to the Gulf, and most of the tankers are Japanese, they reminded us.

The Japanese government, however, was not ready to accept the U.S. demands. Prime Minister Kaifu was personally against dispatching the SDF. He kept saying, "Not the SDF," and we were told that the prime minister was telling us not to let uniforms get close to the Prime Minister's Office. It was beginning to look like it was all about cash, after all.

Was that going to solve the problem? The MOFA had to consider the remaining options. A task force was set up in Vice Foreign Minister Watanabe's office to discuss how Japan could cooperate with the coalition force in the Gulf. The task force met in Watanabe's room every morning at 9:00 a.m. and again at night to review each day's progress. After that, we would go to Vice Minister Kuriyama's office for a meeting at midnight and then to another meeting at the office of Director-General of the North American Bureau Matsuura from 2:00 a.m. (!). This went on every day. We finally decided on contribution measures based on four pillars of cooperation: financial cooperation, transport cooperation, medical cooperation, and supplies cooperation.

Financial cooperation was dealt with by the Ministry of Finance alone. They would not allow the involvement of the Ministry of Foreign Affairs. My office at MOFA oversaw supplies cooperation and helped out with transport cooperation. Another team was in charge of medical cooperation.

Prime Minister Kaifu's Fateful Press Conference

Having canceled his visit to the Middle East so that he could take decisive leadership in formulating contribution measures, Prime Minister Kaifu was scheduled to hold a press conference at the unusual time of 9:00 pm on August 29. He had the attention of the media worldwide. How would he show the Japanese flag? What would be Japan's contribution? The American media especially showed interest in Japan's funding. How much money would Japan, the world's second richest nation, be willing to pay?

MOFA requested that the Ministry of Finance (MOF) supply 1 billion U.S. dollars. MOFA came up with this figure based on a report from the Japanese Embassy in Washington because no matter how much we asked, the U.S. said it was impossible to calculate the cost of war. Vice Foreign Minister Kuriyama visited Vice Finance Minister Masami Kogayu and conveyed our request. He almost begged Kogayu, saying that judging from the way things were going then, if Prime Minister Kaifu could present figures at his press conference on the 29th, the U.S. would surely offer some praise. Not only that, the offer would include airlift and sealift support, albeit using private vessels chartered by the Japanese Government, as well as a dispatch of a 100-strong medical team to the coalition forces. Kuriyama told Kogayu that this would set the tone for a favorable reaction from the U.S. Congress and media thereafter.

Kuriyama briefed the anxiously waiting staff that Kogayu had sympathetic ears and accepted most of what Kuriyama had to say, but he said that squeezing such substantial funding would require time. But MOF would not present its figure for financial cooperation to MOFA. We waited anxiously at Kuriyama's office, hoping that somehow, they would make it in time for the Prime Minister's press conference, which the world would be watching. But the numbers did not come. In the end, what made it into the statement was, "Japan will spend 10 million dollars on Jordanian refugee relief." I had argued strongly during a Ministry meeting against including any reference to such minor funding as the only specific number in the Prime Minister's statement. It would have an adverse effect and should be removed, I urged, but I wasn't heard. As I feared, the 10 million dollars was perceived as the only Japanese contribution and the Statement was ridiculed.

At 8:00 p.m., one hour before the press conference, Prime Minister Kaifu received a telephone call from President Bush. I was the note-taker, listening to the two of them on the extension. No specific amount was discussed, but President Bush's reaction was extremely positive. "Thank you, very, very, much," he said. "Your decision will be welcomed in the United States, I'm sure. I hope you use this as a first step in your continued cooperation." I wasn't sure why President Bush seemed so pleased.

And so, Prime Minister Kaifu's press conference was held as planned at 9:00 p.m., a rather unusually late-night conference. After stating that Japan would cooperate decisively to support peace and stability in the Gulf region, Prime Minister Kaifu announced the four pillars of Japan's contributions, as recommended by MOFA:

1. Transport cooperation using commercial aircraft and ships rented by the Japanese government.
2. Supplies cooperation to support forces in the desert through providing equipment to protect from the heat and to secure water, among other things.
3. Medical cooperation by dispatching a medical team of about 100 personnel to cooperate in medical care for each country.
4. Financial cooperation to supply funds for the countries that rent aircraft and ships. In addition, Japan would provide Jordan, Turkey, and Egypt with economic cooperation and 10 million dollars to support refugees in Jordan.

Then the Q&A began. Prime Minister Kaifu was confident as he stated phrases such as "Peace in the region is a major national interest for Japan," and "We certainly cannot leave the reconstruction of peace in the Gulf region to a third party," and so on. He was from Waseda University's debating club after all. When asked about tangible contributions, however, his remarks turned passive. "Japan does not transport weapons, ammunition, or soldiers," He said, and "Japan's aid to the coalition forces is monetary and not military power." Then followed the Prime Minister added: "People from around the world are sweating to protect peace. Japan is unable to do that, so our scope of contribution is to share the cost." In other words, let the other countries go to the danger zone and Japan will pay for it. The world was listening.

The Kaifu press conference ended up nullifying and reversing Japan's 10-year effort to become a "normal nation" ever since Prime Minister Masayoshi Ohira's 1980 speech in which he declared that "there are things that Japan needs to sacrifice for the world." It wouldn't be fair to blame Prime Minister Kaifu alone. At the time, the Asahi Shimbun had conducted a survey of the House of Representatives members regarding the dispatch of the Self-Defense Forces for overseas missions, and 60% opposed. The overwhelming response from Diet members was that to help the Gulf Crisis, Japan should conduct "refugee relief" and "economic cooperation." They had missed the point from the get-go.

A "super" safety principle towards risking lives is a lesson Japan learned from its great defeat in the Pacific War that has continues to this day. Should we give priority to human life or to more abstract principles? When faced with a choice, human life has been the priority. This was exemplified in 1976 by then-Prime Minister Takeo Fukuda, who, when six Red Army terrorists hijacked a Japan Air Lines plane in Dhaka, accepted every one of the hijackers' demands, stating that "human life weighs more than the earth." In Japan, there is no support for taking up arms to fight for freedom.

It all came down to leadership. This emerged during the Gulf War as well. That is why Prime Minister Kaifu said that he would not send Japanese people near dangerous areas. The international community turned this logic on its head. If one human life is heavier than the earth, then it must be far heavier than money. This is why the 27 countries that risked the heavier-than-earth lives of soldiers, technicians, and doctors by sending them to the Gulf are classified as first-class citizens of the world, while the countries that just sent money were labeled second-class, no matter how many tens of billions of dollars they spent. Japan's attitude was interpreted as, "Japanese lives are heavier than earth, so let other countries handle the dangerous places."

Just as I feared, when the prime minister's press conference ended

the foreign media response was disastrous. After the press conference, gathered in Kuriyama's office in the middle of the night, we
were all overwhelmed by a sense of defeat. My anxiety had been spot
on. The 10 million dollars became a target of ridicule. The American
media especially criticized Japan's contribution measures as "too little, too late," saying, "It is a hamburger without the meat." The U.S.
Congress started moving toward a resolution to denounce Japan.

The biggest shock for all the MOFA people came the next
morning. At 9:30 a.m., Chief Cabinet Secretary Misoji Sakamoto
announced that Japan would contribute 1 billion U.S. dollars to the
activities of the forces in the Gulf. We soon learned that this major
decision had already been communicated to the Secretary of Treasury, Nicholas Brady, by the Ministry of Finance vice-minister, who
was in Washington, and from there, to the President.

For a moment, I was dumbfounded. Then a fierce anger crept into
my mind. There was no way that MOF could have suddenly decided
on a financial contribution of such magnitude in the middle of the
night after Prime Minister Kaifu's press conference.

That meant MOF already had a hold of its 1 billion dollar bullet by the time of the press conference the day before. In order to
teach the Americans that Japan's financial budget is not controlled
by MOFA, nor even by the prime minister, but by MOF itself, they
kept it a secret from MOFA and even from the prime minister, while
conveying the information to the United States!

When President Bush called Kaifu on the telephone the night
before, my conjecture—really, almost my conviction—was that the
1 billion dollars that even the prime minister of Japan did not know
about had been conveyed to the Treasury Secretary, and through
him to the president. That was why President Bush expressed such
appreciation for the Japanese contribution that the press had dubbed
'a hamburger without meat'.

The image of Japan dramatically worsened. After the reporters
left the press conference in the middle of the night, they filed their
critical articles, expressing disappointment in Kaifu's announcement.
There was no way that they would report on the subject again, even if
a 10-billion-dollar announcement were made the following morning.

In those days, 1 billion dollars was not insignificant. Had Prime

Minister Kaifu announced this figure at the press conference, it would have decorated the headlines, and even might have set Japan in a virtuous circle. This press conference stands as Japan's greatest public diplomacy of the Gulf War.

It was the worst-case scenario. The U.S. saw it this way: "It's the same old story. Japan keeps its purse strings as tight as possible until Bush, who is unhappy with the initiatives, makes a phone call. Then Japan runs around and comes up with the big money just 12 hours later. If you shake this country upside down, they'll pay, and they won't pay unless you do."

The time-lagged announcements continued. Whenever Japan prepared to make a substantial financial contribution, MOF would first report it to Washington through its own channels. Only after that would MOF notify MOFA in Tokyo. The public announcement would be just that much later. MOFA couldn't quite keep up with MOF, which had both budgeting and executive powers. MOF kept blaming MOFA. The high-ranking official who was dealing with the U.S. was well known for his rancor toward MOFA. He said "The blunder of the press conference on August 29 was entirely MOFA's fault. The only thing MOFA thinks about is how to please the U.S. Government, so it couldn't wait even half a day," and so on. (The date and time of Prime Minister Kaifu's press conference had been set in advance.)

Japan had set itself up to be defeated in the international PR battle over its response to the Gulf War. A series of telegrams arrived daily from Ambassador Ryohei Murata in Washington warning about deteriorating U.S. sentiment toward Japan. From then on, the U.S. Secretary of State James Baker was no longer Japan's contact. Instead, Treasury Secretary Brady came to the front door. Strategic talks concerning the Gulf War were no more to be seen. The conversation was all about money, and Japan had it coming.

From start to finish, the Ministry of Finance tried to convey the message to the United States that Japan's cooperation in the Gulf War came under the leadership of Minister of Finance Ryutaro Hashimoto, not Prime Minister Kaifu. Perhaps they thought that if they could impress upon the U.S. that the true powerhouse was Ryutaro Hashimoto, Japan–U.S. relations would get off to a good start when the Hashimoto Cabinet was eventually formed.

Nevertheless, why was Prime Minister Kaifu denigrated to this extent? Let me explain some intricacies of the political structure of Japan. Politics in Japan is driven by the balance of power between factions within political parties. It remains so today, but back then it was even more so. Here is what I heard about the Kaifu Cabinet from insiders. In August 1989, a womanizing scandal forced Sosuke Uno to resign after only three months as prime minister. The Takeshita faction was the most powerful, but several of its members were involved in the ongoing Recruit Scandal and Noboru Takeshita was in a bind as to how to respond to the public's demand for cleaner politics. Takeshita was a kingmaker and could effectively appoint the leader of the Liberal Democratic Party, and the LDP's leader would become prime minister. He decided it would be wise, one time, to hand over the post to someone outside his own faction. He chose Toshiki Kaifu, head of the smallest faction in the party. This way, Takeshita and his faction could easily maintain control.

Takeshita had another complicated situation to think about. Former Deputy Prime Minister Shin Kanemaru, another bigwig in his faction, was hostile toward Takeshita himself. Takeshita wanted to make Ryutaro Hashimoto, the sharpest man in the faction, the next leader, but Kanemaru stood behind strongman Ichiro Ozawa, who wanted to prevent Hashimoto from becoming prime minister. Takeshita told Hashimoto to work it out himself with Kaifu.

A deal was stuck. Kaifu was made prime minister and the Takeshita faction maintained power when Ozawa became chief cabinet secretary with a grip on LDP elections and money, and Hashimoto became Finance Minister in the Kaifu Cabinet. This created a delicate three-way relationship between Kaifu, Hashimoto and Ozawa. There were repercussions. The Japanese political scene subsequently turned more turbulent than usual. Ozawa left the LDP to form his own party and masterminded the creation of a coalition of opposition parties that took over the government. As a result, Hashimoto had to wait until 1996 to become prime minister.

Airlift Denied. Sealift Denied

What the United States sought most was Japan's cooperation in airlifts and sealifts. U.S. military shipments to Saudi Arabia were increasing at a rapid pace. The U.S. military presence grew from zero in August to 200,000 men and women by October. The demand was enormous, not only for troops, but also for the transport of equipment and supplies to support them.

The U.S. did not have enough vessels to meet that demand. Their naval ships were needed for combat, so they relied on allies for transportation. For that reason, among the four pillars of contributions that Kaifu announced on August 29, 'transport cooperation' should have become Japan's most important contribution. The U.S. had repeatedly told us that it was essential to see airplanes and ships carrying the Japanese flag, actively supporting the multinational forces. In particular, Washington was requesting that more than 10 aircraft be dispatched to the Gulf per week.

In the end, this did not go well. In response to the wishes of the Prime Minister's Office, Haruki Miyamoto, who as Director of the Civil Aviation Bureau of the Ministry of Transport was oversaw transportation, persuaded Japan Airlines to cooperate. The government had wrongly assumed that just because JAL was flying regular passenger flights to Saudi Arabia, it would surely cooperate. JAL opposed, asking, "Why should we go where our government isn't willing to?" In a sense, they were right.

Finally, Transport Minister Akira Ōno directly summoned JAL President Matsuo Toshimitsu, and as a result, JAL agreed to cooperate, with certain conditions. The Government complied and announced that it would lease commercial aircraft and ships to transport food, water, and medical supplies. MOFA thought this would be too restrictive and objected to these conditions, saying that there was really no transport need for water, food, and medical supplies, but the Transport Ministry did not yield.

Additionally, JAL had its own terms. When I heard them, I was at a loss for words. JAL insisted that the cargo leave from Narita Airport. In other words, the U.S. military should bring the cargo there. Since U.S. military aircraft did not have clearance at Narita, the supplies would have to be flown in civilian aircraft. Not only that, JAL would fly only as far as Jeddah, where it flies commercially, but not to Riyadh. JAL was essentially saying: Bring the American cargo on a civilian airline to Narita, transfer it to a JAL flight bound for Jeddah, then put it on a separate flight to Riyadh. Given that 23 JAL staff members had been taken as hostages by Saddam Hussein at that time, they argued, JAL had no choice but to minimize its involvement.

Nonetheless, there was no way the U.S. was going to agree to this proposal of transferring cargo three times, taking a week to travel three-quarters of the way around the world when a direct flight would only take eight hours, and to top it off, only carry water and food, which was not needed in the first place.

It was my job to convey this to the United States. In my mind, I was thinking, "If I tell them this, there goes my reputation in Washington," but I told them anyway, because that was my role. They probably saw no use in commenting. They didn't even reply.

Our team gave up the idea of leasing Japanese commercial aircraft through the Transport Ministry. I did not know what to do next. There was an officer on my team named Toshihiro Araki. He was chubby and panted a lot, but he was quick at solving difficult problems. He was cheerful and everyone loved him, but sadly he died at an early age. Araki sat right next to me and started flipping through the Yellow Pages. We didn't have the Internet back then. Instead, he found the phone number of an American airline company called Evergreen in McMinnville, Oregon. Araki started dialing. He was calm and smiling as he explained to the other party. Making the call from Japan with no introduction, no groundwork, and not even a word from the U.S. Government, he was talking about a transportation contract worth more than 100 million dollars. We all were flabbergasted.

Thirty minutes later, Araki hung up the phone with a broad grin. Evergreen had accepted our proposal. I felt more bewildered than relieved. For Japan, this had been a national project. It had gone to the Transport Minister and JAL President, and the two organizations had negotiated for days, only to come up with an official proposal that sounded like a joke. Meanwhile, it took a private U.S. airline, Evergreen, 30 minutes to respond to our request and agree to accept the job. What a difference!

A few days later, Evergreen was fully loaded with U.S. military supplies, making its first flight to Saudi Arabia. From then, I don't remember how many flights flew. The Japanese government paid this company more than 10 billion yen. If the cost of a one-way charter was 200,000 dollars, that means there were approximately 170 roundtrip flights. The U.S. government never once expressed gratitude to Japan, perhaps because Evergreen was an American company. Moreover, the soldiers—much less American civilians— had no idea who was paying for the charters, so the operation did nothing to change feelings toward Japan. It was a case of "damned if you do, damned if you don't."

American criticism of Japan gained momentum. Verbal attacks on Japanese airlines and shipping companies began. Things didn't go as planned with the airlines, but we needed to find a way to supply the promised vessels. The Ministry of Transport turned serious in its search. Kiyoshi Terashima, Director of the International Transport Bureau, used his personal connections and convinced a small shipping company called Satokuni Kisen Ltd. to lease one of its ships, the Hirado Maru. Six weeks had already passed since the U.S. request. When we told them that we had found one vessel, they replied: "We have already arranged for vessels. Japanese ships are no longer needed." The United States could not afford to waste even a day waiting for Japan to provide transport. And, Japanese vessels could not carry ammunition, anyway, just food and water, for which there was no transportation need. Suppressing anger, the U.S. politely turned down Japan's proposal.

It was the Japanese government who felt troubled this time around. After all the effort that went into finding this ship, they insisted it be used somehow. The U.S. reluctantly agreed to incorporate the Hirado Maru into its emergency transport plan. The Hirado Maru set sail from the sunny Honmoku Pier on September 25. And then there was trouble in Los Angeles, where the ship went to be loaded with U.S. military cargo. An officer from the Japanese Consulate arrived to check for weapons, to assure they would not be loaded onto the Japanese vessel. Let's just say that the Japanese definition of weapons is much broader than that of the international community.

While U.S. military officers were ready to explode, they also understood that this Japanese ship needed to be used politically. After much ado, Hirado Maru finally departed for Al Jubail, Saudi Arabia.

Then something happened that could have completely shaken Japan–U.S. relations. As the Hirado Maru approached its destination, her crew suddenly declared that they would not enter the Strait of Hormuz because it was dangerous. After some quick persuasion, they reversed their refusal to enter, but the anger of the U.S. military was beyond description. "If you can't load weapons, then don't make an offer in the first place," they said, adding "After finally coming to an agreement to load U.S. military supplies and finally setting sail, you're turn back *en route* saying that you don't want to go to the destination anymore. This is not merely a matter of not cooperating with the U.S., it is interfering with the war." The young officers who became angry with what they saw as Japan's non-cooperation eventually became senior officers charge of American defense policy and carried bitter feelings towards Japan. Naturally, Japan–U.S. relations would not improve. If this discussion had been exposed, Japan–U.S. relations would have been finished.

The fact that the Hirado Maru was not able to carry weapons has to do with the "Integration with Armed Forces" theory of the Cabinet Legislative Bureau. It is a claim that Japan's transportation of U.S. military weapons and ammunition is equivalent to Japan joining the United States to deploy armed forces. Even if a ship belongs to the private sector, the Japanese government cannot charter it for this purpose. The Ministry of Foreign Affairs tried hard to convince the Legislative Bureau that "transportation" is not an "exercise of force" and thus does not constitute exercising the right to collective self-defense. They did not agree.

Yet, Japan's civilian ships commonly transport U.S. tanks and cannons. However, if the Japanese government gets involved, the same activity is deemed unconstitutional. Extending the logic of the CLB, if a national Japanese hospital treated American soldiers who were injured on the front line, and once healed, these soldiers returned to war, the Japanese would be "joining armed forces" with the U.S. This idea is absolutely ridiculous. As we have seen in earlier chapters, the Cabinet Legislative Bureau is a part of the Japanese Cabinet, and it reports to the Prime Minister. Some prime ministers have asserted their power over the CLB, but during the Gulf War, the Prime Minister did not give any instructions.

Human Contribution Failed and Japan became a Cash Dispenser

We had to make a "human" contribution. Our last hope was the dispatch of a possibly 100-strong medical team that Prime Minister Kaifu had announced at a press conference when asked about human contribution. Expectations by the U.S. government were also high. On September 4, Secretary of State James Baker testified before the House Foreign Relations Committee, "Japan has agreed to foot $1 billion and will dispatch medical personnel. This is an unprecedented responsibility-sharing effort." Yet this also led to a miserable result. What happened?

The Foreign Ministry naturally thought that dispatching a medical team would be valued by the coalition forces. This is precisely why the statement issued on August 29 clearly stated, "medical cooperation for every country." Given that this could involve the treatment of injured and ailing soldiers on the front lines, it would be ideal to dispatch SDF medical doctors. A Self-Defense Forces Medical Team is a self-contained team consisting of a dozen or so doctors, nurses, and guards. How many of these teams would the Defense Agency offer?

Prime Minister Kaifu did not agree to the dispatch of defense medical officers, saying that the Ministry of Foreign Affairs should be the ones organizing the teams, not the Defense Agency. It was Minister of Health Yuji Tsushima, not the Secretary of Defense, who received instructions from Prime Minister Kaifu to "Do everything you can."

Coming from the Prime Minister, there was no other choice. The Ministry of Foreign Affairs switched plans to dispatching a medical team from the private sector with the idea that only coalition soldiers would be receiving treatment. the Ministry of Health and Welfare (MHW) showed reluctance from the start, insisting that refugees and civilians would be the target for medical assistance. Where in

Saudi Arabia would we find refugees? MOFA was dumbfounded, but MHW would not give in.

The MHW's concerns and requests continued. Before dispatching the main unit, a survey team needed to be sent to understand the medical needs. Without that, medical services could not be performed. Also, the status of the survey team must be "diplomatic officers." Diplomatic passports can only be issued to government officials, so doctors had to be chosen from national hospitals and hospitals attached to national universities. This made the process that much more complicated. University hospitals are under the jurisdiction of the Ministry of Education, not the Ministry of Health and Welfare. The Ministry of Education has little to do with international issues.

The advance dispatch ended up being nothing more than pathetic: The doctors sent from national universities were denounced for participating in the American war, criticism which the Ministry of Education tried to wiggle away from by saying, "No, they're going to treat refugees." Many of the doctors individually opposed the war, so when MOFA asked them to treat injured and ailing soldiers in Riyadh, they flatly refused, declaring that they would not help people who went out to kill others.

After all this much ado, it was September 19 by the time a 17-member team including five doctors and five nurses was dispatched as the advance party. The U.S. was greatly disappointed to see Japan's international pledge decrease from 100 members to 17. The doctors who arrived in Saudi Arabia went searching for the so-called "refugees," but of course there were none. The advance team of doctors was sent without any agreement as to whom they would focus their medical efforts on or for what reason. Once they arrived, they had to start by debating their very purpose.

Meanwhile, the Saudi government welcomed the arrival of the Japanese doctors and asked them to head immediately to the army hospital at Khafji to help with treatment there. The Japanese refused. "Well then, please go to a hospital in Riyadh," they said. The Japanese again refused, as this was also an army hospital. From this point on, the team refused to treat soldiers, demanding a search for the non-existent refugees in Saudi and becoming a total nuisance to the Saudi government. Finally, it was all the Saudis could do not to tell them just to go home.

In the event, the advance group stayed in Saudi Arabia for nearly one month, during which time they drew up a survey report on things such as equipment that Japan could possibly provide, handed it to the Saudi government, and came home. The main group never went. The 100-member team ended up being zero, not 17.

This is how the dispatch of the doctor team, which was meant to be the focus of personnel dispatch, failed. Something had to be done, so it was decided that the least we could do was offer ambulances. We gathered 20 ambulances at the port and had them ready to load and on their way to Saudi Arabia when the Saudi government said they wouldn't take them unless they were left-hand drive. We suggested that in the middle of the desert where there was not traffic, it wouldn't matter if the vehicles were left or right-handed. Besides, all British military vehicles were right-hand drive. The Saudi government was no longer listening to Japan. By the time left-hand-drive ambulances were ready to go, it was the end of the year.

As expected, the United States emphasized the financial contribution. After the first billion-dollar contribution was announced on August 30, they were already pressing Japan for additional funding. On September 7, Treasury Secretary Brady was in Japan, wasting no time coming to the Prime Minister's Office. With him, he brought heavyweight officials, Deputy Secretary of State Lawrence Eagleburger, Assistant Secretary of Treasury David Mulford, and Deputy Secretary of Defense Paul Wolfowitz. On the Japanese side were Prime Minister Kaifu, Foreign Minister Taro Nakayama, and the new Finance Minister Ryutaro Hashimoto. Hashimoto, the Minister of Transport when I was running around trying to dispatch Japan Coast Guard patrol ships to the Persian Gulf, remembered threatening me over the phone. He looked at me with a grin as I attempted to sit at the very back. "Oh, it's you again. What are you up to this time?"

At the table, Secretary Brady asked for an additional three billion dollars: one billion to support the coalition forces and two billion for the front-line states, Egypt, Jordan, and Turkey. Japan ended up agreeing to the full amount after Secretary Brady left the country, but the timing of the announcement couldn't have been worse. In the U.S. Congress, amid anti-Japan sentiments, Representative David Bonior was about to propose an amendment requiring Japan to pay the full cost of stationing the United States armed forces in Japan. The Foreign Ministry strongly urged the Ministry of Finance to dish out the three billion dollars before the resolution passed, since it was going to be paid anyway, but the Ministry of Finance did not change its schedule. The announcement was delivered one day after the U.S. Congress passed Bonior's resolution, by a whopping 370-53. This confirmed the image that Japan would make huge contributions only under pressure from the United States.

To make matters worse, the same theatrics were repeated. The three-billion-dollar contribution was first mentioned when Finance Minister Hashimoto called Treasury Minister Brady on the phone and asked him to "Please tell the President." Once again, Prime Minister Kaifu was only notified of Japan's decision after the President of the United States. The testimony on September 19 by Deputy Assistant Secretary of State Richard Solomon at the U.S. House Sub-committee on Asia and the Pacific was accurate: "For the past two or three weeks, Japan has been criticized for its poor timing. ... The view that the only way to trigger a decision from Japan is to bash the country has been reinforced."

On September 29, Prime Minister Kaifu attended the U.N. General Assembly in New York, during which time he visited President Bush at his hotel, the Waldorf Astoria, for a Japan–U.S. Summit meeting. Without any apparent worry, Prime Minister Kaifu called the President by his first name, George, and explained that Japan had taken all possible non-military actions, which was the reason for the four-billion-dollar total contribution. President Bush said that he was pleased that Japan and the United States were making a common effort to combat aggression and didn't forget to add a request for increased funding of United States military stationed in Japan.

I carefully studied the President's face. He was smiling and soft-spoken, but the expression he had shown in earnest engagement with Prime Minister Kaifu in Palm Springs five months earlier was gone. According to a report by the *Asahi Shimbun*, President Bush had spoken a month earlier with Finance Minister Hashimoto when he was in Washington. Reportedly putting his arm around Hashimoto's shoulder, Bush said, "I am aware that you, acting in the center of the Japanese government, have made great efforts and a significant impact on this decision."

The Ministry of Finance's strategy was successful: They gave the United States the impression that Hashimoto was a central figure in the Japanese government while showing their own organizational power. However, the alliance would not function effectively if Japan's Prime Minister were merely a contact person to receive U.S. requests rather than a partner who makes policies together with the U.S. President. Surely this would backfire within the Ministry of Finance too, would it not?

The following year on January 20, news broke that in New York, Finance Minister Hashimoto promised Treasure Secretary Brady nine billion dollars. How did the Ministry of Finance let the U.S. government drive them this far? Nine billion dollars was an outrageous amount of money for which the need was never explained. U.S. senators were treating Japan like a cash dispenser, but actually, ATMs are handled more carefully. The American way of withdrawing cash from Japan was violent. After criticizing everything there was about Japan to criticize, they madly shook the machine and then kicked it away.

Huge Order of Equipment from Tokyo to CENTCOM

The Largest Supply of Humanitarian Aid in History Begins

OF THE FOUR JAPANESE contribution measures, the scheme I oversaw was "in-kind contributions," which would become the largest operation in Japan's contribution to the Gulf War. U.S. military men and women in the field showed us deep gratitude but Washington, which had changed its policy to accept only money from Japan, did not appreciate this. Even Tokyo didn't fully understand, suggesting that it would be easier to unify with financial support rather than adding contributions in kind.

However, I was adamant. Japan ended up not being able to send people. If it was not possible to send SDF vessels, transport planes, civilian planes, or even medical teams, at least we could contribute in ways that Japan excels at. Instead of just handing over the money to pay for things, let's put in our own "sweat" by procuring, paying for, and transporting the materials and equipment that the coalition needed in the desert.

Vice Minister for Foreign Affairs Watanabe supported my recommendation that Japan's major contribution should be in-kind. Wasting no time, I went to the head of the personnel department and created a task force of young people. I also asked the Defense Agency to dispatch personnel from the Ground, Maritime, and Air Self-Defense Forces with experience in procurement operations. For important duties, I appointed Kunihiko Miyake, who was the chief official of the Status Agreement Division. In addition to having a wealth of ideas, he was a man with unwavering nerve and leverage and was a rising start in the Foreign Ministry. After forming this team of talented staff members, I made a declaration: "Japan imposes risks on other countries yet receives more fruits of peace than anyone else. Is it enough only to pay money for that benefit? If that is all Japan does, our reputation will take 10 years to recover. Let's make a more direct contribution!"

The U.S. military must buy huge amounts of supplies but when war preparations are so extensive, there are bound to be urgent procurements that cannot be met. Japan can provide quick support and rush supplies to the U.S. military deployed in the desert. Let's deliver the materials and supplies with our own hands. Miyake and his young team were on fire as they lunged forward.

On August 20, I visited Defense Director Yusuke Matsushima (later Middle Army Commander) and Section Chief Tsuneo Isoshima (later Chief of Staff) of the Japan Ground Self-Defense Force at the Ground Staff Office in Roppongi. General Matsushima was a decisive man, whom I had always respected. However, in the years that followed, he was not able to become the Chief of Ground Staff, the top position of the Ground Self-Defense Force. This may have been because he was unjustly criticized for the delayed response to the Great Hanshin-Awaji Earthquake that struck before dawn on January 17, 1995.

As commanding officer of the JGSDF Central Army, General Matsushima had been in charge of the Self-Defense Forces in the region at the time. He had all of his units on standby as soon as the earthquake hit and waited for a request from the stricken Hyogo Prefecture, as this was the law. However, Governor Toshitami Kaihara, who was famous for his ideological opposition to the SDF, delayed requesting deployment of the SDF for four hours. At a later press conference, he said, "It seems that the Self-Defense Forces were slow to mobilize..." At his press conference, the soft-hearted general shed tears over the 6,400 casualties. Television repeatedly broadcast scenes of Governor Kaihara's remarks and General Matsushima's tears but explained only that "the Self-Defense Forces seemed to be late."

My visit with General Matsushima occurred five years earlier. When I arrived at the Joint Staff Office, he and Section Chief Isoshima were waiting for me, wondering what was going on. "Can you make a list of the materials and supplies you would need for battle in a desert?" I asked. Within two days they handed me a list created at the Ground Staff Office that included four-wheel-drive vehicles, seawater desalination systems, water supply vehicles, reefer trucks, generators, tents, housing construction materials, heat resistant equipment, office equipment, and other things.

I took the list to Katsusada Hirose, director general of the Ministry of International Trade and Industry (later Ministry of Economy, Trade and Industry Vice-Minister before becoming Governor of Oita Prefecture). I told him that I wanted to send the listed items to the Gulf and asked him for his cooperation. I asked him to find out as soon as possible which materials and supplies could be procured in Japan. It would be a huge amount of goods. Some of them would have to be gathered from warehouses across Japan. In some cases, if the goods had already been earmarked for other buyers, we would have to ask them to cancel those contracts. Moreover, we didn't have any means yet to secure the funding. No public office would welcome this offer.

But Hirose's response was loud and clear. "Understood. The Ministry will handle it." Section Chief Hirose instructed each department in charge of supplies and to help create a list of supplies for the desert that Japan could provide. It was surprising. MITI even categorized each item by inventory status, and what could be provided in one month, or three months. To begin with, Japanese companies do not have large inventories because they produce products after the orders come in. MITI studied the flow of these items within Japan and contacted each department of each company. By doing so, they effectively earmarked all of the materials and equipment that the U.S. military might need.

On August 26, I handed the completed list to Deputy Director General for North American Affairs Minoru Tamba (later Ambassador to Russia), who was on his way to Washington to explain Japan's contribution strategy. On the 28th, Tamba was subjected to severe criticism from U.S. government officials over Japan's response to the Gulf War. Most tankers in the Persian Gulf were Japanese but it looked as though Japan wasn't going to do anything about it. Later, Tamba told us that what changed their attitude was this list. His bag was nearly empty (the Self Defense Force dispatch and the Airlift Sealift both being virtually null) and the only thing he had to show the American side was this "Tamba List." Later, Tamba thanked me again and again.

We knew we had a daunting task ahead of us. Procurement of a large volume of goods, a mechanism to transport it to the Gulf, a mechanism to enable payment and settlement—these were all areas that had never been explored before. And since we did not yet have an approved budget, it all had to be done using estimates. Legally, it was touch and go. Only a go-getter would be able to pull this off. In that respect, Miyake, the gutsy team leader was perfect. Our team was not composed only of MOFA and SDF staff. Staff from the U.S. military in Saudi Arabia and from MITI were also members.

After our plan went into full swing, CENTCOM's Major Jim Hake was dispatched from Riyadh to Tokyo and commuted to MOFA nearly every day, along with U.S. Army J4 representative Colonel Johnson and Secretary Kevin Meyer, who was in charge of U.S. administration in Tokyo. We had thought that there was no need for CENTCOM officials to come all the way to Japan and that they could just send us a fax, but their list was too long to send by fax. The list that Hake brought with him from Riyadh was as thick as a telephone book.

Meetings took place with Major Hake and the others at MOFA and MITI nearly every day. The meetings at MITI were particularly efficient. Director for Policy Planning Eiichi Hasegawa (later Special Advisor to Prime Minister Abe) of the Trade Policy Bureau Americas Oceania Division gathered young members from each department in the ministry on a schedule to fill in the details for each item in the "phone book," in conveyor belt style. It took a day and a half just to check all of the items.

The relationship between our task force and CENTCOM grew close; we were like brothers and CENTCOM J4 and the Japanese government's in-kind contribution team were one and the same. The challenge was whom to appoint to receive the funding. There was no mechanism to directly provide Japanese government funds to developed countries, not to mention the existence of any sort of framework of support for military purposes. Institutionally, it was almost impossible.

After some moaning and groaning, we decided to form a new international organization. The organization would be named the Gulf Peace Fund. Japan would invest in this fund and through it, procure materials and supplies for the coalition. We instructed ambassadors stationed in member nations of the Gulf Cooperation Council (GCC) excluding Kuwait, namely Saudi Arabia, Oman, Abu Dhabi, Qatar, and the United Arab Emirates, to sign an exchange of notes in order to set up a fund between each government and Japan. It was hard to explain to the Gulf States why we had to make such a fund. However, the Japanese ambassadors stationed in the countries prevailed, and were able to persuade the Arab nations in the Gulf to establish a GCC Gulf Peace Cooperation Fund on September 21, with a representative office in Tokyo. This was completed in a very short time, and it was all due to the wisdom and efforts of the young people, especially Kunihiko Miyake.

Once the system had been established, Japanese government leaders realized that this was an effective measure, and steadily increased its budget allocation. The materials and supplies purchased for the coalition in the Gulf—essentially the U.S. military—finally reached 84 billion yen. The remaining problem was that the Cabinet had not yet made its decision on reserve expenses. So, despite the nominal allocation, there was no actual money. Miyake kept telling the trading companies that were involved in supplies procurement to trust him and that he would be sure to pay the money. All of us were prepared to resign in the slight chance the reserve funds were for some reason not approved.

We knew that there would be scrutiny of a plan that required suddenly raising a large amount of money to procure a large amount of goods. If there were any questionable funds, that would be the end of it. We set up a fund secretariat in the Kayu Kaikan Hotel in Sanbancho, and we invited experienced experts from MOFA, MITI, trading companies and banks. This team procured and shipped 84-billion-yen worth of materials and supplies to the Gulf. The team rigidly managed the budget, processing it to the very last yen and completed the project without causing a single problem.

It would have been impossible to handle this within Japan's regular budget system, but the Ministry of Finance Budget Bureau was able to make it happen. I tip my hat to the flexibility of the Budget Bureau. The Gulf Contribution strategy could not have been realized without Budget Director Hiroaki Taya and Chief Budget Inspector Shigehiro Kuwahara (later Executive Director of BOJ). Later, Taya would be ousted from the Ministry of Finance for a different reason. Destiny is truly harsh.

Longest Day of My Life

U.S. Ambassador Mike Armacost reported to us that U.S. military need was urgent and repeatedly requested MOFA to supply the coalition with four-wheel drive vehicles. My team decided to respond to his request, and our first in-kind contribution involved 800 4WD vehicles. For vehicle procurement, MITI's Automotive Division commandeered vehicles that were intended for other customers and arranged to secure 500 Land Cruisers from Toyota and 300 Pajeros from Mitsubishi Motors.

But, as mentioned earlier, there was no money. The decision to spend one billion dollars would have to come from the Cabinet meeting, which would be held September 21 at the earliest. Until then, nobody had spending authority. Also, would we be able to find a transport ship to carry the vehicles to Dammam, Saudi Arabia? Amid public opposition to war contributions, we anticipated resistance from the Seamen's Union and longshoremen's groups.

Internationally, the "idle Japan" image started taking form. I insisted that this four-wheel drive vehicle grant be announced as Japan's first contribution measure. The Ministry of Transport, however, argued that if it were publicized, the opposition parties would make a big fuss, so it should remain a covert operation to the end. It was MITI that finally announced that the 800 vehicles were to be loaded onto Kawasaki Kisen's 12,000-tonne class cargo ship, the Sea Venus, to set sail from Nagoya Port on September 5. On several occasions before the announcement, I had visited the Transport Ministry's International Shipping Director Nobuo Murakami to discuss shipping options. While he had a list of vessels headed to the Gulf, he cradled it in his arms like a child so that I couldn't see it, telling me time and again that they had not decided on the transport ship.

To the bitter end, the Ministry of Transport did not let us know the name or the sailing date of the ship that would be carrying the four-wheel drive vehicles.

Criticism toward Japan spread throughout the world. Japanese commercial ships sailed in and out of the Persian Gulf every day, yet when it came to cooperation with the coalition, there was not a Japanese vessel in sight. In the United States, longshoremen unions started refusing to load and unload Japanese ships.

Not everything could be kept secret as the Ministry of Transport wanted. The provision of 4WDs would of course become widely known, as soon as the Cabinet decision on the budget went through. Any fuss that arose at that point would only anger the Seamen's Union, who would likely call the ship back, if it were *en route*. The announcement had to be made before the vessel left Japan. I tried again to persuade the Chief of International Shipping for an early announcement, but he refused, saying that it would become a problem in the Diet, Japan's parliament. It was obvious that the Ministry of Transport had its own plan in case the project caused problems: It would claim that it had not been aware that the vehicles were supplies for the coalition.

After thinking it through, I decided to tell an American newspaper. I was not about to cause North American Affairs Bureau Director Matsuura any trouble by consulting him, so I took the initiative and visited Steve Weisman, the Tokyo bureau chief for The New York Times. I explained at length, saying that in the very near future, we would be transporting 800 four-wheel drive vehicles to the Gulf for the multinational forces. Weisman was excited. He had never imagined that Japan would go out of its way to do this. He wrote a long story about the 800 cars and a big article was posted in the New York Times on September 2. It was the only favorable coverage about Japan during the Gulf War for the American audience,

On the day of departure, word had gotten out that the cargo comprised support supplies for the Gulf War. The All-Japan Seamen's Union refused to let the ship depart. It was chaos at Nagoya's Kinjo Pier. I received a call from Murakami, the shipping director. Before slamming the phone down, he told me "I won't have any part of this, Okamoto. You are responsible!"

I immediately reported to Foreign Affairs Vice Minister Watanabe. His instructions were very clear. "Okamoto, go and become friends with the Seamen's Union!" At ten o'clock, I headed out to the All-Japan Seamen's Union headquarters in Roppongi. A central executive committee member Hideo Nomura and international shipping manager Yamato Matsuoka were there to greet me. I figured my only choice was a head-on collision. I honestly explained the sequence of events. Nomura declared that "the ship will not sail." I told him that "this is not for the coalition. It is for Japan." He didn't budge, and repeated: "The answer is no. We cannot carry military supplies." They were intransigent, so I pulled away for the time being and returned two hours later to ask again. They refused again. Nomura wanted clarity: "The Ministry of Transport says that the 4WD vehicles are for civilian use. What's the story?" I told him that "there's no use playing dumb. The truth will come out with the Cabinet decision. They are to support the coalition."

At Kinjo Pier in the port of Nagoya, several newspaper helicopters circled over the Sea Venus, which was being loaded with Mitsubishi Pajeros. The seamen were increasingly nervous, and confusion was escalating. To make things worse, in a panic Kawasaki Kisen had painted over the logo on its ship's funnel to hide it. A secret voyage with the ship's company name invisible? This made the crew even more uneasy.

In the early afternoon, I received a call from Director Murakami of the Ministry of Transport. "Those cars are being unloaded, Okamoto. How are you going to take responsibility for this?" I was about to give up. But on my way to the Prime Minister's Office to give my report, I called the MITI automobile department, that had procured the 800 four-wheel drives for me. I spoke with young assistant director, Hajime Ito (later Director General of Minister's Secretariat, METI), and did not expect to hear what he said: "Okamoto, Sea Venus has only temporarily left port to avoid confusion! We will not let them unload the cars! MITI will not back down one inch!"

His tone pounded against me. I felt embarrassed, but his determination moved me to tears. Okay then, it's back to the All-Japan Seamen's Union one more time. So, I headed for Roppongi. It would be my third visit that day to the Seamen's Union. I was prepared to sit there and not move until they allowed the ship to set sail. Central Executive Committee member Nomura came out of an emergency meeting. I spoke first:

> These four-wheel drive vehicles are Japan's key contribution to the coalition. Japan cannot get away with simply dishing out money. Japan is being criticized all over the world. In the United States, there are movements beginning to refuse handling cargo from Japanese ships. Nomura, please help. It's for the interest of our nation. You people are the only ones who can help the country right now.

Then I bowed my head deeply. Nomura thought hard about it, and then slowly opened his mouth. "Okamoto, last year I lost my wife. I have nothing more to lose. I may lose my job over this, but I will talk to the others about releasing the ship."

A little while later, we received some good news via the Ministry of Transport: "The All-Japan Seamen's Union agrees to the departure of the ship on the condition that the safety of the seafarers is secured." A written agreement between the Seamen's Union and the Ministry of Transport was drawn up immediately. Thankfully, at the Ministry of Transport, the Seafarers Department was in charge and not the International Shipping Section, so we could finally have normal conversations. We started our meeting in the evening that day. Just around the same time, Land Cruisers started being loaded at the Toyota quay in Nishi-4-ku at Nagoya Port. MITI must have given the orders. All the cars were loaded, and the ship pulled away shortly after six. Once it was outside Kinjo Pier, it anchored and waited for the results of negotiations in Tokyo.

The Kaiin Building, where the All-Japan Seamen's Union is located, was packed with media. Bathed in TV lights, the concerned parties, Nomura, Union President Shoshiro Nakanishi, Administration Director Yasuhiko Kimura from the Ministry of Transport seafarer's department, Director Yasuhide Sakinaga (later president) of Kawasaki Kisen as the charterer, and I made our way to the special conference room on the fifth floor. It was all was very professional. Finally, an agreement was exchanged between the All-Japan Seamen's Union, Kawasaki Kisen, and the Ministry of Transport stating that "in the event that the ship is damaged, or a crew member injured, regardless of the situation, the government shall be responsible and act accordingly." It was past midnight. Even at that hour, a huge crowd of press remained outside.

Before dawn the next day, Sea Venus set sail for Dammam, Saudi Arabia, carrying 800 4WDs. Miyake and I, after staying up all night at the office, were glued to the 6:00 a.m. NHK news. The TV showed the Sea Venus after leaving the Irako Channel. She shone a bright orange, reflecting the morning sun, and gained speed as she entered Kumano Pass. We continued to watch, silently. In just two weeks since the request from Ambassador Armacost, we managed to procure and send 800 four-wheel-drive vehicles to the Gulf. At that moment, I was naïve enough to think that this would set the U.S.–Japan relationship right.

Later that morning, I went to the office of Vice Foreign Minister Watanabe's office and submitted my resignation, saying that I wished to take responsibility for risking Japan's Gulf contribution measures. He did not accept it. After that, I visited executive committee member Nomura to thank him. He spoke in a way that was full of meaning for me. "Okamoto, I was sincere in responding to your request because you explained things just as the way they were. If the ship had left without any explanation and I had later found out about the nature of that load, as a union member, I would probably have called the Sea Venus back to Japan, even if it was already in the Indian Ocean."

The Obstacles of Japanese and American Bureaucracy

Full-scale procurement of supplies had finally begun. Following the 800 vehicles, supplies requested by the U.S. included water tank vehicles, 135 large truck chassis for reefer trucks, vehicles such as trucks and forklifts, seawater desalination equipment, computers, copy machines, fax machines, radio equipment, and base camp construction materials to accommodate 140,000(!) people.

This in-kind cooperation program had started to become transformative. It was too serious to laugh at- but there were moments. One day Miyake came to me grinning. "Okamoto-san, the U.S. military is requesting the construction of a runway. It is to be used for combat operation." I replied: "You know it would infringe upon the ban on weapons exports. Theoretically we must tell Americans that the runway should only be used for medical missions, but of course we cannot say such unrealistic things."

"You know Okamoto-san, the J4 logistics and planning guys at CENTCOM are insisting that a 'runways' are 'buildings', and therefore they are not 'weapons. They want to us to interpret the runway as 'a horizontal building.'" We burst into laughter. As it turned out, the U.S. military ended up building its own runway and Japan separately built a heliport for emergency medical care. Anyway, we were consistent in responding to CENTCOM's requests as best we could.

Among purchases made in a short period of time, this was the largest procurement in history. The MOFA team, the MITI team, and the Communications team worked through the night. While in Washington, officials of the State Department and Department of Defense went home every night and together with the U.S. media and Congress criticized Japan, in Kasumigaseki, dozens of Japanese bureaucrats were spending their nights at government offices getting work done for the U.S. military.

It wasn't only the officials who were working hard. Branches of Japanese trading companies all over the world cooperated. Mitsubishi, Mitsui, and Sumitomo were among those trading companies whose locally stationed employees had been taken hostage in Iraq. If the Iraqis found out, there was no telling what would happen. There was fear of terrorism as well. For these reasons, the heads of the local offices even took on clerical jobs. Adjustments of specifications required by the U.S. on procured goods and contract wording—none of this could be done without the help of the trading companies. Not only that, because the involvement of trading companies was in the service of national policy, it had to be carried out on a non-commercial basis, which meant practically zero profit for them. This would be unthinkable for American businesses.

Still, the U.S. response was as expected. "Japan's cooperation is just fulfilling its own commercial interests." There was always a bone to pick when it came to what Japan was doing. Huge resources were secured thanks to Japanese funding and purchasing procedures and sent to the Gulf. Nonetheless, in Washington, where the image of

Japan was one of non-cooperation, none of this was worthy of mention in Congress. As a result, neither the Ministry of Defense, not the Department of State expressed any appreciation regarding the in-kind contribution project.

There was a problem on the Japanese side, too. As this developed into a serious problem, the decisive factor that tore the relationship between Tokyo and Washington apart was the 500 trucks that the U.S. had strongly requested. A major controversy broke out within the Japanese government about whether these were weapons or not—something Americans would not understand. The truck was a drop side version military 4-ton truck that could deflate its tires to operate in the desert, a robust six-wheel drive manufactured by BMY in the United States. It had no special armor, so in that respect, it was just like any other truck. The only difference was that the roof was reinforced so that it could be fitted with a machine-gun turret. The U.S. military strongly hoped to procure these 500 trucks in the United States with money from Japan's Gulf Fund.

Our team was on the phone with BMY in York, Pennsylvania nearly every day so that Japan could directly purchase the trucks and send them to the Gulf. In MITI, however, the Director of the Trade Administration Bureau would not back down on his claim that this truck was a weapon and that its export from Japan is prohibited by the three principles on weapons exports. The Foreign Ministry countered that it could not be a weapon just because it has an iron plate attached to its roof. If so, then if you wanted to, you could "arm" a civilian truck, for that matter. Besides, there was no way that the Foreign Exchange Act and Export Trade Control Ordinance, which define the three principles of Japan's weapons exports, would apply to an "outside to outside" transaction where the Gulf Peace Fund procures U.S.-made trucks in the U.S.

Even in MITI, people up to the section manager level with whom we worked agreed with us. But the Director of Trade did not give in, not even to the persuasive efforts of MOFA's North American Affairs Bureau Director Matsuura. The Director of Trade said that turning down the American request would not be fatal, and that Washington's "people of importance" would understand. If this were to be pursued in the Diet, the current cabinet would not be able to win the support of the prime minister.

The Ministry of Foreign Affairs couldn't give up either, so it became a negotiation between the top players. MOFA Vice-Minister Kuriyama set out to see MITI Vice-Minister Koji Kodama, but typically in a bureaucratic organization, a vice-minister who takes one position in a negotiation with another government office will not be ready to compromise. If Kodama were to let the Ministry of Foreign Affairs win, he would be criticized from below for being weak. As expected, the vice ministers' negotiations ended unsuccessfully.

These conflicts between ministries are usually mediated by the Deputy Chief Cabinet Secretary. Important matters that even he cannot settle are taken to the Chief Cabinet Secretary. If that doesn't work, the Prime Minister makes the final decision. However, I could easily imagine the weak Prime Minister and Chief Cabinet Secretary at the time succumbing to the Director General of the Trade Bureau's threatening concern that "this is going to be a problem in the Diet."

In a Japanese administrative organization, matters do not proceed if the director of the bureau that has jurisdiction over the matter takes a firm stance. The director is the almighty in defending the status quo. Only a strong Prime Minister or Chief Cabinet Secretary can overturn this. There was nothing more that the Ministry of Foreign Affairs could do, but a consensus was reached within the Japanese government to transfer the 50 million dollars in funds to purchase 500 BMY trucks from the "in-kind contribution budget" to the "monetary contribution budget," and the money was transferred into the U.S. government's bank account in November.

But the U.S. government's reaction to this was excessive, if not hysterical. In Washington, the BMY truck was labeled a "killer truck" in contempt for Japan defining an ordinary truck as a weapon, and it was touted as a prime example of the Japanese government's non-cooperative stance. For us reformist bureaucrats in Japan, MITI's intransigence was shameful. To put it simply, because the Japanese had a problem with its purchasing procedures for U.S. military trucks, they just handed over the money and asked the U.S. to handle it. The fact remains that this was a gift to the U.S. military from the taxpayers of Japan. Nonetheless, Washington bureaucrats used this as an excuse to lecture and ridicule Japan. Bashing Japan was an effective tool for winning over the U.S. Congress and media. The attitude of the American officials this time was diametrically opposite to that in the era of Defense Secretary Weinberger. The "killer truck" episode grew from Japan's turning down the American request for a single iron plate on the truck's roof and remained a symbol of Japanese non-cooperation.

After the killer truck incident, I felt the need to explain the in-kind contribution project to the U.S. government one more time. I asked Miyake to go to Washington for me, but when he arrived, he encountered hostility from all sides from U.S. government officials. Miyake reported that the meeting in Washington was extremely uncomfortable right from the start. Nobody was willing to listen to any explanation from the Japanese side. Of course, there could be no hope for gratitude for providing the trucks. The essence of the killer truck issue was not whether the BMY truck fell under the Japanese law as a so-called weapon, but whether Japan would decide to overcome domestic difficulties as an allied party. This was where the criticism lay. That is probably a valid point. However, it does not justify such cold evaluations of an ally. I felt the arrogance of the American bureaucrats.

CENTCOM was Our Only Ally

Miyake felt miserable as he left Washington. From there, he headed for Riyadh and visited U.S. CENTCOM. He felt depressed thinking about having to explain the killer truck issue again. Waiting for him were people such as the major general in charge of CENTCOM's logistics and planning office (J4), and his senior staff. Certain that he would be criticized again, Miyake gave an overview of Japan's contribution to the Middle East and explained the reason we could not purchase the BMY trucks.

Then, to Miyake's surprise, the major general stated that he understood the situation and that Japan should just buy what they could, that CENTCOM highly valued Japan's in-kind cooperation. Miyake reported to me from Riyadh: "His words were so warm, I couldn't believe what I was hearing. I traveled halfway around the world and finally met an American who understands the hardships that our in-kind contribution team went through the past three months. It brought tears to my eyes."

From August to October, about 200,000 U.S. troops were rapidly dispatched to Saudi Arabia. It was not easy for CENTCOM to provide sufficient logistical support to these units. They had to procure necessary materials and supplies locally with limited funds, and 90% of allocated war expenses disappeared into weapons and ammunition. For that reason, it was not easy to find resources for the procurement and transportation of materials and supplies, for soldiers' accommodation and for securing food. Moreover, with the high prices in Saudi Arabia it was impossible to procure supplies at unit prices determined by the Washington accountants. CENTCOM J4 was at a loss. Japan's cooperation with the U.S. provided invaluable support for U.S. military officers and soldiers in the field, much more important than Japan had imagined.

An additional 200,000 troops were deployed in November, including a ground force stationed at NATO, and many supplies were needed for logistical support. Our in-kind team was flooded with orders from CENTCOM including 1,000 vehicles, hundreds of office computers, computers for air traffic control support, asphalt, concrete, wood, and so on. We worked desperately and large numbers of contracts were signed in a hurry. Procurement procedures under the In-Kind Contribution Program continued until 1992. This was because CENTCOM had to continue providing logistical support for tens of thousands of U.S. soldiers stationed in Saudi Arabia after the Gulf War had ended.

Walkman

Many people helped us with the in-kind contribution program, but I will never forget Chairman Akio Morita of Sony. In November, as nearly 500,000 American soldiers were stuck in the fiery desert, CENTCOM asked us to send 40,000 Walkmans. Spending all day from morning to night in the monotonous desert was not mentally healthy for the soldiers. They were feeling desperate, saying things like, "This is torture! I need music! I want a Walkman!" CENTCOM asked the U.S. government but were told that every penny was needed for weapons, and they had no intention of providing music. Knowing that this was asking a lot, CENTCOM asked if they could rely on the good faith of Japan.

I understood the meaning of their request. When I worked as a diplomat in Egypt, I had visited the tents of U.S. soldiers in the Sinai Peninsula ceasefire surveillance team. I could imagine the severe working conditions amid the scorching sand and rocks. I wanted to help. Could it be possible to find a place for this in the in-kind co-operation scheme? I went to the Ministry of Finance. Hiroaki Taya, the chief officer in charge. To make up for Japan not being able to dispatch personnel, he made his drawings with thick lines when deciding financial support measures. However, even the big-hearted Taya, who had been helpful for other requests, refused, saying that there were no troops anywhere in the world who had Walkmans as official supplies.

After exhausting my bureaucratic options, I visited Sony Chairman Akio Morita at the ARK Mori Tower in Tameike. It was November 13. Morita's decision was quick. "Of course! Anyone spending months in a place like that would go mad. Sony will donate the Walkmans!" Just as soon as he said that, he picked up the phone next to him and gave instructions to the officer in charge. And that was that. 10,000 of Sony's goodwill Walkmans were sent to the Gulf, and the soldiers had music to take turns listening to.

Yet this became another cause for criticism from the U.S. media. Japan didn't do anything when they were needed and are now they are trying to cover it up with Walkmans. It was almost ridiculous. The press didn't bother reporting that it was the U.S. military who had requested the Walkmans to begin with, or that the relief came from a private company because Japan's Defense Ministry had refused. I apologized to Morita for the way that the American media was handling this. Morita pursed his lips and said in his usual fast clip, "If it made the soldiers happy, that's all that counts, isn't it?"

The Walkman request had come from General Norman Schwarzkopf. CENTCOM's treatment of Japan was completely different from Washington's, where bureaucrats, politicians and the media treated us like garbage. The hero, Norman Schwarzkopf, wrote in his famous memoir as follows:

Had it not been for the Japanese, Desert Shield would have gone broke in August. While Western newspapers were complaining about Tokyo's reluctance to increase its pledge of $1 billion to safeguard Saudi Arabia, the Japanese embassy in Riyadh quietly transferred tens of millions of dollars into Central Command's accounts. We were able to cover our day-to-day operations before anybody in Washington could lay claim to the money.[30]

There are some mistakes in General Schwarzkopf's description. Japan delivered goods, not cash; the support was directly from Tokyo, not the embassy in Riyadh, and the amount was more than 800 million dollars, not millions of dollars. However, those details don't matter. The important thing is that the commander-in-chief was deeply aware that Japan's sweat and effort helped save CENTCOM from failure. At a time when criticism of Japan was going viral in the U.S. and nobody wanted to defend Japan, only General Schwarzkopf spoke up for us.

Quite a while after the war ended, in August 1991, we received a letter of thanks from General Schwarzkopf addressed to Koichiro Matsuura, Director-General of the North American Bureau. Kunihiko Miyake's name was mentioned, too. It was the only time gratitude was shown officially to the Japanese government concerning the Gulf War.

JAPAN'S HUMILIATION

The Victory Parade to which Japan was Not Invited

ON MARCH 11, 1991, the Kuwaiti government issued an advertisement of gratitude through major American media. Thirty countries were listed, with the U.S. at the top, but Japan was excluded. It is said that the American embassy in Kuwait reported the names of 29 countries, excluding their own.

But after that, something more serious happened. On June 8, three months after the war ended in a victory for the coalition, a parade was held on Pennsylvania Avenue in Washington, DC. President Bush and government leaders, U.S. Congress representatives, and diplomats lined up and 8,800 servicemen led by General Schwarzkopf marched past them. Some 800,000 spectators filled the sidewalks.

Ambassadors from 35 countries were invited, but Japan's Ambassador's name was not included. Thinking that the invitation must have been delayed, the embassy called State Department to inquire and was told that Japan was not on the list. No name? There must be a clerical mistake. Surely, they would just add another chair on Pennsylvania Avenue. The embassy was optimistic that the situation would quickly be resolved, but the U.S. government would not offer a chair for a Japanese representative.

Soon, the embassy discovered that it had not been a clerical error, rather a directive from a high-ranking White House official to delete Japan's name from the list of invitees. Infuriated, the Embassy held several rounds of high-level negotiations until a seat finally was made available for the Japanese ambassador. This was settled only just before the parade. Even the smallest countries, which only sent a handful of troops to the Gulf, were invited to the parade, while Japan was excluded. This was the final episode of Japan's humiliation in the Gulf War.

Why did this happen? There are three reasons from the Japanese side. The first was that Japanese leaders, including Prime Minister Kaifu, did not have an accurate vision or theory of alliance when it came to Japan's role in the Gulf War and therefore, did not understand what Japan was supposed to do. The second was that a few of Japan's key bureaucrats were afraid of rocking the boat, or else simply put their own interests ahead of national interests. The third reason was that the government, afraid of backlash from the opposition party during the parliamentary session, did not publicize Japanese contribution measures. If they openly told the U.S. how much Japan was contributing, the opposition would attack the administration during the Cabinet meeting, saying, "That's too much. It's absurd." And with Japan not announcing it internally, nobody else was going to offer it publicly.

Aside from the United States and Saudi Arabia, Japan contributed more funding than any other country toward the cost of the Gulf War. It is the only country that even raised taxes on people to cover the costs, through the law. The money that the United States ripped away from Japan, while criticizing the country for being a mere cash dispenser, totaled almost 1.4 trillion yen. That amounts to around 10,000 yen each from every Japanese person. Moreover, Japan's contribution was not only funding. Japan's In-Kind Contribution Team collaborated with CENTCOM like a brother and procured a large amount of war-related materials and sent them to the Gulf.

To the bitter end, however, the U.S. government did not help Japan with public relations, no matter how hard the Japanese government tried. In the initial stages, after the U.S. media placed Japan in the enemy group along with Iran and Jordan, no matter what Japan did, it was bad. Japan was plagued by "Damned if you do, damned if you don't." There were no people in the government then like Secretary Weinberger, who would defend Japan to Congress Officials in Washington focused only on what Japan did not or could not do, completely disregarding what Japan did do.

The United States is the type of country where once the national sentiment has been decided, the whole nation criticizes another country like a stampede. It's as if people are competing to see who can be the toughest against Japan and how high they can climb up the stars-and-stripes flagpole.

For Japan and the U.S. to recover as allies emotionally, we had to wait for the inauguration of the Ryutaro Hashimoto government. I've already spoken about how poor Japan's response was during the Gulf War. Still, that bitter experience was a road that Japan had to traverse. It was to become a turning point that would provoke major changes in Japan's security policy. The flow from the Act on Cooperation for United Nations Peacekeeping Operations (PKO Act) → Self-Defense Force Dispatch to Cambodia → Self-Defense Force Act Amendment → Emergency at Periphery Law → Armed Attack Situation Response Law → Maritime Self-Defense Force Dispatch to the Indian Ocean → Land and Air Self-Defense Force Dispatch to Iraq, would not have been possible without the humiliation Japan experienced during and immediately after the Gulf War.

Humiliation of Heroic Japanese Ambassadors

Throughout the Gulf War, the American attitude toward Japan was unfair. In 2013, the movie *Argo*, directed and starred in by Ben Affleck, won an Academy Award for Best Picture. It was an inspiring true story from 1979 about six American embassy employees who sheltered in the Canadian Ambassador's residence after escaping the American embassy in Tehran when it was taken over by Iranian revolutionaries. They eventually were able to flee the country with the help of a CIA operation. The actions taken by Canadian Ambassador Ken Taylor were commendable. Banners saying, "Thank you, Canada!" were put up across the country, and in American bars everywhere, people treated Canadians to drinks. The U.S. was overflowing with gratitude toward Canada, and Ambassador Taylor became a hero.

When the Gulf War began, Japan's Chargé d'Affaires Akio Shirota also sheltered more than 20 American embassy employees in a similar heroic act in Kuwait. However, contrary to Ambassador Taylor's treatment, Shirota was basically humiliated by the U.S. Secretary of State. At 2:00 a.m. on August 2, 1990, Iraq's Republican Guard crossed the Kuwaiti border and it reached Kuwait City at dawn. The Japanese Ambassador had temporarily returned to Japan and 41-year-old Shirota was temporarily in charge of the embassy. Shirota was born four years after the atomic bombing of Hiroshima in Saka Town, eight kilometers from the hypocenter.

The Iraqi army initially controlled the coastal area where Dasman Palace and government buildings are located and were approaching the U.S. embassy. Koji Naito, a 28-year-old Japanese embassy employee who had been staying in a room on one of the upper floors of the International Hotel next to the U.S. embassy, was sending detailed reports to Chargé d'Affaires Shirota. Shirota forwarded these reports to the American embassy, which was unaware of the Iraqi troop movement.

At around 9 p.m., Shirota received a message from the guard: "Some Americans are here to see you. They say they're with the U.S. Embassy." The American embassy was about three kilometers southeast of the Japanese embassy. Without seeking or waiting for instructions from the ministry, Shirota decided to accept them on the spot. The Iraqi military leader was already approaching the Japanese embassy and there was no time for indecision. Seeking protection were Counselor Emille Scodon and her family. They had been at home and were unable to approach the U.S. embassy, which was under siege.

The two embassies had a strong trusting relationship. Prior to this, when the situation had become tense in July, Chargé d'Affaires Shirota and Deputy Chief of Mission Barbara Bodine of the U.S. embassy had discussed a plan to evacuate Americans to the Japanese embassy in case of an emergency. The basement of the Japanese embassy had a large hall usually used for receptions, along with compartments and a kitchen. It was an open space with a semi-underground design that allowed in sunlight, so it did not feel claustrophobic. Shirota sheltered the Scodon family there.

After that, called Bodine called Shirota to seek protection for more employees who were unable to enter the U.S. embassy. Shirota accepted the U.S. embassy members one after another, while he had his staff check on conditions from the rooftop. Some of the U.S. personnel were soldiers attached to USLOK (U.S. Liaison Office

Kuwait), and their security was especially important. If the Iraqi army took them as prisoners, their treatment would be cruel, and Saddam Hussein would likely use his hostages as cards for negotiations with the U.S. With this in mind, on August 2, 16 Americans and their families were welcomed into the Japanese embassy. The Japanese embassy was the only refuge for American diplomats there.

Later, Japanese people living in Kuwait began to evacuate to the Japanese embassy. In the end, the number of Japanese people accommodated in the same embassy basement reached 261. Before taking them in, Shirota told the Japanese evacuees about the Americans in the basement and warned them not to tell anyone about that because it could endanger their lives.

The cooperation shown by those Japanese citizens toward Shirota, who took great care not to put the Americans at any risk, was touching. They had several discussions among themselves about what they could do for the safety of the Americans, not to mention living together and sharing their food. Later, 213 of the Japanese were taken hostage by Saddam Hussein but they all kept their promise to Shirota, and never said a word under interrogation about Americans being at the Japanese embassy in Kuwait.

Shirota traveled around the city day after day in an embassy car, observing the situation and visiting other embassies. He instructed the driver to drive slowly to avoid being shot. He did not display the national flag on the car except when visiting the Iraqi military command. Different embassies responded in different ways. Eventually, a group of embassies that shared the same stance began to cooperate and communicate with each other using code names. Shirota's code name became "Jade Tree" and DCM Bodine used the name "Snow White."

How could Shirota move these Japanese people and American people safely out of the country? Several plans were considered. Tokyo arranged a rescue aircraft and negotiated with the Iraqi side to start bringing Japanese people home. However, among the Japanese people in the basement—including Japan Airlines staff members—it was unanimous that the Americans be allowed to join them. An escape plan team of these citizens made up mainly of engineers carefully put together a plan to get the U.S. embassy employees on board the JAL plane. Although it was the CIA that helped U.S. embassy members escape from the Canadian ambassador's residence in Tehran 11 years earlier, in Kuwait, this escape operation could only be carried out by ordinary Japanese citizens.

They found one problem when they were devising their plan. After everyone was on board, someone had to close the door from the outside. Who would do that? Shirota assigned himself to that mission and decided to stay behind, alone. Before the plan was implemented, however, the Americans were transferred to the U.S. embassy at DCM Bodine's request.

It was decided that the transfer would begin at noon on August 13, when the Iraqi military's vigilance eased because of the heat. That morning, several Americans cried when they said farewell. They were then separated and driven away by Japanese embassy vehicles cars at different times. Shirota also loaded two embassy cars with luggage that might look suspicious and sent them ahead. The luggage included old radio equipment. While the "suspicious" cars caused a fuss at the checkpoint, the cars carrying the U.S. embassy employees would pass through. It was past 3:00 p.m. when word came from Snow White that all had arrived safely at the U.S. embassy.

Most of the 261 Japanese people who had evacuated to the embassy on the 18th were taken to Baghdad. Only embassy employees remained. One of them was an American local employee by the name of Judy. On August 20, the Japanese embassy was surrounded by the Iraqi army and could have been invaded at any time. Shirota decided to get her out. He told her to dress in long black clothing that covered her entire body and entrusted her to a Kuwaiti acquaintance. Judy cried while she was putting herself together in front of the mirror. Shirota, who was fluent in Arabic, took her to the embassy gate and declared to the surrounding Iraqi soldiers, "This is an embassy servant. Someone is coming to pick her up," and had them clear the way for her after some questioning. The Kuwaiti who came to retrieve her waited on the other side, and wasting no time, he took her into his arms. Soon after that, the Japanese embassy became the first embassy to have its electricity and water supply cut off. Shirota and Naito were the only two who remained, and Judy safely returned home to Florida.

After all that, the treatment that Shirota subsequently received from the U.S. government was almost humiliating. In March the following year, after the Gulf War had ended, Shirota headed to Kuwait to reopen the closed embassy, but on the way, at London's Heathrow Airport, he was ordered to go to Washington. He was told that there would be a ceremony organized by the U.S. government to thank him for his heroic behavior in protecting the U.S. embassy employees.

On March 21, Shirota went to the seventh floor of the State Department building and stood waiting in the corridor outside the Office of the Secretary of State. Secretary of State James Baker appeared and handed him a printed Certificate of Appreciation. Shirota had not even been offered a chair, much less invited into the Secretary's office. The "ceremony" was over. The Secretary of State hurried back to his room as if five minutes was too long to spare. That was the entirety of the "U.S. government-organized ceremony of gratitude" for Shirota, who was summoned from a great distance. Shirota thought that he had witnessed a display of American power, but he did not mention this to anyone.

Shirota, who had put the safety of the Japanese civilians who had evacuated to his embassy at risk to protect the American embassy employees to the end, did not mention this to anyone. The American people were never told about his actions nor about the 261 Japanese people who helped.

On January 17, 1991, the battle between the multinational forces and Iraq began and Operation Desert Shield became Operation Desert Storm. Japan's role became financial funding only and there was no more work for me to do. Unable to resist an instinctive desire to seek a new frontier, I resigned from the Ministry of Foreign Affairs at the end of January, after working there for 23 years.

PART FIVE

Iraqi War—American Failure, Japanese Bureaucracy

SUCCESSFUL PRELUDE—DISPATCHING OILERS TO THE INDIAN OCEAN

Prime Minister Koizumi's Decision

THE YEAR WAS 2001, 10 years after the Gulf War that had left Japan facing numerous challenges and criticism. This time, President George W. Bush decided to attack the Taliban and Al Qaeda in Afghanistan in retaliation for the 9/11 attacks. I was serving for the third time, as Special Advisor to the Cabinet, this time under Prime Minister Junichiro Koizumi. All I could think about was that in this relationship with the U.S., if Japan messes up its response, it will be the Gulf War nightmare all over again.

With permission from Prime Minister Koizumi and Chief Cabinet Secretary Yasuo Fukuda, who would become the Prime Minister six years later, I visited Washington from October 9 to 11 to meet National Security Advisor Condoleezza Rice, Deputy Secretary of State Richard Armitage, Deputy Secretary of Defense Paul Wolfowitz, and Chairman of the Joint Chiefs of Staff Richard Myers among others. I was seeking clues on ways Japan could respond as an ally if the United States advanced into Afghanistan.

I felt that the U.S. operation in Afghanistan would be based on a long-term strategic perspective with an eye on preventing terrorism in the future by stabilizing that country. America enjoyed an overwhelming advantage in fighting power, so there was no "do-or-die" or doubts on their side. The strategy was to capture Al Qaeda and Taliban after cornering them with successive attacks. The United States had no thought of engaging in large scale combat over the course of years.

The rapid deterioration of U.S.–Japan relations during the Gulf War had traumatized the Japanese government. This time, I was convinced of the need for Japan to offer what it could before the U.S. requests began to flow in. From the start of the Gulf War, Richard Armitage and others who knew Japan well also did not like using Japan as a cash dispenser. This time, the mood in Washington was that there would be no "tin-cup operation," one where the U.S. government would merely ask Japan for financial assistance. Instead, they completely agreed with me that Japan should propose its own contribution measures first.

Armitage is a legend in the field of U.S.–Japan relations. He is not afraid of criticism. He follows only his own beliefs. Japan has relied on him as the guardian of the Japan–U.S. Alliance, but he values Japan only because it is in the interest of the United States to do so. He says that patriotism toward the United States is what moves him, not a love of Japan. Many in Japan hold a similar view—that judging from every angle, it is to Japan's benefit to remain an ally of the United States.

Former-U.S. Deputy Secretary of State Richard Armitage and Yukio Okamoto attend the IISS-hosted Shangri-La Dialogue in Singapore on June 3, 2007. Okamoto knew Armitage for more than 30 years.

However, so far as the United States is concerned, Japan is only one among dozens of military allies. Japan's response to international contributions tends to lag and the two countries have been mired in trade friction. Considering the U.S. as a whole, the view of Japan is not a mirror image of Japan's perception of the United States. Given this, the continued focus by people like Armitage and Joseph Nye of Harvard University on Japan as central to American national interest has served as a stable lynch pin between the United States and Japan. These are the people who make U.S.–Japan relations strong and unique.

Armitage is a man overflowing with interesting stories. He once visited Cairo as a member of a U.S. government delegation. Salah Salem Road from Cairo city center to Cairo International Airport in Heliopolis is always congested. When the American delegation got stuck in traffic, the Egyptian police in the escort car started shouting orders at the cars filling the street to clear the road and let the convoy through. They even banged into non-compliant vehicles, pushing them out of the way—a sight I witnessed myself, when I lived in Cairo.

The American delegation was both surprised at the rough Egyptian police behavior and worried. The knowledge that Americans were being driven in those cars would arouse public antipathy. Just then, Armitage leaned out of vehicle and shouted at the other cars: "Простите (*Prostitye*)!" "I'm sorry" in Russian. With his large muscular torso and bald head, he resembled a typical villain in a Russian movie. The surrounding Egyptian people likely all thought that a Russian delegation was forcing the Egyptian police to clear the way.

It was Saturday night when I returned from Washington, but I went straight from Narita airport to see Prime Minister Koizumi and Chief Secretary Fukuda. I reported roughly as follows: "What Japan needs to consider this time is how effectively we can combine Japan's defense roles with America's offense to deliver results as an ally. For example, Japan could take over security surveillance, transportation, refueling, and other tasks that the U.S. needs to perform far away from the battlefield, thereby freeing up U.S. units and equipment deployed there. This would allow the U.S. military to relocate extra squadrons to combat zones. Please consider this, conceptually."

I explained that what matters are symbolic actions as an ally. For example, if we can send Japan's airborne early warning and control (AWACS) aircraft to non-combat areas, this will free up American AWACS to fly over Afghanistan. Or we could engage in refueling and medical assistance to the U.S. military outside combat zones. I also pointed out that there were high expectations for humanitarian assistance for war victims and for Afghan reconstruction. Since the 9/11 terrorist attack, the United States had been recognizing the importance of close coordination with its allies, shifting from the unilateralism of the Bush administration when it first started." "Okay," Prime Minister Koizumi said. "Give it a try." He had made his decision.

Maritime Self-Defense Force Ships Assume Defense in the Indian Ocean

As soon as I received the prime minister's permission to begin examining our specific options, I visited Deputy Chief Cabinet Secretary Shinzo Abe (who would become the longest serving prime minister in Japanese history) and Deputy Chief Cabinet Secretary Teijiro Furukawa. I offered my report to Abe and trusted him to come up with an effective policy once I gave him some input. He agreed with what I was trying to do. Then I visited Defense Agency Vice Minister Ken Sato and Deputy-Vice Minister Takemasa Moriya to debrief them on my Washington visit. Moriya, who became Vice Minister of Defense, would later play a major role in the Futemma issue.

At night, at the residence of the Minister for Foreign Affairs often used for secret meetings, I consulted with Vice-Minister Yoshiji Nogami (later Ambassador to the United Kingdom), Director-General of Foreign Policies Shotaro Yachi (later chief of the National Security Secretariat), and Ichiro Fujisaki, Director-General of the North American Affairs Bureau (later Ambassador to the United States). So what specific measure did I need to offer the administration? I consulted with Captain Katsutoshi Kawano, known as the Maritime Self-Defense Force "brain."

Kawano, who 13 years later became the Chief of the Joint Staff, the highest-ranking uniformed officer, was then a captain in the Maritime Staff Office. He was a resourceful man of great creativity. Ten days after the 9/11 attack, there was information that terrorists would target a U.S. military base overseas. The Seventh Fleet in Yokosuka was to evacuate 1,200 kilometers south to Iwo Jima. The U.S. Navy asked Japan's Maritime Staff Command to send ships to escort the Seventh Fleet as it navigated south of Tokyo Bay, where there was heavy shipping traffic.

Japan's Self-Defense Forces Law rigidly defines what the SDF is allowed to do. It prohibits any activity it does not specify. As there is no provision in the Law for "guarding U.S. fleets," an escort operation would not be permitted. Kawano was convinced however, that such an urgent U.S. military request must be accepted. After giving it much thought, he came up with Article 5 of the Ministry of Defense Law, which states that the SDF may conduct research. His logic, albeit rather hilarious, was that the SDF would investigate and research the behavior of the U.S. fleet during an emergency evacuation, and for that purpose they would need to send escort ships. It sounded ridiculous, but it was the only way to make the operation possible.

After reporting to the higher ranks, he ordered two escort ships to be dispatched. This exposed him to a rebuke from politicians, who worried about accusations from opposition parties in the Diet of such a transparent stretching of the law. Nevertheless, Capt. Kawano's decision had a major impact. Images of the Seventh Fleet traveling south in Tokyo Bay alongside Japan's Maritime Self-Defense Forces were broadcast on CNN many times, impressing the American people. What would have happened if Japan had refused?

Kawano and I spread a large chart of the Indian Ocean across my small office in the Prime Minister's Office and discussed it over and over again. What could we do? The conclusion we came up with was to send Maritime Self-Defense Force (MSDF) refueling vessels to the Indian Ocean with escort ships to guard them. At the time, the Taliban had been transporting narcotics to Yemen and Somalia in exchange for weapons, which they carried back to Afghanistan. An eight-nation multinational fleet led by the United States was organized to interdict the Taliban traffic. Japan, unable to exercise its right to collective self-defense, could not join the multinational fleet itself, which might possibly engage in battle with the Taliban ships. Instead, the idea was to position Japanese vessels in adjacent waters to refuel foreign navy ships as needed.

There was no constitutional issue regarding the dispatch of escort ships to Japanese supply vessels because that is the exercise of the right to individual defense. Their roles may be different, but Japan's presence would be secured in the Indian Ocean. This is close to what Armitage meant by "boots on the ground."

I wasted no time explaining this to Deputy Chief Cabinet Secretary Abe, Chief Cabinet Secretary Fukuda, and Prime Minister Koizumi, in that order. Kawano and I had especially in-depth discussions at Fukuda's office. With the approval of Prime Minister Koizumi, the chief cabinet secretary gave instructions to the Ministry of Defense and Ministry of Foreign Affairs to start working on legislation to enable such operations.

Since Japan can only legally conduct activities specified in the Self-Defense Forces Act, new legislation was needed to deploy an MSDF fleet to the Indian Ocean. For this, Prime Minister Koizumi introduced an Anti-Terrorism Special Measures Law. He chose the path of persuading citizens face-to-face, even if that meant turbulence. He did not seek "the safe way" and carried on without fear of the political landmines associated with security policy. In this way, he enabled Japan to make substantial contributions within the constitution for international security.

What a difference this was from the Kaifu Cabinet during the Gulf War! Before any constitutional revision, what Japan needs for its security is a strong political attitude. The refueling ship Hamana sailed from a base in Kure on November 9 with two escort ships, the Kurama and the Kirisame. In just two months after 9/11, the Koizumi Cabinet enacted "the Anti-Terrorism Special Measures Law" and sent SDF vessels to fight terrorism. This was something Japan had never done before. It was accomplished with unusual speed and without any prodding from the United States.

Over the next eight years from November 2001, Japanese supply ships and escort fleets replenished the ships of 11 countries participating in Operation Enduring Freedom a total of 939 times. Although some critics, both within and outside Japan, jeered at this activity by calling it a "Gas Station Operation," refueling played a major role. The U.S. government was pleased. After a long 10 years, Japan finally contributed concretely to preserving international security. The replenishment of fuel for the warships of various navies was not simply a symbolic activity but also a substantial one. We were told that some developing countries could participate in the multinational fleets only because the Japanese refueling operation reduced their financial burden.

Dispatching MSDF vessels to the Indian Ocean meant that the Japanese SDF was finally participating in the international fight against terrorism. The United States, which had demanded payment of 11 billion dollars during the Gulf War, appreciated the decision and did not demand any additional financial contribution from Japan.

The reception at home was positive too. Japan had six high-performance Aegis destroyers. When the decision was made to dispatch these to escort the refueling vessels, much of the media hurled criticism. Once the ships were sent, the criticism stopped. That was because the people regarded the Aegis destroyers simply as highly efficient escort ships. Sending the Self-Defense Fleet to the Indian Ocean freed the SDF from preposterous hindrances in the future, and at the same time blew away American skepticism about the U.S.–Japan alliance. Twenty-seven supply ships and 44 escort ships were dispatched during those eight years.

As I have written earlier, the abortive dispatch of patrol boats to the Persian Gulf in 1990, during the Nakasone years, ended in a miserable failure for Japan. A decade and a half later, refueling vessels were dispatched to the Indian Ocean as a prelude to Japan's involvement in the Iraq War. This operation fulfilled Japan's responsibilities to the extent possible. While I had great respect for Masaharu Gotoda, the man who adamantly blocked the sending of Japan's Coast Guard ships to the Gulf, if he had been Chief Cabinet Secretary this time around, we would have been crushed. But it succeeded this time because of the decision by Chief Cabinet Secretary Yasuo Fukuda. The United States and Japan were able to enter another honeymoon era due to the personal affinity between Prime Minister Koizumi and President Bush. The "individuals" make a difference in every decision.

Challenges remained, however. Sure enough, there was "sweat" involved, unlike the Gulf War. While they did a superb job, maritime refueling under the scorching sun was technically difficult and physically tough for our MSDF sailors. Fundamentally though, the operation was a scheme carried out in safe waters without having to take the risks that other countries were taking. The SDF dispatch after the war in Iraq was based largely on the same framework. It wasn't until 2015, after Shinzo Abe formed his second cabinet, that more advanced operations, such as defending foreign naval ships, were legalized.

In contrast, Democratic Party Secretary-General Ichiro Ozawa and Foreign Minister Katsuya Okada who came to power in the 2009 election, said that dispatching a refueling vessel to the Indian Ocean was a violation of the constitution that touched on the right to collective self-defense, and was not based on the UN Security Council resolution. Following the expiration of the Replenishment Support Special Measurements Law in 2010, no renewal measures were taken, and the operation was terminated. Of course, Japan's act of unilaterally halting its contribution was criticized, and Japan eventually made a financial contribution of 500 billion yen to cover half of the salaries of Afghan police officers. As logistical support, there actually was no issue as far as the constitution was concerned. Refueling activities that had been highly valued by other countries were discontinued, and the alternative put a huge financial burden on the state.

I was particularly disappointed in Ozawa. During the Gulf War, he had insisted on dispatching the SDF, saying that Japan should become a "normal country." He was the hope of young bureaucrats. But his subsequent behavior made me suspect that his actions were actually political and partisan, and hinged on calculating whether they would help lift him to power. Although the SDF fleet dispatch to the Indian Ocean was an implementation of the very philosophy he had claimed to support during the Gulf War when he was in the LDP, now because it was an LDP decision and he was a leader of a new party, he opposed it. After taking power, his party's Hatoyama Cabinet withdrew the MSDF from the Indian Ocean to fulfill a campaign promise. This sudden policy shift by Ozawa and the Hatoyama Cabinet drove Japan's security policy back to one that dictated no dispatch of personnel, no sweat, and payment of a fortune, just as in the Gulf War.

THE WAR BEGAN

Black Hawk Down

BY JANUARY 2003, the U.S. Army had already amassed a 70,000-strong military force in the Persian Gulf. Once a massive army is deployed to the front lines, the possibility of their being utilized becomes quite high. When I heard the news, my memory rushed back to the days of the Gulf War of 1990 when tents were pitched in the Saudi-Arabian Desert and for five months, 400,000 U.S. army soldiers waited for the opening of hostilities. Again, a heavy and ominous feeling crept over me. If war were to start, America would need the cooperation of Japan. Would we be ready?

At that time, I was appointed by Prime Minister Koizumi as his Special Advisor to deal with Iraq. My assignment was: How would Japan cooperate in the reconstruction of Iraq after the end of the anticipated Iraq War? It was a job worth doing, so I happily accepted the post. I wanted not only to help Iraqi people but also to make up for Japan's failure in contributing to the Gulf War of 1991–92—a failure that damaged U.S.–Japan relations for a long time.

Working for Prime Minister Junichiro Koizumi, a man of resoluteness, I would be able to assist in a way that had not been possible during the Gulf War 13 years earlier. During the First Gulf War, there was a demand for Japan to come up with a graduate course level contribution, that is, to cooperate with the United States while the war was still going on. But this time, in Iraq, the task for Japan would be to provide "peaceful cooperation" after the hostilities ceased. It seemed to me like a college level task.

Besides, I already had experience as a Special Advisor to the Prime Minister when Prime Minister Ryutaro Hashimoto was in office. I prided myself on having achieved some significant results. I naively thought that a similar assignment under Koizumi should not be too difficult to handle. But my positive experience with the Hashimoto Cabinet turned out to become my undoing. In retrospect, I should not have accepted that post.

In my previous assignment, I was under the protection of the Prime Minister and the powerful Chief Cabinet Secretary, Seiroku Kajiyama, the man whom I still consider to be more statesman-like than any other politician I have ever met. I was provided with a sufficient budget and staff, based on which I was able to carve out a new front line for the government.

But things were different this time. I was given a comfortable office at the Prime Minister's Office Building not very far from the office of the Prime Minister, but I was given no staff throughout my assignment, nor the political protection needed to win the turf battles with other agencies. I often wondered why. I came to realize that Prime Minister Koizumi, albeit a man of independence and decisiveness, needed no advisor, as he would totally depend on the

As Special Advisor to the Cabinet, Yukio Okamoto (right), 57, greets U.S. President George W. Bush at a welcome reception at the Prime Minister's residence in Tokyo on December 8, 2002.

existing bureaucracy except for a small number of items he wanted to put his own stamp upon. So, I had to engage in a one-man battle with other government offices, particularly the Ministry of Foreign Affairs (MOFA), which wanted no independent persons acting independently on a diplomatic issue.

Although the predominant atmosphere within the government was that a firm approach should be taken against Iraq, which was suspected of holding weapons of mass destruction, I was critical of America's launching a war against Iraq. I even wrote a newspaper article entitled "The U.S. should not make an armed attack on Iraq." My reasoning was that an attack on Iraq would entangle many citizens, and it would deepen the hatred of America in the entire Arab world.

The Prime Minister's Office had a tolerant atmosphere that encouraged differing opinions, and I was not chastised for the article. The domestic conservative faction on the other hand, had ways to criticize me. And I was told that in Washington, some people were saying, "Okamoto must make his position clear as to whether he is an ally or an enemy of the United States."

Inside the Prime Minister's Office, it was again Deputy Chief Cabinet Secretary Teijiro Furukawa who supported me. The Cabinet has three Deputy Chief Cabinet Secretaries. By convention, one is appointed from the House of the Representatives, one from the House of Councilors, and one from the bureaucracy. The bureaucrat-turned-Deputy Chief Cabinet Secretary is the highest position in the bureaucracy. His or her duties are to adjust important policies before they go to the political level. These judgments determine the policy content and direction at the bureaucratic stage. In the case of Furukawa in particular, not many Americans know that he was the one who promoted many of the new positive policies regarding the Japan–U.S. alliance.

The prevailing mood within the Japanese government was that firm measures needed to be taken against Saddam Hussein. A brilliant U.S. victory was predicted, as in the Gulf War, but I knew it wouldn't be so easy. One day in February, I went to see the Prime Minister with a projector and a screen. I showed him some scenes from the movie "Black Hawk Down." The movie was about the mess in Somalia in 1993 when U.S. Marines were trapped in urban guerilla warfare and killed, their dead bodies dragged behind trucks. I spoke frankly: "The U.S. will proceed easily to Baghdad. The problem is the guerilla war that will take place in the cities afterwards. Iraq will turn into a quagmire."

Bob Woodward wrote of an interesting episode in his 2006 book, *State of Denial*,[31] in which U.S. military officers imagined that Saddam might have been planning a strategy of urban terror in which his units would melt away, and then "resurface periodically and randomly to attack U.S. forces, creating a long-term insurgency." At exactly the same moment, I was making the same argument to Prime Minister Koizumi in Tokyo.

Although I was against the United States starting a war, if a war were to begin, I also firmly believed that Japan should unequivocally support the United States. Criticizing the U.S. after the outbreak of war would be tantamount to helping Saddam Hussein's campaign to divide world opinion. Japan needed to be different from France or Germany, which were openly critical of U.S. policy. I knew from experience that criticism from foreign countries when American soldiers started to die would incur a severe emotional reaction from the United States

On February 26, when war became inevitable, I flew to Washington to hear U.S. government views. On the eve of war Washington was full of tension. Amidst this, people gave me time, spoke about the prospects of war, and the position American allies would be placed in. In addition to speaking to private experts, I met Steven Hadley (Deputy National Security Advisor) and Eliot Abrams (Special Adviser) at the White House. At the State Department I spoke with Richard Armitage (Deputy Secretary) and Jim Kelly (Assistant Secretary), and at the Pentagon I consulted with Paul Wolfowitz (Deputy Secretary) and Richard Myers (Chairman, Joint Chief of Staff).

My longest meeting was with Paul Wolfowitz. A war was about to begin, and we talked for nearly two hours. He has been described as an architect of the Iraq War and attracted global criticism when no weapons of mass destruction were found in Iraq after all. This, I thought, was a bit unfair to him. I later learned that European countries had also communicated information to the United States regarding the existence of WMD in Iraq. I had been friends with him

Prime Minister Junichiro Koizumi (left) appointed Yukio Okamoto, 57, Special Advisor to the Prime Minister on April 15, 2003, assigning him the responsibility for reconstruction in Iraq.

for many years. Wolfowitz had no personal agenda, he was simply a man who easily sympathized with others. His explanation of the U.S. offensive strategy was persuasive, but I also felt that he was overly confident in the ability of anti-Saddam forces in Iraq to govern their country. Perhaps that was because I was aware that one could not readily trust his sources, Ahmad Chalabi and other exiled Iraqis, who would later return to Iraq to become key ministers.

Immediately after returning to Tokyo, I went to see Prime Minister Koizumi and Chief Cabinet Secretary Fukuda and reported as follows:

1. War Preparations and Optimism

(1) Since 9/11, the U.S. has been in a state of war, and Bush is a "war president," much as President Franklin D. Roosevelt had been. Washington thinks that some disruption of international order may be unavoidable, but ensuring the safety of the American people has

a higher priority. They have decided to enter a long war with Islam extremists. The sense of crisis is now fueled by the behavior of Germany and France, whom Americans think are making things easier for Saddam Hussein and extremists.

(2) The U.S. government is gathering intelligence and information, preparing for war, developing UN diplomacy, dealing with neighboring countries, and holding covert negotiations with Iraqi dissidents—all under a unified strategy and without a single loose thread. It is only the United States that could undertake such an integrated set of activities.

(3) There was overwhelming confidence in the military equipment and ability of the U.S. Armed Forces. The combat would end in a comparatively short time. Washington is convinced that the morale of the Iraqi military is very low. The major fields of battle are expected to be in Baghdad and Tikrit, and the U.S. thinks that both the regular army and the Republican Guard will surrender if surrounded. Washington has optimistic expectations that both the southern Shia and the northern Kurds will welcome the American forces as a liberation army, and there will be no objection from the majority of the central Sunni faction.

(4) They think it is definitely possible to discover chemical and biological weapons.

2. Occupation and Governance

(1) Governing Iraq is seen as fundamentally different from Afghanistan, and the U.S. expects to handle the situation to the end. They estimate that an almost 100,000-strong American military presence will be necessary until the end of hostilities.

(2) In the beginning, a GHQ-type military administration will be established and then transferred to civilian jurisdiction (led, for example, by an experienced former economic cabinet minister). As Iraqis are recognized as competent people, the existing Iraqi government body would be utilized as the executing agency. A Baath Party cadre would be purged.

(3) The funding needed at the initial stage is estimated to be around 10 billion dollars. Since the Iraqi economy is far more advanced than that of Afghanistan, its reconstruction will require much more money. As much as possible, the funding will be gleaned from sales of Iraqi oil.

(4) Many international specialists will be required, including civil engineers who are expert in building infrastructure, as well as experts in administration, judicature, medicine, and translation. The desire is to make it as "internationalized" as possible.

At the end of my report to the Prime Minister, I added that if war starts, Japan must support the United States with a unified and powerful voice in order to keep Washington linked closely to international society and avoid its heading toward isolationism. I stressed the need to separate other important issues like the protection of Japanese nationals and the need to assist neighboring countries from any announcements. I concluded my report by saying that Japan must contribute to the reconstruction of Iraq in a broad way, such as rebuilding infrastructure, political governance, humanitarian assistance, debt relief, removal of mines and so forth. In doing so, I felt that the most important element would be the 'speed of execution'. Even today, I think the report was correct.

The war began on March 20, 2003. Prime Minister Koizumi remained firm when he received the report from his Embassy in Washington and immediately held a press conference at which he declared unequivocal support for the United States. I was impressed. Just a few days earlier, when MOFA submitted a draft of "the Prime Minister's statement" for Koizumi to read at a press conference, he had responded angrily: "I don't need this! I will speak in my own words. Just bring me the necessary information." I watched as he literally threw the documents back at the MOFA officials.

He knew that the manuscript prepared by bureaucrats would just be playing it safe and would not elicit the sympathy of the nation's citizens. He wanted to speak to the Japanese public in his own words. According to a survey conducted on March 22 and 23 by Yomiuri

Shimbun, the largest-circulation Japanese newspaper, 76% of the respondents said that they would approve of an attack on Iraq, resonating with Prime Minister Koizumi's candid address, with 12% responding that it was the obvious thing to do and 64% saying it was unavoidable. This was truly impressive leadership. Never before had Japan had such a prime minister.

Prime Minister Koizumi prioritized foreign policies without fear of criticism. Given its geopolitical position, Japan cannot adopt an "evenhanded foreign policy" and maintain the same attitude toward all other nations. Still there have been many situations in the past in which Japan did not unequivocally state its position in order not to displease somebody. This was called "omni-directional diplomacy."

This time Japan could have kept its position ambiguous by simply expressing an "understanding" of the U.S. action, but Prime Minister Koizumi made it clear that Japan would "support" the United States. By that time, Japanese public opinion had matured enough to understand the foreign policy of the Government, as long as the prime ministers spoke to them with candor and in earnest.

As expected, it didn't take long for the war to end in a military victory for the United States, given the overwhelming American strength and the stupendous advances in its military technology. The brutal deaths of the Marines in Somalia had shocked the United States, which thereafter used all of its ability to study ways of war that could keep humans as far away from combat as possible. In Iraq, the use of unmanned surveillance aircraft and bombers brought them one step closer to remote-controlled war. As such, the frontal war ended in complete victory for the U.S.

Nonetheless, the story of Black Hawk Down stuck in my mind. From my experience serving in the Middle East, I could not think things would continue to go well in that region.

Saddam Hussein's Palace

In Tokyo, preparations for the restoration of Iraq began. In Washington, Deputy Secretary of State Armitage had told me that I would never learn the U.S. strategy for Iraq restoration in Washington. He had said, "Jay Garner is in command of restoration. Go and talk with him in Kuwait." So, on April 7, two days before the fall of Baghdad, I visited Jay Garner in Kuwait at the headquarters of the U.S. Office of Reconstruction and Humanitarian Assistance (ORHA), an organ created by the United States to reconstruct Iraq after the war.

How could Japan contribute to Iraq restoration? I was determined to figure this out. Since the Gulf War, my conviction was that Japan needs to do something itself before being told by someone else. At ORHA, I was met by Katsuhiko Oku, Councilor of the Japanese Embassy in London, who was on loan to ORHA. Oku was 13 years behind me at MOFA. I had met him for the first time in 1987. He was a lively and refreshing man. He loved to remind me of our first encounter, which he remembered very well: "I brought a paper for you to sign, and you scared the hell out me by staring and roaring at me, he said. He was, of course, exaggerating, but we immediately reaffirmed to each other that we were cut of the same cloth. Oku was later assigned to the Japanese Embassy in Baghdad and became the lead diplomat for Japan's activities in Iraq, and my invaluable partner.

ORHA Director Jay Garner, was a retired Lieutenant General who had experience in the Kurdish area in Northern Iraq and looked like a tough bulldog. He was not interested in diplomatic conversations. He meant business. He startled me by asking abruptly, "Which area does Japan want to take the responsibility for? At this early stage you can pick any area you want. Nasiriyah? Diwaniyah? Just name it." He apparently knew the subject well and loved Iraqi people. I immediately liked him and wanted to develop a good relationship with this confident, if a bit impatient official

Maybe it was this confidence that prompted his early departure from his job. He was at his post in Baghdad for hardly any time at all. Garner's straightforwardness must have created enemies in Washington, and he was forced to quit the job he had barely begun. He returned home in early May. He was unable to keep his promise to greet me in Baghdad.

Garner had his chief staffers lined up in the meeting. Seated next to him was his deputy, British Major-General Tim Cross. I met him subsequently in Baghdad and was always impressed with his deep thinking about Iraq. Little did I know then, however, that he would become a severe critic of U.S. governance of Iraq, calling it "fatally flawed." He declared at a public hearing in 2009 at the British Parliament[32]: "Although I was confident that we would secure a military victory, I offered my view that we should not begin that campaign until we had a much more coherent postwar plan."

While Garner was introducing his staff, Oku whispered into my ear, "These people will be very cooperative because they are grateful for what you personally did during the Gulf War." "The Gulf War?" I wondered. The Japanese were thrashed and treated like a pariah because no one knew what we actually did.

It was Cross who began to speak, with his eyes pinned on me. "I was here in the desert during the Gulf War as Commander of the 1st Armored Division. I drove a land cruiser—one that you people sent to us from Japan. It was because we had these vehicles that we were able to carry out our duties. Thank you very much."

I was stunned. When I dispatched 800 4WDs amid international attention and turmoil in September 1990, there was nothing but criticism at home and no word of appreciation from the United States. Now, 13 years later, I was hearing words of gratitude for the first time from someone who had actually used the vehicles!

I stared at Maj. Gen. Cross's face without responding. The meeting went on to the next item, but my mind flooded with memories of the Gulf War and the humiliating ingratitude we had endured. At the meeting, aside from Garner, Cross, and the chiefs of Restoration, Humanitarian Support and Civilian Rule, there was a tall, attractive woman at the meeting. She was the Coordinator for Central Iraq, which included responsibility for Baghdad. Her name was Barbara Bodine. The name sounded familiar, but I could not recall where I had heard it before.

Then she spoke: "I was at the American Embassy in Kuwait when Iraqi Forces reached Kuwait City on August 3, 1990. I was the one in charge of protecting the American Embassy staff, who were given shelter in the Japanese Ambassador's residence. I was the counterpart of Ambassador Shirota during the operation, and I will never forget his courage." So *that* was why I recognized her name! I was again moved.

I was hearing words of gratitude for what Japan did during the Gulf War, this time for the way our Embassy in Kuwait had rescued more than 20 American Embassy personnel and their families. Hardly anybody knew about the episode as it was deliberately buried under the layers of hostility Washington harbored against Japan at the time.

Later, the ORHA changed its name to the CPA (Coalition Provisional Authority). Oku moved to Baghdad in April with the CPA team, to the Saddam Hussein Palace, where the CPA headquarters had been established. The palace also housed part of the Multinational Forces Headquarters, so soldiers came in and out of the building around the clock. The palace contained about 300 rooms, and Oku was able to secure a small empty room on the second floor. He brought in a bed and a refrigerator, and it became his operations room.

After my return to Tokyo, Oku said on the phone: "Okamoto-san, the power of "Host Nation Support" (Japanese financial support for U.S. Forces in Japan) is amazing! Every U.S. military officer I talk to tells me how indebted they are to the HNS. They're friends with Japan right from the start! Thank you, thank you, Okamoto-san, for helping to make my job easier."

Oku thanked me simply because at MOFA, I was always in the position of working to increase the HNS budget, but it was astonishing to hear how the HNS was appreciated, even in such a remote place. "Okamoto-san, please come to Baghdad as soon as you can," Oku said.

I did just that. Per his request, I went to Iraq several times. And traveled with Oku all over Iraq, from Baghdad, to Mosul, Arbil, Sulaymaniyah, Kirkuk, Tikrit, Karbala, Hillah, Najaf, Diwaniyah, Nasiriyah, Samawah, Amarah, Basrah, Umm Qasr, and many other small towns. Oku was a forthcoming man. Usually, Japanese officials first say "no" to everything and then look for something within the proposal to which they can say "yes." Oku's approach was the opposite. He would start with a positive answer, and from that eliminate the parts that he thought would have to be a no. I was determined to help this man till the end, and as it turned out, Katsuhiko Oku was a true hero.

FAILURE OF U.S. GOVERNANCE IN IRAQ

Occupying Iraq is Not the Same as Occupying Japan

IN EARLY MARCH just before the war began, I presented two scenarios in writing to the Prime Minister and the Chief Cabinet Secretary and frankly explained my assessment: While America believed in the optimistic scenario, my frank judgment was that the pessimistic scenario was more likely.

The Optimistic Scenario: "The Road to Middle-East Peace Begins in Baghdad"

The Iraqi citizens enthusiastically welcome the American Army. ... As a joint effort with the Iraqi advisory group, a constitution is created and peace is established. ... In one or two years, a democratic Iraqi government is elected. ... The Iraqis brilliantly take charge of the country and a market economy takes firm root. ... Iraq becomes a showcase for democratization in the Middle East. ... Seeing the success of Iraq, the monarch states in the Gulf Area carry out internal reforms. ... The flow of funds to terrorists from both Iran and Syria stops, and the Palestinian problem also improves. ... The entire Mideast moves toward stability. ... The Middle East turns pro-America.

The Pessimistic Scenario: "Long-term Confusion and World Disunion"

Saddam Hussein's loyalists continue resistance at great cost in human life. ... World opinion turns against the United States. ... Even after the American occupation, resistance continues. ... Hostilities and arms spread within and beyond Iraq. ... American occupation

continues for a long time and terrorism proliferates. ... The entire
Arab world takes on an anti-U.S. mood. ... The U.S.-friendly Arab
regimes become unstable. ... The Palestinian situation worsens.

Of the two scenarios, optimistic and pessimistic, the situation
in Iraq was already unfolding along the pessimistic path only six
months after the U.S. victory in the war. In no small part, I was convinced, the deterioration was due to two strategic errors.

Failure of U.S. Governance: the CPA

The first was the failure of U.S. governance. After serving in Baghdad for barely a month and a half, Lt. Gen. Garner was replaced by
Jerry Bremer as the Administrator of Iraq. Secretary Bremer was the
special envoy of President George Bush and was treated as such. I
visited him every time I went to Baghdad. Bremer was the opposite
of Garner, who was informal affable, and casually dressed. Bremer
was formal, wore an impeccable business suit, and came across as a
proper Washington bureaucrat. The only aberration in his presenta-
tion was the big desert boots he always wore, which showed promi-
nently when he would throw his feet on the table. That was his style.

I could see he was an able and hard-working official, but how
much love he harbored towards the citizens of Iraq, I could not
know. His most important goal was to quickly advance the political
process in Iraq—create administrative institutions, hold elections,
set up a congress, promulgate a constitution, and thus establish a
democratic government. However, he and Washington made some
major mistakes in the early stages that undermined efforts to stabilize Iraq. Bremer and his CPA lacked a well-thought-out strategy.
The best evidence was their rush to de-Baathify the government and
their cavalier dismissal of Iraqi military personnel.

Immediately after the U.S. occupation of Iraq in May 2003, Secretary Bremer abolished the Baath Party and removed all party members from public institutions in one fell swoop. First, some 85,000
individuals holding positions in the top three levels of management,
which included government agencies, national hospitals, national
universities and other public institutions, were removed from their

offices. De-Baathification later spread to schoolteachers and medical doctors in level four, resulting in the expulsion of most government officials before an agreement could be made on a mechanism to restore the nation.

The far-reaching extent of De-Baathification without an agreed mechanism for reconciliation exacerbated the problem. The term itself meant the exclusion of 1,500,000 Baath Party members from the future administration of Iraq. The truth was that most of these people had registered themselves as Baathists simply to get jobs. They had signed up for the sole purpose of making a living and not out of loyalty to the party or ideology. They could have become friends of America.

I have subsequently met many professionals, bureaucrats, engineers, medical doctors, teachers, and city council members who were Baathists resolved to rebuild their own country. I lost contact with many of them, however. Many disappeared from their workplaces. Due to the exclusion of these people who had served as the middle management of the government, the Iraqi government was in a state of collapse at the most important juncture.

Judging from President Bush's frequent comments about the successful democratization of Japan after World War II, it was evident that Americans tended to think that it wouldn't be hard to use the experience in Japan and apply it to Iraq. The fact that General Douglas MacArthur, Commander-in-Chief of the allied forces who ruled Japan, democratized Japan without deploying any military power is noteworthy in world history. However, Gen. MacArthur had studied Japan thoroughly in preparation for occupation. It is said that a library of books about Japan lined the shelves of his personal study in the Philippines.

General MacArthur had dismissed 200,000 bureaucrats and politicians from public duty, but he did so over a period of nearly three years, in alignment with the Japanese people building a new system of governance. Added to that, MacArthur's successor General Matthew Ridgway, ended this policy of expulsion from public office in 1951, and by 1952, most of the expelled had returned to their former positions. Unlike these two generals who stabilized and democratized Japan, CPA Administrator Paul Bremer's expulsion of Ba'ath members was too hasty.

One person I knew who did not completely follow the de-Baath-ification order was a Major General named David Petraeus, stationed in the city of Mosul. He was responsible for the stabilization of Northern Iraq. He resisted Secretary Bremer's orders and got an exemption to run a local reconciliation process that allowed most of the Baathist school teachers, Mosul University professors (120 Level Four members), and other key ministry representatives in Nineveh Province to remain in their positions. These individuals had signed up as members of the 1.5 million-strong Baath Party because they needed jobs. This policy served as one of the reasons for the stability in the provinces under Petraeus.

I visited primary schools in Mosul where teachers, possibly Baathist members, were teaching eager children with passion. The region under Petraeus' control was stable until the insurgency took root there in 2004, when it became clear that Iraqi leaders in Baghdad were not going to approve the local reconciliation initiatives there, and the local governor was assassinated in June 2004.

After expelling the Ba'ath members, the CPA brought in exiles to rule Iraq who had fled to other countries. These people, who included Ahmad Chalabi, had skillfully led the U.S. government into the Iraq War with their fluent English. After the war, they returned to Iraq under asylum granted by the United States to clear old grudges in their home countries and to spearhead the expulsion of the Baath Party. They were not popular among the Iraqi people however, so from the onset, American rule in Iraq was destined to fail.

The second strategic failure cannot be over-emphasized: The complete dismantling of Saddam's Army without pay created strong and determined enemies—hundreds of thousands of them—of the United States. Later research revealed that this was one of the first decisions Jerry Bremer made in Iraq, but I had no way of knowing. Bob Woodward writes in *State of Denial*[33] that the United States failed to govern Iraq after the war and that the CPA turned the soldiers of the former Saddam Hussein regime into enemies. Woodward cites an episode in which the CPA denied a request for former Iraqi soldiers and Baath party members to be given an "emergency payment" of roughly $20 to help them survive. The approval would have created friends for the American troops and cost merely 200 million dollars.

Had the request been granted, I am certain that most of Saddam's soldiers would have participated in the national reconstruction corps. Instead, they were left full of vengeance and in possession of plentiful weapons as they turned to kill American soldiers everywhere.

Since I do not have supporting information of my own, I will not write further, but the fact remains that the security environment in Iraq quickly deteriorated. Although the planning and execution of military operations was flawless, the U.S. had not considered governance plans carefully. The people known as neo-conservatives, who were directing the war in Washington, were burning with idealism. The Iraqis who lived in exile in the United States took advantage of this idealism—and their naivete—and led them to believe that the Iraqi people would welcome American occupation as a liberation army. One of my good friends was a well-known neo-conservative who held a key position in the government. What fueled him was not his fighting spirit, nor his right-wing ideology, nor even his desire for merit. It was his sense of justice.

This brought to mind the history of the successful democratization of Japan engineered by the American Occupation Forces in Japan, which I experienced first-hand as a boy. General MacArthur did not use military force to achieve his goal of pacifying Japan, and in turn, not a single shot was fired at the Occupation Forces by a Japanese national.

Of course, the foundations of the two occupations were different. First of all, the Japanese Emperor declared defeat and told the citizens to "beware most strictly of any outbursts of emotion which may engender needless complications, or any fraternal contention and strife which may create confusion, lead you astray and cause you to lose the confidence of the world," in an NHK radio broadcast[34], proclaiming that the people must change and create a peaceful society. It was the first time that a Japanese emperor had directly addressed the people. The photo of the Emperor at GHQ alongside MacArthur presented an undeniable message to the public that times had changed. Also, Imperial Army chief General Anami committed ritual hara-kiri to acknowledge Japan's defeat to the entire army of 5.5 million soldiers, thereby asking the still-belligerent officers not to resist the United States.

In Iraq, there was no declaration of surrender. In stark contrast, Saddam's men were ordered to continue fighting. They had been instructed by Saddam's intelligence organ, Mukhabarat, to resist and create chaos in every way possible. Furthermore, Saddam, before fleeing, had set free all the criminals from prisons to disrupt the legal and social order.

Of course, there are differences in national character. Japanese people don't often rebel against orders given to them by a higher authority. During World War II, Japanese chanted slogans calling Americans and British demons, but once a new day began with Japan's defeat, they became friendly with the Occupation Army, referring to them by the affectionate name of "America-san." Surely, there was a shortage of supplies throughout Japan and people lived in utter poverty, but social order was maintained even amid the hustle and bustle of reconstruction. The diligence of the citizens became the driving force for recovery.

The CPA should have understood this was not the case in Iraq and sought something different from the Iraqi people. Speaking from my experience working in the Middle East, I believe the answer to this would have been to understand Islam and the people's obedience to God. How many Muslim Americans were in the CPA? Did the U.S. officials ever try to solicit the help of imams in Iraq?

I attempted a visit to the hardline cleric Muqtada al-Sadr in Najaf, the sacred land of the Shi'a Muslims, but the CPA stopped me. Does that mean that the CPA solicited the help of the Shi'ite Grand Ayatollah Ali al-Sistani? Just as MacArthur used the Japanese Emperor, Bremer should have paid more respect to Iraq's spiritual authority and asked for his support to stabilize Iraq.

Saddam Hussein, who was of the Sunni minority, had persecuted the Shi'a majority. Removing Saddam's ruling structure, which was Sunni-based, would inevitably invite Shi'a retaliation, and then subsequent retaliation from the Sunni. The only way I can see that could have prevented the endless retaliatory cycle was for the Shi'ite Ayatollah to show "forgiveness" to the Sunnis.

In my view, the CPA over-emphasized the process of political democratization as a means for the restoration and improvement of the lives of Iraqis. It created an interim ruling structure, conducting a national election, establishing the People's Assembly, creating a democratic government, and producing a constitution, all of which are politically more salient and sellable in Washington than in Baghdad.

By doing so, they lost the momentum to improve the lives of citizens and also alienated the highest-quality Iraqi technocrats at the working level. Improving living conditions, albeit not as politically impressive as institution-building, was a *sine qua non* for winning popular support for the American presence, the most important element in rebuilding the nation under American governance. Unfortunately, the CPA did make this a high enough priority.

An example of getting priorities wrong was the CPA's failure to quickly fix the Dura Power Plant in the southern district of Baghdad, which provided half of the city's total electric power. The plant had been so badly damaged that in the summer of 2003, amid the blistering heat, it was only providing electricity for a few hours per day. The plant had been poorly maintained under Saddam and would break down no matter how often it was repaired. Moreover, there was rampant theft by robbers who would steal and melt the power cables to sell. CPA had tried to fix the problem but did not succeed. Still, did it try hard enough? It was a matter of only one power plant in a safe area at the time. The U.S. could have sent an engineering corps together with civil experts and spared a platoon to guard the power plant against petty thieves. Japan could have participated in the repair process. No doubt, Baghdad citizens would have felt the positive change in their lives and appreciated the U.S. governance more. It was all about what priority would be assigned to improving essential infrastructure.

One Iraqi government official who tried to restore the Dura plant told me about this episode: "We pleaded to CPA to have the power plant fixed as quickly as possible. The CPA accepted our point and said: 'You can order new generators from the manufacturers immediately.' We were very happy, but when we told the CPA that the manufacturer was Siemens, they told us, 'No, nothing from Germany'. And that was the end of that."

Summer in Iraq is oppressively hot; temperatures can reach nearly 50 degrees Celsius. People feel if they are standing with a hairdryer constantly blowing at their faces. It did not take long with no electricity before citizens began to feel, "Things were better during the Saddam days." These feelings ultimately turned into anti-U.S. Army sentiment. The citizens who had waved to welcome Americans in Baghdad had not been cheering about the demise of Saddam Hussein. It was because they thought the new ruler, the United States, would improve their living conditions.

The United States had several hidden goals in managing Iraq, entangled with the official manifesto of democratic action. One was, of course, to obtain Iraqi oil. Another was to secure oil-rich Iraq as a future market for American goods. If the United States was concentrating on securing economic interests backed by Iraq's future purchasing power, this strategy was short-sighted. This was the critical phase of stabilization. It was a bizarre contrast to the well-conceived battle plan.

Another example that I experienced was the U.S. objection to Japan's proposal to help Iraqi hospitals. Oku and I were close to securing a budget of 300 million dollars out of Japan's total assistance of 5 billion dollars for Iraq. With the help of Iraqi hospital officials at the Ministry of Health, we identified 24 major hospitals out of more than 150 public hospitals nationwide to receive donated medical equipment and materials.

The discussions with Tokyo were proceeding smoothly but we had to inform the CPA of our intentions. Expecting blessings and encouragement, we explained our plan in detail, including the names of the intended recipient hospitals. The American reply did not respond for some time. "We are confirming Washington's disposition," they told us. And when their answer finally came, we were stunned: "We ask that Japanese donations of medical equipment be limited only to the 13 hospitals built previously by Japan under its economic aid program." This was an unreasonable restriction when all 24 hospitals were badly in need of new equipment.

When we asked a friend at the CPA, he told us that "there are some people in Washington who are suspicious that Japan is trying to seize this opportunity to take over the medical equipment market in Iraq after the reconstruction of the country. Washington thinks such commercial rights should be given to U.S. companies. Therefore, Japanese cooperation should be limited only to the hospitals where Japan has had historical ties."

This was a stereotypical example of how Americans perceive that whatever Japan does for the public good, it is always with the purpose of bringing profit to Japanese companies. When in 1990, Japanese companies responded to the government's request to furnish the American Forces in the Gulf desert with needed supplies without any profit, the American response was the same. The CPA's lack of tough action to suppress the large-scale plundering and looting by citizens that began immediately after the fall of Baghdad eroded the citizen's confidence in law and order at the incipient stage of the occupation. Looting went on throughout the country. Valuables were stolen and industrial infrastructure was destroyed. I personally saw numerous factories that had been raided by looters, where all the electrical equipment, computers and office supplies had been ripped out and carried away. In libraries, books were scattered all over the floor. The plunderers had no interest in books, they stole the bookcases.

In August 2003, the director of Baghdad Central Hospital spoke to me with indignation: "The looters were all normal citizens, and they came to plunder this hospital's medical equipment. I stood at the entrance raising my hands to stop the crowds. I begged the American soldiers who were guarding the entranceway with guns to help me. And what do you think the soldiers said? I couldn't believe my ears! They told the crowd, 'Everything here belongs to you people. Take what you like.' The crowd shoved me aside and burst into the hospital." Then the director added in a sad tone: "The only equipment we were able to save was in a room where looters, upon opening the door, fainted. I had anticipated the raid and had filled the room with anesthetics."

The response of the American soldiers indicated that they had no clear orders to prevent plundering. It must have been left to the judgment of individual soldiers. The consequences were profound. Over the first several critical months of stabilizing the society, the public sense of the need to observe laws was undermined. Even after nationwide looting subsided, there was a tendency among citizens who had participated in this sort of lawlessness to find it easier to follow avarice and injustice, rather than rules and restrictions.

The lootings had an infinite adverse impact on the reconstruction of the country. Particularly serious was the fact that various government ministries had all been broken into and looted. The single exception was the Ministry of Petroleum, which was guarded by U.S. soldiers because of the perceived interests for the United States. The fact that government organs were crippled hampered the recovery of the country. If the U.S. could protect the Ministry of Petroleum, why couldn't they protect other important government offices? As a result, the U.S. occupation lost the assistance of a functioning Iraqi government as well as the trust of Iraqi bureaucrats.

Iran's Willingness to Cooperate

I must also write about my own failed attempts. The United States, which continued to loathe Iran, believed that Iran was sending thousands of Shia insurgents across the border to the area around Basra at the southeastern tip of Iraq. In Basra, I asked the British Commander who was responsible for public order in the region if the American assertion had any truth to it. He laughed, "There are no Iranians here." It would have been quite simple for Iran to bring Basra under its influence, but there was no sign of Iran making such an attempt. Today, Basra is the area that has the most stable public order in all of Iraq.

Iran was a touchy subject, and I knew I had very few friends who would support me in approaching Teheran for cooperation. Nobody thought Iran would be forthcoming, much less engage in projects to help Iraq. People in Washington would surely raise their eyebrows. But I thought that Iran could be an important part of the Iraqi equation and that somehow, if we could obtain their cooperation, even if tacit, it would be a substantial contribution to stability in Iraq.

Certain that Iran was hoping for Iraq to stabilize, I visited Teheran in June and again in November 2003 for meetings with Foreign Minister Kamal Kharazi, National Security Council Secretary Hassan Rouhani, Congressional Foreign Policy Committee Chairman Mohsen Mirdamadi, and others.

I was deeply impressed especially by Hassan Rouhani, who 10 years later, in 2013, was elected President of Iran. He constantly smiled as he spoke calmly about Iran's position of wanting to support Iraq's rehabilitation. Rouhani's sense of balance and his realism, I thought, was no different from that of Western intellectuals. He emphasized that Iran needed a stable neighbor, and maintained that Iran had no interest in meddling with Iraq, much less placing Iraq under its sphere of interest.

I was convinced that Iran wanted the situation in Iraq stabilized. I was reminded of an experience while visiting Afghanistan in March 2002, the year before the Iraq War. The United States, which had invaded Afghanistan in October 2001 to wipe out Al-Qaeda and the Taliban, were anxious about the large number of Iranians who had come to Afghanistan by crossing the border into Herat Province.

When I arrived in Afghanistan, however, I was surprised to hear otherwise from Ismail Khan, Afghanistan's most powerful mujahideen warlord who ruled the three western provinces. I had expected Khan, a passionate patriot, to maintain strong vigilance against Iran but he said that he felt grateful to the Iranians who were crossing the border voluntarily to help the construction of infrastructure for poor Afghans.

I told a U.S. representative about this episode. He curtly replied, "Iran is simply building roads in Herat to make it easier for their troops to invade Afghanistan." I never heard of any Iranian ambition regarding Herat Province after that, but the United States never deviated from viewing Iran as an evil state that never does anything out of good intentions.

To digress for a moment, the charismatic white-haired leader, Ismail Khan, was a quiet man with charismatic power. He and I stood on a hill together and talked for a long time as the sun went down. Twenty-three years prior to that, the Herat people had stood up against the Soviet occupation troops, killing more than 200 Soviet military advisors and their families. The reprisal against the uprising was fierce, with Soviet troops killing 25,000 Herat citizens in one day. Ismail Khan was a soldier in the government army working with the Soviet Union at the time and was ordered to fire at the people. He instead suddenly turned around on them and started firing at the Soviet Army, and became a hero.

Afghan mountains are steep, with bare rocks. Humans are deterred by the overwhelming nature. In that environment, the mujahideen fought the Soviets. Then the Taliban, Al-Qaida, and the U.S. military continued to fight. Whether in Afghanistan, Iraq or Iran, the region is not a place where the West can expect to perform well unless they know what they are doing.

Iranians said they were ready to establish firm border control with Iraq and that they would stop additional Iranians from entering Iraq. Simply put, the border police would permit one Iranian national to cross the border into Iraq only when one Iranian had returned. They also pledged that no potential terrorist would pass the border. I felt this offer was quite meaningful and immediately conveyed it to Tokyo and asked them to relay the Iranian proposal to Washington.

Oku had thought up a scheme for Japan to provide the Iranian government with patrol vehicles for that purpose. There was no reaction from MOFA in Tokyo. I directly communicated to my friends in Washington that since Iran is indicating a cooperative stance, now is the time to open dialogue with them. But, in the final analysis, I was only able to convey this as a personal opinion, so there was no urgency for the United States to act on it.

The situation worsened with the change in Iran's president in August 2005 from the moderate Mohammad Khatami to the fundamentalist Mahmoud Ahmadinejad. At long last, it had seemed that the United States might begin to move in the direction of seeking the possibility of Iranian cooperation, but then it was too late.

At an international conference in Geneva in October 2006, I had the opportunity to meet Sir Hilary Synnott, who was the U.K. representative in Iraq responsible for coordinating with the CPA. He had been enthusiastic about Iraq's reconstruction, so I decided to share my thoughts with him. Sir Synnott, who later became a strong critic of the American CPA approach, told me that he had shared my opinion about the relationship with Iran.

THE DEDICATION OF THE SOLDIERS

American Soldiers and Iraqi Citizens

BACK IN IRAQ, Oku and I were both moved by the dedication of the American soldiers to their duties. Units of American Army troops in Baghdad were in a constant state of alert, faced as they were with the possibility of an armed attack. But they had to meet Iraqi citizens every day if they were to be able to restore the structures and rhythms of daily life in the city.

Oku, with his typical openness, had become close friends with Lt. Colonel Eric Nantz of the 1st Battalion of the 325th Airborne Brigade of the 82nd Airborne Division. Nantz was a North Carolinian who looked like the actor Paul Newman and smiled constantly. He never went anywhere without photos of his three children. When Oku took me to meet him, the handsome colonel was sitting in a small room in a house that was still half constructed as he explained the difficulties of his duties. Most Baghdad citizens at that time welcomed and co-operated with the U.S. military, but there were hostile forces as well. Nantz explained to me that his order, "Be friendly, professional but prepared to shoot," was not easy order to observe, but he had great hopes for the future.

Early in the occupation, I was surprised when I went out into the city with Nantz and his troops in his APC. Not only did children chase after us, but adults also waved at us. Men waved from in front of their houses, while women huddled inside the houses and waved shyly. It almost made me think that Iraq might move right into the era of democratization and peace after several months. How wrong I was.

The American Army that was deployed across Baghdad at that time to look after the life of citizens consisted of 12 battalions of 850

Yukio Okamoto visits Mosul, Iraq in September 2003. Yukio was surrounded by many welcoming children when he tried to take a picture. At the time, many citizens appreciated American soldiers for their efforts to restore civilian life.

soldiers each. It was not a small number. Nantz's battalion was in charge infrastructure restoration of the sections called Ashraf and Azamia, which together had a population of 850,000. Every morning a planning meeting was held to decide on the order of work. The battalion then scattered into the city to restore necessary facilities.

At that point, most citizens openly welcomed American soldiers not as conquerors, but as liberators. It was clearly a honeymoon moment between the U.S. Army and the citizens of Baghdad. This was the case not only in Baghdad. In many cities across Iraq, I witnessed the American Army arduously working on the rehabilitation of citizens' lives.

In the Shiite holy cities of Karbala and Najaf, too, Nantz was engaged in reconstruction work with local representatives. Often, when Oku and I visited regional cities to discuss restoration plans with city officials, American Army officers who were stationed there would attend to observe the discussions, with no fear of being attacked by insurgents. They believed that their goodwill would communicate itself to the people.

So, early on, it seemed as though Iraq would continue to democratize and stabilize. But not long afterwards, the security situation in Iraq visibly began to deteriorate. The eyes of senior CPA officials and Iraqi leaders were not directed at the public. They were working in a direction that would negate the hard work of the soldiers in the field like Nantz. Here is when I was first struck by how different this governance was from that of MacArthur's GHQ.

Major General Petraeus and the 101st Airborne Division

Iraq has both vast areas of parched earth, and rich greenery blessed by the two great rivers, Tigris and Euphrates. These are the two rivers that nurtured the Mesopotamian civilization. Both rivers start in the fountainhead of Turkey's Anatolian plateau. The Tigris flows along the east, and the Euphrates along the west of Iraq from north to south until they meet 430 kilometers south of Baghdad to become Shatt-al-Arab, before pouring into the Persian Gulf.

The Tigris is especially important. Once past Mosul, the Tigris becomes a gorge with tall cliffs rising on both sides. From Baghdad

Commander of Coalition Ground Forces, General Ricardo Sanchez (left), meets with Yukio Okamoto at Camp Victory military base near Baghdad on September 16, 2003. Yukio admired General Sanchez's compassion for the Iraqi people.

The Tigris River flows through Mosul, Iraq, as photographed on September 16, 2003 by Yukio Okamoto, who was impressed by the beauty of the city. Later, much of Mosul was destroyed following ISIS attacks in 2014.

400 kilometers to the south, it slowly flows along flatlands amid date palm groves, wheat fields, and wasteland where houses are built out of sun-dried bricks. The Tigris flows through the cities of Mosul and Baghdad, bringing greenery to the desert. Once, it created the civilizations of Babylon and Ur, some 90 and 330 kilometers south of Baghdad, respectively. It is the great mother river of Iraq that supports the lives of the people. When it passes through Mosul, the flow is clear and blue, but becomes murky in Baghdad.

Mosul, with a population of 2.2 million, is the second largest city in Iraq, and spreads out from the banks of the great river. The town is brownish and dry, lined with medieval-like houses made of stacked sun-dried bricks. It was also once home to Nineveh, the capital of Assyria. General Ricardo Sanchez, U.S. military Commander-in-chief for all of Iraq, used to tell me at his office in Camp Victory in Baghdad that Mosul had been given high priority as a model city for post-war Iraq. Mosul was not only the center of northern Iraq, it was also a strategic point near the borders of Syria and Turkey. It was also an "experimental city" outside the Kurdish region to test the coexistence of the Sunni, Shia, and Kurdish communities.

Right from the beginning, I liked this general for his human touch and his apparent compassion for the Iraqi people. It was later that I learned through the press about the conflict between Sanchez and Paul Bremer, and subsequently, Sanchez's dismissal. The analysis that Sanchez shared with me was always much closer to my own understanding of the situation in Iraq.

Six months after the end of the Iraq war, Mosul became the base for stabilization in northern Iraq. The 22,000 officers and soldiers of the U.S. Army's 101st Airborne Division who fought their way to Baghdad then moved north and stationed themselves in Mosul and the surrounding province. Air Assault divisions are task forces that operate mainly by helicopter. The 101st was a powerful force with 250 assault helicopters, including the Sikorsky UH60 Blackhawk, the helicopter I had spoken about with Prime Minister Koizumi in February. The division had jurisdiction over Nineveh, as well as the Kurdish Provinces of Dahuk, Arbil and Sulaymaniyah to the northeast. In each of these provinces, security was stable.

The 101st Airborne Division had a wide range of activities, from public safety to setting up administrative structure and executing civilian assistance projects. The man in charge of the 101st Airborne Division was Major General David Petraeus. He was intelligent and capable of strategic thinking and at the same time very caring. He was a hero long before he became the commander of the "surge" in Iraq, then head of the U.S. Central Command (USCENTCOM), and finally Director of the CIA. His lifestyle was frugal. His "bedroom" was a screened off corner of a room with only a sleeping bag. It was unbelievably austere.

Many of the citizens of Mosul came to know the name Petraeus as if to idolize him. He was convinced that in order to stabilize security, it was most important to earn the trust of the people. Pro-U.S. sentiment among the Mosul city councilors and the general population was quite apparent. Whenever I met with community leaders, the mayor, city council members, hospital directors and school masters, I heard nothing but praise for the American military leader in the town. Under Petraeus, the number of police officers grew from zero immediately after the war, to 7,000 by the summer of the same year. I was told later by his deputy, Brigadier General Frank Helmick, that the usual mission of an Airborne division is to drop in on an enemy-occupied region, get the residents on your side, and support combat on the front lines from behind the enemy. Petraeus was a superb commander who could win the hearts and minds of the people.

Petraeus secured a large chunk of the commanders' discretionary fund named CERP (Commander's Emergency Response Program). It totaled 2.6 billion dollars and was intended to be spent across Iraq on a variety of civil projects. The source of CERP, I suspected, was partly money Saddam Hussein had kept at the Palace. Petraeus just smiled when I asked him that, but he admitted to securing enough of the funds to conduct more than 4,500 civil projects in the four provinces under his jurisdiction—from police reconstruction and industrial recovery to education and medical assistance, improvement of residential environments, roads, bridges, water supply and sewer services.

His deputy, General Helmick, was also a very warm man. One day, I visited a bank in Mosul with Helmick. Financial institutions had started to function, so we went to check the situation. In the bank, which unfortunately was the first target of ISIS when it occupied the city, an elegant elderly woman wrapped in a scarf came running up to Helmick, thanking him over and over again.

"What's up?" I asked. Helmick responded with a shy grin. "One day, as I was walking through the Division Headquarters, I heard a loud commotion of men and a woman talking. A lady was accusing my soldiers of stealing her treasure, a 100 dollar bill she said was her life savings, when they had entered her house to search for weapons. She was demanding the money back, but nobody would listen to her plea. I approached the crowd and heard the commotion, and then I ordered my military aide to give her 100 dollars. Helmick had the aide carry an emergency supply of dollars for such occasions, which were accounted for in the CERP program. The soldier was dissatisfied, saying that the woman had no evidence for her claim. I told him, "'If you're going to make a mistake, better err on the side of the weak.' That's all." I could easy tell how grateful she was from the tears she shed.

Oku and I visited Mosul's 101st Airborne headquarters countless times. It was the only place in the north that was safe to spend the night, and it was the most efficient for carrying out Japan's civilian assistance project in cooperation with Petraeus' Division, with which we had established trust. The 101st Airborne was compassionate toward the residents. The attitude of the leaders showed their men how to behave.

General Helmick would accompany Oku and me in his Black Hawk helicopter when we needed to inspect sites to determine if they were appropriate for Japanese assistance, because U.S. and Japan's efforts could complement each other. In the helicopter, Helmick would keep the door open while flying and always waved his hands even as they rested in his lap. To my quizzical look he said: "Oh this? I'm showing my gratitude to the Iraqi citizens," he said. "But nobody can see you from down there." "Oh no, Iraqis can see me waving in their hearts." From Petraeus and Helmick on down, the entire division, I felt, had a respect for the Iraqi people. This was also the way Helmick's loyal interpreter Sadi Othman, a tall soldier who seemed big as a mountain, felt about his American colleagues.

So, when the news broke that U.S. soldiers tortured Iraqis prisoners at Abu Ghraib Prison in 2004, I could not believe the story. Would even the soldiers in the 101st Airborne do this kind of thing when faced with prisoners? I sent Petraeus an e-mail, asking "Could this happen in your prisons too?" Petraeus wrote me back:

Yukio,

Abu Ghraib was a shock to all of us. It was, in fact, sickening and, in a sense, was like a blow to the solar plexus, literally knocking the wind out of us. I don't know what led to the actions in the photographs; however, I can say that we worked hard in our area to ensure that detainees were treated properly—even to the point that we had the ICRC, an Imam, and various Province Council members visit our facilities. And when they asked for improvements, etc., we did our best to make them.

Beyond that, I would hope that the world will not judge the hundreds of thousands of soldiers in Iraq by the actions of a few.

The vast majority of soldiers were fierce in war but compassionate in peace, and I think you saw that during your visits.

We sacrificed greatly to bring freedom to the Iraqi people, and then went to work to try to improve their basic services, governmental institutions, infrastructure, and so on. Again, I believe you saw a great deal of that, and I hope that you can convey what you saw to your readers.

Sincerely,
Dave Petraeus

After General Petraeus and the 101st Airborne Division departed, however, the security of Mosul began to deteriorate rapidly. Partly, this must have been due to the fact that not enough troops were left in Mosul to continue the efforts of the 101st, and partly it was the population's frustration with Iraqi leaders in Baghdad who had

David Petraeus, then a Major General and Commander of the U.S. 101st Airborne Division, meets in his office in Baghdad with Yukio Okamoto on September 16, 2003. Petraeus went on to become Commander of the U.S. Central Command and later, Director of the CIA.

resisted approving the reconciliation initiatives that Petraeus had brought to them, all of which Ambassador Bremer had approved.

One further reason, I thought, was the U.S. attack on Fallujah in November 2004. Militants were encamped in many mosques in that city. Under the full-scale attack of the U.S. military, Sunni fighters quickly escaped the city and expanded their bases in the northern region. It was from then that the security of the largest northern city, Mosul, took a plunge. And when President Barack Obama, reversed every Iraq-related policy of his predecessor George Bush and withdrew all U.S. forces stationed there before the country's security system was in place, the chaos in Iraq deepened.

Mosul's security deteriorated to the point that it finally fell into the hands of Islamic State of Iraq and Syria (ISIS) in June 2014, when ISIS leader Abu Bakr al-Baghdadi declared the founding of his Islamic State and was inaugurated as its supreme leader "caliph" in Mosul. The first thing this most powerful, most horrible terrorist group did was rob the Central Bank of Mosul, the bank where the elderly Iraqi lady had shed tears of gratitude thanking General Helmick 10 years earlier, of an estimated $400 million. That money became a major source of funding for the IS in its early days.

Looting and destruction continued under ISIS rule for three years until Iraqi government forces and a coalition of volunteers recaptured the town in July 2017. The fighting left the beautiful town that had once flourished on the Tigris River in complete ruins.

The Japanese Engineers Who Impressed the 101st Airborne

Petraeus' was most interested in the citizens' welfare and reconstruction of the economy. Repairing cement factories was crucial for that. Cement was Iraq's third largest industry, after crude oil and petroleum products. There was a cement factory in the town of Singer, 80 km west of Mosul, which again became the site of a carnage when ISIS seized the town in 2015. This was where residents had been controlled by violence until they were finally released in the summer of 2017.

One day, I received a request from Petraeus and his civilian advisor Dick Nabb:

The Sinjar cement plant is vital for the local economy, but where the maintenance had been quite bad to start with, looting caused operations to completely stop. However, the morale of the workers is surprisingly high and they have taken the 24,000 dollars that was left in the company's safe to do some makeshift repairs, and are now producing what little they can. Still, this is nowhere near their original production capacity of 6,400 tons a month.

The northern part of Iraq can be reconstructed if they can obtain cement. Many jobs can be secured. Part of the cement produced can be sold across the border to Syria, only 50 kilometers away, to earn foreign currency. The problem is that they do not know how to repair the plant. Can you send cement experts from Japan?

I asked Nabb why they didn't ask for American experts. The answer was that American experts did come, but they said it would cost 23 million dollars to repair the plant. There simply was no such budget.

General Helmick took Oku and me to the cement plant in his Black Hawk helicopter accompanied by the security force that escorted us everywhere we traveled. The factory stood twenty kilometers east of Sinjar, alone in the middle of a desert. The facilities were large, but there was no movement on the premises. Dead silence. The sun glared through the bright blue sky into the completely soundless factory. The electrical system had been looted and destroyed so the workers were trying to run the plant manually and the employees eagerly asked for the factory to be revived. There was something sparkling in their eyes. I knew I had to find a way to do something for them.

So I telephoned Tokyo and talked with Akira Nishikawa, the President of Mitsubishi Materials Co., which aside from being a major copper smelter, was also one of the largest cement manufacturers in Japan. I asked him for help and requested that he send several experts to Iraq. I was an outside board member of the company, and I knew Nishikawa well. I emphasized that Iraq was not a safe place, but visiting experts would be under the full protection of American soldiers.

Holding the telephone, I wasn't sure how Nishikawa would respond because Japanese cement companies were not in the least bit interested in doing business in the Middle East. Besides, even if the Sinjar plant were to be restored, it would not be the cement making company that would benefit, but the equipment manufacturers that supplied the cement manufacturing machinery. Not only that, since the plant was built by Romania, there would be no benefit to Japanese machine manufacturers either. It was also a dangerous place to be.

Would Nishikawa risk his staff to come to Iraq, and on top of that, be willing to pay the experts' expenses? Nishikawa's response was immediate.

"We'll do whatever is necessary." I was moved, but little did I know then that asking Nishikawa would put us in political difficulties later.

On October 3, two experts, Michio Fujita and Masanori Hirayama arrived from Japan. They were both Mitsubishi executives. They said that they could not send union members to the dangers of Iraq with no remuneration. As executives, they were not union members and they volunteered to come to Iraq. The next day, Fujita and Hirayama boarded a Black Hawk escorted by the American soldiers and took off. It was almost dusk when the two returned to the base where Petraeus, Helmick, Nerve, Oku and I waited.

They told us that the kilns at Sinjar for baking cement powder would have to be heated up to 1,450 degrees Celsius. To do this, the heavy oil blown into the burner unit has to be preheated to 150 degrees. Because the boiler isn't working properly, the heavy oil is only heating up to 60 degrees because the high-pressure pump linked to the burner unit had been stolen. In addition, they pointed out that the compressor was not working, so the amount of air was not controlled. By replacing the boiler, the high-pressure pump and the compressor, the first kiln should reach 70% of its intended capacity. They said that reactivating one kiln out of two should suffice. It won't cost more than one million dollars."

This surprised Petraeus and Nabb. "You're saying it won't cost a million dollars?," they asked. The Mitsubishi executives explained that Sinjar didn't need extravagant machinery, and inexpensive boilers from China or Eastern Europe would do. They reminded us that Iraqi technicians at Sinjar are skilled people, and assured us that it would go well. Then they added, "If anything goes wrong, call us in Tokyo. We will come back to help." Before leaving Iraq, they also visited a cement factory in the important city of Kirkuk, which they found had less well-trained technicians and less promise for a quick and inexpensive repair.

Of course, we kept silent about this story because of the political sensitivity that was surfacing in both Japan and the United States. But the difference between the U.S. experts' estimate to restore the Sinjar factory and the estimate of the Mitsubishi executives was reported in *The Washington Post* on Nov. 10, 2003. In Tokyo, Diet Member Nobuhiko Suto of the Democratic Party started attacking me in the powerful Budget Committee of the House of Representatives. "Yukio Okamoto, Special Advisor to the Prime Minister, took engineers to Sinjar from Mitsubishi Materials, where he serves as an executive board member. It is obvious he did this for the company's profit. He should be removed from the position of Prime Minister's Special Advisor."

Representative Suto had completely mistranslated the *Washington Post* article, which had praised the MMC expert team, and relentlessly came after me in the Diet, saying that major American newspapers were also criticizing Japan's actions. It is rare to find a former university professor who has no understanding of English, but this was enough to cause trouble for me for a while. I had to visit Nishikawa to apologize about having his purely goodwill episode become a target of criticism in the Diet. Nishikawa, the President of the multi-billion-dollar Mitsubishi company, was a short man with large glasses who never ceased to smile. He was like a jovial boss down at a small-town mom-and-pop shop. He interrupted his meeting and came out to see me.

I apologized for having brought him to an embarrassing situation. He shook his head and grasped my hands: "Okamoto-san, I am very thankful that you gave us the opportunity to work for the country. It was the most important thing." Here was a contrast between a vulgar Diet member and a businessman with higher aspirations. I put my hands together as I watched President Nishikawa return to the meeting. The Japanese are some of the most benevolent people in the world. It takes a long time to reach a decision on economic cooperation, but once a decision is made, you can depend on a reliable completion of the tasks, in good faith.

JAPAN'S ASSISTANCE FOR THE RECONSTRUCTION OF IRAQ

Cooperation with Arab Nations

WHILE OKU was working in Baghdad, the process to support Iraq's restoration began in Tokyo. In accordance with the traditional method of economic cooperation, the support would be directed toward Iraq's humanitarian and industrial sectors. Totaling five billion dollars, Japan's contribution ranked one of the highest among the international donors. This was a huge amount to contribute to the restoration process, but the painful memories from the Gulf War were still with me. In addition to the large funding commitment to the Multinational Iraq Assistance Group, I was convinced Japan needed to "sweat" by sending human resources, not just money. Japan must show its human face and leave its footprints on the ground.

A thought hit me about how Japan could deliver effective assistance when we had little experience with Iraq. The Arabs! We need their cooperation. Why not create a high-level mechanism together with the Arab countries to coordinate our aid efforts? That way Japan could take advantage of the good relationship it had enjoyed with Arab countries and satisfy the United States which wanted to 'internationalize' the reconstruction of Iraq. Let Arabs participate in the building of social stability in Iraq through joint projects. Japan was able to do this because it was not perceived as having a political agenda in the region. But which project should be targeted?

I discussed my idea with Hiroyasu Ando, Director General of Middle East Affairs at MOFA, who later became President of the Japan Foundation. Ando was a tall dark guy, dubbed by women in the office as "the Black Panther." Always warm and friendly, he spent his student years engrossed in theatrical playwriting and even missed his own graduation. He had no interest in turf-battles. He gave me his sincere agreement and started working with me. My relationship with the Ministry was very smooth until a new Director General in charge of Middle East Affairs rotated in. He had worked for me before, but was quite protective of his turf, and my relationship with MOFA deteriorated.

Still, I pressed ahead. In Cairo, I met with Prime Minister Atef Ebeid and Foreign Minister Ahmed Maher and explained the concept. Thanks to the groundwork Ambassador Kazuyoshi Urabe had done prior to my visit, both of them welcomed the idea of Japan and Arab countries working together to assist Iraq. But from my previous service as a young diplomat in Cairo, I knew I had to see someone in addition to the Prime Minister and the Foreign Minister.

So, I went to see Osama El Baz. He was still the Presidential Foreign Policy Advisor, as he had been when I left Cairo 20 years before. I hit him with the idea, and his reaction was more enthusiastic than I had expected. He immediately went to speak to President Hosni Mubarak and reported back to me that the President's response was also positive. He said that the President himself would select people to represent Egypt in the forum.

I was greatly encouraged as I set out for Riyadh. Despite his poor health, Foreign Minister Saud Al Faisal met with me. He came alone, with no one else present. That meant he had the absolute power to decide. I was impressed with his quiet intelligence. He agreed to the concept of setting up the forum, but when I suggested the possibility of increasing the number of participants to include other nations, like Jordan, Tunisia, and Kuwait, he told me that nobody would complain about Egypt and Saudi working together with Japan, but if we were to expand the number of participants, even by one, we would likely head for trouble.

I accepted his judgment, and the forum of the three nations, Japan, Egypt and Saudi Arabia, was officially agreed upon on May 24, 2003, at a meeting between Prime Minister Koizumi and President Mubarak. Koizumi asked former-Prime Minister Ryutaro Hashimoto to represent Japan. Subsequently, the forum became the most im-

Yukio Okamoto (at left) attends a summit meeting of Prime Minister Junichiro Koizumi (center) and Egyptian President Hosni Mubarak, also attended by then-Deputy Chief Cabinet Secretary Shinzo Abe (left of Koizumi), in Cairo on May 24, 2003.

portant venue for Japan to discuss Iraq and the Middle East situation with Arab partners. The forum continued for five years.

Egyptian Doctor Fikri

But I am getting ahead of myself here. I thought we should kick off the nascent forum with a medical project because no one could object to a humanitarian contribution. Theoretically, Egypt would be an ideal partner because it was the center of medicine in the Arab world. The Egyptian medical community had a strong sense of mission, had highly trained personnel, and there was an extensive human network. We could not afford *not* to use this. I presented a plan to Prime Minister Koizumi in which Iraqi doctors and nurses would be sent at Japan's expense to Egypt for specialized training. Japan would also furnish Iraq with the medical equipment that the Egyptians recommended. The Prime Minister responded with an unusually powerful voice: "This is good. Definitely do it."

Back in Cairo, I visited the Minister of Higher Education, which had jurisdiction over Cairo University, to solicit cooperation. With approval, I then went to the Cairo University Pediatric Hospital, the largest medical facility in the Middle East, with a total of 13 affiliated hospitals, 2,000 doctors and 5,000 beds. A man waited for me in a hospital room. His name was Doctor Asem Fikri. He was both the hospital administrative manager and a surgery professor at the university. He had handsome features and a smiling face that made him seem like a boy who had grown to manhood without losing his original naïveté.

I began the conversation with a direct request. I explained that the Japanese government wanted to help the doctors in Iraq and asked him to come with me to Baghdad. Although this was our first encounter, it was as if he had always expected to be asked. "I have been waiting for a long time to hear someone say those words," he said. "As soon as the war ended, we went to the Iraqi border via Jordan, but we were unable to enter. Yes, we are happy to be a part of your project and go with you to Baghdad."

Three minutes into our first encounter, Fikri was already a strong ally. Encouraged by Fikri, I went back to Foreign Minister Maher to obtain the support of the government. he responded cautiously. "I am in favor of that personally," he said, "but Egypt cannot take actions that will be seen as legitimizing America's occupation. The decision must be made by the President himself." So I returned to meet presidential advisor El Baz. And once again, he told me to leave matters in his hands.

When Prime Minister Koizumi met with President Hosni Mubarak on May 24, 2003, in Cairo, he asked for Egyptian participation in this medical support project. I was not sure what the President would say, given the country's critical view of the U.S. occupation of Iraq. But Mubarak showed no hesitation and expressed powerful agreement. "Let's definitely do this together." Foreign Minister Maher, who was sitting next to the President, gave me a broad smile.

On July 9, a joint survey team of 13 Japanese aid experts from MOFA and JICA, and seven Egyptian doctors met in Jordan's capital of Amman and headed for Baghdad. Katsuhiko Oku was elated about the project and came all the way from Baghdad to meet the team. Oku led a convoy of 10 four-wheel-drive cars, leaving Amman early in the morning. The team arrived at the Iraqi border before noon. At the checkpoint, a long queue of trucks waited to head towards Baghdad, and it took some time to get through, but finally we crossed the border and entered Iraq. We had 575 km to go.

Before we left, the Japanese aid agency's office in Amman warned us that the road to Baghdad was extremely dangerous. They explained that hostile parties roam the 270 km before Baghdad, and pointed out that there was a violent battle raging in Fallujah along the way. They advised us to drive along the entire stretch of the road at the highest possible speed, to absolutely avoid stopping, and to be prepared with first-aid kits and fire extinguishers in case of an attack.

Our convoy of Toyota and Mitsubishi 4WD vehicles ignored the 90 km speed limit and dashed to Baghdad at 150 km per hour without ever stopping. We arrived in Baghdad in the late afternoon. On the way, we could see smoke billowing into the sky in the distance in Fallujah, perhaps the result of shelling.

No doctors were included in the Japan team. This was because of the bitter experience during the Gulf War, when Japanese doctors who opposed the war had ruined an international medical cooperation project in the Gulf. Also, we decided that it would be better for Egyptian doctors to be in direct contact with Iraqi doctors.

As expected, there were objections from the Japanese side about not including Japanese doctors. One concern was that Egypt is a Sunni country and Iraq had become a Shiite country. Would Egypt help Iraq? Some in Tokyo emphasized the point that Shiite doctors of Iraq may not accept guidance from Egyptians. They wanted the Iraqi doctors trained in Japan. But I held my ground. "If you're going to talk about the sectarian differences among Muslims, what about the difference between monotheistic Iraq and polytheistic Japan?" I retorted. But in truth, I knew they had a point, and was not entirely sure Sunni Egypt would work well with Shiite Iraq. I had to confirm. "Dr. Fikri, all of Egypt is Sunni. Iraq is now a Shiite country. Does this matter?" Fikri looked at me incredulously and laughed. "There is absolutely no need to worry," he said. "We are Arab brothers."

So, our joint survey began in Baghdad. The Egyptian doctors who inspected Iraqi hospitals had flattering things to say about Japan's long record of aid in Egypt. "Visiting Iraqi hospitals is like looking at Egypt 30 years ago. Thanks to Japan, we have achieved our present standards. We will repay your kindness by helping Iraq."

The Egyptian doctors worked arduously. Fikri hardly slept. He continued to write up survey reports and the minutes of agreements with the Iraqi side even after the Japanese members had gone to bed. This unique Japan–Egypt joint project began in March 2004. The first dispatch consisted of 100 Iraqi doctors and nurses selected from hospitals in Iraq. They received intensive training at Cairo University Medical Hospital. Japan took responsibility for covering the expenses as well as providing the necessary equipment. Under the plan, which continued for three-and-a-half years, a total of 502 doctors and nurses from about 30 major Iraqi hospitals received training at the University in Cairo. After returning to their home country, they have remained engaged in medicine. There was no end to the number of Iraqi doctors who had hoped to go through this program.

Thanks to the devotion of Cairo University and the efficiency of Japanese bureaucracy, the program was carried out perfectly. For Japan, it was another example of how the country excels at implementing non-controversial projects once the plan is set.

Dispatching the Self-Defense Forces to Iraq

The United States was clamoring for Japan to put "boots on the ground." Troops from nearly 30 mainly U.S.-friendly countries already had been dispatched to Iraq to assist the reconstruction.

Peacebuilding in places where there are risks is the job of the military. Only a competent force, equipped for self-defense and trained to protect itself, could do the job. Even in 2003, however, the Japanese people remained in a state of alarm over the Japanese military's invasion and occupation of countries overseas that began in 1931. Various arguments were presented against the deployment of the SDF to Iraq. The scope of the SDF's activities was strictly limited by law, which made it necessary to create a "special measures law" each time the government sought to dispatch the SDF overseas. This time, Prime Minister Koizumi stood firm. While deliberations were difficult, the Special Measures Law to dispatch the SDF to Iraq for Humanitarian and Reconstruction Assistance in Iraq was enacted on July 26, 2003.

Again, the opposition politicians argued that sending Self-Defense Forces overseas as a violation of the Constitution. For me, the opponent I needed to convince was—just like back in 1987 when we planned to dispatch Coast Guard patrol boats—Masaharu Gotoda, the former Chief Cabinet Secretary and the most powerful pacifist among the conservatives. This is what he told me:

"The Self-Defense Forces are a strictly nonaggressive defense unit. To send them overseas, you had better have a very good reason. Koizumi has said that he will not use force and will not enter combat zones. Do you think it will end there? Have you people ever been in a battle? Prime Minister Koizumi probably sees this is as a sort of gamble. Is it safe? Let's hope the bet works. This is going to change Japan. But have you told the people what that's going to look like? You're thinking that change is a good thing, aren't you?"

This was the conviction of an ideological heavyweight conservative who, at more than 90 years of age continued to bear the burden of war. Still, I wanted to persuade Gotoda. I knew that Japan's security policy would only move to the extent that he, a respected benchmark for conservative opponents, would allow.

The Special Measures Law for Humanitarian and Reconstruction Assistance in Iraq had already been passed in July of that year. Under the strong direction of Prime Minister Koizumi, every effort was made on the political side, and a law was created only four months after the war in Iraq broke out. After that, however, the bureaucratic side moved slowly, which worried Oku and me. When Oku and I visited the headquarters of the Multinational Forces in Babylon in July 2003, we were greeted by senior officers of the First U.S. Marine Expeditionary Force.

When we visited the same headquarters again only two months later, it looked completely different. There was no sight of the more than 20,000 U.S. marines who had been stationed there earlier. We were greeted by General Andrzej Tyszkiewicz of Poland and General Ricardo Isidro of Spain, who were overseeing the coalition forces in Iraq's mid-south. Guarding the headquarters was a Filipino military police unit.

We were briefed by the two generals that the building of social infrastructure was being carried out by Romania, Thai and even an Asian country with scarce military resources like Mongolia. In this region alone, 9,000 officers and soldiers from 21 countries had come to participate in peace-keeping and reconstruction. In addition, more countries were participating in peace-keeping operations in southern Iraq. The utter absence of Japanese participation embarrassed Oku and me.

Politically, Japan's biggest problem at the time was dispatching the Self-Defense Forces to Iraq. Where should they be stationed, and for how long, and to do what? Discussions continued in Tokyo. The Defense Agency was extremely careful about selecting a location, but the situation surrounding multinational forces in Iraq was evolving too quickly to leave it to the slow-paced bureaucratic process in Japan. Oku and I were convinced Japan must move much faster.

One after another, support troops from many countries were arriving in Iraq. Asian forces included hundreds of Thai, Filipino and Mongolian soldiers, who had no experience in such matters. More than 30 countries had already participated, but still Japan was not there. Another political defeat like the one following the Gulf War of 1990 was about to take place for Japan.

It felt like Japan's "Gulf War syndrome," a humiliation that supposedly had been overcome, was reoccurring again. On the field, the attitude toward Japan was quickly deteriorating, and the Gulf War trauma of Japan was beginning to emerge.

But the issue this time was more serious. Unlike during the Gulf War when fighting was still underway, the battles in Iraq had already ceased. So, the absence of Japan would mean its non-participation even in a peace-building process, even after the war had ended. It was becoming clear that the coalition forces would likely treat the countries that lagged and arrived late as a 'second class group'.

Yet, it also was apparent that deploying the SDF in southern Iraq would take quite some time. So why not send a small number of SDF soldiers before then? Oku and I thought of "embedding" a small unit of SDF engineers and private experts in the U.S. 101st Airborne.

General Petraeus welcomed the idea, and General Sanchez said that they would be pleased to accept such a proposal from Japan. He was happy at the prospect of Japan contributing its unique capabilities to restore industrial facilities in the north. He also said that the Japanese team would be escorted at all times by American soldiers. This way, the Self-Defense Forces could have a visible presence six months ahead of any full-fledged SDF activities.

Unfortunately, Tokyo did not share the same sense of urgency, and turned down the concept. Meanwhile, it sent nearly a dozen teams to investigate how the SDF might be deployed. The United States was getting tired of receiving waves of Japanese investigation teams. "Other countries came once or twice to investigate and sent in troops right away. How many times does Japan have to investigate before they're satisfied?"

Finally, Washington had had enough. In mid-September, they sent notice that the next time would be the last time an SDF dispatch inspection team would be accepted. "We don't need your SDF. Just stop wasting our time." As one would expect, Tokyo decided not to send any more survey teams.

Japan's Gulf War syndrome had recurred. Although the relationship between Koizumi and Bush as leaders was strong due to their good personal chemistry, the atmosphere on the ground was like that of August to October 1990, when Japan–U.S. relations deteriorated drastically. The sense of crisis that Oku and I had from experiencing that during the Gulf War was not shared in Tokyo. On the contrary, Tokyo was beginning to find our presence a nuisance. I should have noticed that.

One day, Oku and I visited a quiet, idyllic small city in southern Iraq. Compared with other Iraqi towns we had visited, it was peaceful and unrelated to war. The place was called Samawah. I said, "There's no need for any army at a place like this. There's no way the SDF will come here, either." Oku grinned. "That's why they *will* come. Do you want to make a bet?" I lost the bet and had to buy Oku dinner in Baghdad.

I have written critically about the circumstances leading to the dispatch of the Self-Defense Forces to Iraq, but on the other hand, there is a backdrop to why ensuring the safety of the SDF was so important. What Japan will never be able to overcome is the shibboleth of "Japanese life." If a Japanese person were to die while on a government mission overseas, it would cause a great commotion. Police Inspector Haruyuki Takada was killed in 1993 when he was dispatched to serve in the Cambodian civilian police force. Kiichi Miyazawa, who had been prime minister at the time, later recalled that he was prepared for his cabinet to fall over that incident. Indeed, since then, the National Police Agency has adamantly refused to dispatch police officers to peacekeeping operations abroad.

The Ministry of Defense would likely do the same, if they were to lose an SDF soldier, sailor or airman. In Japan, the death of a single person changes everything. In 1960, a female university student named Michiko Kaba was trampled and killed during a demonstration against the renewal of the Japan–U.S. Security Treaty. After her death, student demonstrations rapidly subsided. There are few countries where the death of one person can slow a political movement or bring down an entire cabinet. In this way, Japan is unlike other countries that dispatch personnel to the Gulf, accepting the possibility that there may be casualties.

It was Japan's duty to send the Ground Self-Defense Force to Samawah but most of the debate over the pros and cons of the dispatch was not about the mission per se but about the safety of the SDF personnel. It was all about how safe it would be and whether the area was a "non-combat zone." The SDF commanders who had been dispatched in succession to research the situation did not define their ambition as "to bring peace and stability to Iraq." Instead, it was "to bring everyone safely back to Japan." The Japanese people felt the same way. If there were to be even one casualty, Japan's system of contributing to international security would collapse.

Yet, Katsuhiko Oku was not provided with Japanese security in Iraq. When Oku and I travelled in the southern part of Iraq administered by the coalition forces, the vehicle that we rode in was escorted by the Polish Army under the command of General Andrzej Tyszkiewicz. But in northern Iraq, where the United States had jurisdiction, we were not protected. The understandable position of the U.S. was, "We are still fighting the remainder of Saddam's Army and cannot divide our forces to protect foreign dignitaries. Each country is expected to use its own troops to escort its mission members."

Oku often said: "Do you get it Okamoto-san? There are two types of lives in Japan's civil service: Those who have to be kept safe, and we, who do not. If we get killed now, they'll just say that we were fools to be in a dangerous place, and that would be the end of the discussion." While all of Japan was busy debating whether it would be safe to send the Defense Forces to Iraq, Oku and his assistant were running around Iraq on their own fighting a lone battle.

A total of 550 men from the Ground Self-Defense Forces arrived in Samawah, Al-Muthanna Province, on December 15, 2003, for the purpose of "humanitarian assistance"—primarily delivery of water to the local residents. They stayed until July 2006. The whole operation left a future challenge for Japan. Because of the political compromise in Tokyo, SDF soldiers were not allowed to carry sufficient weapons to protect themselves in Iraq. They had to be protected first by the Dutch, and later by Australian troops. Furthermore, only Japan's SDF, among all multinational forces, had to stay away from the role of preserving the security in Iraq, limiting its activity only to 'humanitarian assistance'.

Notwithstanding the constraints on military contributions, the dispatch had historical importance: Japan had stepped forward to contribute to international peace by sending troops abroad for the first time.

DEFEAT

My Partner's Death

A WONDERFUL FORMER COLLEAGUE of mine, Tsukasa Uemura, was serving as Chargé d'Affaires at the Japanese Embassy in Baghdad. He helped Oku and me do our work in Iraq. Uemura, who later became Ambassador to Saudi Arabia, would protect the Embassy and Oku would travel around the country. They had joined the Ministry of Foreign Affairs in the same year. Uemura was fluent in Arabic and above all, was a man of courage.

In April 2004, two Japanese men traveled to Baghdad, ignoring the Japanese government's recommendation against it. They were taken hostage by militants. Uemura went to the scene and negotiated with the militants using his own channels and eventually won their release. In the process, however, there was a possibility that he would be captured. Uemura was well aware of the danger but went to negotiate anyway. I don't know the right words to describe Oku and Uemura, except to note just that there are brave diplomats like them.

Oku was a generous man who would willingly take a risk. One day, he and I were at a hospital in Hillah. Doctors, one after another, pleaded: "We are under-stocked in all medical supplies. We're out of medicines, we have only 60 sheets of x-ray film available each month." The crucial element was speed. Oku gave it a thought and answered: "Go ahead gentlemen, buy what you need." Even I was surprised at this. "Hey, Oku, aren't you too quick to make that promise?" Oku smiled and said, "It shouldn't cost more than 5 million yen. I've got about that much in personal savings. If Tokyo doesn't approve, I'll pay for it myself."

We heard several people in Tokyo say, "Oku ought to be asking

the ministry first. It will be authorized in a few months. Taking personal initiative without waiting doesn't work in government." But
Oku knew well that while we waited half-a-year for authorization,
patients at this hospital would die. All I could say to Oku was, "Let's
do it, I'm in."

Oku and I visited city councils in every town we went to in Iraq.
The city council members made requests, one after another. They
needed medical equipment, pharmaceuticals, drinking water, sewage
treatment, education, emergency vehicles, small generators, city hall
building repairs, and more. All of these areas were in dire straits after
13 years of international sanctions and looting. Oku wrote everything
down and took on what he could promise on the spot. He relayed
major projects to Tokyo.

We were free to travel anywhere in Iraq. In hindsight, that era
was like a dream. Oku trusted the Iraqi people's goodwill and dealt
warmly with people at every destination. He was fearless. When
people were in trouble, he did not fail to respond. The devotion
that he poured into Iraqi society was unlimited. Oku often said: "I
don't agree with the reason the U.S. started the war, but looking at
the results, it's a good thing they got rid of Saddam Hussein. Take a
look at the Iraqi people smiling and speaking freely with nothing to
fear! Iraq is liberated. We must help these people."

Iraq is different from other Mideast countries. Both of us felt that
we should help Iraq's strong layer of mid-level citizenry to stand at
the front line of Iraq's reconstruction. But Washington was trying to
reconstruct Iraq from the top by appointing as cabinet ministers and
governors Iraqis who had lived in exile during the Saddam Hussein
era. That, Oku and I thought, would never work. Those people were
not trusted by the public. People who do not belong to the top elite
in the central government—people like local mayors, city council
members, hospital doctors, school principals and teachers—should
serve as the core to rebuild Iraq. Oku felt optimistic. "Iraq is a nation of highly capable middle-class people who surely will rebuild
their country." It was through these people that Oku and I began to
implement projects for localities throughout Iraq.

Every time I came back to Tokyo, I was asked by the media why
Japan had to take care of the debris that Americans left by launching

a misguided war based on false allegations about chemical weapons. It was a good question. I, too, was disappointed by the poor intelligence the United States used as the basis for its decision to start the war. But I told the media the story of a town called Halabja because that hideous incident had blinded the Americans and fed their excessive zeal for the war.

Halabja lies in the land of the Kurds, where Saddam massacred more than 5,000 people by poison gas in 1988. The victims were women, children and the elderly, since the men had been hiding in the mountains to fight against Saddam's forces. It was heart-breaking to see so many helpless senior people still suffering from the sequelae of the poison gas. They pleaded with me to build more hospitals in the region. I felt strongly that medical projects in Halabja must be included in Japan's assistance program.

On July 16, Fikri and I visited U.N. representative Sergio Vieira de Mello at the U.N. headquarters in Baghdad. He was a fine Brazilian diplomat with a strong sense of mission. Smiles never left his face. He was pleased to hear our plan, saying he needed every bit of assistance the international community could extend to Iraq. Before we met him, we chatted with his friendly secretary, who told us how happy she was to work for such a wonderful boss.

It was a warm and friendly meeting. De Mello expressed a lot of hope in the chances for the democratization of Iraq. We shook hands firmly and promised to meet again soon. But security in Iraq had already begun to deteriorate. Just a month later, on August 19, 2003, the first large-scale terrorist attack inside postwar Iraq occurred. A huge car bomb targeted the U.N. mission and blew away and killed de Mello and his friendly secretary, along with other 22 U.N. staff.

Three weeks after the attack, I flew to Baghdad. Oku and I visited the site to pay our respects to Representative de Mello. I stood there, speechless. There was no trace of De Mello's office. His room had turned to concrete rubble. Yet the building still flew the U.N. flag, at half-mast. With his eyes fixed on the flag, Oku let out a cry from deep inside. "Can you look at this flag and just walk away from Iraq?"

Iraq was very close to stabilization. However, U.S. rule in Iraq failed, and toward the end of 2003, the situation across the country began to crumble with what seemed like a death rattle.

Oku and I traveled all over Iraq, and when we went south, we felt safe. Central and southern Iraq were under the jurisdiction of the multinational force which maintained a very good relationship with the general public. General Tyszkiewicz of Poland, who was the overall commander had a platoon of Polish troops escort us. They had two APCs with machine guns moving in front and behind our vehicle.

The excellence of Polish soldiers was proven in the Battle of Karbala in April 2004. In this famous battle, 40 Polish soldiers, together with Bulgarian soldiers and with only a limited amount of equipment and food were surrounded by militants with several times the number of men, but protected the city hall in the Shiite holy city of Karbala for four days. Armed militants had attacked the city. The Iraqi government troops fled, and the militants laid a mortar barrier in front of the city hall and forcing the children of Karbala to remain in the area as human shield hostages so that the Polish could not counterattack. They then attacked the city mercilessly with an overwhelming majority. Ultimately, the Polish army rushed in and released the children and launched a fierce counterattack. They defended the city hall without a single casualty to their own forces.

I learned of the story later and was reminded of the Polish soldiers who had guarded us. I was not surprised that they had the ability to perform such a miracle.

We were also safe in the Kurdish region in the northeast. This was because we were escorted by the Kurdish militia, the Peshmerga. They were a disciplined elite unit and provided us with full protection wherever we went in the Kurdish region. When Kurdish President Masoud Barzani learned that we weren't usually provided with our own escort, he offered to protect us outside the Kurdish region as well, but this was not possible because of the political problems it would surely have caused.

One area Oku and I were interested in was the land of the Kurds consisting of the two provinces, Arbil and Sulaymaniyah. Peace and stability reigned there. We became good friends with Jalal Talabani, the Kurdish leader who later became the President of Iraq in April 2004. He invited us to his house in Suleymaniyah, where we talked about the possibility of Japanese nationals engaging in aid operations in Kurdistan guarded by the Peshmerga. Contrary to our recommendations however, the importance of the Kurds was lost on Tokyo. It was the Koreans who later came to station 2000 soldiers in the Kurdish capital of Arvil.

The most dangerous part of the country for us was northern Iraq. The U.S. military, in charge of the entire north, told us that because of ongoing fighting between U.S. troops and Saddam Hussein's remnants in the north, they could not send troops to protect foreign dignitaries. They expected each country to be responsible for its own protection. That was natural enough. However, as I mentioned earlier, there was no way that the Japanese Self-Defense Forces could protect us. For the Self-Defense Forces to guard the Japanese Embassy in Baghdad was an invocation of the right to individual self-defense, not collective, and thus it was not a constitutional issue.

But at the same time, there was one subtle problem. Japan is a super-equality conscious society, which makes it difficult to create two classes of people—those who protect and those to be protected. The reason is emotional. Are our SDF lives less important than other lives? Does that make us second-class citizens? Why should we act as shields for other groups of Japanese people? This is the psychology that lies deep within the SDF.

Of course, firefighters and police officers willingly take risks and act as shields to protect the lives of others because that is their job. But it is difficult to ask the SDF, which had been kept in the postwar political shadows, to suddenly come out and protect diplomats. This is not an issue for the individual SDF personnel. Each and every one of the troops has a high sense of mission and morale. The problem is that the organization and system do not work that way.

However, the enactment of Japan's Legislation for Peace and Security in 2015, initiated by Prime Minister Abe, made the protection of Japanese citizens overseas an inherent mission of the SDF. Eventually, the day will come when the SDF will guard and protect our diplomats in Iraq.

But that day had not come before Oku was killed on November 28, 2003, while *en route* to an information exchange conference for the reconstruction of the north, held in Tikrit, where Saddam Hussein was once based. He was shot on the road that he and I had often traveled along together. When Oku left Baghdad for the north on that fateful day, he was accompanied only by a single Iraqi guard hired by the Embassy. The attack was carried out by several terrorists. It occurred 80 km north of Baghdad, as they were returning to the Embassy. We were to meet two days later at the Syrian border.

It is speculated that the intention was to interfere with the stabilization of Iraqi society, but that cannot be confirmed. The attackers fired 36 rounds of ammunition from AK47 rifles while driving alongside the Embassy SUV, killing Oku, a colleague of his, and the driver. Further details are unknown. A small boy testified that he saw from a roadside farm an attacker vehicle driving in front of Oku's car to slow it down while a second car drove alongside and attackers opened fire. Local farmers notified the police, and the bodies of the victims were rushed to a hospital in a pick-up truck. While the other two were already dead, Oku was still alive, but his wounds were fatal. He died on the way to the hospital. Perhaps Oku took his last breath thinking of his wonderful family. They say he died smiling.

My Defeat

After Oku was killed, I was left with a void in my heart. And with him gone, there was no one to tell the Ministry of Foreign Affairs that they ought to cooperate with me, and my relationship with the ministry slid further downhill. As my activity intensified in Iraq, generating a great many policy recommendations for Tokyo, I was feeling increasingly frustrated. The bureaucrats were reluctant to listen to outsiders' opinions and would say they don't need someone else doing their job. Giving credit to outsiders weakens their position and their raison d'être. It seems that like the human body, bureaucratic organizations reject contamination by alien elements from the outside.

And like members of the long ago disbanded Japanese Imperial Army, most of those in the contemporary Japanese bureaucracy show absolute loyalty to the organization to which they belong. This is because the organization will take care of them for the rest of their lives. In Japan, there is no completely open system nor society. Opinions and information from the outside are considered, basically, "noise."

Out of all the information that they gather, only what is convenient for them ever publicized. The "don't let the people know, just let them obey" mentality still pervades Japanese bureaucracy today. The Ministry of Foreign Affairs in particular, which has no domestic support base, tries to secure its own identity by keeping others off its lawn. And now I was wrestling with myself, and spinning my wheels without any support from MOFA.

At the time, MOFA would not send officials to Iraq, notwithstanding my plea to send staff to Baghdad to support Oku. The reason was simple: "Iraq is not safe." The Japanese press started to criticize MOFA for not going to Iraq while Okamoto was often visiting there. The result was a request from MOFA to Chief Cabinet Secretary Yasuo Fukuda to put an end to my visits to Iraq. One day Fukuda grinned at me and said amusingly, "Hey, Okamoto, your beloved MOFA's Vice-Minister asked me to stop you from going to Iraq. They say you are a bad influence on their safety-first policy." Luckily, Fukuda never stopped me from going to Iraq.

Oku died with many unfulfilled dreams. I could not abandon ship if I lost my co-pilot halfway. I knew it was not going to be an easy job to fight the battle against the bureaucracy alone, without Oku, but I was determined to do it. But one incident at Oku's funeral led me to the excruciating conclusion that I must resign my post. The trigger was the words of Mrs. Yoriko Kawaguchi, the Minister of Foreign Affairs, a fine intellectual. She took me aside at the funeral, placed her hands on my shoulders and said gently: "Okamoto-san, you don't have to feel responsible and blame yourself, you know." She was obviously saying this out of genuine sympathy for me. But, still, it was strange. Feel responsible for what? She could have shared her grief for Oku with me, but to mention my sense of guilt? I started to ask my close friends, "Why did she have to say that?"

It proved easy to find out why. I soon learned from media friends that several people in the ministry were promoting the story that it was Okamoto who caused the death of Oku. The story was that Oku was influenced by Okamoto's vision of dealing not only with Shiites, but also with Sunnis, and that was why Oku headed out to the Sunni region, where he was killed. It was obvious that some in MOFA used Oku's death as an occasion to make their Foreign Min-

istry colleague, a hero, which he deserved. At the same time, some
saw it as an opportunity to eliminate my role using the charge that
I was the one who led Oku to his death.

Tsukasa Uemura, who was Oku's right-hand man in Baghdad,
consoled me by saying, "Okamoto-san, I know better than anyone
that this is not true, and I will go anywhere and testify." But I had
had enough of MOFA officials and didn't want to see their faces
anymore. I knew that unless I resigned, the slander would not stop.
It would infuse an image on Oku's wonderful family that aside from
the terrorists, there was someone else responsible for the death of
their beloved husband and father. I could not bear that prospect.

I told Prime Minister Koizumi of my determination to disembark
from the ship. He invited me for dinner, just the two of us. As we
dined, he brushed my explanation aside and said, half laughing, "I
always get attacked from all sides. It's not a big thing. Why are you
letting it bother you?" "Mr. Prime Minister, you are a politician. But
I am not."

I had been happy to work under Prime Minister Koizumi. He
prioritized his diplomatic actions and was not afraid of criticism. He
chose the path of persuading the public head-on. Koizumi always
stayed a loner and thus was able to achieve many results as a politician. But I was much weaker as an individual.

The Ministry of Foreign Affairs is an organization that includes
many fine individuals. As long as I was not tangled up in a battle for
authority, they were wonderful to get along with. My relationship
with the Ministry of Foreign Affairs soon improved after I left my
position in the Prime Minister's Office.

Oku was a hero in my mind. He did not become a hero because
he was killed. He was a hero who was killed. Oku's death made big
national news. Some 3,000 people lined up to lay flowers at his funeral in Tokyo. I received moving condolence letters from Generals
Petraeus and Helmick. In 2015, during a visit to Tokyo, General
Petraeus and MOFA colleagues of Oku held a brief ceremony and a
moment of silence at a modest memorial to Oku outside the ministry
building. At the end of the ceremony, Petraeus saluted and remarked
on what a hero Oku was to him. I was not invited.

In early 2012, several months after the war in Iraq ended, I visited Frank Helmick's home at Fort Myer—a military Base near the Pentagon across the Potomac River from Washington D.C. At that time, General Helmick was the Military Assistant to the Deputy Secretary of Defense. I wanted to spend an evening with him absorbed in memories of Oku. Although Helmick looked at me with his usual warm eyes and spoke kind words of sympathy, I saw his mind was not totally absorbed in mourning for Oku. I understood why only when we sat down to dinner with his wife Melissa and their two wonderful children, and he said grace. "Dear God, please protect my 20 sons killed in Mosul and my friend Katsu Oku, who are with you now." I felt like a lightning bolt hit me. The entire country of Japan had lost only two lives, Oku and his junior officer, Masamori Inoue. But Helmick alone lost 20 men who, along with Katsu, tried to help the citizens of Iraq live peacefully in their newly won freedom.

A few months later, I was in Cairo. As security in Iraq worsened, civilians were banned from traveling there and I could no longer go without an official title. Still, wanting to be as close to Iraq as possible, I went to Egypt. I also wanted to see Dr. Fikri again. In Cairo, traditional wooden sailing boats called *felucca* ply the river. One night, I sat on a small *felucca* alone with an Egyptian driver as he sailed along the Great Nile. The Nile resembled another great river, the Tigris, in Iraq. I felt as if I was in Mosul. I could not stop my tears, thinking about the fallen heroes.

PART SIX

DIFFICULT NEIGHBORS—
THE MOST IMPORTANT
DIPLOMATIC TASKS

JAPAN'S SEMI-ETERNAL YOKE

Kuala Lumpur

IN 1958, just a bit more than a decade after the Pacific War ended, we accompanied my father to work in Kuala Lumpur for two years in the Federation of Malaya. For this 13-year-old boy, the time we spent there was like a dream.

Japan had invaded the Malay Peninsula on December 8, 1941, at the same time as Pearl Harbor. Earlier that year, the United States

Yukio Okamoto, at 13-years-old, stands at the right of his teacher from the British School he attended in Kuala Lumpur, as she prepares to return to her home country, England. His teacher is holding flowers as Yukio and his friends see her off at the airport.

had cut off its supply of oil to Japan, so Japan tried to secure oil by occupying the Dutch territory of Indonesia. To do so, it was necessary to capture Singapore, the British base for Southeast Asian domination. Breaking the British supply line in Asia was something that Germany also strongly hoped for.

Recognizing that it would not be possible to take hold of the impregnable Singapore from the tightly protected seaside, the Japanese military planned an attack from Johor in the north. This meant that it had to capture the entire Malay Peninsula, all the way to Singapore.

Attempting to dominate the Malay Peninsula before the British Army could fortify its defenses in Singapore, Japan deployed its most advanced troops for the operation, including the Imperial Guard. The forces had been well trained in anticipation of combat on the Malay Peninsula.

The timing of the commencement of the operation was vital. For both the Pearl Harbor attack and the landing on the Malay Peninsula, it was an absolute requirement that it be a "surprise." If one of the operations started independently, the other would no longer be a surprise. As such, the fighting began in the middle of the night in Malaya, and early morning, in Hawaii, at basically the same time. Japan had not declared war on either the United States or the United Kingdom.

This is how the Southern Operations began. The British Commonwealth military comprised a force of 89,000 men, including Indian and Australian troops. The Japanese Army landed at the northern tip of the Malay Peninsula with a total force of 35,000, defeated the British troops using a bicycle infantry ("bicycle blitzkrieg"), and occupied the whole peninsula in 55 days. Some 1,800 Japanese soldiers and 5,000 British soldiers were killed. The Japanese occupied Kuala Lumpur on January 12, 1942, before landing in Singapore on February 8. Following a fierce battle, Lieutenant-General Arthur Percival surrendered to Lieutenant-General Tomoyuki Yamashita, who came to be known as "the Tiger of Malay." One-hundred thousand British POWs were captured, making it Great Britain's greatest humiliation in modern times.

The Japanese Army achieved its military objectives by occupying the Malay Peninsula and Singapore, and then Indonesia and British

Burma with phenomenal speed. However, this early success ultimately led to the retreat and failure of the Japanese military. Excessive hubris vis-à-vis the British Army led to the catastrophe of the Battle of Imphal. Advancing along the agriculturally rich Malay Peninsula, a combination of advantageous conditions meant that food could be procured locally, providing smooth supply and logistics. However, this good fortune resulted in neglecting logistics in subsequent battles, where a great number of soldiers died from hunger. Moreover, the Imperial Japanese military repressed citizens of Chinese heritage in Malaya and other occupied Asian countries. The antipathy this caused has afflicted Japan for decades since.

By the time my family arrived in Kuala Lumpur, the town was already dazzling. Coming from the monotone atmosphere of Japan, I plunged into a world of primary colors. British colonial rule had just ended and compared to Japan which had not yet recovered from the war, the beautiful, wealthy city was stunning. To me, it was what the future looked like. Although it was more than 10 years after the War had ended, however, there was still an unhealed antipathy among the Malaysian Chinese toward Japan.

My father's policy was to send us to local schools, so I started at a school where most of the children were of Chinese heritage. The first Malay I learned was the name my classmates called me: *babi, binatang*. It meant *pig, beast*, and it was what they used shout at the Japanese soldiers during the War.

The next words they made me learn were *kapala potong*, meaning *executioner*. Using gestures to indicate decapitation, my classmates tried to show me that this is what the Japanese did to them. In Singapore, the 25th Army led by Lt.-Gen. Tomoyuki Yamashita killed 5,000 Malaysian Chinese (British military prosecutors estimated 6,000) after charging them with espionage. A large number of these Chinese migrants were likely executed in the city of Kuala Lumpur.

It was my first encounter with the "history issue" that was to continue to plague Japan. Being children, we were able to get along and become friends, but that dismal feeling stayed with me for a very long time, coloring my subsequent mental landscape.

Then my father transferred me to a British school. My classmates there were children of British businessmen who ran tin mines and

rubber plantations, or employees of American and Dutch companies attempting to expand their business in the newly established
Federation of Malaya.

Memories of the War remained among them, too. Perhaps it was
just a coincidence, but one of my Dutch classmates, who had experienced the Japanese military conquest in Indonesia, was particularly
hostile toward me. Most of the other children were British, but they
never turned a cold shoulder to me just because I was Japanese. My
best friend was American. Most of my teachers were British, and
they were all kind. It was at this school that I came to like the British.

My classmates at school were European and American, but we
lived in a settlement of Malays, Chinese and Indians with whom I
played after school. There were also mixed-race kids called Eurasians,
who had both European and Asian parents. I guess you could say it
was a racial melting. My first love, Jenny, lived across the street. She
was Malaysian Chinese.

I spoke English in my daily life. At school, I studied French as
my second language, and at home, a tutor taught me Malay. If I am
intrinsically cosmopolitan in any way, without a doubt it became a
part of me while I lived in Kuala Lumpur.

Why did Japan go to war with people like this? Would these people ever forgive us for what the Japanese Army did? From childhood,
"War" became the story of my life. I wanted to be a diplomat when
I grew up. Perhaps that was partly because Kaoru Hayashi, who was
Japan's first ambassador to Malaya, was dazzling and cool, but it was
most likely because my childhood heart told me that it was necessary
for Japan to get along with all countries.

Japan's Understanding of History

In Asia, the Pacific War is not yet history. This is the crucial premise
when speaking of Asian politics. In particular, the "history issue"
remains a cause of tension, fueling sharp confrontations in the relationship with China and Korea.

If, as the average Japanese person imagines, World War II started
with the attack on Pearl Harbor in December 1941, then it makes
sense to say that historically, responsibility for the War has been

taken. Japan started a war that was wrong, in a manner that was wrong. As a result of this misjudgment and these actions, Japan was devastated by massive U.S. attacks that incinerated her land and killed 3.1 million people. (The United States, meanwhile, lost 400,000 lives across two theaters of war, 112,000 of them against Japan.)

Even now, there remains a strong-rooted awareness in Japan that goes something like this: The War started with Japan recklessly challenging the United States, but then it was completely battered. Japan was thoroughly punished. Seven men were sentenced to death by the Tokyo Tribunal and 934 more were executed after judgements in courts around Asia. We Japanese have made our amends. From now on, we should strive to live as a peaceful nation. There is no need to look back. We started the War, but there has already been enough punishment. In the end, *war* is to blame for everything, not Japan. And that is how history has become summarized.

General Prince Naruhiko Higashikuni, who was appointed Prime Minister immediately after the War, asked the American people to forget Pearl Harbor, suggesting that the Japanese people in turn should forget Hiroshima and Nagasaki.[35]

"Dear American people," he wrote. "Please forget Pearl Harbor. Let us Japanese also forget the devastation caused by the atomic bomb and let us start this year as a completely new and peace-loving nation."

Although Higashikuni's proposition was pathetically simple and cheap, his feeling that Japan's aggression was offset by its suffering remains widespread in Japan. The Pacific War now remembered by Japanese people involves buildings and civilians burnt to ashes by the fire and heat of the U.S. Air Force's incendiary bombs, and soldiers starving to death or killed by U.S. military flamethrowers on the Pacific islands—and then, finally, the two atomic bombs. These are the visions of victims.

Prime Minister Higashikuni's misconception was that the War began in Pearl Harbor in 1941. Even though his statement does have a bit of truth to it in relation to the United States, it means nothing to China and Korea. Modern Japanese perceptions of history have dropped most of the 10 years from 1931 to 1941.

Japan started the War with China on September 18, 1931, almost exactly 10 years before it attacked Pearl Harbor. The Kwantung Army seized Manchuria when it blew up the Manchurian railway at Lake Liutiao, which was operated by Japan, pretending it was an attack by the Chinese Army. Using the Lake Liutiao Incident as an excuse, Japan occupied all of Manchuria as well as Northern China. This was eight years before the Nazi invasion of Poland. The Pacific War was an extension of the war in mainland China.

China's claim is correct. Its grudge against Japan dates to 1931, when Japan began seizing Chinese wealth and territory. Unlike during the Pacific War, when Japan's position went from aggressor to victim, during the preceding years, Japan was the perpetrator and China the victim. A considerable number of Japanese recognize only that there was some sort of conflict with China on the mainland, and nothing more. This is in part because the Japanese Army tried its best to trivialize the meaning of the Sino-Japanese war. For this reason, the large gap in perspectives between the Japanese and Chinese has made Sino-Japanese relations unstable and vulnerable to this day.

The Japan–Korea relationship is different, but the lack of awareness in Japan regarding Japan's colonial rule over Korea has widened the gap with Korea in the same way as with China. Japan insists on opening a new page because it believes it already was punished for the War. But both Korea and China insist that Japan's crimes in Asia have not been settled, and demand more sincere apologies. Some 75 years after the end of the War, this break has yet to be mended. Japan's reputation throughout Asia is not bad. Japanese "reconciliation" relates today only to its relationship with these two countries. Japan still cannot pursue stable diplomacy in northeast Asia without directly confronting historical issues.

In 2004, Japan, along with Germany, Brazil and India, made a bid to become permanent members of the U.N. Security Council. A certain number of co-sponsors were needed to submit the necessary amendments of the U.N. Charter to the U.N. General Assembly. In Europe, a joint proposal was made by 11 nations including France, in support of Germany. Japan approached Asian countries, hoping to receive a joint proposal in the Pacific region. Unbelievably, the only countries that expressed support for Japan were three distant nations, Afghanistan, Bhutan and the Maldives. The proposal to

make Japan and the three other nations permanent members of the
Security Council was soon withdrawn.

Why didn't the countries that Japan regarded as friends raise
their hands? Without a doubt, China's fierce opposition campaign
in Asia, saying that Japan still has not repented for aggressions of
the past, had a major impact. Still, why did even the friendly Southeast Asian countries accept China's claim? After all, these countries
received war compensation, massive economic cooperation, direct
investment, and workforce training from Japan. In the end, it all came
down to the "history issue." Japan has not yet succeeded in breaking
away from the past.

Apology and Compensation

The Japanese government did apologize to China and South Korea, of
course. The words "apology" and "remorse" were included in the 1972
Joint Communique with China, and in the 1998 Japan-Republic of
Korea Joint Declaration when President Kim Dae-jung visited Japan;
they were even in the Japan-DPRK Pyongyang Declaration with North
Korea during Prime Minister Koizumi's visit to North Korea on September 17, 2002. But this has not been enough because Tokyo has only
issued bits and pieces of an apology and has not come right out with
it. No direct apology has been given in writing to China since 1972.

Germany takes the position that World War II was a crime committed not by Germany as a country, but by a group of Germans
called Nazis. That is why in December 1970, when Chancellor Willy
Brandt knelt in front of the memorial to the victims of the Warsaw
Ghetto uprising, he made a huge impact around the world. Still, he
did not issue an apology as a nation, like Japan.

Asians interpreted Chancellor Brandt's dramatic photo as a gesture to mean that Germany's apology was deeper than Japan's. The
question I'm most often asked by audiences when I speak in Asian
countries, especially by young people, is, "Why can't Japanese leaders
be like Brandt?"

Japan has paid enormous war reparations to Asian countries such
as Indonesia, Burma, the Philippines, and Vietnam. For example, the
550 million dollars paid as compensation to the Philippines in 1956

accounted for 18% of Japan's national budget and 58% of its foreign reserves at the time. Japan also waived ownership of foreign assets then valued at 28 billion dollars.

Meanwhile, Germany, although not in the form of state reparations, in many ways paid more compensation than Japan did. It's not about who has apologized more deeply, Japan or Germany. It's that the way the two countries are held responsible is different. In one case, it is called "the Nazi War" and in the other, "a War for which all citizens are responsible."

Organizations in Korea are developing a movement to erect statues around the world commemorating "comfort women." One of these statues was erected in a town in Bavaria, Germany, in March 2017. It was also in Berlin, where Chinese leader Xi Jinping violently criticized Japan on March 28, 2014, saying Japan's wartime atrocities were still "fresh in our memory." Perhaps he figured that the German audience would be highly sympathetic, second only to China and Korea in disliking the Japanese.

Germany partnered with France to undertake a grand project of European integration to promote postwar reconciliation. Recognizing that bilateral reconciliation between Germany and France could not be achieved easily, the leaders of both countries sought to resolve hatred and hostility through the process of forming a larger, pan-European framework, which has continued for more than 50 years. The Élysée Treaty requires summit meetings between France and Germany at least twice a year. Between Japan and China, aside from multilateral occasions such as APEC Summits, Japanese prime ministers have made fifteen visits to China, and China's presidents have visited Japan only three times.

Would leaders of victim nations such as France take a view of history and form strategies to forgive their opponents? Would perpetrators establish conscious policies and make concrete efforts rather than merely advocating pacifism? In the victimized nation of China, former Premier Zhou Enlai was such a politician. So was former President Hu Jintao, although his power base was weak. There also weren't many such leaders in Japan, the perpetrator. In any age, the most important thing is which direction leaders point the public to follow.

Yasukuni Shrine

A single shrine has aggravated Japan's relations with foreign countries: Yasukuni Shrine, in central Tokyo. The most intractable problem persists with China, but some Americans also view the shrine as a symbol of Japanese militarism. Recently, criticism has arisen even from South Korea, which originally perceived no connection.

Yasukuni Shrine is a sacred place that enshrines 2.47 million souls who died in war since the Meiji period. Many young men who died wrote letters before departing on suicide missions, "Dear Mother, Do not cry if I shall die. You can come and see me any time, at Yasukuni." Having lost my uncles in the war, I too, visit Yasukuni often. It is a place for the spirits of the dead, dominated by silence.

For these reasons, the Japanese do not see Yasukuni as a military facility, much less a "War Shrine." Public opinion polls reveal that the overwhelming majority of Japanese do not view Yasukuni as a symbol of militarism, while the same sized majority of Chinese and Koreans do. The opinions of the Japanese, who visit Yasukuni for personal reasons, have nothing to do with militarism. At the same time, the Japanese people are sensitive about how foreigners see Yasukuni Shrine. When Prime Minister Junichiro Koizumi visited the shrine in 2001 despite criticism from China, an opinion poll showed that slightly more than half of the Japanese respondents opposed his decision to visit, while just under a third supported it. It is the public's considered opinion that it is fine for the people to visit the shrine, but for a prime minister to do so takes on a political aspect, which is unacceptable. Although public sentiment has evolved, more Japanese polled after Prime Minister Shinzo Abe's visit to Yasukuni in 2013 opposed than supported it.

China does not object to Japanese people consoling the souls of the war dead, including those who died during the Sino-Japanese War. In 2005 and 2006, I took part in a debate program emceed by the popular Chinese commentator Bai Yansong, with the famous Japanese anchorman Soichiro Tahara, at Phoenix Television in Hong Kong. This program was covered by China's CCTV, and I was told that the program enjoyed an audience of millions from across China. Not letting Bai Yansong's questions intimidate me, I said that I had visited Yasukuni Shrine numerous times and that this was natural because my uncle and others were enshrined there. Apparently, this did not provoke much opposition from the Chinese viewers. Even if Yasukuni Shrine was seen as a symbol of militarism, the attitude among the Chinese was that as long as Japan as a state—that is, its leader—does not honor Class A war criminals, it isn't a problem.

So, what solution is there for the Yasukuni problem? The easiest move would be to enshrine Class A war criminals separately and return things to the state that they were until 1978, by which time many Class B and Class C war criminals from the Pacific War were already enshrined there, but not the 14 Class A war criminals. These 14, including the top government and military leaders, were enshrined there in a secret ceremony in 1978, by a head priest who rejected the war crimes tribunal's verdicts. The Japanese Emperor never visited Yasukuni Shrine again.

The families of those 14 no longer oppose a forced separation. However, the shrine severely resists, saying that a soul is like a flame, and it is impossible to remove specific individuals once their souls have become part of the collective flame. It only sounds like rhetoric to me, but if that is the case, there is nothing I can do about it. The most reasonable thing would be to leave Yasukuni Shrine as it is and build a new national community memorial that excludes the Class A war criminals, and have the Japanese leaders visit only there. Many Japanese people agree.

A Difficult Neighbor: Improving Relations with China

Apology and Atonement

CHINA SAYS THAT JAPAN has yet to face its history—that it has never apologized. Japan's official statement of apology was issued in the Japan-China joint statement for the normalization of diplomatic relations in 1972: "The Japanese side is keenly conscious of the responsibility for the serious damage that Japan caused in the past to the Chinese people through war, and deeply reproaches itself." However, the Chinese did not accept this, responding with another document that brushed aside Japan's words, and expressed "hope for the Japanese to learn from the lessons of history."

In 1995, in a more in-depth reflection from Japan, a statement on the 50th anniversary of the end of the war, was issued by Socialist Party leader and Prime Minister Tomiichi Murayama, leader of a coalition government with the conservative Liberal Democratic Party. It read, in part;

> *During a certain period in the not-too-distant past, Japan, following a mistaken national policy, advanced along the road to war, only to ensnare the Japanese people in a fateful crisis, and, through its colonial rule and aggression, caused tremendous damage and suffering to the people of many countries, particularly to those of Asian nations. In the hope that no such mistake be made in the future, I regard, in a spirit of humility, these irrefutable facts of history, and express here once again my feelings of deep remorse and state my*

heartfelt apology. Allow me also to express my feelings of profound mourning for all victims, both at home and abroad, of that history.[36]

The statement was unprecedented in its acknowledgement of Japan's "colonial rule and aggression" in Asia. However, it was addressed to the 'people of the Asian nations' broadly and not specifically to China, where the greatest human and material damage had been inflicted.

In addition to issuing written documents, Japanese leaders have made numerous verbal apologies. Prime Minister Kakuei Tanaka expressed the first apology in Beijing during the two nations' first post-war summit meeting on September 29, 1972, with Premier Zhou Enlai. Tanaka's choice of words was unfortunate, however, when he used the phrase, "*gomeiwaku wo okakeshimashita.*" *Gomeiwaku* is a Japanese idiom that is commonly used as an apology. But the phrase was perceived as too informal and led to trouble. The Chinese interpreter translated it as *tian le mafan*, which is more like saying "excuse me" when you accidentally spill water on a passerby. This Chinese expression spread throughout China, leading to the perception that Japan had not apologized.

On April 23, 1979, almost five years after Tanaka's ignominious resignation after the Lockheed scandal, I had the opportunity to talk with him at his residence. I was merely a young clerk from the foreign ministry but when I was finished with the business I had there, he asked if I'd stay and talk for a while. For more than an hour, he spoke of Japan's journey and the importance of friendship with China. He was a man of strong personality and spoke with sincere compassion. There was no mistaking that he felt Japan had atoned for the sins it had committed. When I asked him what he meant by "*gomeiwaku wo okakeshimashita*" he emphatically replied, "I apologized to China!"

I'll never forget what I was told by Noboru Takeshita, who served as prime minister in 1987 and had orchestrated positive Japan–China relations in the 1980s: "Until China is satisfied, we should apologize over and over again. Because if you do that, people eventually will forgive. And it actually won't take forever."

Deng Xiaoping made the first formal state visit to Japan in 1978, and the next such visit didn't happen until Jiang Zemin in November 1998, 20 years later. This was two months after Korean President Kim Dae-Jung's historical visit, when he declared the conclusion of historical issues between Japan and Korea. The host was Prime Minister Keizo Obuchi, who naturally intended to offer an apology to China in writing, just as he had with Korea. However, the response was not the same. Kim Dae-Jung wrote in the same joint declaration that the two sides would end the dispute over historical issues, but Jiang Zemin did not agree to draw the curtain.

Jiang remained adamant about the position of *yi shi wei jian, mian xiang wei lai* (using history as a mirror to face the future), telling Japan it must continue repenting. This caused Prime Minister Obuchi to bristle, asking, "Does Japan have to keep apologizing forever?" This ended up stalling Japan's war recognition with China at the impasse reached back in 1972.

The Chinese government does not tell its people about the "good deeds" that Japan has performed since 1979. From the very beginning, Japan's voluntary economic cooperation with China (Overseas Development Assistance) was intended as reciprocation for Chiang Kai-shek's generous offer at the end of the War to abandon liability claims against Japan. This amounted to trillions of Japanese yen in loan and grants. China used this money to construct energy and transportation infrastructure, starting a virtuous cycle for its economy. Japan's contributions played an essential role in helping to lay the foundation in China in the 1980s that enabled its economic breakthrough in the 1990s. At its peak, Japanese assistance provided for as much as 20% of China's gross fixed capital formation.

Although Japan has supported China's economic development more extensively and more effectively than any other country in the world, the Chinese government since the Jiang Zemin administration not publicized this to the Chinese population. Normally, if a facility is built with the economic support of another country, the name of that partner country is attached. China does not do this for Japan. China maintains that since it is money that must be returned, there is no need to express thanks, even though Japanese yen loans to China are redeemable in 30 years at an interest rate of just 0.1%, and the "grant element" is set according to international standards at 60%. So, although it is a loan, 60% of the money is provided free of charge, as a gift, and the rest is almost interest-free, too.

In 2000, China eradicated polio, which had long plagued its children. This could not have been possible without the hard work of dedicated Japanese physicians under Japan's economic cooperation program. For 10 years, Japanese doctors dispatched by the Japan International Cooperation Agency (JICA) had traveled throughout all 10 Chinese provinces—even the most remote—to distribute vaccines. That year, President Zhu Rongji delivered a speech proudly declaring the extinction of polio, but at no time did he mention Japan.

Many Japanese scholars and government officials have traveled to China to consult on how to develop a modern economic structure. But these things have been long forgotten. To solidify the people's loyalty to the Communist Party, it was inconvenient for Japan to be virtuous. This is why the Chinese leadership repeatedly has fed the public with images of atrocities committed during the War by the Imperial Japanese Army.

"Inconvenient Truths" on Both Sides

How many people died in China during the Sino-Japanese War? In Japan, many documents and materials exist regarding the *Sankō Sakusen*, later known as the "Three Alls Policy," under which the Japanese Army, in the name of sequestering Communist Party sympathizers, evacuated millions of Chinese from their villages to concentration camps with no shelter, leaving a vast number of them to die. Horrifying anecdotes of that policy abound. A friend of mine at Lee Kuan Yew School of Public Policy recounts a sad family history in which his grandfather, a village chief, was tied to a tree and stabbed in front of all the villagers as a warning to them when he didn't share information regarding the Chinese Communist Party with the Japanese Army.

It was the Imperial Japanese Army that started the Sino-Japanese War, and it was the Imperial Japanese Army that killed Chinese citizens. You can call it "resident protection" all you like, but sending troops to another country to occupy their land and build a puppet government is not acceptable in a civilized world. The verdict of history is clear. Japan should have apologized in a way that convinced China. What our fathers and grandfathers did to China is that important.

Just as Prime Minister Nobusuke Kishi pushed his way through domestic opposition to establish the highly controversial alliance with the United States, Japan should have made amends to China for its actions from 1931–1945. However, this opinion provokes strong opposition from other conservatives—"In those days, Western imperialists did the same thing, it wasn't only Japan … Japan liberated Asia from Western colonization … Japanese soldiers were humane, they didn't commit atrocities … The Nanjing Incident didn't happen," and so on.

To begin with, when the Sino-Japanese War began in 1931, the American Neutrality Act prohibited the transport of goods to warring countries anywhere in the world. For this reason, Japan did not call these acts of war, but "Incidents," obscuring what they were really up to: The Manchurian Incident, the Marco Polo Bridge Incident, and the China Incident. For this reason, many Japanese students do not even understand that there was a war between China and Japan before the Pacific War began. Japan invaded China. There is no doubt that violent destruction and slaughter were carried out by the Imperial Japanese Army.

Meanwhile, it is also true that the scale of Japanese barbarism publicized in China has increased based on Chinese domestic political circumstances. The numbers that the Chinese use have grown with the times. The Chinese government and official textbooks have pronounced that the Japanese killed 20 million Chinese people and injured 15 million more. This figure of 35 million killed and injured was invoked by President Jiang Zemin when he lectured at Waseda University during his 1998 visit to Japan.

If Japan denies or tries to clarify these figures every time China announces them, Japan is accused of revising history. It is now impossible to investigate the entire picture of the slaughter carried out by the Japanese military. There are many people in Japan who deny that there were even six million victims. However, there is no doubt that the Japanese army killed an incredible number of Chinese people. No defense can justify that.

In the 1970s, my seniors at the Ministry of Foreign Affairs were told by their Chinese friends, "Japan is lucky because of what happened after the war. Maybe they killed six million Chinese, but 40 million people were killed in the Communist Party's Great Leap Forward era and the Cultural Revolution after that, so nobody remembers what Japan did."

This is the Achilles' tendon of the Communist Party. In order to sweep away the memory of the Communist Party's Great Leap Forward and the Cultural Revolution of the 1950s and 1960s from the minds of its citizens, it was necessary to teach them that the Japanese army's barbarism was even worse, and that the Communist Party drove away the invaders. That's why images of Japanese atrocities are repeatedly spread through education, TV dramas and in publications.

As the market economy progressed and information became more available through the internet, people grew increasingly disillusioned with communism. Indeed, due to sense of crisis, the Chinese Communist Party revised the constitution in 2004. When the people begin to abandon Communism and party authority is shaken, the simplest way to prevent collapse is to promote the victory story that Communist forces repelled the demonic Japanese imperialists. In fact, it was not the Communist Party but the Kuomintang (KMT) that repelled the Japanese, but that didn't matter to Jiang Zemin. He bolstered public support with this thesis: "The Communist Party Eliminates the Evil Empire of Japan."

China-Japan relations went downhill especially during Jiang Zemin's 10 years as China's premier. At the time, Jiang Zemin was faced with the rapid spread of a socialist market economy that began with Deng Xiaoping's Southern Tour lectures in 1992. This caused alienation between the people and communist ideology, and the public's loyalty to the Communist Party of China was eroding. Information about the outside world started to enter the country through the internet, and people began to notice contradictions in the Communist Party's words and deeds. It was at this time that Jiang Zemin thought of anti-Japanese war sentiment as the most effective means to fortify the power and legitimacy of the Communist Party.

Is Reconciliation Possible?

I was born in 1945, and I believed that if you gave it another 50 years, a true friendship could develop between Japan and China. However, in 1995, half a century later, and now, even 75 years later, there is still no true friendship between the two countries.

Setting the tone for the relationship between Japan and China is difficult. Although I hear the comforting words, "Most of Japan-China relations over the history of 2,000 years have been good. This friction is only temporary," anti-Japan sentiment among the Chinese is quite severe, especially among Chinese youth. Reconciliation is based on the premise that the victim nation—in this case, China—accepts the apology and remorse of the perpetrator, in this case, Japan. Unfortunately, China is not ready.

The source of China's anti-Japan sentiment obviously lies in Japan's violence during the War. It is natural for victims not to like their aggressor. Then why does Japan, the perpetrator also dislike the victim, China? Japanese people originally had strong friendly feelings towards China. Much of Japanese culture—architecture, food, written language, etc.—originated in China, and in the first decade after Sino-Japanese relations were normalized in 1972, most of the Japanese people felt favorable sentiment toward China. By the turn of the millennium the sentiment had turned sour. In response to the violent anti-Japan demonstrations in China and the constant hatred aimed at Japan, people began saying, "We have apologized over and over again, we've had enough." This feeling is rapidly intensifying, and the territorial dispute over the Senkaku Islands, which deepened after 2009, has radicalized the awareness of people in both countries.

The bilateral relationship started worsening concerning the War in the late 1980s. It is rare that relationships between two nations worsen as the years go by due to historical issues. I think that the cause for this was escalating Chinese nationalism. The problem is serious in China because the feeling of dislike toward Japan is stronger among the younger generation than among seniors who experienced the War. The younger the generation, the more intense the aversion toward Japan. There is only one reason for this: education.

In fact, according to various surveys, nearly 80 percent of the respondents in China report that they do not like Japan. It seems that most of their information about Japan comes from indirectly, through the media and school. Anti-Japan historical education introduced by Jiang Zemin in 1994 especially had a great impact on the young generation. There are more than 100 patriotic memorial sites in China that commemorate the war against Japan and other anti-Japanese themes. These facilities show visitors barbaric acts by the Japanese army through photos, models and relics. Objects filled with horror are lined up on display. The number of these museums across China increased, especially after the anti-Japan education of the Jiang Zemin period. Anti-Japan memorial halls started being built in the late 1980s; the huge anti-Japan memorial museum in Shenyang was built in 1991 and then expanded and reopened in 1999.

No matter which museum I visit, I am disturbed by the number of children visiting there. Millions of elementary school children visit the anti-Japan memorial museums as part of their school curriculum and shout *Xiao Riben!* ("Small Japan"—a derogatory name for Japan). The reproduction of anti-Japanese sentiment in China is never-ending.

True reconciliation requires a certain amount of mutual understanding regarding historical issues. Would a renewed apology from Japan in writing change the CCP's interpretation of history? Is the Chinese Communist Party capable of making its propagandistic data more objective? Is it possible for Beijing to change its anti-Japan history textbooks?

Above all, for Japan and China to be able to discuss viewpoints on history objectively, it is essential for China to ensure freedom of expression and freedom of association and establishment of political parties. In short, a democracy needs to be in place. When the time comes that various opinions can be heard within China—for example, when a Chinese Democratic Party is formed and its members declare interpretations of facts that differ from the Communist Party—that will be the beginning of an age when two-way constructive dialogue will be possible between Japan and China.

Education and the Younger Generations

The way history is taught in Japan has exacerbated the history issues with China. Dozens of different history textbooks are approved for use in Japanese high schools. China has objected only to one edition. There is no doubt that these textbooks are all written objectively, at least more objectively than those used in China. However, the biggest problem in Japan is that high school teachers, pressed to prepare students for their college entrance exams, typically end their history lessons about the War with the Manchurian Incident in 1931, soon after the Showa Period began. In high school education, it is necessary to make "modern history" a compulsory subject after designating it as an independent curriculum. Ultimately, whether or not a nation seriously reflects upon its past is determined by how those events are communicated to their children.

It is not impossible to improve the atmosphere between Japan and China. In the first half of the 1980s, Japan-China relations were calm, showing possibilities for reconciliation. In 1992, the Emperor made a trip to China. We should first try to return to that age within the next decade or so. This will greatly depend on the Chinese leader's way of thinking. For example, briefly in the 2000s, under the Hu Jintao administration, a section of the display in one of the main anti-Japan memorial museums at Lugou Qiao (Marco Polo Bridge) was revised to something not quite so provocative.

Japan-China relations bottomed out in 2015 but have gradually improved since then. One reason is the sharp increase in the number of tourists coming from China to Japan. In 2018, the number of tourists from China was more than 8 million. Adding the total number of visitors in the past, it won't be long before this number surpasses 100 million. When Chinese people experience the present peaceful Japan, where the residue of 75 years ago has been wiped away, they generally return home with a favorable impression of Japan. These positive feelings are quietly influencing Chinese national sentiment.

Still, it will take at least several decades for the two countries to go beyond an improved political atmosphere and to achieve "true reconciliation." How can we get there? The main prerequisite would be for the Chinese leader to make a political decision to reconcile with Japan. Even if Japan had met every condition that China had laid out thus far, this would not be the way for China to restore relations with Japan. First, there must be a political decision to reconcile with Japan. Only then can its leaders decide how to use Japan's conciliatory actions as explanatory material for its citizens.

The changing generations in China also have important implications. China-watchers call Mao Zedong and Zhou Enlai the first generation, Deng Xiaoping the second generation, Jiang Zemin the third, Hu Jintao the fourth, and Xi Jinping and Li Keqiang the fifth generation. All of these people received strong ideological education from the Communist Party, including during the Cultural Revolution, and naturally maintain a strong sense of wariness toward Japan. They studied abroad in the Soviet Union and former Soviet-bloc countries.

However, Deng Xiaoping introduced educational reform in 1978, inviting the winds of liberalism onto campuses and shaping university education into something more moderate and well-rounded. It was followed by the Japan-China honeymoon era, when Hu Yaobang favored Japan. This was when the sixth generation, whose opinions are considered to be the most neutral toward Japan, grew up. Hopeful candidates of that generation included Hu Chunhua and Sun Zhengcai, until they were crushed by Xi Jinping, with his aims of becoming a lifetime president.

I fear that the opportunity has been lost for Japan and China to go back to basics and reach a fundamental reconciliation in the form of "Japan's apology" and "China's forgiveness." The Japanese have apologized to China in various ways, but China's sullen reaction every single time has left Japan exhausted. Generations have passed hands in Japan and the young people are uncomfortable about the need to apologize forever for a war fought not by their grandfathers, but by their great-grandfathers.

The Japanese side has its own political problems. The LDP has many so-called "factions" and their power relations have determined policies toward China. While the Kochikai, an Ikeda-Ohira-Miyazawa succession, had a liberal policy agenda and the Fukuda faction (Fukuda-Mori-Abe) traditionally took a policy closer to the Taiwanese, Kakuei Tanaka, who had normalized diplomatic relations between Japan and China, and the later Tanaka faction (Prime Ministers Takeshita, Hashimoto, and Obuchi) actively promoted positive policies towards China.

In the past, conflicts between LDP factions were extremely aggressive. Into the 2000s, the Tanaka faction was battered by the Fukuda faction and lost momentum. When Junichiro Koizumi said that he would "destroy the LDP," what he really meant was that he would destroy the Tanaka faction. There is no denying that improvement of Japan-China relations slowed down as the Tanaka faction lost ground.

Even more fundamental are the qualitative changes in relations with Japan, as China sees them. Now that China has become a superpower, public sentiment demands even more energy when it comes to apologizing or forgiving. In the 20th century, when China was politically and economically weaker, they considered it important to meet face-to-face with the more powerful Japan. Achieving settlements with Japan had significance for China. The power balance is now reversed and the importance of Japan to China has declined. For Chinese leaders, it isn't worth it to spend energy on improving relations with Japan if extremist students are going to accuse the leadership of being weak-kneed. Most Chinese are probably happy with a superficial friendship.

The anti-Japanese sentiment among the people fostered by the Chinese government is strong and will likely take a long time to reverse. It may be impossible to change the position of Japan as perennial adversary until China is democratized and a multi-party system is established. Managing the long years until then is a major task, especially for Japanese leaders.

AN EVEN MORE DIFFICULT
NEIGHBOR—SOUTH KOREA

Japan Will Not Be Forgiven

THE "HISTORICAL ISSUES" between Japan and South Korea are even more complicated than those between Japan and China. In August 1910, Japan annexed Korea with the Japan-Korea Annexation Treaty, which stated that "His Majesty the Emperor of Korea makes the complete and permanent cession to His Majesty the Emperor of Japan of all rights of sovereignty over the whole of Korea," forcing the Korean people to become *subjects of the Empire*, thereby imposing obligations on them as Japanese citizens. This forced Koreans to change their names to Japanese names, forbade them from using the Korean language, and even made them follow the Japanese Shinto religion. In other words, it was a policy to make all Koreans *children of the Emperor*, just as the Japanese were. Although they became, in effect, Japanese nationals, the peoples were distinguished by two separate family registers—the Domestic Family Register for the Japanese, and the Korean Family Register for Koreans. So, the ultimate purpose was to create second-class Japanese citizens on the Korean peninsula.

Japan's colonial policy was designed to deny the uniqueness and culture of the Korean people and to cram Koreans into the lowest class of Japanese people. Japan's actions during the war in China were physical aggression and acts of war, at the expense of many civilian lives. In Korea, meanwhile, although anti-Japanese activists were suppressed, violence against civilians was less than in China because Koreans were formally considered to be Japanese. As a result, the Japanese people are not fully aware of the crimes committed by

Japan in Korea. Between 1910 and 1945, Japan tried to wipe out the national and ethnic identities of Koreans. The reality was that Japan sought to eradicate Korea (Chosun) as a nation.

Despite deep fissures and ongoing stresses, when Kim Dae-Jung was the president of South Korea (1998–2003) there was optimism on both sides that Japan-Korea relations would make great progress. In the Japan-South Korea Joint Declaration of 1998, Prime Minister Keizo Obuchi "expressed his heartfelt remorse and sincere apology for the great damages and suffering caused by Japan's colonial rule to the people of Korea … and that in appreciation, Kim Dae-Jung expressed his intention to develop future-oriented relations."

Kim Dae-Jung's speech to the Japanese parliament at the time, in which he declared "the closing of past pages and a joint progress into a new era" was moving to many. Under Kim, the South Korean people regained access to Japanese culture that had long been banned in Korea, and in Japan, Korean TV dramas and movie stars moved up the popularity charts. In 2002, Japan and South Korea cohosted the FIFA World Cup. This even created hopes that Japan and South Korea were beginning to head toward a process of final reconciliation. Albeit temporarily, President Kim's achievement was significant—he had convinced people that reconciliation would eventually be possible.

After that, however, Japan–South Korea relations quickly cooled. Kim's successor, President Roh Moo-Hyun, undermined the Japan-South Korea rapport that President Kim Dae-Jung had built. I doubt that Roh himself was anti-Japanese, however. During his visit to Japan in 2003, I served as an adviser to Prime Minister Koizumi and had the good fortune to sit next to President Roh Moo-Hyun at the Prime Minister's house. We spoke for quite a long time, and my impression was that Roh was rather pro-Japanese. Not long after that, Roh's comment to U.S. Defense Secretary Donald Rumsfeld that South Korea saw Japan as a "hypothetical enemy" seemed to me to be purely based on domestic political calculations.

Diplomatic relations with South Korea are more complicated than Japan-China relations. In China's case, the intentions are clear when the demands on Japan escalate, whether concerning the Senkaku Islands or the handling of historical issues. For example, the Chinese government encouraged anti-Japanese riots in 2005 as a way to obstruct Japan's bid for a permanent seat on the Security Council. In 2009, riots were to gain an upper hand on the Senkaku Islands issue. So, regardless of whether Japan is willing to accept China's demand of the moment, the prospect of future anti-Japanese policies and Japan's response to China are easy to anticipate.

This is not the case with South Korea. At the root of South Korea's actions toward Japan is not national interest but a grudge held against Japan, rooted in the distinctly Korean concept of "han." This is what makes South Korea's behavior unpredictable. With Korea, even after a decision has been made between the two countries, the next administration may easily deny it. The goal posts continue to move.

That successive presidents have condemned Japan and cooled relations between Tokyo and Seoul is not in South Korea's national interest, given the many ways its economic structure complements that of Japan. Yet South Korean presidents—other than Kim Dae-Jung—have increased their domestic approval ratings by leading the public in an anti-Japan direction. In the South Korean psyche, Japan carries more weight that it should. For South Korea, Japan is a benchmark. Success means beating Japan. Not beating Japan means failure.

Like Japan, China also has a history of conquering Korea. In the Korean War, the Chinese Volunteer Army invaded and advanced until just before wiping out the Korean Peninsula. Curiously though, Korean resentment is not directed toward China. Perhaps this is due to *Sadaejuui* (lit. «serving-the-Great ideology»), a somewhat pejorative term for another Korean concept with historical roots. The grudges are always directed at Japan. One week after her inauguration, President Park Geun-hye gave a speech on March 1, 2013, marking the anniversary of the independence movements, stating, "The historic dynamic of one party being a perpetrator and the other party a victim will remain unchanged even after 1,000 years have passed. It is incumbent on Japan to have a correct understanding of history."[37] After that, anti-Japanese sentiment accelerated in South Korea.

Anti-Japanese sentiment among young people is created by their education and fueled by the media. The media is particularly responsible in South Korea, where emotions fluctuate wildly. Events that happen in Japan are reported in detail, but because of the deeply rooted bias the reports often sound like a joke.

On May 5, 2013, Prime Minister Abe stood on the pitcher's mound to throw the ceremonial first pitch at a baseball game for the popular Yomiuri Giants team. His uniform number was 96. It was a gift from the Yomiuri Giants to Prime Minister Abe, Japan's 96th prime minister. South Korean media reported, however, that this was Abe's campaign to amend Article 96 of the Constitution—the clause that defines constitution amendment procedures—to facilitate militarization. Then, in October that same year, President Park Geun-hye stood on the mound in Seoul to throw the first pitch at a Samsung team game wearing a uniform that had no number at all. The South Korean media attacked her, as well. She was wearing Japanese sneakers.

On May 12, one week after the pitching ceremony, after inspecting recovery efforts of the Great East Japan Earthquake, Prime Minister Abe climbed into the cockpit of a T-2 training plane at the Air Self-Defense Force base in the disaster-stricken area of Higashi Matsushima city. The number on the aircraft was 731. South Korean newspapers reported that Prime Minister Abe was once again emphasizing militarism by boarding an airplane honoring the demonic bacterial unit 731. Prime Minister Abe didn't even look at the number on the aircraft when he boarded the plane. The plane had belonged to the 73rd squadron, famous for its acrobatic flights. This happened to be the captain's plane, hence the number 1 after the squadron number.

Miracle on the Han River

After the Korean War, South Korea's economic growth rapidly outstripped China's. Under President Park Chung Hee, the annual GDP growth rate for 36 years from 1962 to when the economic crisis hit in 1997 was 8.9%; the nominal GDP expanded more than 200 times, from 2.7 to 560 billion U.S. dollars.

The Vietnam War created special demand, and industrial conglomerates such as Samsung and Hyundai grew rapidly. With military assistance from the United States, national capital was invested in industry. Business conglomerates, called "chaebol," enjoyed full support from the government, including tax exemptions, subsidies and low-interest funds. The priority shifted from an agriculture-centered structure to light industry, and by the 1970s, it expanded from spinning and cement-making to export-oriented heavy industries such petrochemicals, automobiles, home appliances, shipbuilding and steel. This was South Korea's great leap forward known as the "Miracle on the Han River," a reference to the large river that flows through the city of Seoul.

As with China, there was no expression of gratitude toward Japan although Japan's economic aid to South Korea greatly supported the Miracle on the Han River, exceeding 670 billion yen by 1990. Meanwhile, there remains a deep-rooted feeling among Japanese companies that South Korea took technology from Japan in a tricky manner. Japanese businessmen acknowledge that Japan also sought to catch up with Western powers after the Meiji Era by desperately pursuing European and American systems and technologies, so they cannot criticize China and South Korea for that. The problem is the way South Korea went about it, the businessmen say, and they cite countless examples.

Let me share one that I know firsthand. Mitsubishi Materials Corporation (MMC), for which I served as a board member for many years, manufactures machine tools. One of them is made by sintering super-hard tungsten to make blades that can cut through any metal. South Korean companies clearly wanted to get ahold of this technology. Of course, MMC would not give it them. One South Korean company then turned to a subcontractor who supplied MMC with its manufacturing equipment. One day, a large purchase order came to this subcontractor from South Korea. The subcontractor was delighted by the large order. The South Korean company asked the subcontractor to provide them with blueprints because they needed to "understand performance details" if they were going to make such a large-scale purchase. The subcontractor was reluctant at first, but couldn't resist the temptation to make a huge profit, so it shared the blueprints. This was the last they heard from the South Korean company.

In the 1990s and 2000s, thousands of Japanese electronics engineers were recruited to work Korea, Taiwan, and other parts of Asia. They were either recruited from major Japanese electronics manufacturers or had been invited as visiting professionals and paid high honoraria. The outflow of technology became a big concern for Japanese companies and some even checked the passports of their employees. In the case of Korea, engineers traveling to and from Seoul on weekends were investigated. In this way, South Korean electronics manufacturers were able to save money on R&D and instead invest in production facilities and beat the Japanese manufacturers by lowering costs through economies of scale. This is the grudge held by Japanese businessmen.

Of course, that was decades ago. Today's South Korean manufacturers successfully outperform Japanese manufacturers using their own technologies and capabilities. Recently I visited the Hyundai shipyard in Ulsan, South Korea. I take my hat off to them. Most of the seeds of technology were from Japan—in the '70s and '80s, the Japanese politely taught Korean engineers shipbuilding technology in great detail. My brother, who was a shipbuilder, has often talked about how he instructed South Korean engineers who came to Japan for training.

Since then, however, it has been the South Koreans themselves who have mastered and improved the technology after incorporating it into their state-of-the-art shipbuilding processes. Contrary to Japanese belief, the wages of South Korean welders and painters are higher than those in Japan, but the large number of designers and planners has allowed companies to respond flexibly to the demands of the ship owners. Having a sufficient degree of protection from the government in comparison with Japan is also a great advantage for South Korea. But more than anything, I was struck by the spirit of challenge and strong morale throughout the factory, not to mention the glowing faces of the employees. This is something that has been lost in Japan since the 1980s.

The shipbuilding kingdom thus shifted from Britain to Japan, then to South Korea. Now, China is threatening South Korea's position in this industry. The competitiveness of a nation depends on its ability to identify the technological trends of the times and make new investments or industrial adaptations as needed.

Comfort Women and Conscripted Workers

The biggest thorn in the side of Japan–South Korea relations is what is known as the "comfort women" issue. A global campaign by South Korea has established an international image of the 20th century Japanese military forcibly taking women from conquered lands and turning them into sex slaves.

South Korea launched this campaign in the United States. It reasoned that the most effective path to win sympathy in the United States, where many organizations and people are sensitive to human rights and the rights of women, would be the comfort women issue. Koreans began to erect statues of young girls in various parts of the United States as symbols of comfort women. It is hard to imagine that girls as young as those in the statues would have been comfort women, but facts don't always matter in a political campaign.

When the chairman of the U.S. House Committee on Foreign Affairs knelt and placed a bouquet of flowers at one of the statues erected on public land in Glendale, California, his gesture was widely welcomed in South Korea, not to mention, of course, by the congressman's many Korean-American constituents.

Of course, this could only result in stirring up hatred against Japan. What benefits would South Korea reap by launching an anti-Japan campaign in the United States? Japanese diplomats think that South Korea wants to increase its political influence in the United States. They often note that while Korean-Americans have a strong sense of attachment to their home provinces in Korea, they do not have a strong sense of loyalty to South Korea as a nation and have become an influential political force in the United States. The Korean government's idea was to use the anti-Japanese campaign to unite Korean-American citizens there, and the campaign to erect comfort women statues was the perfect project.

A friend of mine who served as Japan's Consul-General in Los Angeles explained: "It all started in 1992, at a Korean-owned store in Los Angeles. The owner shot and killed a Black girl, who he suspected of shoplifting. This led to a five-day shootout between the Korean-American and African-American communities in Los Angeles. At the time, the Korean community was left with a strong feeling that the Los Angeles Police Department (LAPD) did not protect them well enough. The South Korean government concluded that this was because Korean-Americans did not have enough political power in the U.S. From then on, as a nation, South Korea engaged in measures to systematically increase the number of Korean-Americans in the population."

Indeed, soon thereafter the South Korean government decided to allow dual (Korean and U.S.) citizenship and began to actively encourage naturalization in the United States. As a result, the Korean-American population grew from 800,000 to 1.42 million by 2010. During this period, the number of Japanese-Americans declined from 850,000 to 760,000.

As much as the Japanese government was concerned about the comfort women campaign, it feared that taking a defensive stance would trigger fierce opposition in South Korea and invite American intellectuals to label them as revisionist. They decided that it would be wiser to continue to bow and apologize rather than argue over historical facts. By doing so, they hoped the storm of criticism against Japan would eventually subside.

I, too, have refrained from speaking out actively regarding this issue, aside from participating as a board member of the Asia Women's Fund, which was established in 1996 to pay compensation to comfort women. Unfortunately, it seems clear that not explaining the facts as Japan sees them has fostered prejudice regarding the issue and negative feelings toward Japan all over the world.

For example, a World History textbook published in 2011 by McGraw Hill and widely used in U.S. high schools included the following passage:

> The Japanese army forcibly recruited, conscripted, and dragooned as many as two hundred thousand women aged fourteen to twenty to serve in military brothels. The army presented the women to the troops as a gift from the emperor, and the women came from Japanese colonies such as Korea, Taiwan, and Manchuria and from occupied territories... The majority of the women came from Korea and China. Once forced into this imperial prostitution service, the 'comfort women' catered to between twenty

and thirty men each day. Others were killed by Japanese soldiers,
especially if they tried to escape or contracted venereal disease. At
the end of the war, soldiers massacred large numbers of comfort
women to cover up the operation.[38]

Surely no American high school student could read this without
feeling disgust towards the country called Japan. Even if it is too late
to change the mindset of South Koreans, who have been inculcated
with the extreme interpretations of South Korean NGOs, it is unbear-
able to see young Americans reject Japan because of these inaccurate
accounts. That is why, at the risk of drawing heated condemnation
from Korean groups and being called a revisionist by Americans
who agree with the Korean perspective, I decided to publicly state
my own opinion in writing.

For years, the *Asahi Shimbun*, known as "Japan's opinion paper,"
had led a campaign to blame the Japanese military and criticize the
Japanese government for its handling of the comfort women issue.
Then, in 2014, *Asahi* admitted that information in many of its past
articles had been mistaken, and it eventually retracted 18 articles that
were printed between 1980 and 1994. In October 2014, the newspaper established an in-house "Third Party Committee" to investigate
how this had happened. As one of the seven committee members,
I spent three months looking into the comfort women issue. The
committee's results were printed in a 110-page report.

The *Asahi Shimbun*'s courage in trying to correct its mistakes
was commendable, but the damage caused by the previous articles
was significant. Those articles were communicated in South Korea
as historical facts originating from Japan, and each one accelerated
criticism of Japan in South Korea.

For example, take the number of comfort women. In a commen-
tary published on January 11, 1992, the *Asahi* reported there were
200,000. The writer had confused the number of comfort women
with the number of Korean women who were conscripted into Japanese factories during the war. The number made its way to South
Korea and caused great commotion. After that, it became known
around the world as the "official number that even Japan admitted."

How many comfort women were there in reality? Professor

Ikuhiko Hata, a historian who has undertaken a restoration of historical facts based on publicly available material and his own research, estimates the number of comfort women at 20,000, a number consistent with the calculations of many other historians, but also disputed. Of these, nearly half were "main islands" Japanese, about the same number were Korean, and the rest were from other locations, such as Okinawa and Taiwan.

The testimony of a man by the name of Seiji Yoshida played an important role in the *Asahi Shimbun* campaign. He wrote extensively and gave numerous lectures that he said were based on his personal experience. In 1982, he declared that he had been ordered by the Japanese military to go "comfort women-hunting" on the Korean island of Jeju, where he had taken 200 Korean women and put them in "comfort stations." Since then, he has been praised in South Korea for his writing and lectures and for his gestures of remorse and apologies. His "confession" became the basis for the famous January 1996 United Nations "Report of the Special Rapporteur on violence against women, its causes and consequences, Ms. Radhika Coomaraswamy, submitted in accordance with Commission on Human Rights resolution 1995/85."[39] It also became one of the grounds for a U.S. House of Representatives resolution demanding that Japan apologize to South Korea in June 2007. Unfortunately, Yoshida's story was completely fabricated. Yoshida had never served in the military and had never been to Jeju island. People who tell false stories for personal gain or public attention are con men. In 2014, the *Asahi Shimbun* announced that all of Yoshida's stories were false.

Still, regardless of whether the individual newspaper articles were false, the comfort women system was tragic and barbaric. At the root of it was Japan's public prostitution system, under which prostitution was legal until the system was abolished in January 1946 during the U.S. Occupation.

My mother Kazuko, who was born in 1915, lived in Tengachaya, Osaka, during the War. Tobita Yūkaku, one of the largest red-light districts in Japan, was located nearby. Many women were regularly recruited from Tobita, where about 200 brothels to serve the Japanese military in China as comfort women. When the women of Tobita left for Osaka Port, from where they headed to mainland China, the people in the neighborhood are known to have waved Japanese flags to see them off, just as they when soldiers were sent off to war. Kazuko's father was the head of the neighborhood association and in charge of gathering people from local families to send these women off properly "to serve the country." Kazuko remembers that her father made sure that she was always there to join the flag-waving. Under the public prostitution system, the women worked for the soldiers. Kazuko sent them off with respect, cheering, "*Gokurohan!* (Thank you for your work!) Be careful out there!"

Although Kazuko was already an adult, she didn't see anything wrong with these women traveling to China, or with waving the nation's flag to see them off. Did she ever think about her husband stationed in Manchuria? I suspect she might have thought, "People like Shuzō, who have families, wouldn't dare." At least for Japan, the barbaric public prostitution system numbed people's normal values and sensitivities.

The above is my understanding of the Japanese comfort women, in particular. The situation on the Korean peninsula was probably different. Many sources show that Korean contractors, not the Japanese military directly, were deeply involved. Professor Hata had in his possession a number of Korean newspapers that carried help-wanted ads for comfort women, offering a monthly income of more than 300 yen. This was at a time when the monthly salary for a Japanese soldier was roughly 10 yen.

Of course, even this is probably not the entire story. Many women were presumably taken to comfort stations by intermediaries on false pretenses or sold by their parents to vendors. In any case, all of the materials I examined suggest that the depictions in the American high school textbook are not true. Professor Ikuhiko Hata researched the testimonies of women who say they resisted but were forcibly taken away, but points out the absence of eyewitness testimony from third-party members such as family, neighbors or friends. (This is covered in Hata's 2018 book, *Comfort Women and Sex in the Battle Zone*.[40] Admittedly, there are arguments regarding Professor Hata's claims.) Similar studies have been published in South Korea, but their authors have been severely ostracized.

Nonetheless, no facts could ever justify the comfort women sys-

tem itself. The comfort women system was a barbaric and abhor-
rent system designed to satisfy the sexual needs of soldiers on the
battlefield. I stated this clearly during the press conference at which
the third-party committee released its report concerning the *Asahi
Shimbun* journalism. The conditions awaiting the women once they
entered these jobs were inhumane. The excuse that the operation was
conducted by private contractors and that the military had nothing to
do with it simply does not hold. The military allowed the construction of "comfort stations" in occupied territories. Japanese military
doctors treated the women for sexually transmitted diseases.

It is only right for Japan to apologize for allowing this barbaric
system to exist. Japan should take the lead in pushing to abolish
public prostitution systems worldwide, as they still exist in some
countries. Until now, Japan has apologized and provided compensation for the comfort women in South Korea. Four prime ministers,
Ryutaro Hashimoto, Keizo Obuchi, Yoshiro Mori, and Junichiro
Koizumi have sent letters of apology to each of the surviving comfort
women. Yet the South Korean government does not have a consistent desire to resolve this issue, which has always been pushed by
the most radical domestic actors who sometimes have even used it
as an anti-Japanese policy card to appeal to the public.

When the Asian Women's Fund, which I was a part of, was established in 1995, the South Korean government at first welcomed it,
proclaiming that it would help to bring the matter to a close. When
national public opinion pushed back, the government turned around
and criticized the Fund. During Park Geun-hye's presidency, the
two governments reached an agreement to confirm a "final and ir-
reversible" resolution of the comfort women issue. Three years later,
President Moon Jae-in dismantled that agreement.

Then there is the problem of conscripted workers. South Korea
has claimed that they were forced laborers, a stance that has rapidly
hardened under President Moon Jae-in. In contrast, the Chinese
forced laborers were essentially abducted and brought to Japan by
the Japanese military during the war and forced to work. The Korean
conscripted laborers are a completely different category. They were
not assigned to forced labor. Moreover, legally, the conscription issue
was settled in 1965 under the Japan–Republic of Korea Agreement

on the settlement of problems concerning property and claims and on economic co-operation.

President Moon also stepped up his policy of investigating Koreans who cooperated with Japanese rulers during the colonial period, confiscating the property of their descendants by applying the Special Law to Redeem Pro-Japanese Collaborators' Property. This law was enacted during the presidency of Roh Moo-Hyun, under whom Moon Jae-in served as Chief Secretary.

The road ahead will not be easy. Grudges and resentment indeed do last a thousand years.

Deteriorating Japan–South Korea Relations

There had been some hope for improvement in Japan-South Korea relations during Kim Dae-Jung's presidency, but as we have seen, three subsequent presidents, Roh Moo-Hyun, Lee Myung-bak, and Park Geun-hye turned them worse than ever.

Roh Moo-Hyun surprised the United States by making it clear that South Korea viewed Japan as a "hypothetical enemy." Lee Myung-bak had made moves to improve relations between Japan and South Korea early in his administration, but as his domestic approval ratings declined, he played the "Japan card" and stoked anti-Japanese sentiment with statements such as, "If Japan's emperor wants to come to South Korea to apologize, he shall visit all of the victims and bend down on his knees."

Park Geun-hye used anti-Japanese sentiment as the basis for strengthening the foundation of her administration from the very beginning of her presidency.

Her strategy was to join China in criticizing Japan. The Japanese Prime Minister's visits to Yasukuni Shrine had always been an issue strictly between Japan and China, which South Korea had never protested. However, South Korea started criticizing Japan, together with China.

China, on the other hand, had never criticized Japan regarding the comfort women, an issue that had until then only been disputed between Japan and South Korea. At the request of the South Korean government, China began criticizing Japan about comfort women and started a movement to designate the remains of Japanese military comfort stations in China as World Heritage Sites.

Then there was President Park Geun-hye's provocative decision to honor Ahn Jung-geun, a Korean nationalist who in 1909 shot and killed Hirobumi Ito, who had been Japan's first Prime Minister, while he was visiting China, at Harbin Station. At that time, Ito was serving as Resident General of Japan in Korea, the head of the Japanese administration in Korea. To Japanese, Ahn Jung-geun is an assassin, but to the Koreans, he is a national hero.

In June 2013, President Park Geun-hye proposed to President Xi Jinping in Beijing to build an Ahn Jung-geun memorial building at Harbin Station, the site of the assassination, as a joint China–Korea project. To Japan's surprise, Xi Jinping agreed. In March 2014, the Ahn Jung-geun Memorial Hall was opened with a lavish ceremony.

Among young South Koreans, Ahn Jung-geun took on an even greater role as a symbol of the anti-Japanese movement. During an East Asian Cup soccer match held in Seoul in July 2013, a portrait of Ahn Jung-geun that reached from the top of the stadium seats all the way to the ground sent the crowd into a frenzy. It is easy to incite the people, but it is not easy to calm them down once they are aroused.

The actions of 110 years ago have placed Japan in a perpetual state of moral inferiority. The South Korean government passed the Special Law to Redeem Pro-Japanese Collaborators' Property during the Roh Moo-hyun administration. It attempts to remove all Japanese color from the nation through an outrageous law that seeks out Koreans who cooperated with Japan's colonial rule more than 70 years ago and confiscates the property of their descendants.

What about the treaty that South Korea signed with Japan? Japan and South Korea normalized diplomatic relations in 1965, signing the Treaty on Basic Relations, to fulfill wartime reparations. However, this did not satisfy Moon Jae-in and his group. How would they water-down this international treaty? Moon Jae-in appointed a local judge from Chuncheon as chief justice of the Supreme Court. In 2018, the Supreme Court ruled that the 1965 Japan–South Korea agreement did not bind Korean victims as individuals, which means that citizens' suits for compensation could have legal standing. Unless the resentment of the people is cleared, there can be no progress in Japan-South Korea relations.

Like Japan and South Korea, there are other pairs of countries that consider each other historical nemeses. There have been many cases of violent conflicts between nations since back when Athens fought Sparta. Even today, it is almost impossible to repair such conflicts as those between Cyprus and Turkey, or Turkey and Greece, or Serbia and Croatia in Europe, or Iran and Iraq in the Middle East, or in Asia, India and Pakistan or Thailand and Myanmar.

The conflict between Japan and South Korea has a better chance for repair than these others. First of all, Japan's ill feelings towards Korea are manifest as a reaction to Korea's anti-Japan policy. The criticism is one-sided. Secondly, in South Korea, the victims consciously instigate anti-Japanese sentiment among the people, but as with Kim Dae-Jung, senior leaders with different views can change public sentiment.

WITNESS TO RECONCILIATION

Chinese Forced Laborers

RECONCILIATION ISSUES also exist at the individual level. During the Sino-Japanese War, the Japanese army marshalled Chinese people as workers. Some of them were Chinese soldiers, others were civilians. Many were taken from their homes, as if they were abducted. Although those concerned are not willing to talk much about it, there are many testimonies that Japanese troops captured Chinese farmers

Yukio Okamoto presents a lecture titled "Challenges and Perspectives for Japan" at the National Committee for American Foreign Policy in New York on April 10, 2014. Upon request from the Prime Minister's office, Yukio traveled throughout the U.S. to deepen American understanding and interest in Japan.

who were peacefully working on their farms and brought them to Japan, just as European slave traders captured Blacks in Africa in the 18th century and took them to various parts of the world as slaves. Their number totaled about 50,600 people, including soldiers and civilians. This is part of Japan's dark history.

Japan also took many Chinese soldiers as prisoners of war. However, Japan had not declared war on China because it wanted to dodge condemnation from the international community and avoid triggering the U.S. Neutrality Act. Still, these soldiers who were taken in the battle with China were prisoners of war. These POWs were brought to Japan as forced labor. Because there was no "war" according to international law, they were subjected to forced labor under poor conditions that did not even comply with the Geneva Conventions.

These forced laborers were thrown into coal and metal mines or construction sites in Japan and forced to work like slaves. Many of them died. The government has burned all the documents concerning this program, but there are still records of these forced laborers and the private companies that received allocations of POWs. Only recently have some Japanese companies begun to apologize and compensate these victims out of a sense of moral responsibility.

In 2016, one company—Mitsubishi Material Cooperation (MMC)—embarked on the daunting task of locating, apologizing to, and compensating the survivors and bereaved families of the Chinese workers who served the company during the war. I served on the company board and helped initiate the program. Upon learning of the effort, the *Global Times*, an English-language Chinese state newspaper, reported "For a company to settle their debts with the Chinese victims face-to-face is historically significant. This will certainly prove to be the right course and have various political implications…."

On June 1, 2016, a brief ceremony of reconciliation with the first three of the several thousand forced laborers took place in Beijing. They were quiet, sincere-looking old men. I wanted to exchange words with them, but I could not. It was all I could do to look them straight in the eye and apologize silently, in my heart.

Japanese people complain about the flood of anti-Japanese dramas and movies in China, but in fact, there is similar opposition to this phenomenon among the Chinese. That kind of anti-Japanese drama does not reflect the full sentiment of China toward Japan. In Japan, meanwhile, the conservatives and right-wingers attacked— and continue to attack—such measures by private companies, saying that this will only fuel Chinese demands. They criticize me by name, too. Let them.

American Prisoners of War

The Pacific War began in December 1941 with the Imperial Japanese Navy's attack on Pearl Harbor. In the subsequent six months before its crushing defeat in the Battle of Midway in June 1942, the Japanese army won battles across Southeast Asia and the Pacific islands, taking many Allied soldiers as prisoners of war. They captured American soldiers on the Bataan Peninsula and Corregidor Island in the Philippines, British soldiers in Singapore, and Dutch and Australian soldiers in Indonesia. Ninety-five percent of the captured POWs came from these four countries and they were brought to Japan. The Asian POWs were released locally.

The Japanese Army's "Guidelines for the Treatment of Prisoners of War" of 1942 stated that "white prisoners of war shall be required for the expansion of Japan's production and for military labor" and that "non-white prisoners of war who are not needed shall be released first, as quickly as possible, and then utilized locally as much as possible."

Why were only white POWs brought back to Japan? This was to counter the Japanese inferiority complex by putting whites into slave-like circumstances. These white POWs were forced to do hard labor in the harsh environments of coal mines, copper mines, construction sites, ports and factories. They numbered 34,000 people in total.

On July 19, 2015, in Los Angeles, I experienced a deeply moving moment as an outside director of Mitsubishi Materials Corporation (MMC). MMC had decided to apologize to the American POWs. American POWs had filed compensation lawsuits against Japanese companies including MMC. Before the War, MMC was called Mitsubishi Mining Corporation. It owned many copper and coal mines in Japan, where some 2,800 POWs had been sent to harsh labor. Al-

As an outside director of Mitsubishi Materials Corporation, Yukio Oka-moto meets with Chairman of the POW Association Lester Penney, and another POW representative, Jim Murphy, in Los Angeles on July 19, 2015.

though the military had been in charge of monitoring escapes and other POW behavior, some members of the board felt that, as operators of the facilities, the company was responsible for participating in this inhumane act. I too argued that the company should make an apology, and, after some debate, everyone on the board agreed. I was deeply moved.

However, it was not easy to reach a consensus in Japan. Even then, there was vigorous opposition outside the company that could not be ignored. Other companies were concerned that if MMC apologized, they would be forced to follow suit. They argued about who suffered more. Didn't MMC know that Japanese POWs were also subjected to inhumane treatment overseas, including by the Soviet Union? Didn't the U.S. military shoot and kill Japanese soldiers who had surrendered because they didn't want to take them in as POWs? What about the indiscriminate bombing raids on Japanese cities by the U.S.? If only Japan apologized, it would be as if to proclaim that Japan's treatment of POWs was worse than that of other countries.

At MMC, we intended to overcome these objections, but the Japanese government opposed our plan, saying that all wartime claims, including personal compensation had been settled under the 1951

San Francisco Peace Treaty. Why would a private company want to undermine international legal stability by complying with demands from the other side, after all this time?

After the Shinzo Abe administration came to power, the government's attitude changed. Yes, as a nation, we had settled any postwar claims through the San Francisco Peace Treaty. Beyond that, however, private companies would now be free to apologize in their own ways.

Just around that time, a Japanese woman named Kinue Tokudome, who was deeply interested in this issue, informed me that Rabbi Abraham Cooper of the Simon Wiesenthal Center was willing to mediate apologies from Japanese corporations to the American POWs. Considering the advanced age of the POWs, this could be our last chance. After intensive discussions within the company and a unilateral report to the Japanese government, we left for Los Angeles on July 19, 2015.

What awaited us was a moving sight. Lester Penney, chairman of the POW Association, bowed deeply to our delegation. I was so moved by his words that I almost wanted to cry. "This is the second time I have ever bowed to the Japanese," he said. "The first time was 70 years ago. I bowed because if I didn't, they would beat me badly. Today is the second time. I bow to show respect to the Japanese who had the courage to come all the way here, to apologize."

I was struck with a strong feeling of remorse. Why couldn't we have done this sooner, when so many more former POWs were still alive? We talked with the men after the ceremony. One of the POW representatives, Jim Murphy, had been forced to work in inhuman conditions in MMC's Osarizawa copper mine. He said, "I understand that the information board at the Osarizawa copper mine site is simply a tourist information board that describes the history of the copper mine. Please indicate in the history that we POWs were used as forced labor there." Although I did not have the authority, I promised to make it happen and when I returned to Tokyo, I appealed to the chairman and president of the company. They both immediately agreed.

The U.S. record is also blemished. Its incarceration of Japanese-Americans in internment camps from 1941 remains a stain on American history. In 1988, the U.S. government passed a law to apologize and pay compensation to Japanese-Americans who had been forcibly interned. Two years later, a ceremony was held where nine elderly survivors received the first $20,000 payments and a formal apology letter signed by President George H.W. Bush. The letter read:

A monetary sum and words alone cannot restore lost years or erase painful memories; neither can they fully convey our Nation's resolve to rectify injustice and to uphold the rights of individuals. We can never fully right the wrongs of the past. But we can take a clear stand for justice and recognize that serious injustices were done to Japanese American during World War II. In enacting a law calling for restitution and offering a sincere apology, your fellow Americans have, in a very real sense, renewed their traditional commitment to the ideals of freedom, equality, and justice. You and your family have our best wishes for the future.

Sincerely, George Bush

In response to Jim Murphy's request, in 2016, MMC installed large metal plaques at the entrances to four mines. The one at Osarizawa copper mine reads:

In Memory of WWII POWs

During World War II, military personnel of the Allied Forces captured by the Japanese military were forced to work in mines and factories throughout Japan. These included the Osarizawa (Hanawa) Branch of the Sendai POW Camp that was under the control of the Japanese military and located at this site. In all, 545 POWs (494 American, 50 British, and 1 Australian) were held at the camp at the end of the war, and 8 POWs died in captivity. Working conditions for the POWs were exceedingly harsh and left deep mental and physical wounds that the lapse of time would not heal. POWs were subjected to similar conditions in the mines of Hosokura (Miyagi Prefecture), Ikuno (Hyogo Prefecture) and Akenobe (Hyogo Prefecture), which were also operated by the former Mitsubishi Mining Company. Reflecting on these tragic past events with the deepest sense of remorse, Mitsubishi Materials offers its heartfelt apologies to all former POWs who were forced to work under appalling conditions in the mines of the former Mitsubishi Mining Company, and reaffirms its unswerving resolve to contribute to the creation of a world in which fundamental human rights and justice are fully guaranteed.

November 2016
Mitsubishi Materials Corporation

PART SEVEN

Japan's Fragile Security and the Future of an Incremental Nation

JAPAN'S FRAGILE SECURITY PHILOSOPHY

THE JAPANESE CONSTITUTION, while deeply cautioning the Japanese government against waging war, declared that Japan is resolved to "preserve our security and existence, trusting in the justice and faith *of the* peace-loving peoples *of the world." In other words, because the Japanese were at fault in the 1930s–40s,* as long as we throw away our weapons, Japan's peace and security will be ensured by the "justice and faith" of all the other countries in the world.

That was the thinking of General Douglas MacArthur, who famously said that Japan has the maturity level of a 12-year-old boy. Under the postwar Constitution, the Japanese were made to believe that they would make their greatest contribution to peace by not becoming involved in any conflict. They have even denied themselves the concept of offensive war, even in self-defense.

This has distorted Japan's security policy. After the end of World War II, rather than Japan itself examining who and what had gone wrong, it was decided that Japan would follow a path of unilateral pacifism and that everything would be fine as long as Japanese don't bear arms. Judging by the behavior of North Korea and China in this century, this is not persuasive.

The contortions caused by this framing in the Constitution range from the semantic to the serious, impeding Japan's ability to respond to the global situation. Under the current constitution, the Self-Defense Forces are neither an army nor a fighting power. Their military equipment is called "special vehicles," not tanks, and "support fighter planes," not bombers. Government officials are always having to explain the constitutionality of the SDF, trying not to bite their tongues in mid-argument. While Japan continues its unique debates, the global security environment grows more dangerous by the minute. Japan's security system, with its patchwork of laws and cabinet decisions that did not change the constitution, cannot meet the task.

Yet domestic opposition to constitutional reform remains strong. Most of the public accepts the existence of the SDF, while polls show that a solid majority of the people oppose changing Article 9, the core of the peace constitution. If the people were to be asked now to vote on revising the constitution to include a Japanese military, and the referendum were to fail, the next opportunity might not come for another 20 to 30 years. Perhaps it would be better to wait to hold a referendum until the threats from North Korea and China have become so pervasive that more people believe in the need for the military to be written into the constitution.

No Priority

The constitution has meant that Japan doesn't prioritize the government's national defense function. This is surprising for a modern state, and it weakens Japan's security structure in myriad downstream ways.

For example, the Tokyo High Court ruled the Yokota Air Base noise trial of 1987 as follows[41]: "Wartime aside, the role of the national defense during times of peace is not different from the roles of other administrative departments such as diplomacy, economy, and education. National defense shall not be allowed sole superior public character nor shall be regarded as priority." As a result, the SDF cannot train its staff on how to conduct interference to jam radio waves, because that would violate the Radio Law. If war were to break out, Japanese units would suddenly need to spring into action to protect Japan, without training.

Or, consider Naha Airport, the gateway to Okinawa. The runway of this congested airfield is shared by passenger aircraft and fighters of the Air Self Defense Force Southwestern Air Command. In 2018, there were 596 scrambles with suspicious aircraft approaching from China. The fact that SDF activities are not given priority during normal times means that scramblers are launched according to when their take-off requests are placed, sometimes waiting behind a long line of passenger aircraft. This is the result of the judgment of the Japanese court.

Of course, this does not enable national defense, so a workaround had to be found. Instead, an emergency launch of an SDF aircraft is treated with priority at the discretion of the air traffic controller. Therefore, the relationship with the individual controller is important. For that reason, I was told that the Air Self-Defense Force team and the air traffic controller team try to improve their friendship by holding regular softball tournaments.

The anti-military sentiment stems entirely from the memory of the Pacific War. As I wrote earlier, the country that wins a war will soon forget it, but the country that loses will let the memory define its direction for 50 to 100 years. Post-war Japan was dominated by a peace movement that arose from deep anger against the military and the government's manipulation of information and recklessness in continuing the war.

National policy cannot exceed the will of the people. Japan is still immature regarding the role it should play in international security. I give lectures all over Japan and I pose this question to the audience: "If there are only three ways for a nation to seek survival—unarmed neutrality, armed neutrality, and an alliance with some other country—which would you choose?" How would these possibilities play out? If we were unarmed and neutral, an invading country might not slaughter Japanese, but we would become enslaved. If we were armed and neutral, we would have to expand our tiny military force of 230,000 to at least 600,000, on par with South Korea. We would have to reinstate conscription, and because China, Russia and North Korea all have nuclear weapons, we would need nuclear arms as well. If we were to pursue an alliance, who should be our partner? An autocracy like Russia or China? Or South Korea, which hates Japan? Or the United States, which shares the liberal democratic values of Japan?

When presented with these options, the audiences invariably choose the alliance option, and choose alliance with the United States. So, they begin to see that regardless of whether they like or hate the U.S., there is no other way to ensure Japan's security.

At the same time, I ask my audiences to think about this: In 1965 when I was 20 years old, the U.S. population was about 200 million, and Japan's was about 100 million—a ratio of 2 to1. By 2050, the U.S. population is projected to increase to around 400 million while Japan's remains around 100 million. The ratio then will be about 4 to 1. Leave aside the vast populations of China or India, this country—the U.S.—is an economic and technological superpower. From an economic standpoint, it is impossible for Japan to choose not to associate with the U.S.

Some media outlets include "dispute resolution through diplomacy" as an option in their public opinion polls. Many respondents naturally prefer that option, me included. But these media are mistaken—the phrasing of the question is misleading. The issue is what happens when diplomacy breaks down.

JAPAN'S GEOPOLITICAL ENVIRONMENT

JAPAN IS THE ONLY COUNTRY in the world that has territorial disputes with all of its neighboring countries and regions—Russia, North Korea, South Korea, China and Taiwan. Amid such instability, the Constitution prohibits Japan from fighting a limited war.

Threats from North Korea—Nuclear Program and Missiles

Nobody ever expected North Korea to abandon its nuclear weapons. The weapons are a central pillar of North Korea's security, not to mention the legacy of the revered Great Leader Kim Il-Sung. Above all, North Korea's GDP is tiny by comparison with South Korea's, so if the two were to integrate, North Korea would be absorbed by its neighbor. Thus, North Korea will keep its nuclear weapons so as to negotiate with South Korea about integration on a more equal footing. Furthermore, although North Korea's economy is about the size of Gabon's, its leader Kim Jong-un attracts as much international media attention as the President of the United States. He must deeply believe that he is a great world leader. Would he ever let go of such a comfortable position? Never.

Moreover, North Korea is rapidly overcoming remaining technical challenges and is emerging as a nuclear-weapon state. Although it is no longer a signatory to the Non-Proliferation Treaty (NPT), it will be difficult for the Washington to exclude Pyongyang from future nuclear arms reduction negotiations.

And what does this mean for Japan? Just the thought of the rogue nation North Korea right next door with a viable nuclear arsenal will keep all of Japan in a grave state of alarm. But the situation becomes more complex and threatening, both militarily and politically, as the scenarios are played out. It has been estimated that North Korea has 300 to 400 Nodong intermediate-range ballistic missiles with a range that covers all of Japan. If it succeeds in miniaturizing its warheads, the threat to Japan will increase significantly. Meanwhile, after its successful ICBM test in 2017, North Korea now has missiles that can theoretically reach Washington, D.C. Ironically, this put Japan and the United States on the same level in terms of the threat they face. It put an end to decoupling.

However, if future disarmament negotiations with the U.S. were to lead North Korea to cease developing ICBMs that can reach the U.S., and the U.S. mainland were no longer in danger of a North Korean nuclear attack, Japan and the U.S. would be decoupled. Japan would face a crisis of a completely different dimension.

Given this, the most important steps Japan can take are to strengthen the Japan–U.S. Security Treaty. The treaty states that any attack on Japan will be considered an attack on the United States. As long as it is in place, North Korea knows that it will need to be prepared to face retaliation from the U.S. if it were to attack Japan. A well-functioning Japan–U.S. Security Treaty is Japan's best deterrent to an attack.

Yet Japan must not only rely on the U.S. nuclear deterrent against the North Korean threat. Japan must itself be capable of retaliating or the deterrent will not be strong enough. Japan needs the ability to strike enemy bases, at least. Even if it could not shoot down a first strike missile from North Korea, it must have the capability to destroy the second and subsequent missiles within a North Korean launch base. This would force North Korea to re-think launching a first strike.

The point is, an enemy base attack capability does not mean the ability to attack North Korea, rather, the ability to prevent North Korea from attacking Japan. It is a matter of deterrence. Liberals in Japan say this would violate Article 9 of the Constitution, but this interpretation has been revised, first by the prime minister in 1956 and subsequently by cabinets and legislative statements, including by Prime Minister Abe's government in 2015. So, this is a matter of interpretation, and the question is political: Is it politically correct for Japan to have this sort of offensive capability?

Of course, Japan should concurrently pursue a peaceful approach toward North Korea. The sooner Japan negotiates a normalization of diplomatic relations with North Korea, the better. North Korea is the only country in the world with which Japan doesn't have normalized relations. At the same time, changing this would likely also alter the rigidified relationship between Japan and South Korea. Bringing North Korea into the mix could open new prospects for Japan and South Korea.

Invasion of Taiwan—A Threat from China

China's phenomenal economic development exploded with tremendous energy in the 1990s. By 2010, China's GDP had surpassed Japan's. From 2000 to 2019, China's military budget increased by 887%, while Japan's increase over the same period was only 1%. The current People's Liberation Army's Navy has more than 3.6 times the tonnage of Japan's and 7.4 times the number of air force aircraft. It has an estimated 2,200 ballistic missiles, compared to zero in Japan.

The biggest threat to Japan is the expansion of the Chinese navy. In 1985, China made a far-reaching plan to build a large blue water fleet by 2020, including building several aircraft carriers. That plan has steadily become a reality. The United States only has one aircraft carrier task force, home ported in the waters from the Western Pacific to the Indian Ocean. China already has deployed two carrier task forces to cover the South China Sea, the East China Sea, and the Pacific waters around Japan.

Other neighbors are taking this situation very seriously. South Korea, Vietnam, and Australia have launched plans to strengthen their submarine fleets. In 1992, China adopted the Law of the People's Republic of China on the Territorial Sea and the Contiguous Zone, unilaterally proclaiming seven groups of islands as Chinese territory—the Spratly Islands, Paracel Islands, Pratas Islands, Macclesfield Bank, Penghu Islands, Taiwan, and Senkaku Islands. In 2012, China declared itself a Maritime Power. China's ultimate goal is to establish military hegemony in the Western Pacific and eliminate the military presence of the United States. If this trend continues, the Western Pacific Ocean could be dominated by the Chinese fleet by the 2030s.

The lack of fundamental reconciliation with this giant nation destabilizes security in Japan and the region. China has pushed in whenever a power vacuum has appeared on its side of the facing island chain—that is, along the line connecting Kyushu, the Okinawan archipelago, Taiwan, and the Philippines. When U.S. forces pulled out of South Vietnam in 1973, China occupied the Paracel Islands. As the Soviet Union collapsed in the late 1980s, China occupied the Johnson Atoll in the Spratly Islands and skirmished with the Vietnamese. When U.S. forces left the Philippines in the early 1990s, China took over the Spratly Islands' Mischief Atoll. China drove the Vietnamese and Filipinos out and occupied the lands.

Based on this pattern of behavior, if the U.S. Marine Corps were to pull out of Okinawa, China would most likely fasten its eye on the Senkaku Islands and make a measured advance. First, they would skirmish with fishing boats, then challenge marine police, and finally, warships. If they were to land there first, Japanese security would be seriously undermined.

China has already incorporated the Senkakus into its domestic territory under its 1992 Law of the People's Republic of China on the Territorial Sea and the Contiguous Zone. In 2009, China adopted the Law of the People's Republic of China on Island Protection, which also covers the Senkaku Islands. Chinese soldiers believe that Japan is illegally occupying the islands, known in Chinese as the Diaoyu Archipelago. For the soldiers, it would be natural to fight to take the Senkakus.

When China seized Johnson South Reef in the South China Sea, more than 60 Vietnamese troops who resisted were killed in action. When China closes in on the Senkakus, can the Japanese government order the SDF to mobilize? Or will it not be prepared to lose the first Japanese lives to military force since WWII and declare that it will "continue tenacious diplomatic negotiations"? If that happens, Japan will lose not only the uninhabited Senkaku Islands. China will redraw the Japan-China exclusive economic zone border, moving it east to between the Senkaku Islands and Ishigaki Island. Japan will lose fisheries and marine resources, and China's border will have moved much closer to Okinawa. Japan's security environment would become even more vulnerable.

Perhaps the most realistic security threat to Japan is the invasion of Taiwan by China. Compared with the conceptual threat of North Korea, this is very real, and the damage to Japan would be immeasurable. Since his inauguration in 2012, Xi Jinping has used the phrase "the dream of the great rejuvenation of the great Chinese nation" many times. What is that dream? Various deductions suggest the absorption of Taiwan. China would probably first call on Taiwan politically, to agree to a "one country, two systems" arrangement. Taiwan, which has been paying close attention to China's governance of Hong Kong, would probably not agree. The remaining option for China, then, would be to pursue unification militarily. On January 2, 2019, Xi Jinping made a speech in which he confirmed that he would not rule out the use of force against Taiwan. In fact, even the name "People's Liberation Army" reveals the intention, as it means "liberating the Chinese in Taiwan."

The most important factor in the event of an armed invasion of Taiwan by China is the U.S. response. Will the U.S. send a carrier force to rescue Taiwan at the risk of a medium-range missile attack from the Chinese coast? If China were to invade Taiwan without a provocation such as Taiwan declaring independence, the U.S. would probably move to rescue Taiwan. If that were to happen, what will Japan do?

Japan would not be able to send soldiers directly to defend Taiwan, but in accordance with the U.S.–Japan Security Treaty, it would support the U.S. military from the rear. China probably would consider this a hostile act, increasing the danger of a military clash between China and Japan. China might, quite naturally, try to seize the Senkaku Islands. Then, an armed conflict between China and Japan at sea would become a real possibility.

The primary focus of Japanese diplomacy in the coming 20 years must be to prevent China from the temptation to invade Taiwan. And it must strengthen deterrence in cooperation with the United States. Despite the tensions, if Japan and China manage to avoid the worst-case scenario of armed conflict for another 20 to 30 years, a new generation of Chinese leaders might change the national strategy. The possibility of a peaceful resolution to the Taiwan issue could emerge. Japan and the U.S. have no choice but to wait and see.

Unable to See Future Prospects with Russia

In the final days of World War II, when Japan's defeat was in view, the Soviet Union abandoned the Soviet-Japanese Neutrality Treaty and declared war on Japan. After Japan surrendered by accepting the Potsdam Declaration on August 15, 1945, and was disarmed, the Soviets fiercely attacked the Japanese army in Manchuria, capturing many Japanese soldiers as POWs in violation of international law. The soldiers were sent to 2,000 prison camps in Siberia and other parts of the Soviet Union as a labor force.

In the northern part of the Japanese archipelago, the Soviets occupied four islands that had been Japanese territory since ancient times and whose inhabitants were all Japanese—Etorofu, Kunashiri, Habomai and Shikotan. The Soviets likely reasoned that the war had officially continued for 18 more days, until Japan signed the surrender document on the deck of the battleship *USS Missouri* in Tokyo Bay on September 2, 1945.

As a result, Japanese people have no sense of closeness to the nation of Russia. The fact that about 60,000 Japanese soldiers died after being captured by the Soviet Union and subjected to harsh conditions at camps in Siberia adds to the antipathy. Moreover, historically, Russia was always a potential enemy of Japan. Since the time of Peter the Great in the early 1700s, Russia put constant pressure on Japan as part of a national strategy to make it a vassal state after conquering the Korean Peninsula. The Russo-Japanese War of 1904 was a battle to stop Russia from moving into Korea toward Japan.

After Japan occupied Manchuria in the 1930s, the Japanese army's primary goal was to fight the pressure of the mighty Soviet Union and push it north, as far as possible from the Soviet-Manchurian border. The attempt to establish the Amur Republic and the folly of the 1939 Nomonhan Incident—the Battles of Khalkhin Gol—were part of this. One could argue that Japan became a military power in order to contain Russian expansionism.

In 1951, Josef Stalin's Soviet Union did not participate in the San Francisco Peace Treaty Conference between Japan and the Allies, so the border between Japan and the Soviet Union was never determined. Indeed, three-quarters of a century after the end of World War II, there is still no peace treaty between Japan and Russia. As tensions between the U.S. and the Soviet Union worsened during the Cold War and the Japan–U.S. alliance strengthened, Soviet hostility became overt. In the midst of a domestic uproar over the conclusion of the 1960 revision of the Japan–U.S. Security Treaty, the Soviets sent Tokyo a threatening memorandum that read: "The conclusion of the new military treaty will in no way bring security to Japan. Rather, it threatens to draw Japan into a new war ... in which the entire nation of Japan will see the tragic fate of Hiroshima and Nagasaki in its first moments ...."[42]

From then on, Japan and the U.S. proceeded in a framework that would jointly confront the Soviet Union. Although the Soviet Union

Yukio Okamoto delivers a congratulatory speech at the graduation ceremony of the National Defense Academy on March 22, 2009. "Only when the Self-Defense Forces ensure national security will the people be able to survive in international competition with confidence and a sense of security," he said. Former Prime Minister Koizumi (left, front row) also attended as a guest of honor.

did not menace Japan directly, its enormous military pressure was a constant threat to Japan, with the Soviet nuclear submarine fleet in the Sea of Okhotsk, and 390,000 Red Army troops deployed in the Far East. Japan's defense system was developed solely from the perspective of how to counter this danger. In facing the Soviet Union, it was necessary to cooperate closely with the U.S. on defense. This led to heightened U.S.–Japan security cooperation in the mid-1980s.

Currently, there is no concern of a "Hot War" between Japan and Russia. Under the persistent unstable situation with territorial disputes, however, normal political and economic relations that should exist do not. For example, Japan's direct investment in Russia is less than half that of its direct investment in China. The number of Japanese businessmen working in China is roughly 100 million, compared with 1,400 in Russia. Japanese airlines fly to all areas of China some 1,300 times a week but have only 40 weekly flights to Russia. If relations were normal, Japan and Russia should be able to cooperate on Siberian development, for example. Russia should be the key to solving Japan's vulnerability in terms of natural resources, but the outlook for that is bleak.

DIVERGENT PATHS

IN 2017, HUMAN RIGHTS activist Moon Jae-in became president of South Korea and a situation developed that threatened to significantly alter the security balance in East Asia. President Moon Jae-in's South Korea began distancing itself from the U.S.–Japan–South Korea alliance and forming stronger ties with North Korea, with an eye on reunification of the Korean Peninsula. In his Aug. 15, 2019, National Liberation Day speech, Moon said, "South Korea will unify with the North and become a bridge between Eurasia and the Pacific. That is the way to overtake Japan and to make Japan act responsibly in East Asia." He was not looking to fortify South Korea–U.S.–Japan trilateral cooperation, rather to unify with North Korea to create a nation of 80 million people and become a world power. He had a goal of achieving this by 2045.

The situation threatened to put the U.S. in a difficult position for ridiculous reasons—a dispute concerning an uninhabited island in the Sea of Japan. About 160 km from Oki Island in Shimane Prefecture, Japan, and 340 km from Busan, South Korea, lies the island of Takeshima, known as Dokdo in South Korea. In 1952, then president of South Korea, Syngman Rhee, unilaterally declared possession of the island and stationed a garrison there. From Japan's perspective, this was an illegal occupation, as Japan had claimed Takeshima since the 17th century. When drafting the San Francisco Peace Treaty, the U.S. did not accept South Korea's claims to the island, which can be understood to mean that the U.S. considered Takeshima to be Japan's inherent territory.

On August 25, 2019, the South Korean military conducted a large-scale exercise to practice defending this island, an exercise that was widely viewed in Japan as aimed at a potential Japanese threat, based on its claim to the island.

The U.S. concluded mutual defense treaties with each country, which protects them both, the Japan–U.S. Security Treaty and the U.S.–ROK Mutual Defense Treaty. In the event of an invasion of either country, U.S. forces in both South Korea and Japan will act to defend the country. But what happens if there is a military confrontation between South Korea and Japan, as Seoul was considering in its training exercise on Takeshima? Would U.S. forces in South Korea join one side, and U.S. forces–Japan join the other? It sounds like an absurd bit of dark humor, but there is no doubt that Japanese people worry about whether the U.S. would prioritize Japan if push came to shove in the region. At times, some Japanese have believed that the U.S. would favor South Korea. There is no guarantee that these Japanese fears won't grow amid strains with South Korea. In that case, both the U.S. and Japan would have to work hard to tackle the public attitude toward the Japan–U.S. alliance.

Japan's Only Security Lies with the United States

The preamble to the Constitution doesn't cut it when it comes to protecting Japan's national security. The belief that all nations around Japan are benevolent and trustworthy belongs in fairy tales and cannot be at the foundation of our national security. Japan itself carried out a daredevil attack on Pearl Harbor, after all. Others could do the same.

If a gap between Japan and the United States were ever to become visible, China and Russia would try to drive a wedge between the two allies. Former Deputy Secretary of Defense Richard Armitage has often said that Americans who say we must choose between U.S.–China relations and U.S.–Japan relations are wrong. He has argued that the Japan–U.S. relationship must be strengthened to improve the U.S.–China relationship. In his view, if China sees the seam between Japan and the U.S. starting to unravel, the first thing it will do is try to break the two countries apart. If Japan–U.S. relations are strong, China will give up trying to divide them and finally engage in serious talks with Washington.

As long as the people who are shaping American foreign policy think this way, there is no problem. In 1998, President Bill Clinton made an unusually long nine-day visit to China, without stopping in Japan. Originally, China requested the China-9, Japan-0 visit. When Armitage heard that the administration had accepted this request, he insisted that the president also visit Japan during the trip, saying, that if China is demanding the president not go to Japan, he should go to Japan for that reason alone. He was adamant that U.S. foreign policy not be dictated by China.

Clinton agreed, and the U.S. government decided the president would stop in Japan on his way home, after visiting China. It never happened. As I understand it, Japan turned down the offer of the visit, saying that Japan is an adult country, and the U.S.–Japan relationship wouldn't be affected by the president not stopping there. That was a shame. Not only did it spoil the momentum of Japan's friends in Washington, we also lost the opportunity to impress upon President Clinton that Japan is different from China.

In Conclusion

The relationship between nations is ultimately shaped by human emotions—especially by the mindsets of their top leaders. As I have mentioned earlier, it was possible for the INF negotiations to become the gold standard for the alliance relationship because President Reagan and Secretary of Defense Weinberger saw the importance of Japan's position and emphasized that the negotiations would have a great impact on Japan as well. Likewise, I reviewed how the excellent personal rapport between Prime Minister Junichiro Koizumi and President George W. Bush was extremely important. Prime Minister Abe understood this when he reached out and built a constructive relationship with President Donald Trump.

From the Japanese perspective what matters most, though, is how the president positions Japan–U.S. relations in the context of U.S. foreign policy. What happens when a president has no special feelings for Japan? On April 4, 1993, when President Clinton met with Russian President Boris Yeltsin in Vancouver, a Russian attendee left behind a memo with notes from the summit on the table. On it,

Yukio Okamoto interviews U.S. President Bill Clinton at the White House for an NHK television program that aired on November 17, 1995.

President Clinton was recorded as having said, "When Japan tells us 'yes', often it means 'no'. It's very important for the Japanese not to behave the same way with you."

After I left the Ministry of Foreign Affairs, I had the opportunity to interview Mr. Clinton for a TV program, and he seemed to feel warmly toward Japan. However, because of this careless mention to an outsider, the fragility of Japan–U.S. relations was communicated to the world. And then, even if a president who values Japan highly does come forward, it is meaningless if Japan cannot respond. Although the leaders of the U.S. and Japan developed a warm personal connection when they met in Palm Springs in 1990, a few months later, when Saddam Hussein invaded Kuwait and the Gulf War began, Prime Minister Kaifu failed to fulfill the requests of President Bush, let alone the expectations of the international community.

As I have explored on these pages, a major rift developed between Japan and the U.S. Two months after Saddam's invasion, at the Bush–Kaifu meeting held on the occasion of the United Nations General Assembly, President Bush was courteous, but the warm atmosphere of the meeting in Palm Springs had evaporated. To share risks or not: The success of Japan–U.S. relations depends solely on this point.

The Japanese public's feeling regarding security is simple: War should be avoided as much as possible, and Japan must never return to militarism. Administrations in the past have dealt with this sentiment by repeating that Japanese public opinion will not tolerate a risk to human life. But it is not the sacrifice of human life that Japanese people detest, it is lives lost to bullets. It seems clear to me that Japan does not operate according to the common sense of countries that have armed services and say that only trained and competent forces should be dispatched to dangerous areas, not civilians. Everything leads back to the Pacific War.

In the past 10 years, however, the public has started thinking about security as an issue that concerns them. The list of situations that can't be ignored has only grown—the Gulf War, the end of the Cold War structure, the Peacekeeping Operations Law debate, the Emergency-at-Periphery Law, the revision of the SDF Law, the East Timor problem, the Okinawa problem and North Korea. Awareness is at an astonishingly high level now.

This maturity shows in changes in public sentiment, from opposition to the Iraq War before it started, to the idea that there probably had been no choice, after it was over. Although the public rejects right-wing, hardline policy, they are coming to understand the theory of security based on common sense.

Yet it will take decades for Japan to break away from its professions of pacifism. The media exacerbates the problem. When a civilian temporarily boards a Japan Maritime Self-Defense Force ship dispatched to the Indian Ocean to maintain the ship's onboard equipment as a protection against terrorism, it is sensationalized as front-page news. Japan will not be able to interface with the international community if it adheres to this creation, which regards human life as the highest value and gunpowder smoke as pure evil.

Japan keeps rattling off rhetoric about itself and the role it can play, like "Beautiful Country," "Gateway to Asia," "Challenging again" and so on, but nobody has seriously thought about creating a system to make any of these ideas real. As we saw in the comfort women issue and the Nanking Massacre, a country that disputes historical atrocities by using technical arguments but does not see the larger problem behind them—has no choice but to stride as if handicapped by deformity. The only people who accept the thesis that Japan is a beautiful country are the Japanese themselves.

So, I worry about the future of Japan. In world history, there are many countries that flourished for about 100 years and then disappeared like bubbles, like the Vandals and the Visigoths. Japan is being overshadowed, even compared with the rest of Asia. We may be at the beginning of our downfall. Even today, the Japanese do not view themselves objectively in the context of long-term trends. Nothing has changed from the wartime national character, in which one evaluated strength based only on superficial numbers. This has led Japan to various maladies. It danced during the bubble economy of the 1980s and neglected to make new domestic investments. It invested in the U.S., the yen appreciated, and bilateral friction intensified. It ignored the shift away from manufacturing by U.S. companies and imagined that Chinese companies would never catch up. Only after the victory and defeat are settled does Japan accept its own failures and recognize its opponents' excellence.

Among themselves, the Japanese show their virtue—a generous and kind spirit—in a completely different way than Americans do. But of course, America has its own virtues, not least of all its ability to reinvent itself. Let me close with a personal experience of these dynamics.

The diversity of American society drives its rapid growth. Netscape offered a free browser in 1994. That was the beginning of the internet age, three years after I left the Ministry of Foreign Affairs. Wanting to understand what was happening in Silicon Valley, I chose 20 startups frequently mentioned in magazines and sent letters to them, asking for appointments. Ten companies never replied and eight turned me down. The only ones that agreed to meet with me were Microsoft and eBay, which were already large and stable. The smaller venture companies would not meet.

As is typical of Silicon Valley, their refusals were as straightforward as the 0s and 1s of computer coding, with no polite decorations. They simply said, "Japanese response to discussion is too slow," or "We are not interested in doing business with Japan." It occurred to me that this may not only illuminate U.S.–Japan differences, but also offer a clue to why Japan started to fall further behind in the global economy.

When I realized that I would not be welcome in Silicon Valley unless I became a player myself, I decided that I must start my own venture capital company. So, I gathered local experts and launched a venture fund called the Pacifica Fund. We invested in startup companies that engaged in technological development (in Silicon Valley jargon, it's called a "technology play"), rather than e-business. My partners were Japanese, American and Indian, and were all IT engineers. I gathered 2.5 billion yen in initial investment capital by calling on several Japanese companies. This was the minimum needed for a fund to survive in Silicon Valley.

Optimists gather in Silicon Valley. There, people don't just dream, they keep challenging technological breakthroughs, believing that they will become millionaires. For example, suppose startup Company A's competitor Company B is acquired by a giant like Microsoft or Cisco. In Japan, Company A would be disappointed that it wasn't chosen. Not only that, it would have to compete with the giant corporation that absorbed Company B. Company A leaders would reflect and try to figure out what they did wrong. But Silicon Valley is different. The leaders there think, "The giant buying Company B is proof that we have potential. This will raise our valuation, too."

Silicon Valley is strong because it is a heterogeneous gathering. Many years earlier, it was Mr. Fujio Cho, manager of Toyota's Kentucky factory (later Chairman of Toyota Motor Corporation), who vividly explained the importance of diversity to me. I had met Mr. Cho in the late 1980s in the U.S. and shallowly remarked, "You must find it difficult to bring together American workers of all different races, different ways of thinking, different behaviors, and different beliefs, to produce a uniform car."

Mr. Cho instantly disagreed. He told me that in Japan, the quality of workers is uniform, and teamwork is smooth. If there is a problem in the manufacturing process, the workers get together to discuss it and solve it on site. As a result, he said, problems do not always rise to the surface. This cannot happen in the United States where, if there is a problem, the production line stops. At that point, the problem is examined thoroughly, and the manufacturing manual is rewritten. Then, he pointed out, the improved platform is then used to build new products.

I deeply understood his meaning and remembered his explanation when I came to Silicon Valley. The contrast to Japan is sharp. In any organization anywhere, the attitude of the "individual" handling a situation is ultimately the most important. This is true in Japanese companies, in Japanese politics. In any organization, there are two types of people: those who think about policy and move forward, and those who think about defense and stay put, in the belief that the best way to ensure that there are no complaints from anywhere is to do nothing.

This applies to national policy, especially. Some leaders line up all the existing tools on a desk—the laws, cabinet orders, Diet responses, precedents, and so on—and looks at them. This school of thought examines the current rules and frameworks, and then tries to develop possibilities using only these things. Others, though, set the goal first, and then apply available tools to achieve it. If there aren't enough tools, or if the tools become obstacles, new ones are created. If there is no precedent, a new one needs to be set.

Each school of thought has its own logic, so this is not about which is better. The problem arises when people become entrenched in one or the other. It's easy to find reasons why something can't be done, but policies should be purposeful and evolve as circumstances change.

I had painful experience acting the first way when I launched the venture investment fund Pacifica in 2000. It was challenging and exciting but involved a lot of work. The pressure of shepherding other people's money was overwhelming. Crushed by the thought that I could no longer live in Japan if I couldn't return peoples investments, I continued to invest in companies that my partners found. Over the course of six years, I invested in more than a dozen startups, after taking almost twice as long to select investments as other funds would take. I figured that by being so careful, everything would go well. However, it was not successful. We were hit by a huge reverse storm. The promising companies we invested in fell to China's low-cost offensive.

Of course, this was a major disappointment. But for me personally, there was no better way to get to know the United States than to work in Silicon Valley. People gather there from all over the world. The diversity is not merely a mixture of different cultures and ideas, but something that creates a completely new culture, the way that light appears colorless when the rays of many colors are brought together. Witnessing Silicon Valley's constant and resilient efforts, I

Yukio Okamoto was named a Robert E. Wilhelm Fellow at the MIT Center for International Studies in Cambridge, MA, in November 2012. He began drafting this book in this research office with the encouragement of Professor Richard J. Samuels, the Center's director, shown at right. Okamoto hoped that the book would be read especially by American youth interested in Japan.

was reminded of what an amazing country this was.

And I also drew lessons for how Japan could survive and prosper in this new era in which it must take the initiative and expand what has been Japan's narrowing frontier. It is time for a fundamental discussion on the state of this nation. Seventy years after the end of World War II, Japan has become a competent and peace-oriented democracy, both physically and mentally. In view of this, the advent of the world's new drifting era will likely prompt Japan to shift away from its current "Japan First" policy and encourage it to start anew as a nation that takes the lead in safeguarding global public goods." At least it should.

If so, then it is time to for Japan to use its accumulated strength and philosophy to usher the world away from the situation of stagnation that it is heading towards, to a brighter future. I believe that this is the road ahead for Japan.

THE END

While a fellow at MIT, Yukio Okamoto enjoyed taking walks during his breaks from writing, in the park near the apartment he rented in Boston.

Endnotes

PRELUDE

1. Shiba, Ryotaro. Showa Toiu Kokka (*A Nation Called Showa*). NHK Shuppan, 1998.

PART ONE

2. Shiba, Ryotaro. Saka No Ue No Kumo (*Clouds Above the Hill*). Bungeishunju, 1999.
   https://www.amazon.com/Clouds-above-Hill-Historical-Russo-Japanese/dp/1138858862
   https://www.amazon.com/%E5%9D%82%E3%81%AE%E4%B8%8A%E3%81%AE%E9%9B%B2%EF%BC%88%E4%B8%80%EF%BC%89-%E6%96%87%E6%98%A5%E6%96%87%E5%BA%AB-Japanese-%E5%8F%B8%E9%A6%AC%E9%81%BC%E5%A4%AA%E9%83%8E-ebook/dp/B018LXS1X0

3. Yamashita, Kazuhito. Ima Yomigaeru Yanagida Kunio No Nousei Kaikaku (*Revival of Kunio Yanagida's Agricultural Policy Reform*). Shinchosha, 2018.
   https://www.rieti.go.jp/en/publications/summary/18020004.html

4. Ishimitsu, Makiyo. Dare No Tame Ni (*For Whom*). Chuo Koron Shinsha, 1979.
   https://www.amazon.com/whom-memoirs-ishimitsu-4122006899-Japanese/dp/4122006899?ref_=ast_author_mpb

5. Tobe, Ryoichi, et al. Shippai No Honshitsu: Nihongun No Soshikironteki Kenkyu (*The Essence of Failure: An Organizational Theory Analysis of the Japanese Armed Forces*). Chuokoron Shinsha, 1991.
   https://www.amazon.com/Shippai-No-Honshitsu-Nihongun-Shoshikironteki/dp/4122018331

6. NHK broadcasted a documentary on August 13, 2017 https://www2.nhk.or.jp/archives/movies/?id=D0009050802_00000

7. Fukuyama, Takuma. Testimony to Grandchildren Volume 26. Chapter in Part 2, "Participated in the Process of Defeat in Unit 731." Shimpu Company, August 2013. ISBN: 978-4-88269-784-8.
   http://www.shimpu.co.jp/bookstore/item/itemgenre/magosho/1538/

8. Shimamura, Kyo. Sanzennin No Seitai Jikken (*Live Experiment on 3,000 Human Beings*). Hara Shobo, 1967.
   https://iss.ndl.go.jp/books/R100000039-I001124056-00?locale=ja

9 Okamoto, Kazuko. Namba no Yuyake (*Sunset in Namba*). Self publication, 2013.

10. Sabata, Toyoyuki. Nihonjin No Sensokan Wa Naze "Tokui" Nanoka (*Why is the Japanese View of War "Unique"*). Shufunotomosha, 2005.
https://www.amazon.co.jp/-/en/%E9%AF%96%E7%94%B0-%E8%B1%8A%E4%B9%8B/dp/4072475688

PART TWO

11. Ikeda, Kiyoshi. Kaigun To Nihon (*The Navy and Japan*). Chuokoron Shinsha, 1981.

12. Hosaka, Masayasu. Ano Senso wa Nandattanoka (*What Was That War*). Shinchosha, 2005.
https://www.amazon.co.jp/%E3%81%82%E3%81%AE%E6%88%A6%E4%BA%89%E3%81%AF%E4%BD%95%E3%81%A0%E3%81%A3%E3%81%9F%E3%81%AE%E3%81%8B-%E5%A4%A7%E4%BA%BA%E3%81%AE%E3%81%9F%E3%82%81%E3%81%AE%E6%AD%B4%E5%8F%B2%E6%95%99%A7%91%E6%9B%B8-%E6%96%B0%E6%BD%AE%E6%96%B0%E6%9B%B8-%E4%BF%9D%E9%98%AA-%E6%AD%A3%E5%BA%B7/dp/4106101254

13. Nomura, Kichisaburo. Nichibei Kaisen: Saishu Kosho no Keiken to Hansei—Chubei Taishi no Kaisonichiroku to Sengo Shori (The Outbreak of War between Japan and the United States: Experience and Reflection of the Last Negotiation—Memoirs and Post-War Process of the Ambassador of Japan to the United States). Shoshishinsui, 2021.

14. Tuchman, Barbara W. *The March of Folly—from Troy to Vietnam*. Knopf, New York. March 1984.

15. Dower, John W. *Embracing Defeat: Japan in the Wake of World War II*. W.W. Norton & Co., 1999.

16. Bix, Herbert P. *Hirohito and the Making of Modern Japan*. Harper Collins Publishers, September 2000.

17. Gen. Douglas MacArthur telegram to the Chief of Staff of the U.S. Army (Eisenhower). https://history.state.gov/historicaldocuments/frus1946v08/d308

18. Fujiwara, Akira. Uejinishita Eirei Tachi (Spirits of War Dead Who Starved to Death). Chikuma Shobo, 2018.

19. https://survey.gov-online.go.jp/h30/h30-life/2-1.html

20. https://news.northwesternmutual.com/2018-09-25-Nearly-half-of-Americans-think-the-middle-class-is-shrinking-and-one-third-believe-it-will-disappear-entirely

21. [AFL-CIO] https://aflcio.org/press/releases/ceo-pay-soars-361-times-average-worker

22. The Institute of Labor Administration (労務行政研究所)
https://jinjibu.jp/article/detl/hr-survey/1925/#heading_3_1

23. Asami, Tamotsu. Hensetsu To Aikoku: Gaikokan Ushiba Nobuhiko No Shogai (*Change and Patriotism: The Life of Diplomat Nobuhiko Ushiba*). Bunshun Shinsho, 2017.
https://www.amazon.co.jp/%E5%A4%89%E7%AF%80%E3%81%A8%E6%8

4%9B%E5%9B%BD-%E5%A4%96%E4%BA%A4%E5%AE%98%E3%83%BB%E7%89%9B%E5%A0%B4%E4%BF%A1%E5%BD%A6%E3%81%AE%E7%94%9F%E6%B6%AF-%E6%96%87%E6%98%A5%E6%96%B0%E6%9B%B8-%E6%B5%85%E6%B5%B7-%E4%BF%9D/dp/4166611410

24. Kissinger, Henry. Years of Upheaval. Boston:Little Brown, 1982.

PART THREE

25. Weinberger, Caspar. *Fighting for Peace: Seven Critical Years in the Pentagon*, pg. 239. Grand Central Publishing, 1990.

26. https://www.asahi.com/articles/ASP893W3SP87PITB00N.html

PART FOUR

27. Weinberger, Caspar. *Fighting for Peace: Seven Critical Years in the Pentagon*, pg. 421. Grand Central Publishing, 1990.

28. Gotoda, Masaharu. Sei to Kan (Politics and Government). Kodansha, 1994. https://www.kinokuniya.co.jp/f/dsg-01-9784062072267

29. Asahi Shimbun Gulf Crisis Reporting Team. *The Gulf War and Japan: Questions about Crisis Management*, pg. 88. Asahi Shimbun Publishing, 1991. https://www.kinokuniya.co.jp/f/dsg-01-9784022562753

30. Schwarzkopf, H. Norman and Petre, Peter. *It Doesn't Take a Hero: The Autobiography of General H. Norman Schwarzkopf*, pg. 365. Bantam, 1993.

PART FIVE

31. Woodward, Bob. *State of Denial: Bush at War*, Part III, pg. 125. Simon & Schuster, New York. 2006.

32. https://www.theguardian.com/uk/2009/dec/07/iraq-inquiry-tony-blair-delay

33. Woodward, Bob. *State of Denial: Bush at War*, Part III, pg. 167. Simon & Schuster, New York. 2006.

34. 昭和天皇 終戦の玉音放送. https://web.archive.org/web/20110719132013/http://cgi2.nhk.or.jp/shogenarchives/sp/movie.cgi?das_id=D0001410387_00000 15 August 1945

PART SIX

35. https://kenpouq.exblog.jp/22436461/ and
https://www.nytimes.com/1945/ 09/15/archives/higashikuni-bids-us-forget-dec-7-survivors-of-the-houston-upon.html

36. Statement by Prime Minister Tomiichi Murayama, "On the occasion of the 50th anniversary of the war's end." 15 August 1995. Ministry of Foreign Affairs of Japan.
https://www.mofa.go.jp/announce/press/pm/murayama/9508.html

37. President Park Geun-hye's 94th March First Independence Movement Day Commemoration Speech. March 1, 2013. Embassy of the Republic of Korea in the USA. https://overseas.mofa.go.kr/us-en/brd/m_4497/view.do?seq=

691507&srchFr=&amp%3BsrchTo=&amp%3BsrchWord=&amp%3BsrchTp=
&amp%3Bmulti_itm_seq=0&amp%3Bitm_seq_1=0&amp%3Bitm_
seq_2=0&amp%3Bcompany_cd=&amp%3Bcompany_nm=

38. Bentley, Jerry H. and Ziegler, Herbert F. *Traditions & Encounters: A Global Perspective on the Past*, AP Fifth Edition. McGraw Hill, 2011.
https://www.amazon.co.jp/Bentley-Traditions-Encounters-TRADITIONS-ENCOUNTERS/dp/0076594386

39. United Nations Economic and Social Council Commission on Human Rights," E/CN.4/1996/53/Add.1, 4 January 1996.

40. Hata, Ikuhiko. *Comfort Women and Sex in the Battle Zone*. Hamilton Books, 2018.

PART SEVEN

41. Judgment by the Tokyo High Court on July 15, 1987. Hanrei Jiho, Vol. 1245, p. 3.

42. Collection of Publications of the Ministry of Foreign Affairs, first half of 1960, pp. 205-209. January 27, 1960. World and Japan database, National Graduate Institute for Policy Studies, University of Tokyo.
https://worldjpn.net/documents/texts/JPUS/19600127.O1J.html

"Books to Span the East and West"

Tuttle Publishing was founded in 1832 in the small New England town of Rutland, Vermont [USA]. Our core values remain as strong today as they were then—to publish best-in-class books which bring people together one page at a time. In 1948, we established a publishing outpost in Japan—and Tuttle is now a leader in publishing English-language books about the arts, languages and cultures of Asia. The world has become a much smaller place today and Asia's economic and cultural influence has grown. Yet the need for meaningful dialogue and information about this diverse region has never been greater. Over the past seven decades, Tuttle has published thousands of books on subjects ranging from martial arts and paper crafts to language learning and literature—and our talented authors, illustrators, designers and photographers have won many prestigious awards. We welcome you to explore the wealth of information available on Asia at www.tuttlepublishing.com.

Published by Tuttle Publishing, an imprint of Periplus Editions (HK) Ltd.

www.tuttlepublishing.com

Copyright © 2025 Okamoto Associates, Inc.

Library of Congress Cataloging-in-Publication Data in process

ISBN 978-4-8053-1843-0

27 26 25 24
10 9 8 7 6 5 4 3 2 1   2406VP

Printed in Malaysia

Distributed by

North America, Latin America & Europe
Tuttle Publishing
364 Innovation Drive
North Clarendon,
VT 05759-9436, USA
Tel: 1 (802) 773 8930
Fax: 1 (802) 773 6993
info@tuttlepublishing.com
www.tuttlepublishing.com

Japan
Tuttle Publishing
Yaekari Building 3rd Floor
5-4-12 Osaki Shinagawa-ku
Tokyo 1410032, Japan
Tel: (81) 3 5437 0171
Fax: (81) 3 5437 0755
sales@tuttle.co.jp
www.tuttle.co.jp

Asia Pacific
Berkeley Books Pte Ltd
3 Kallang Sector #04-01
Singapore 349278
Tel: (65) 6741-2178
Fax: (65) 6741-2179
inquiries@periplus.com.sg
www.periplus.com